INUYASHIKI 4

HIROYA OKU

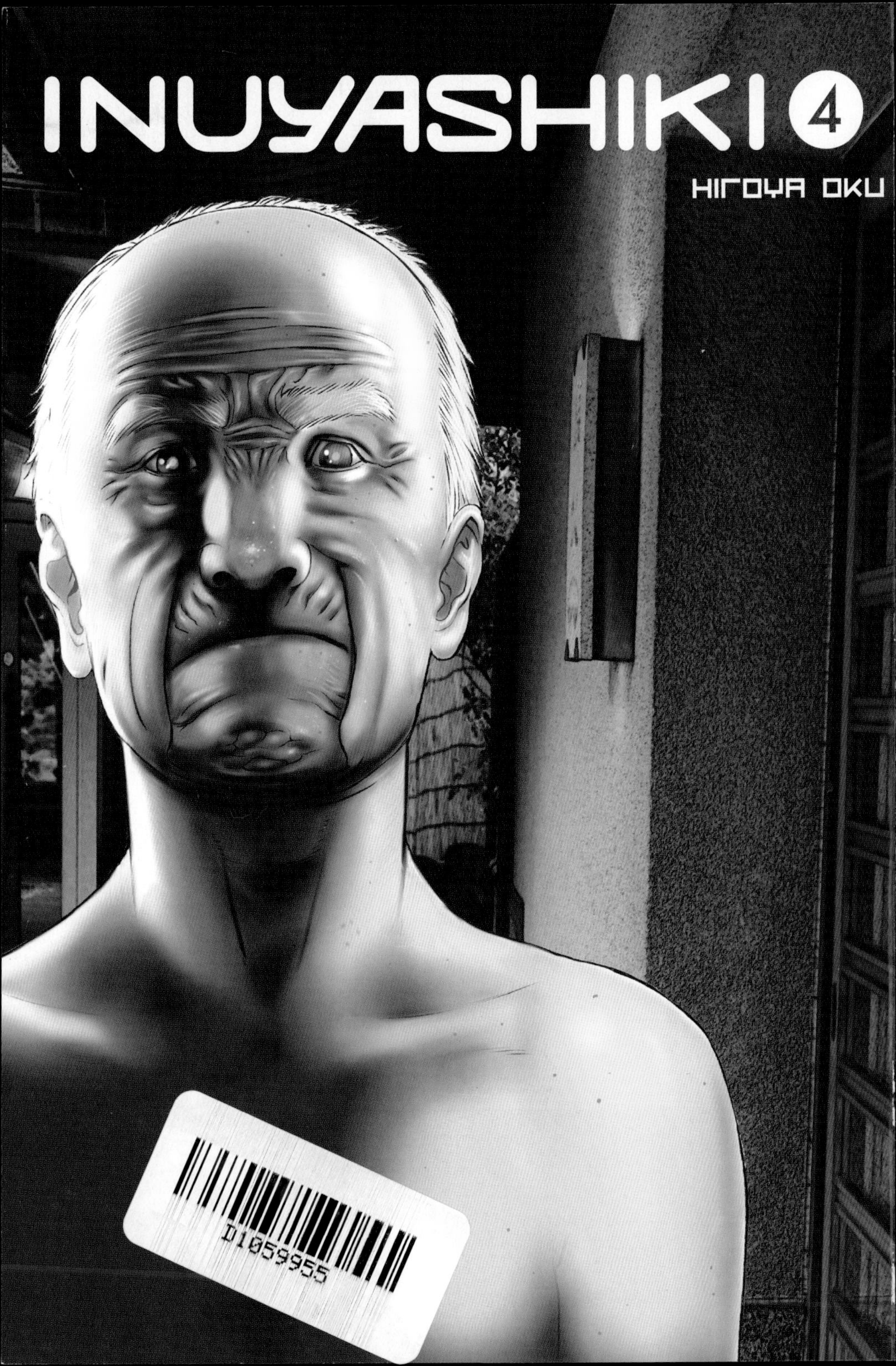

INUYASHIKI 4 CONTENTS

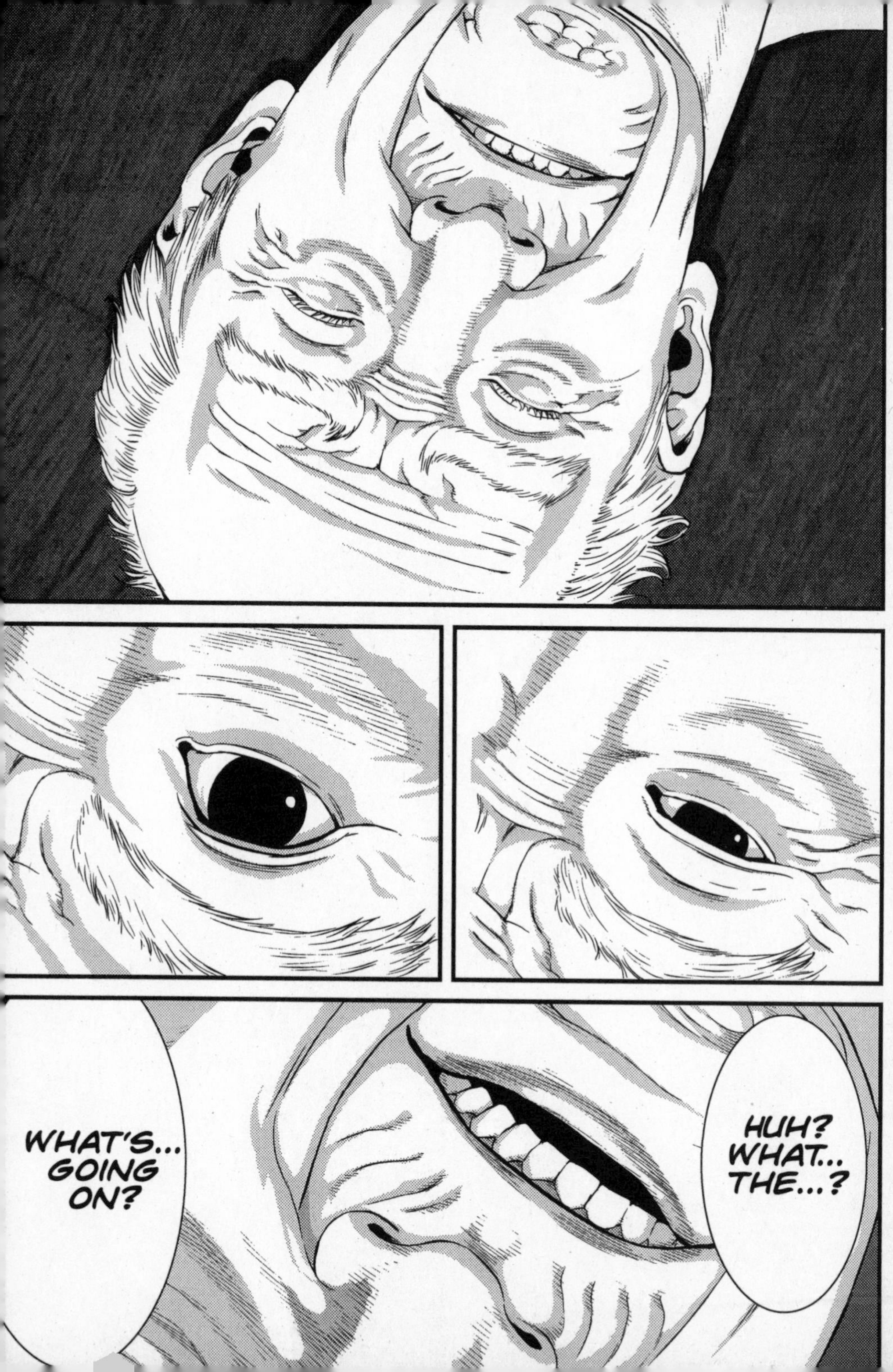
HUH? WHAT... THE...?
WHAT'S... GOING ON?

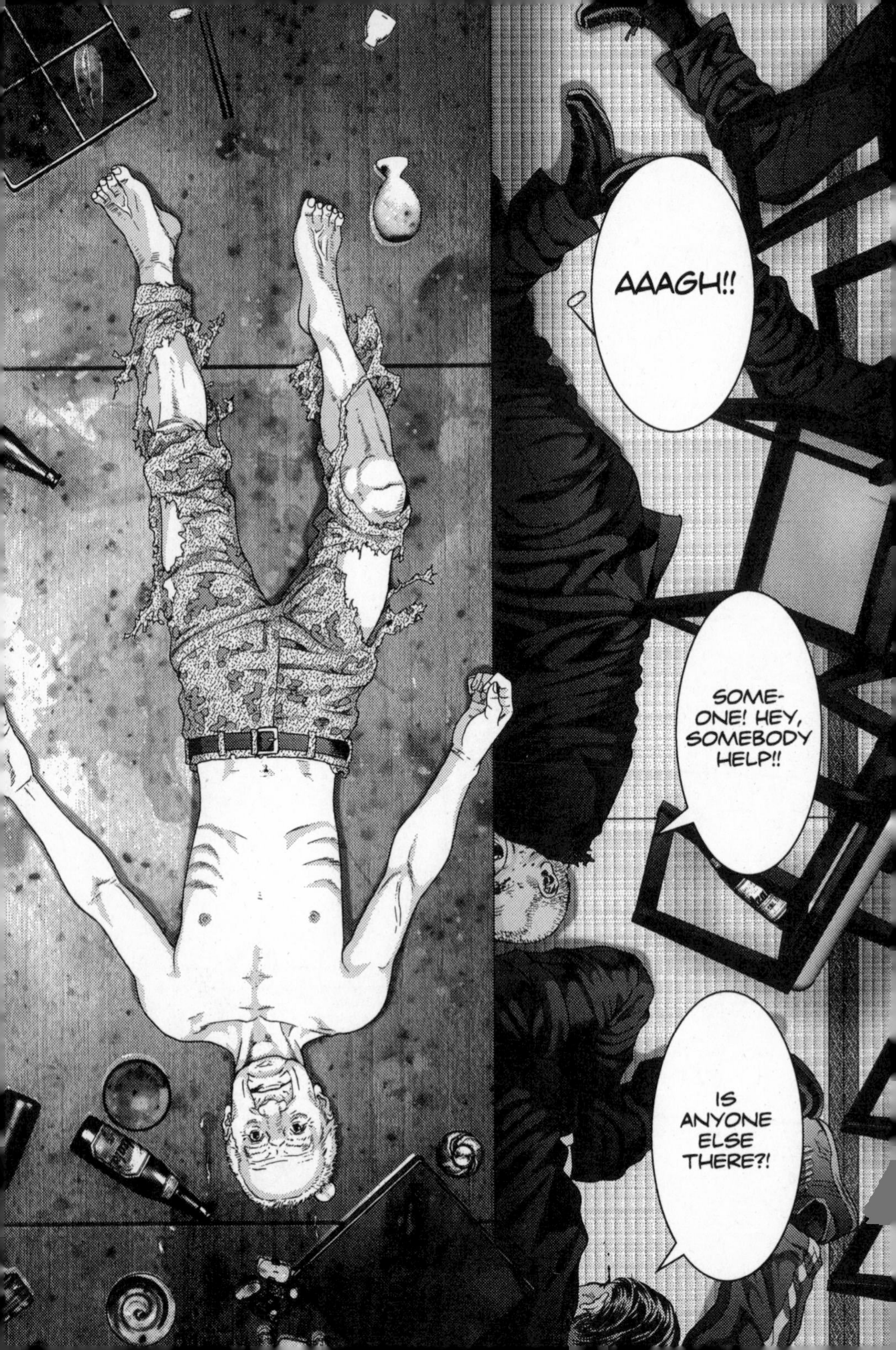
AAAGH!!
SOME-ONE! HEY, SOMEBODY HELP!!
IS ANYONE ELSE THERE?!

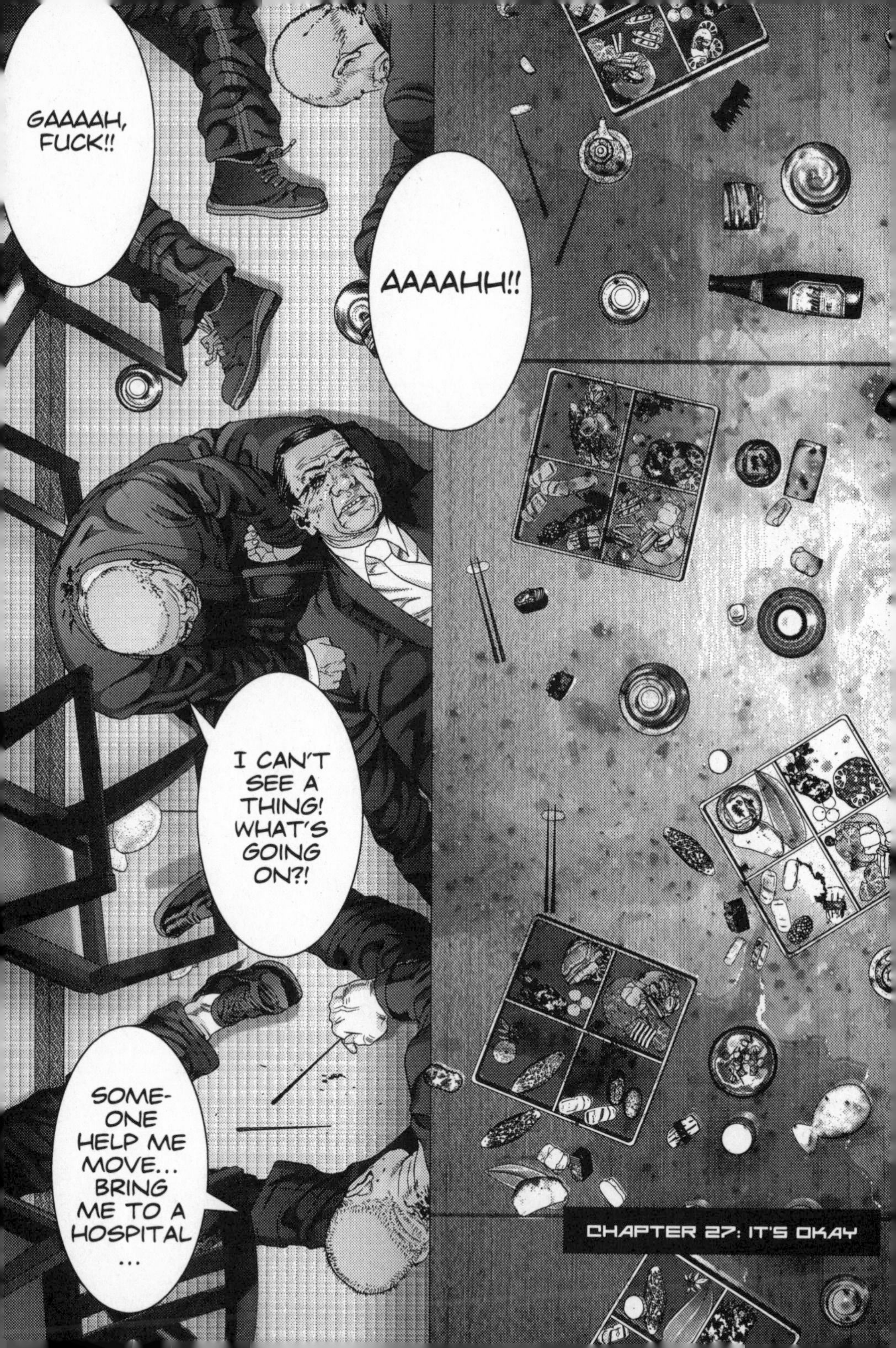
CHAPTER 27: IT'S OKAY
AAAAHH!!
GAAAAH, FUCK!!
I CAN'T SEE A THING! WHAT'S GOING ON?!
SOME-ONE HELP ME MOVE... BRING ME TO A HOSPITAL ...

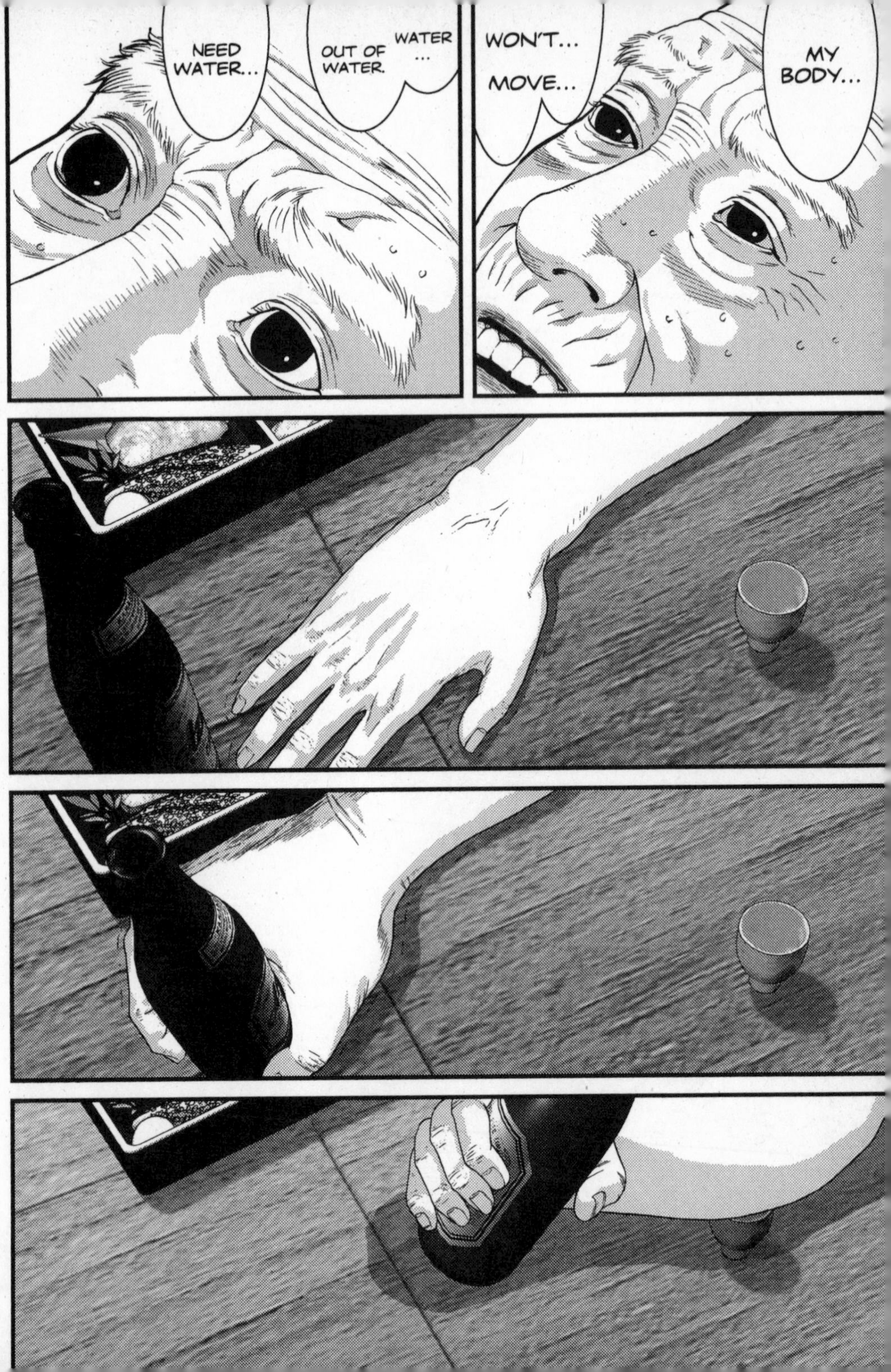
MY BODY...
WON'T... MOVE...
WATER ...
OUT OF WATER.
NEED WATER...

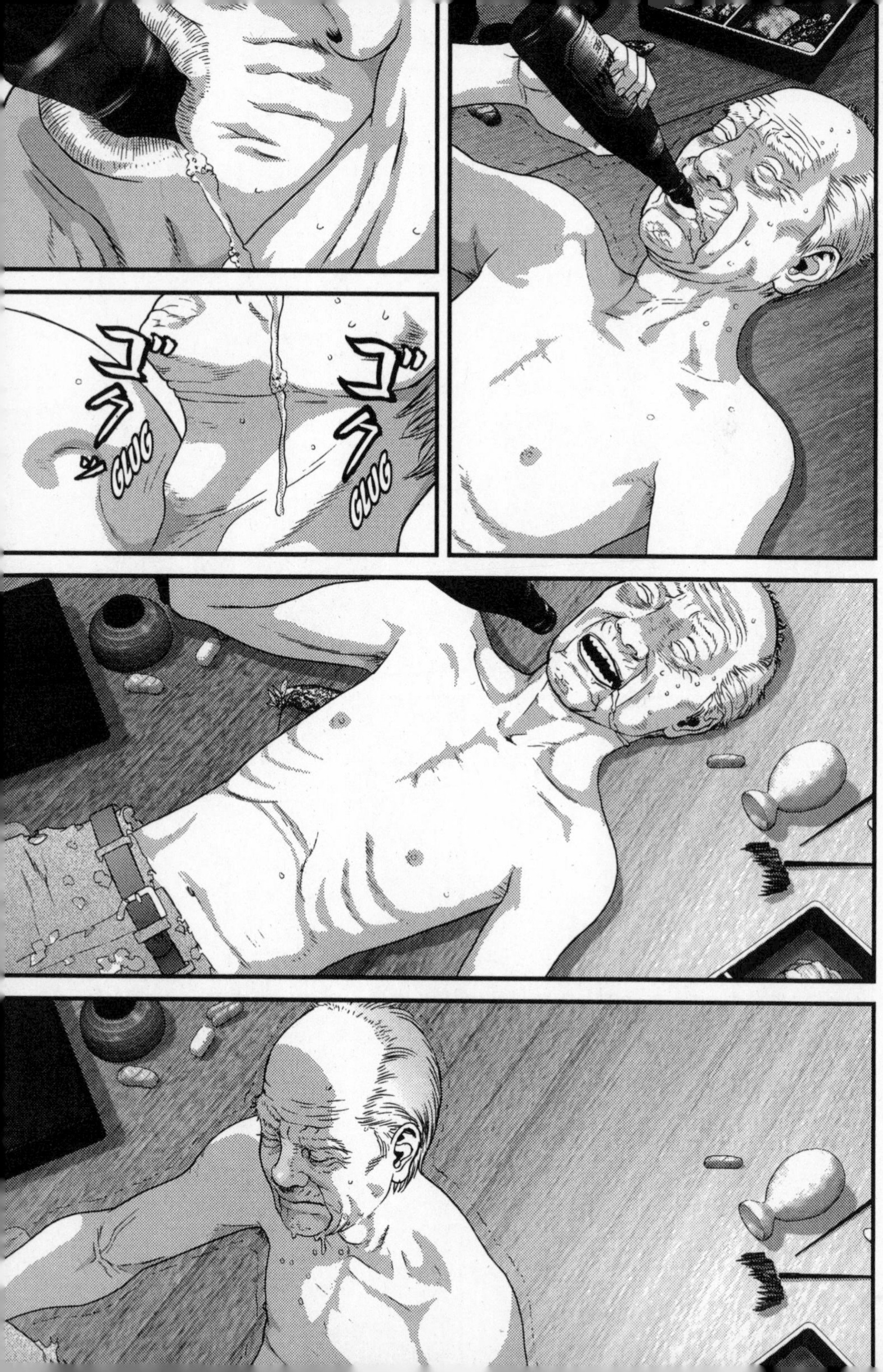
ゴク
GLUG
ゴクッ
GLUG

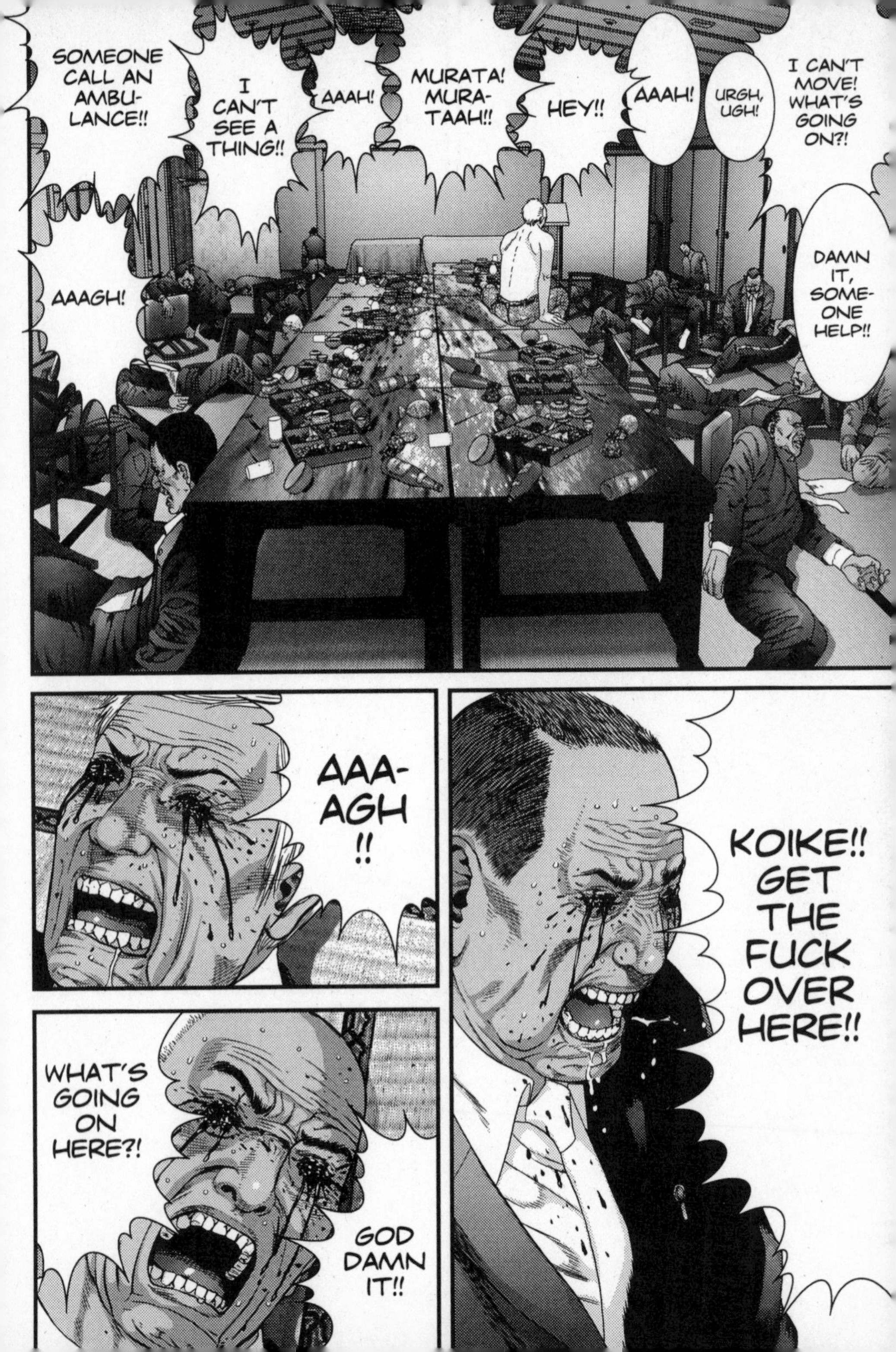
I CAN'T MOVE! WHAT'S GOING ON?!
URGH, UGH!
AAAH!
HEY!!
MURATA! MURA-TAAH!!
AAAH!
I CAN'T SEE A THING!!
SOMEONE CALL AN AMBU-LANCE!!
DAMN IT, SOME-ONE HELP!!
AAAGH!
KOIKE!! GET THE FUCK OVER HERE!!
AAA-AGH !!
WHAT'S GOING ON HERE?!
GOD DAMN IT!!

SHIKAMA! ARE YOU THERE?!
AAAH! AAAGH!
GAAH, DAMN IT!!
I CAN'T SENSE ANYTHING! IT'S ALL DARKNESS!
ME NEITHER!!
THE FUCK IS ALL THIS?!
SHIT! GODDAMN IT!
SOMEONE HELP!
RAAAAAGH!!
DID I...
...DO THIS?

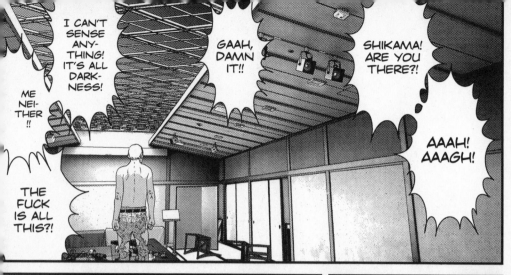

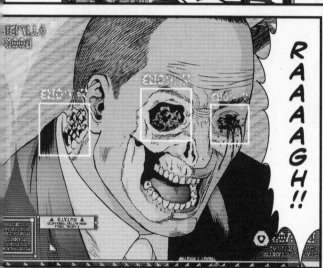

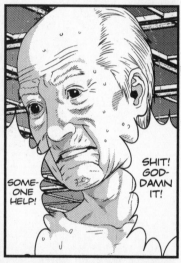

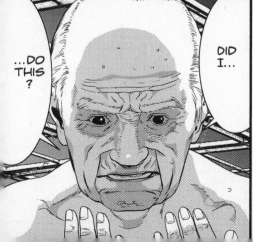

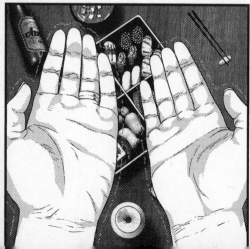

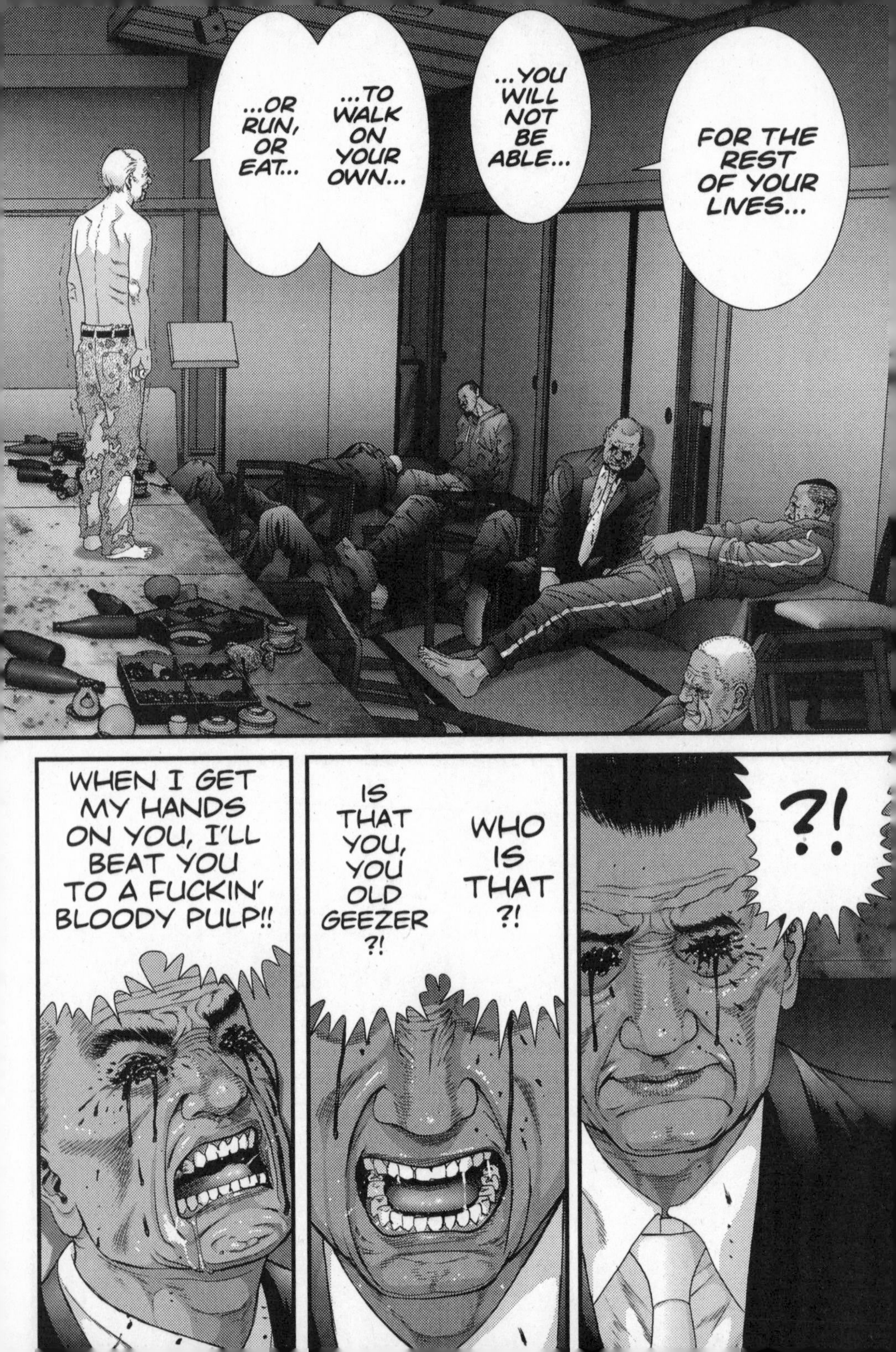
FOR THE REST OF YOUR LIVES...
...YOU WILL NOT BE ABLE...
...TO WALK ON YOUR OWN...
...OR RUN, OR EAT...
?!
WHO IS THAT ?!
IS THAT YOU, YOU OLD GEEZER ?!
WHEN I GET MY HANDS ON YOU, I'LL BEAT YOU TO A FUCKIN' BLOODY PULP!!

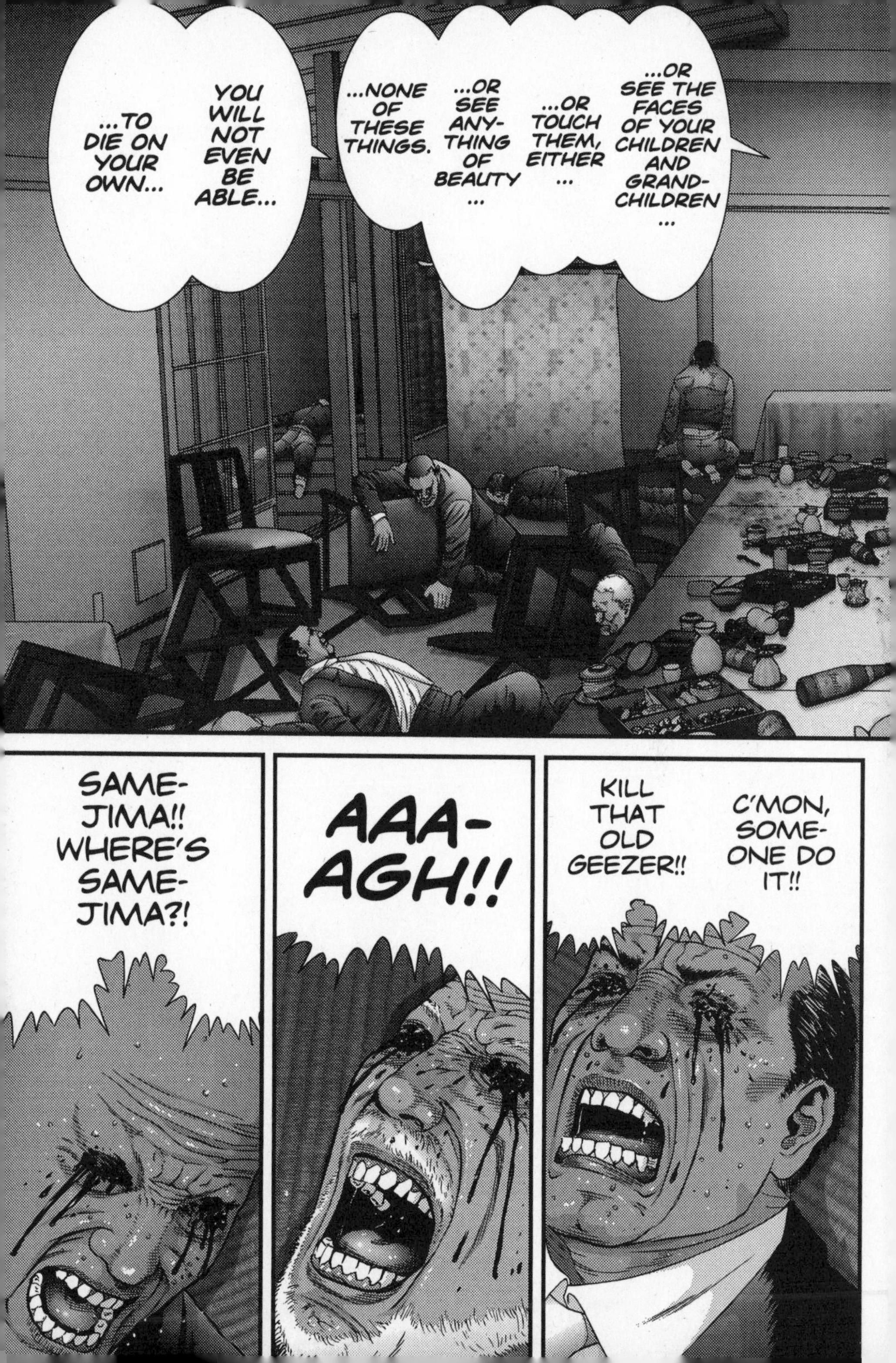
...OR SEE THE FACES OF YOUR CHILDREN AND GRAND-CHILDREN ...
...OR TOUCH THEM, EITHER ...
...OR SEE ANY-THING OF BEAUTY ...
...NONE OF THESE THINGS.
YOU WILL NOT EVEN BE ABLE...
...TO DIE ON YOUR OWN...
C'MON, SOME-ONE DO IT!!
KILL THAT OLD GEEZER!!
AAA-AGH!!
SAME-JIMA!! WHERE'S SAME-JIMA?!

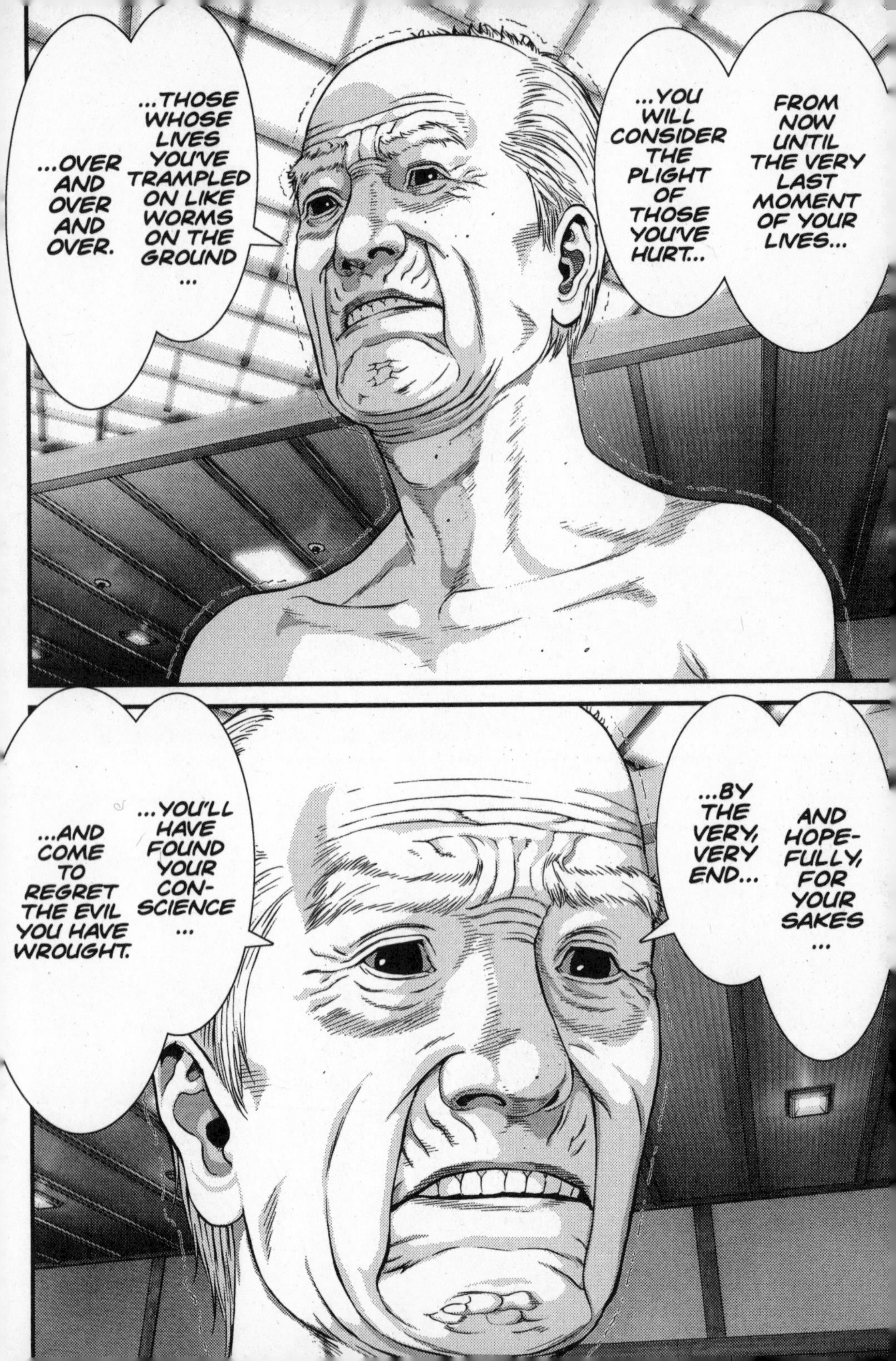
FROM NOW UNTIL THE VERY LAST MOMENT OF YOUR LIVES...
...YOU WILL CONSIDER THE PLIGHT OF THOSE YOU'VE HURT...
...THOSE WHOSE LIVES YOU'VE TRAMPLED ON LIKE WORMS ON THE GROUND...
...OVER AND OVER AND OVER.
AND HOPE-FULLY, FOR YOUR SAKES...
...BY THE VERY, VERY END...
...YOU'LL HAVE FOUND YOUR CON-SCIENCE...
...AND COME TO REGRET THE EVIL YOU HAVE WROUGHT.

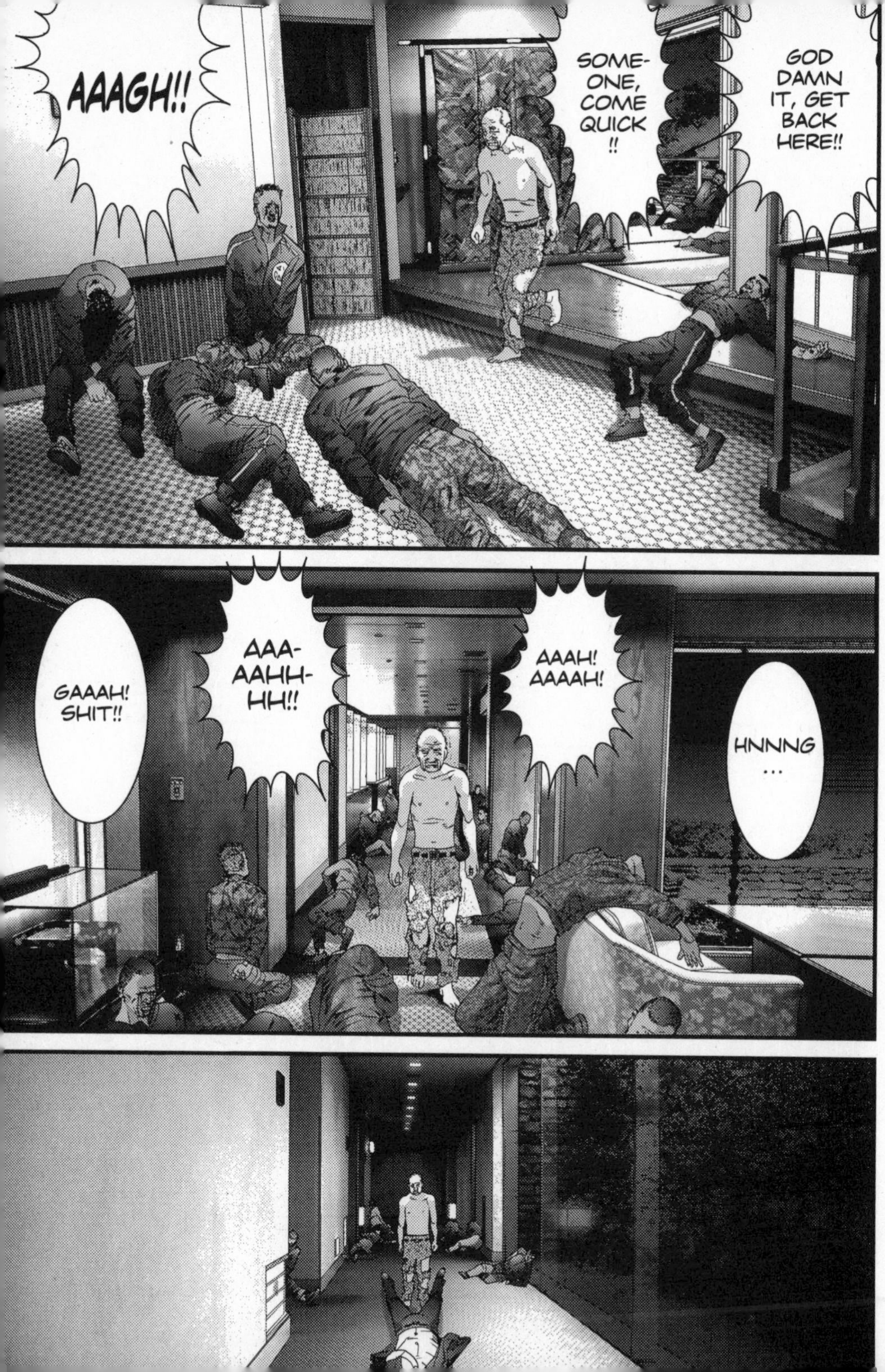
GOD DAMN IT, GET BACK HERE!!
SOME-ONE, COME QUICK !!
AAAGH!!
HNNNG ...
AAAH! AAAAH!
AAA-AAHH-HH!!
GAAAH! SHIT!!

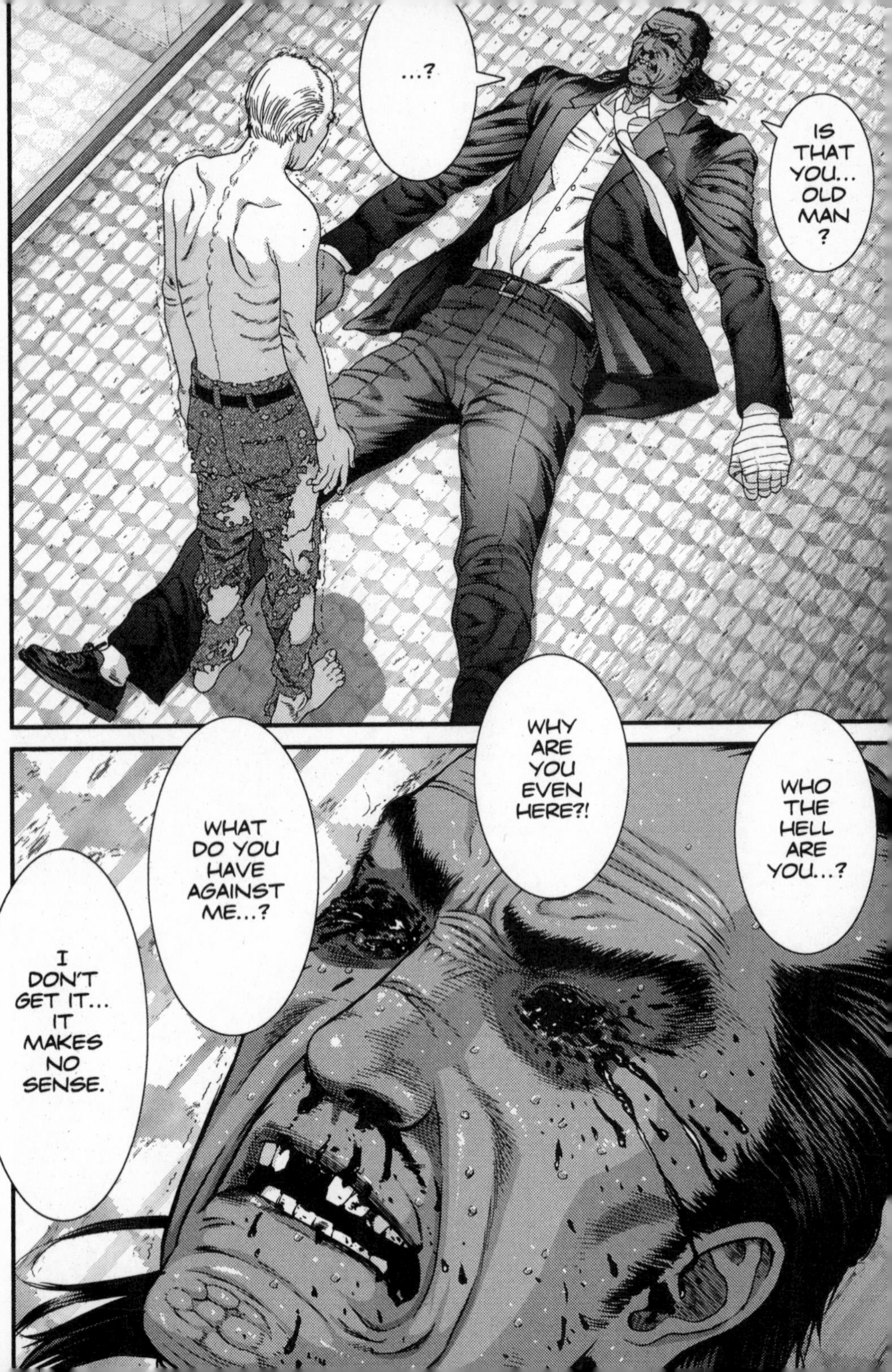
IS THAT YOU... OLD MAN?
...?
WHO THE HELL ARE YOU...?
WHY ARE YOU EVEN HERE?!
WHAT DO YOU HAVE AGAINST ME...?
I DON'T GET IT... IT MAKES NO SENSE.

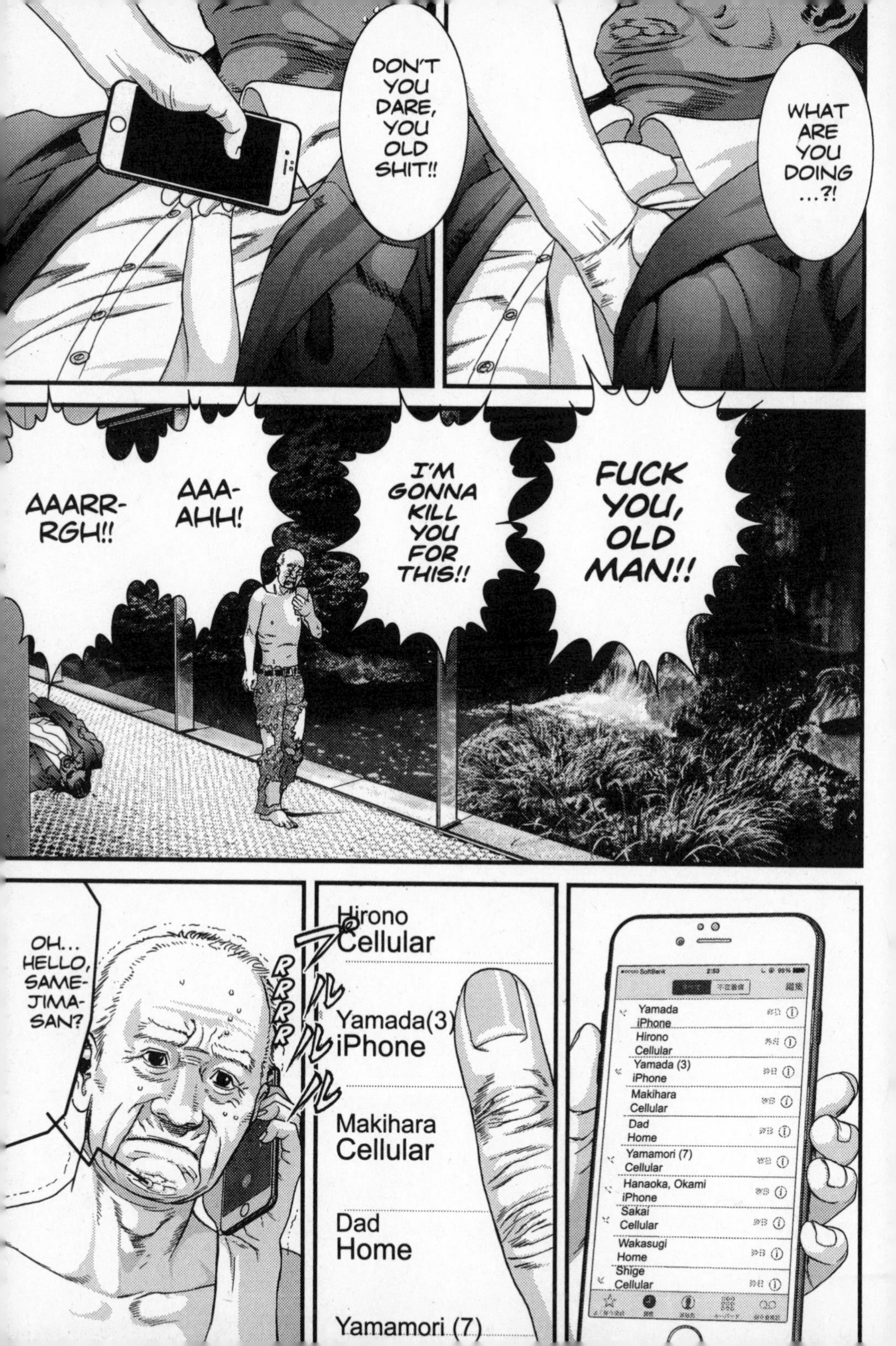
WHAT ARE YOU DOING ...?!
DON'T YOU DARE, YOU OLD SHIT!!
FUCK YOU, OLD MAN!!
I'M GONNA KILL YOU FOR THIS!!
AAA-AHH!
AAARR-RGH!!
SoftBank
2:53
99%
Yamada iPhone
Hirono Cellular
Yamada (3) iPhone
Makihara Cellular
Dad Home
Yamamori (7) Cellular
Hanaoka, Okami iPhone
Sakai Cellular
Wakasugi Home
Shige Cellular
Hirono Cellular
Yamada(3) iPhone
Makihara Cellular
Dad Home
Yamamori (7)
RRRRR
プルルルル
OH... HELLO, SAME-JIMA-SAN?

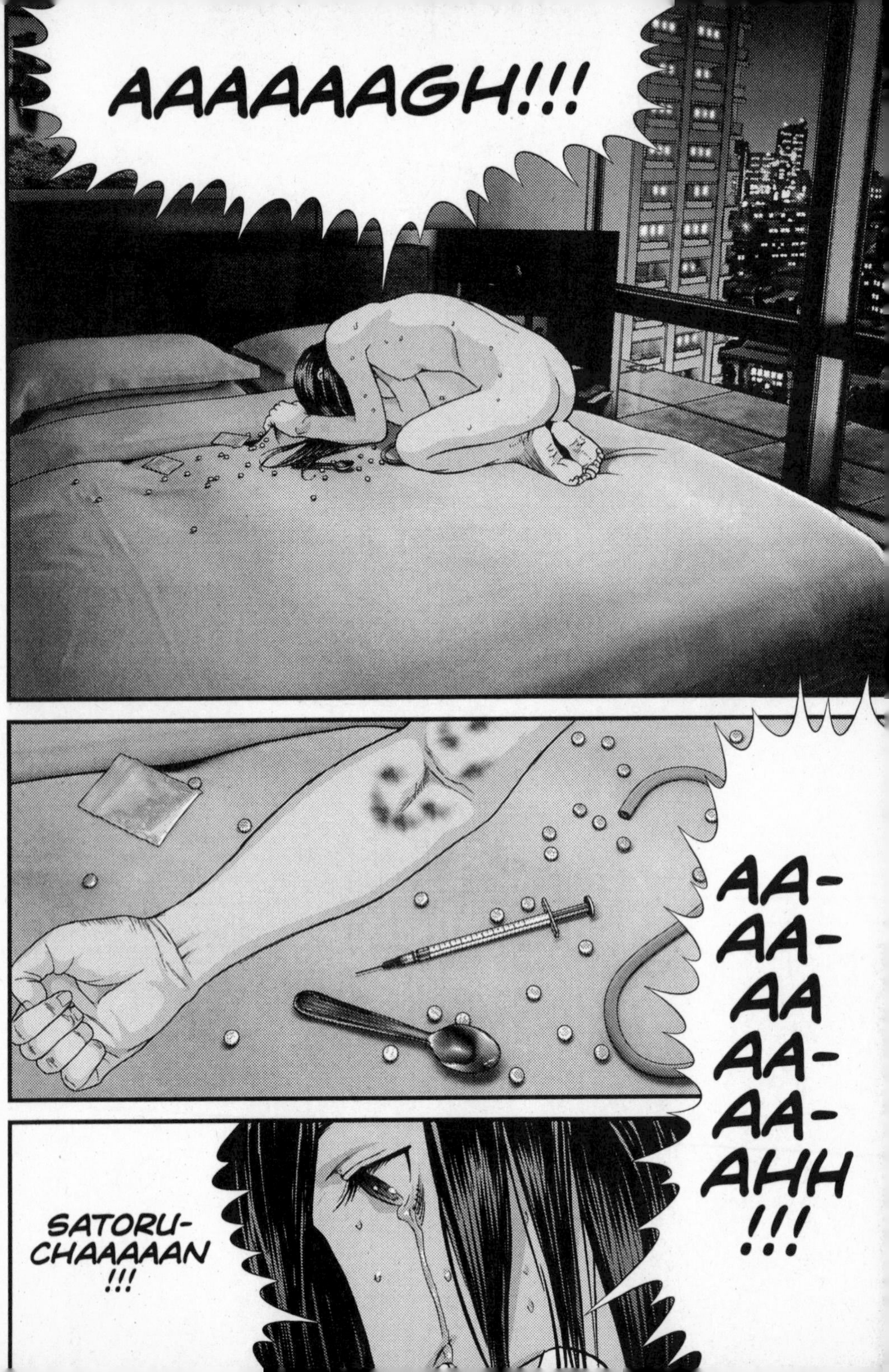
AAAAAAGH!!!
AA-AA-AA AA-AA-AHH !!!
SATORU-CHAAAAAN !!!

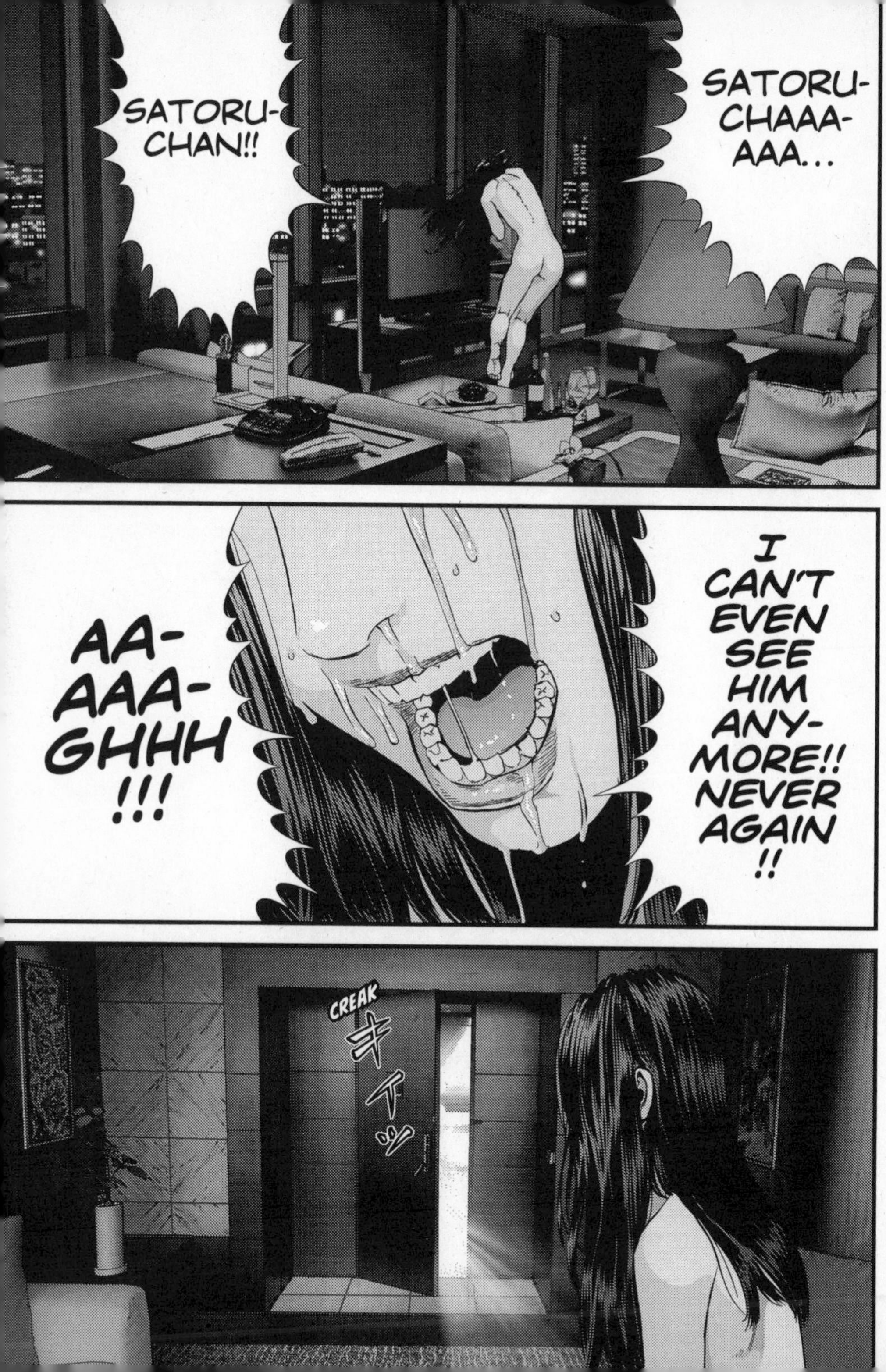

SATORU-CHAAAA-AAA...
SATORU-CHAN!!
I CAN'T EVEN SEE HIM ANY-MORE!! NEVER AGAIN !!
AA-AAA-GHHH !!!
CREAK
キイッ

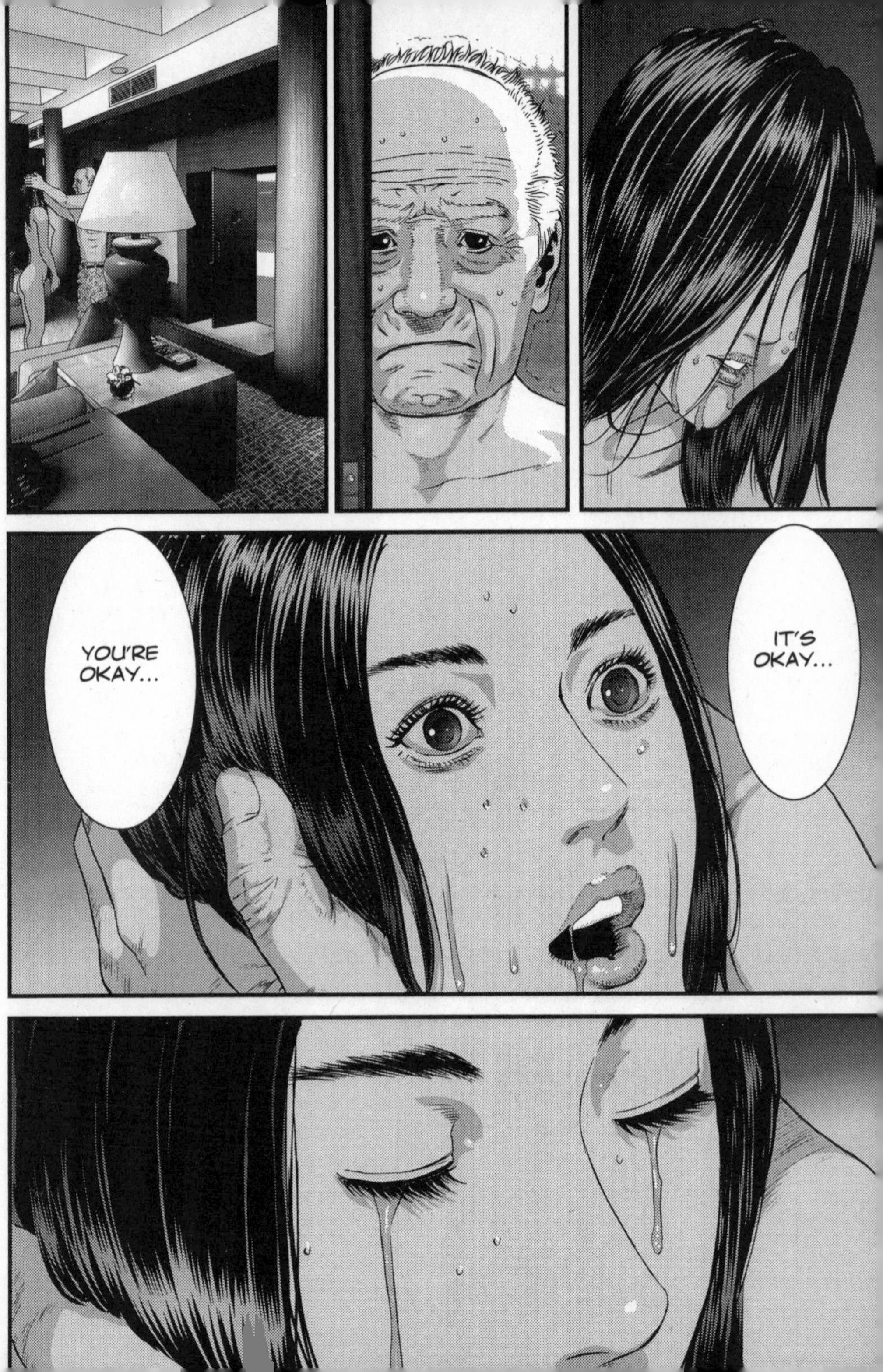
IT'S OKAY...
YOU'RE OKAY...

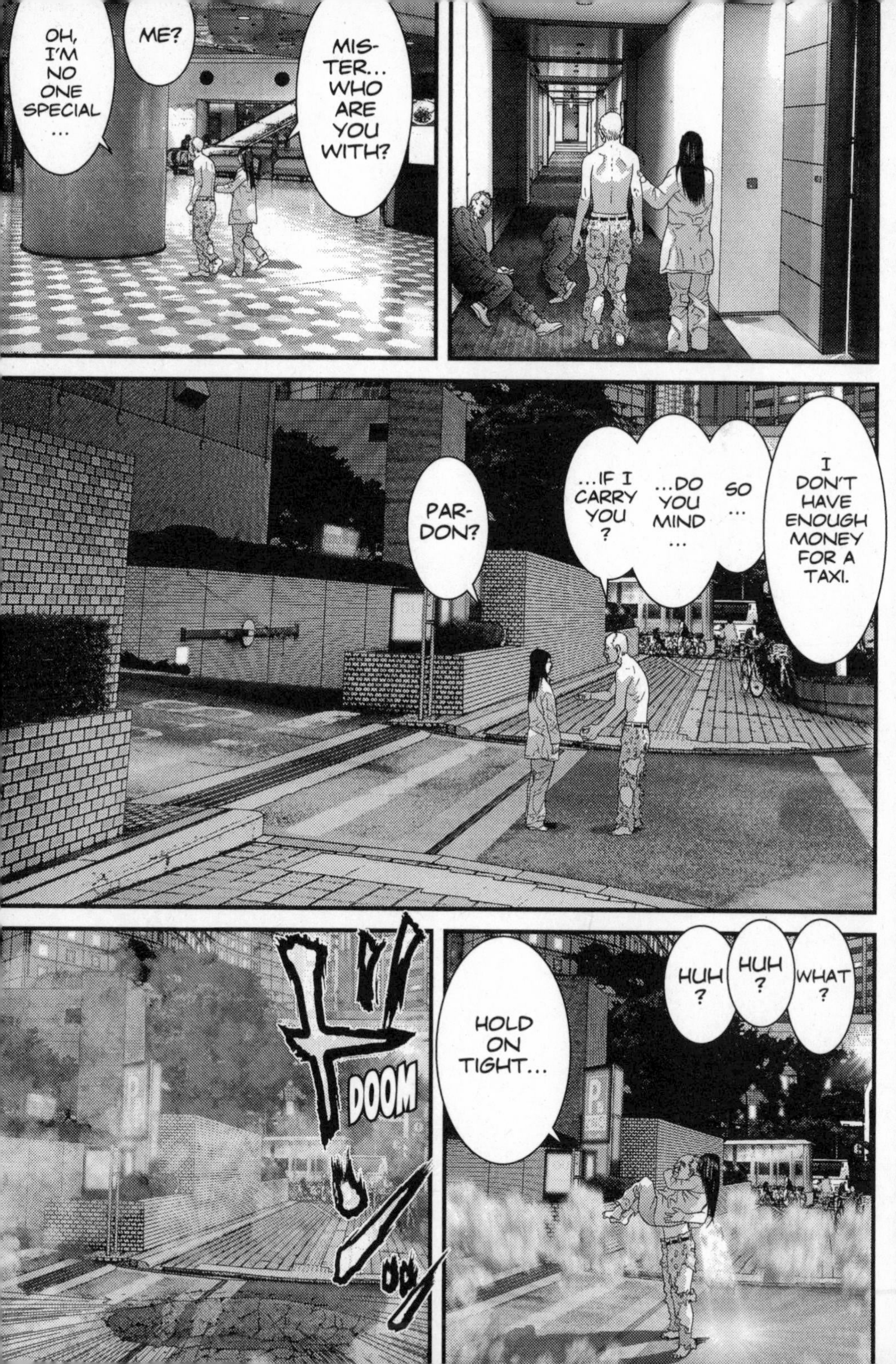
MIS-TER... WHO ARE YOU WITH?
ME?
OH, I'M NO ONE SPECIAL...
I DON'T HAVE ENOUGH MONEY FOR A TAXI.
SO...
...DO YOU MIND...
...IF I CARRY YOU?
PAR-DON?
WHAT?
HUH?
HUH?
HOLD ON TIGHT...
DOOM

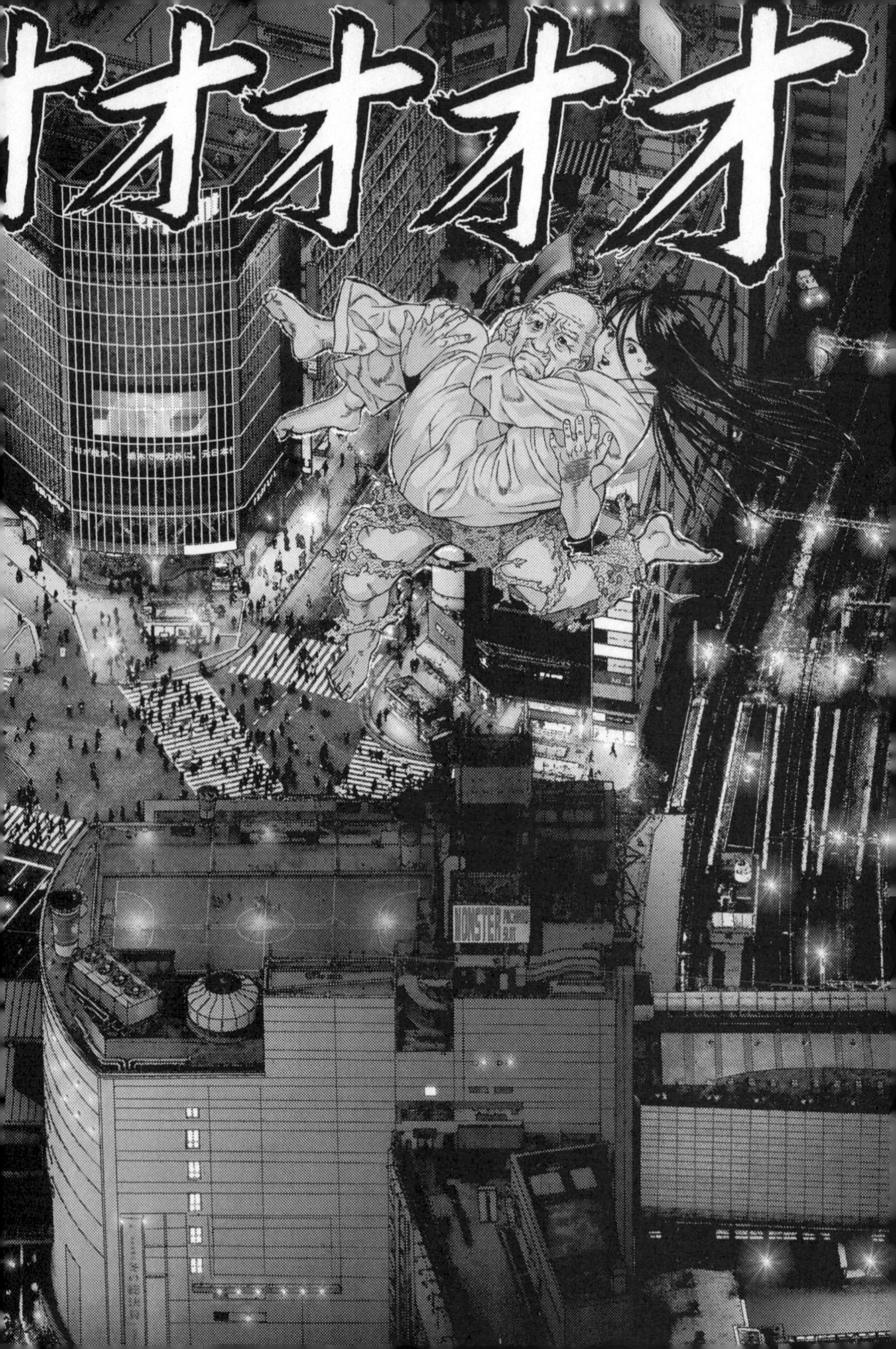
オオオオ

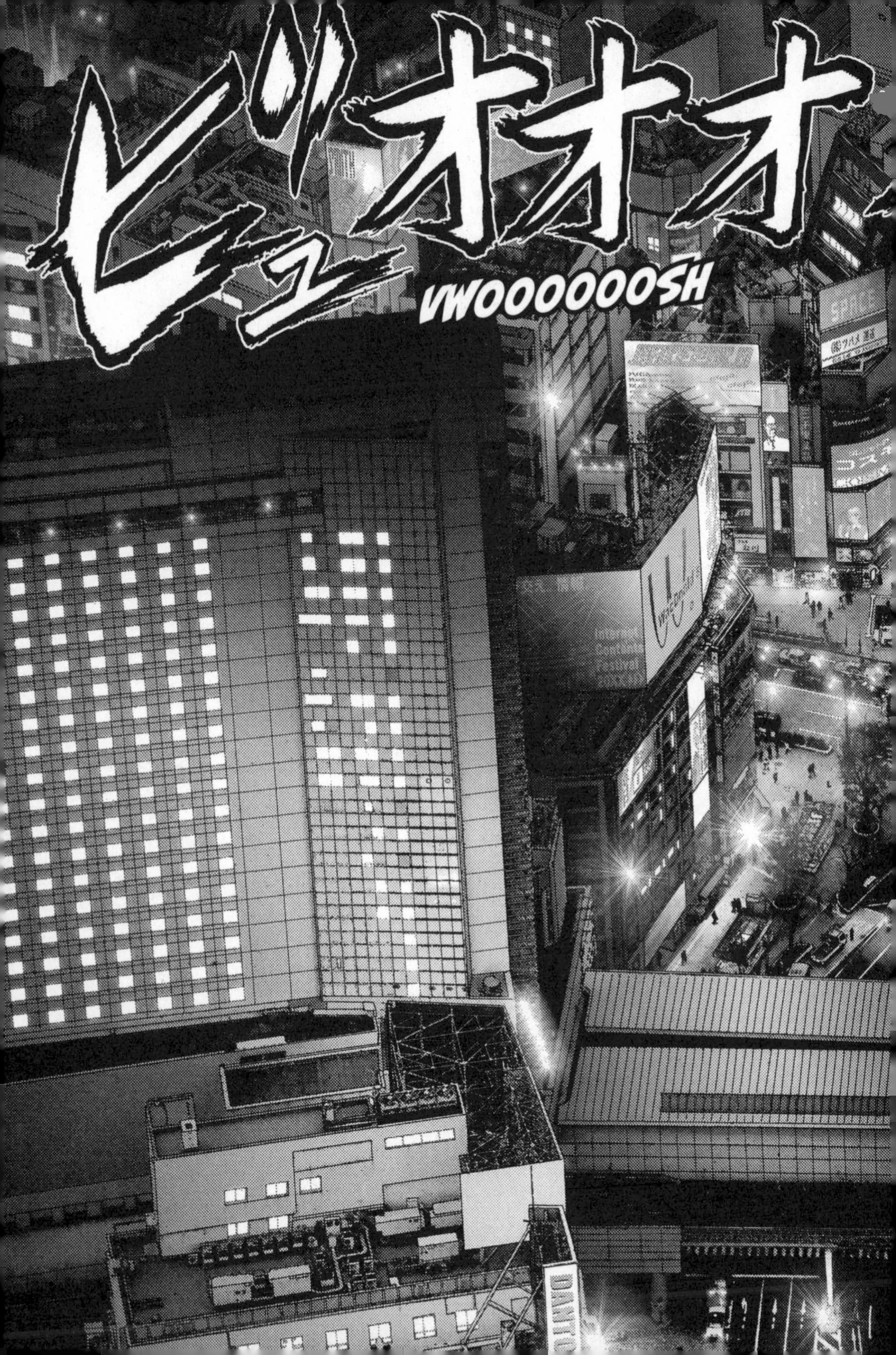
ビュオオオ
VWOOOOOOSH

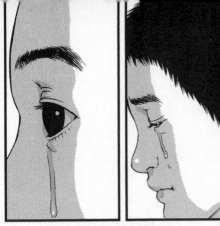

CHAPTER 27 - END

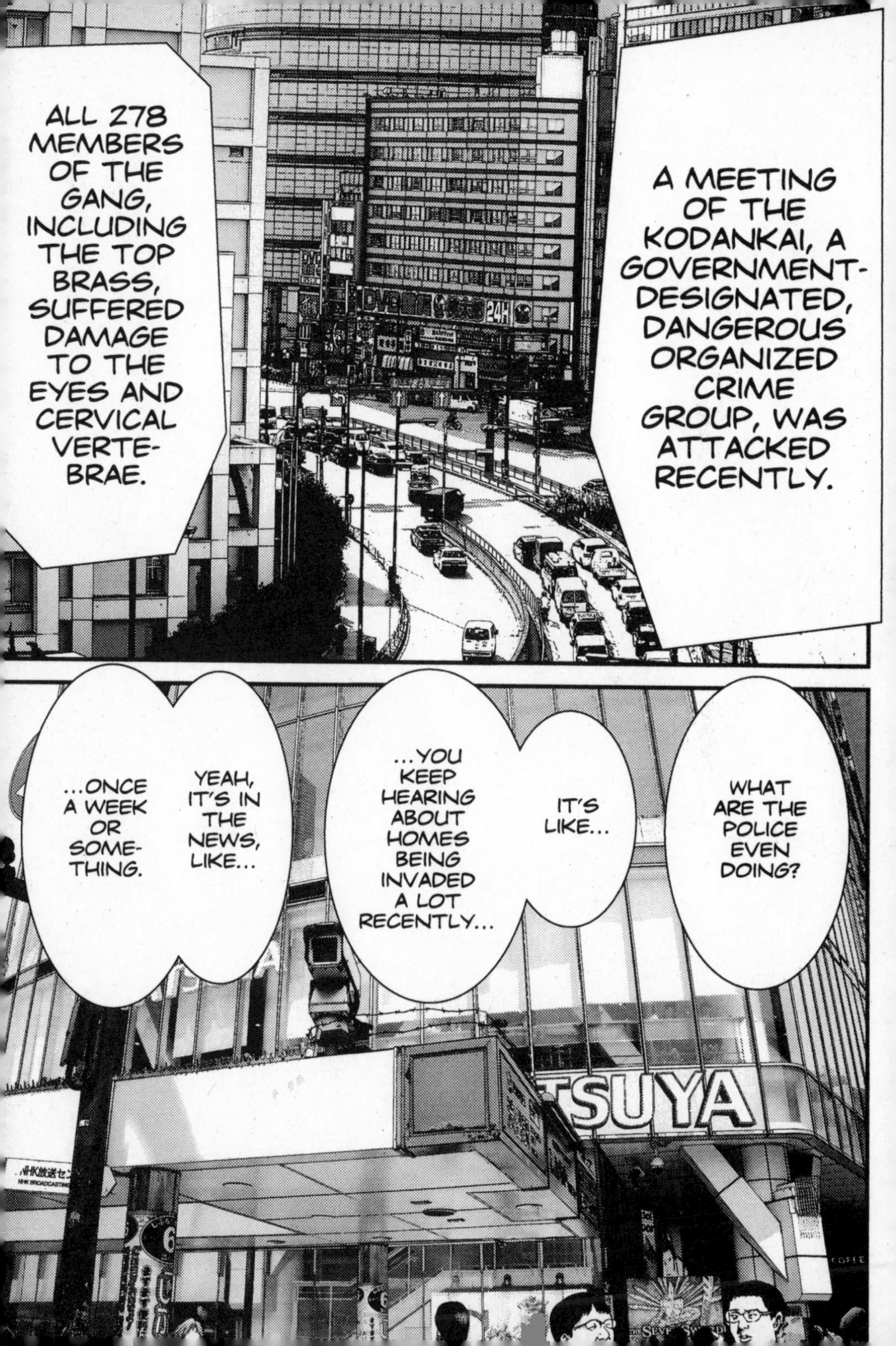

A MEETING OF THE KODANKAI, A GOVERNMENT-DESIGNATED, DANGEROUS ORGANIZED CRIME GROUP, WAS ATTACKED RECENTLY.
ALL 278 MEMBERS OF THE GANG, INCLUDING THE TOP BRASS, SUFFERED DAMAGE TO THE EYES AND CERVICAL VERTE-BRAE.
WHAT ARE THE POLICE EVEN DOING?
IT'S LIKE...
...YOU KEEP HEARING ABOUT HOMES BEING INVADED A LOT RECENTLY...
YEAH, IT'S IN THE NEWS, LIKE...
...ONCE A WEEK OR SOME-THING.
TSUYA

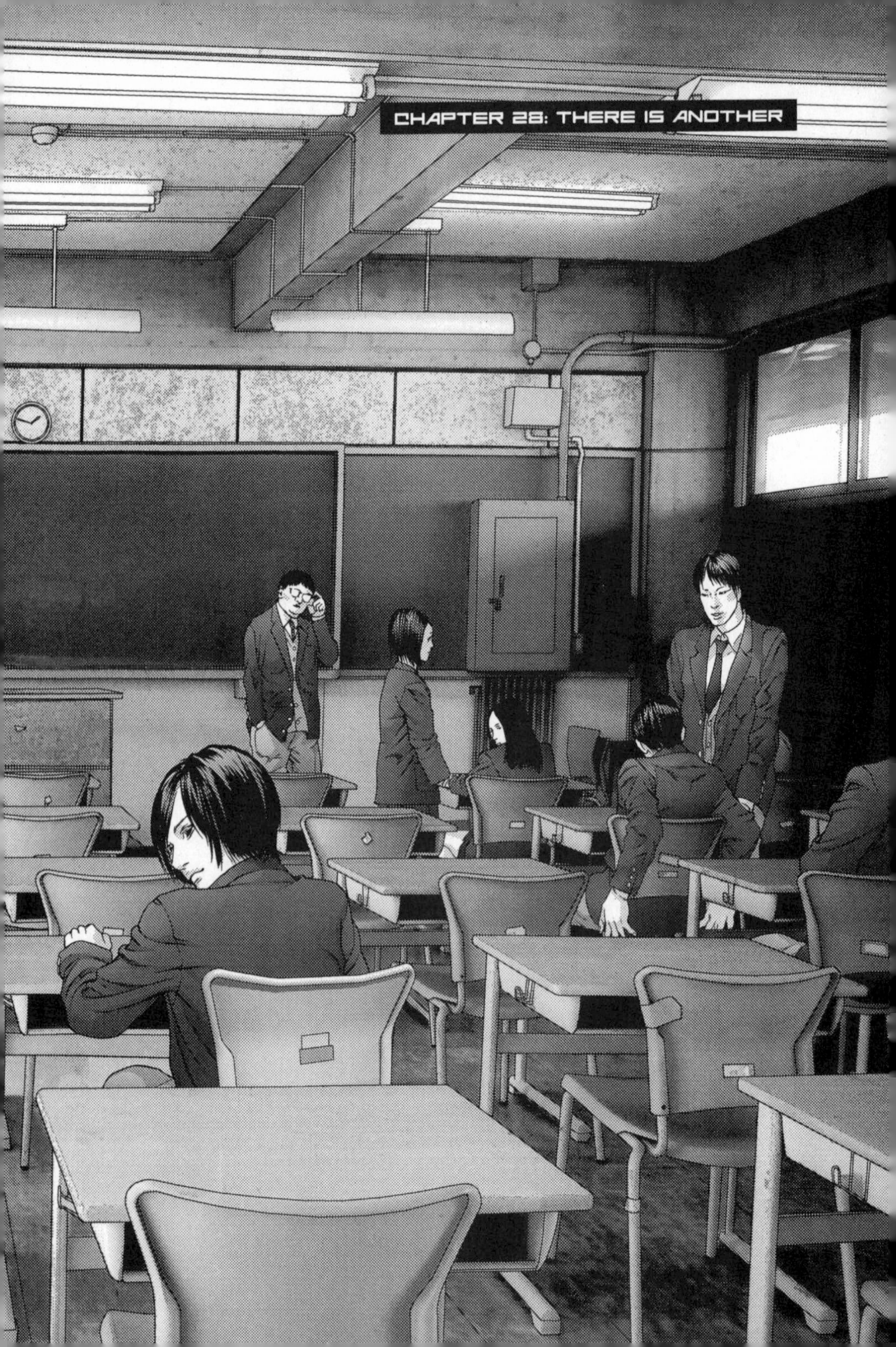
CHAPTER 28: THERE IS ANOTHER

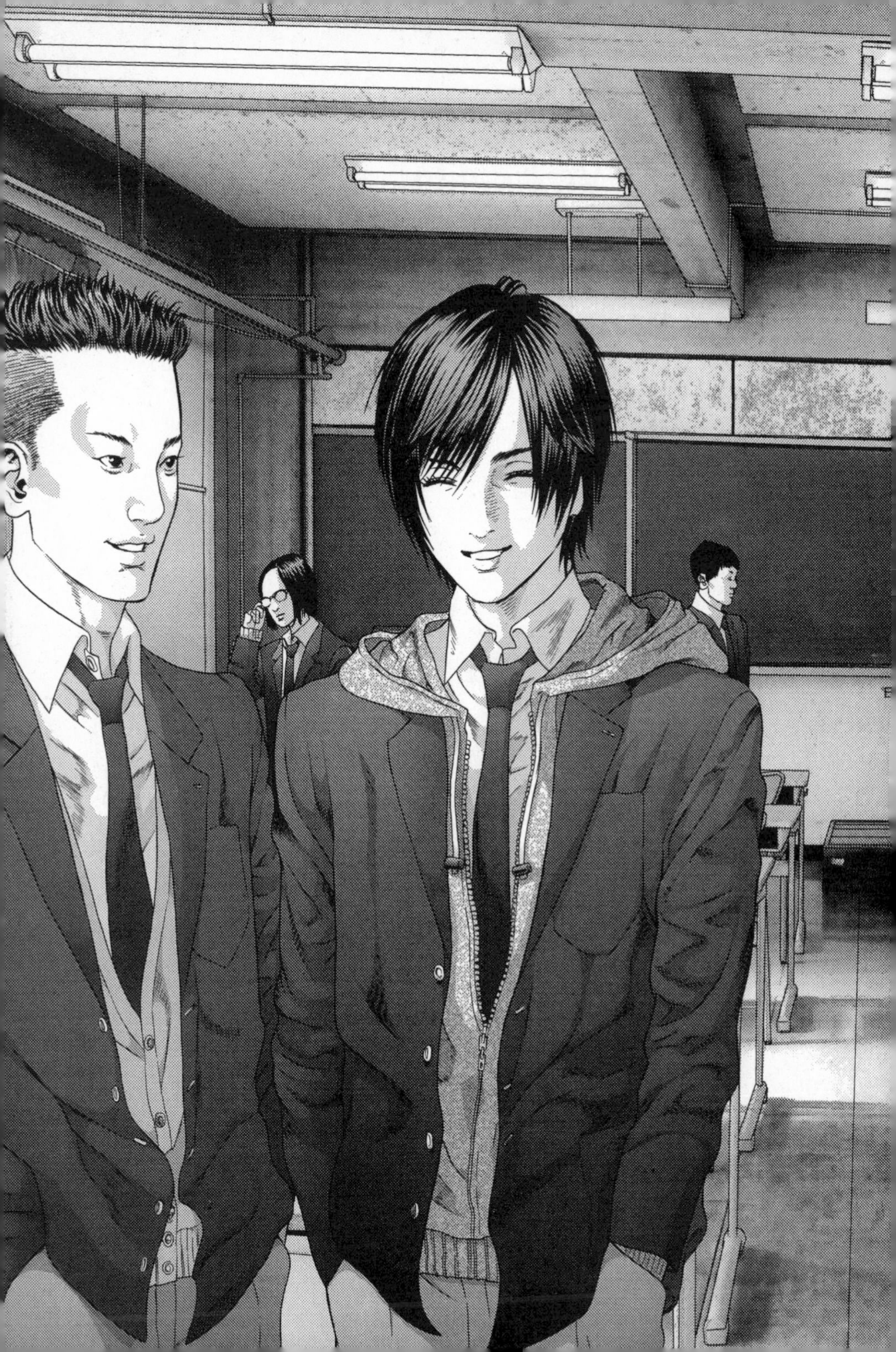

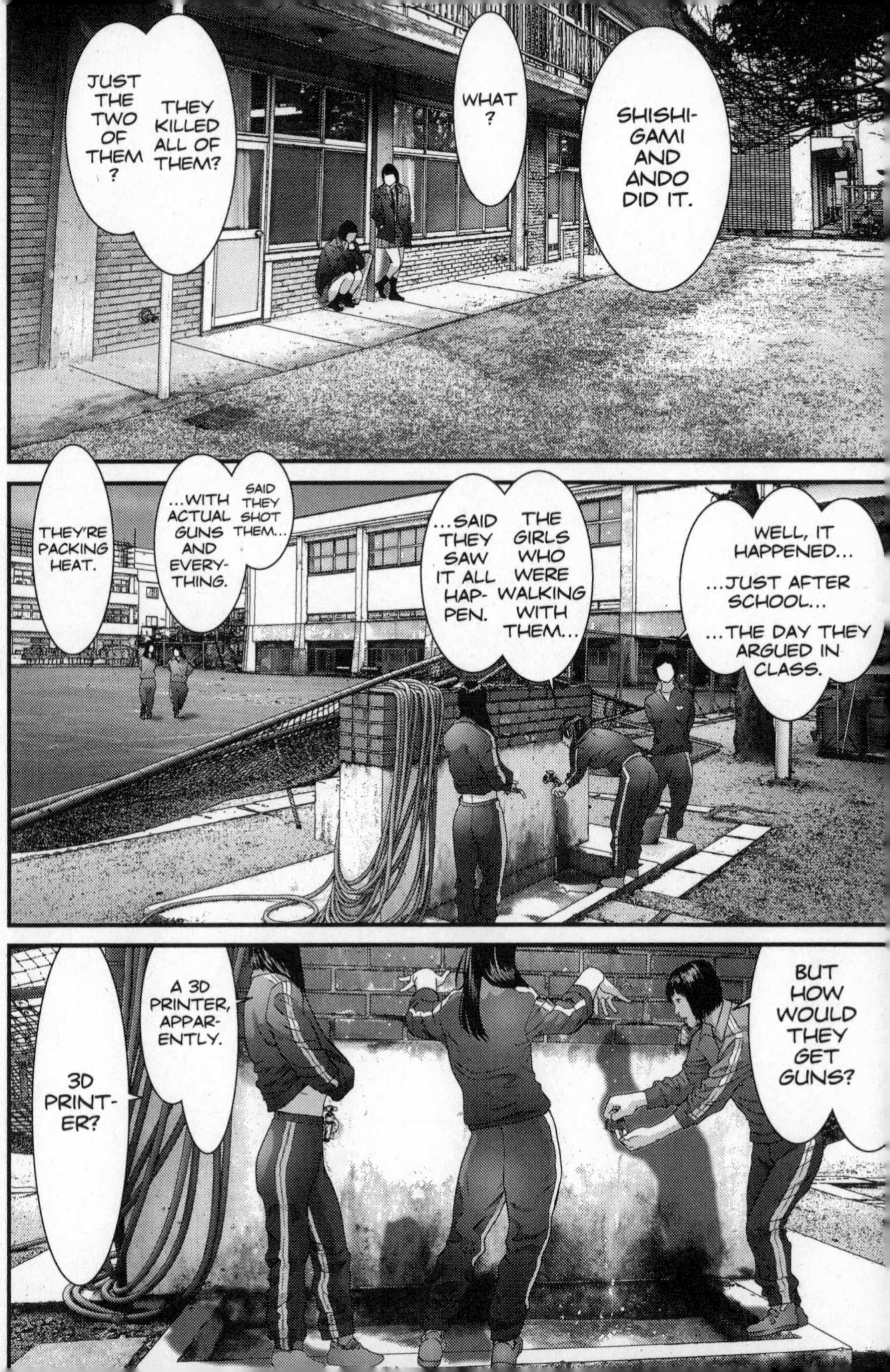
SHISHIGAMI AND ANDO DID IT.
WHAT?
THEY KILLED ALL OF THEM?
JUST THE TWO OF THEM?
WELL, IT HAPPENED... ...JUST AFTER SCHOOL... ...THE DAY THEY ARGUED IN CLASS.
THE GIRLS WHO WERE WALKING WITH THEM...
...SAID THEY SAW IT ALL HAPPEN.
SAID THEY SHOT THEM...
...WITH ACTUAL GUNS AND EVERYTHING.
THEY'RE PACKING HEAT.
BUT HOW WOULD THEY GET GUNS?
A 3D PRINTER, APPARENTLY.
3D PRINTER?

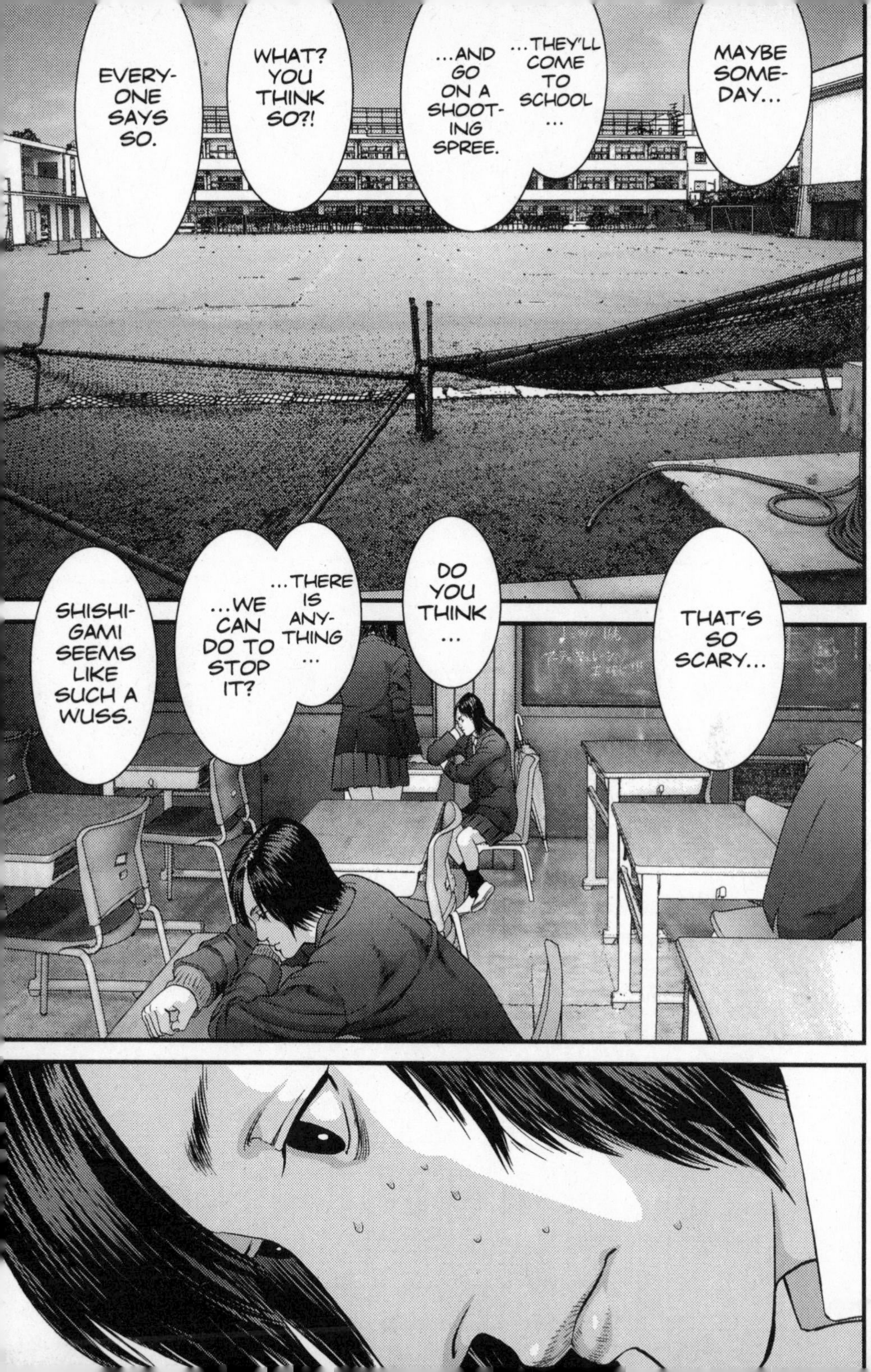
MAYBE SOME-DAY...
...THEY'LL COME TO SCHOOL ...
...AND GO ON A SHOOTING SPREE.
WHAT? YOU THINK SO?!
EVERY-ONE SAYS SO.
THAT'S SO SCARY...
DO YOU THINK ...
...THERE IS ANY-THING ...
...WE CAN DO TO STOP IT?
SHISHIGAMI SEEMS LIKE SUCH A WUSS.

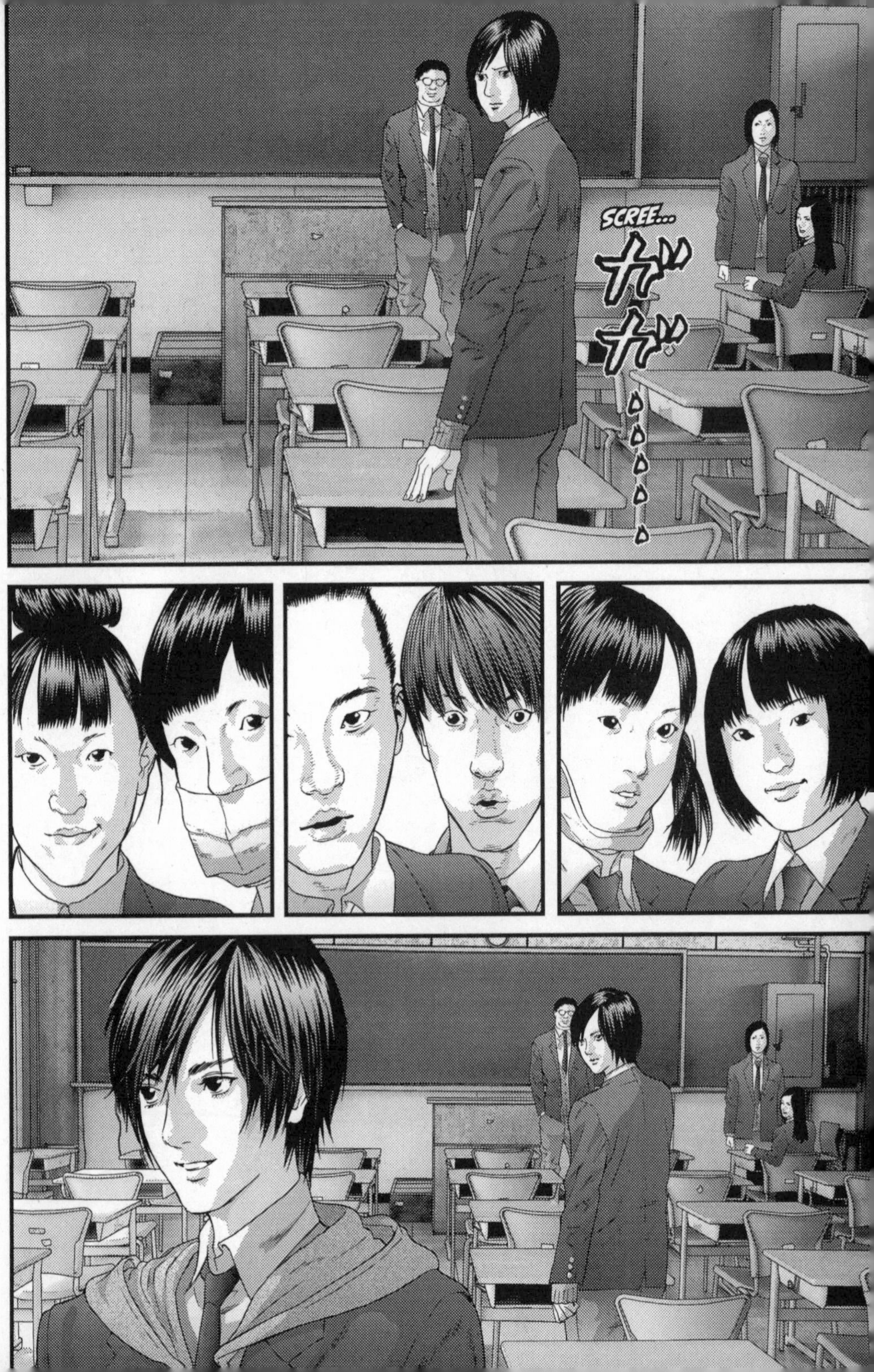
SCREE...
ガガ
ああああああ

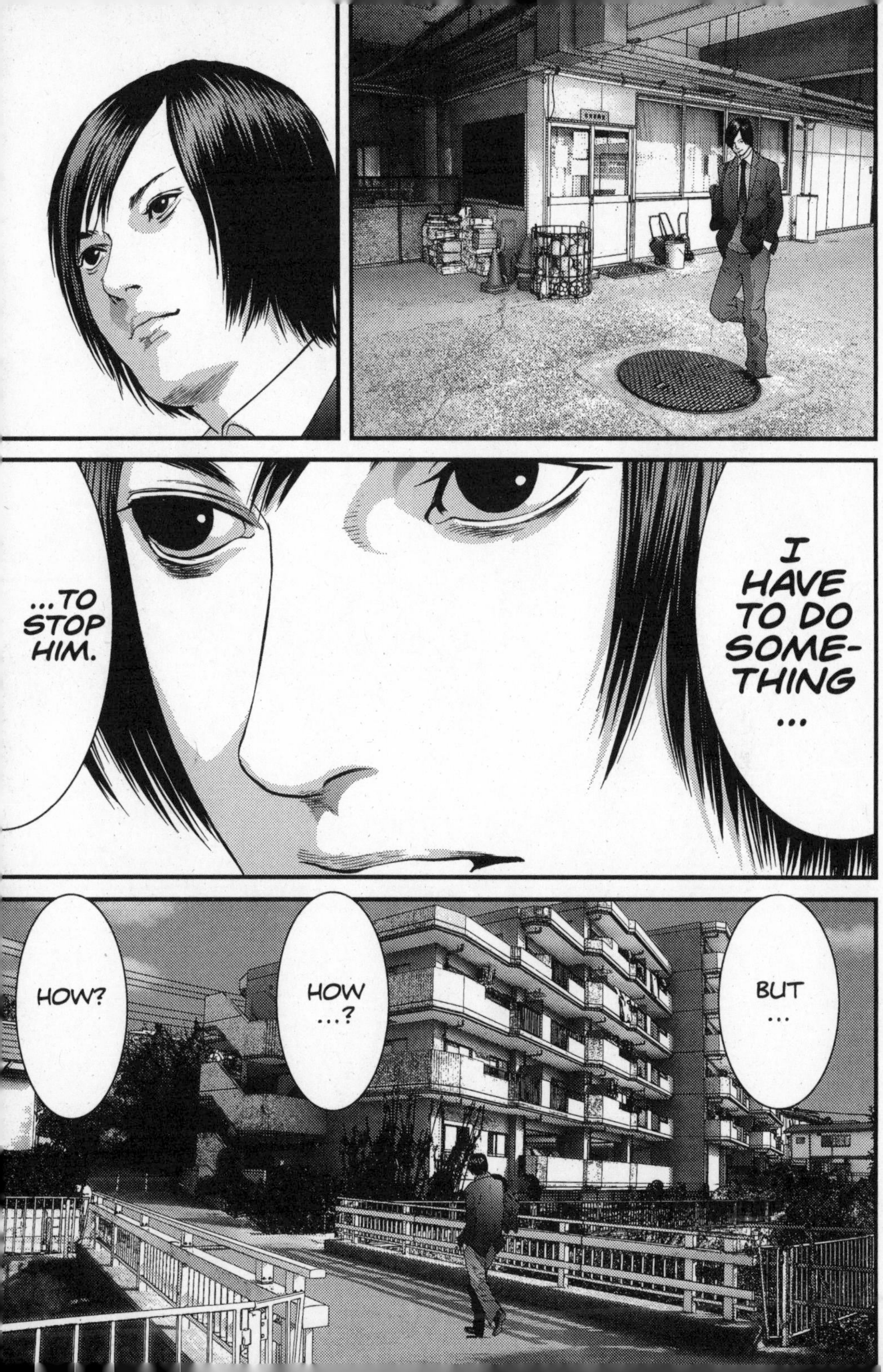
I HAVE TO DO SOME-THING ...
...TO STOP HIM.
BUT ...
HOW ...?
HOW?

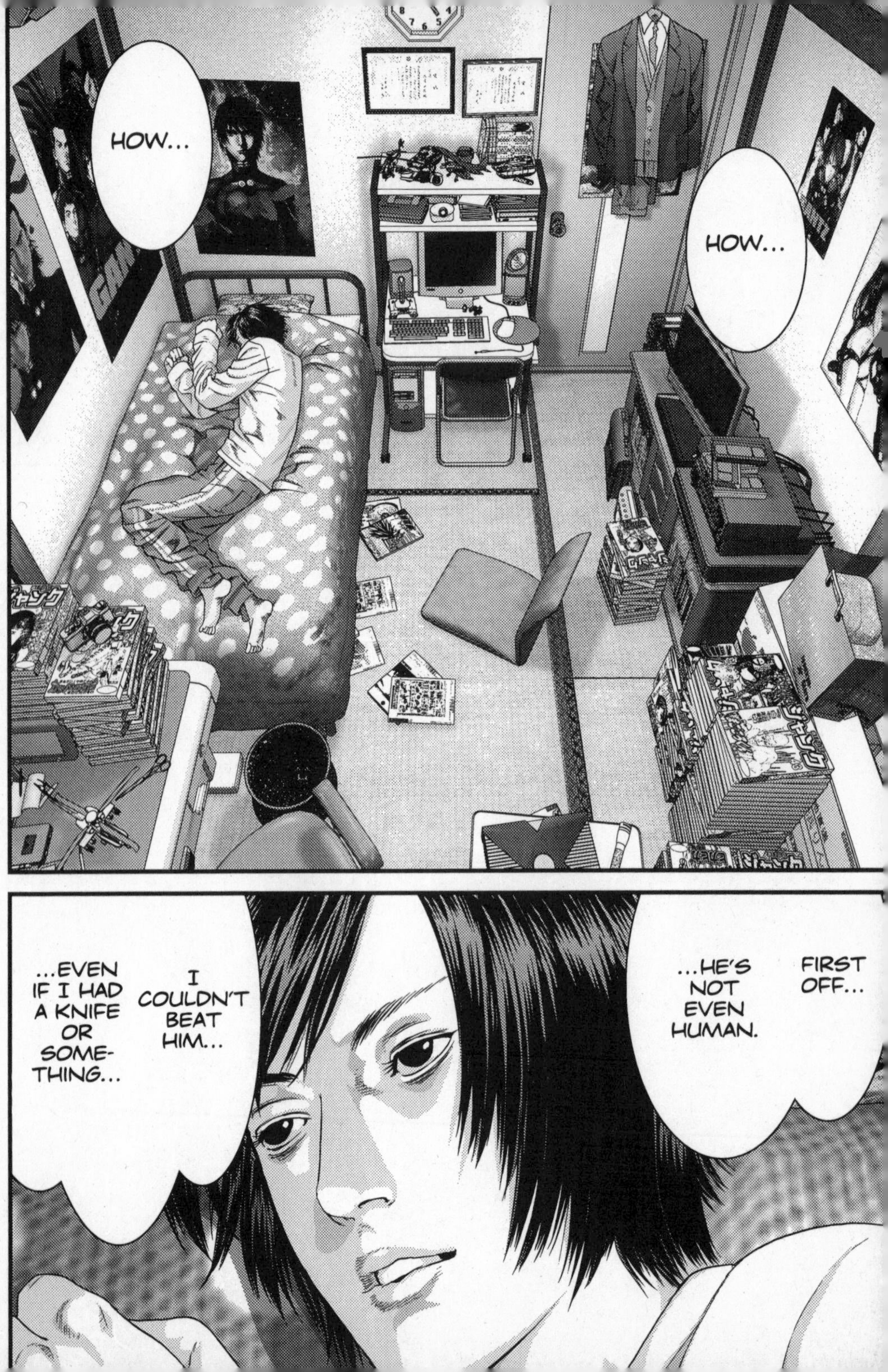
HOW...
HOW...
FIRST OFF...
...HE'S NOT EVEN HUMAN.
I COULDN'T BEAT HIM...
...EVEN IF I HAD A KNIFE OR SOME-THING...

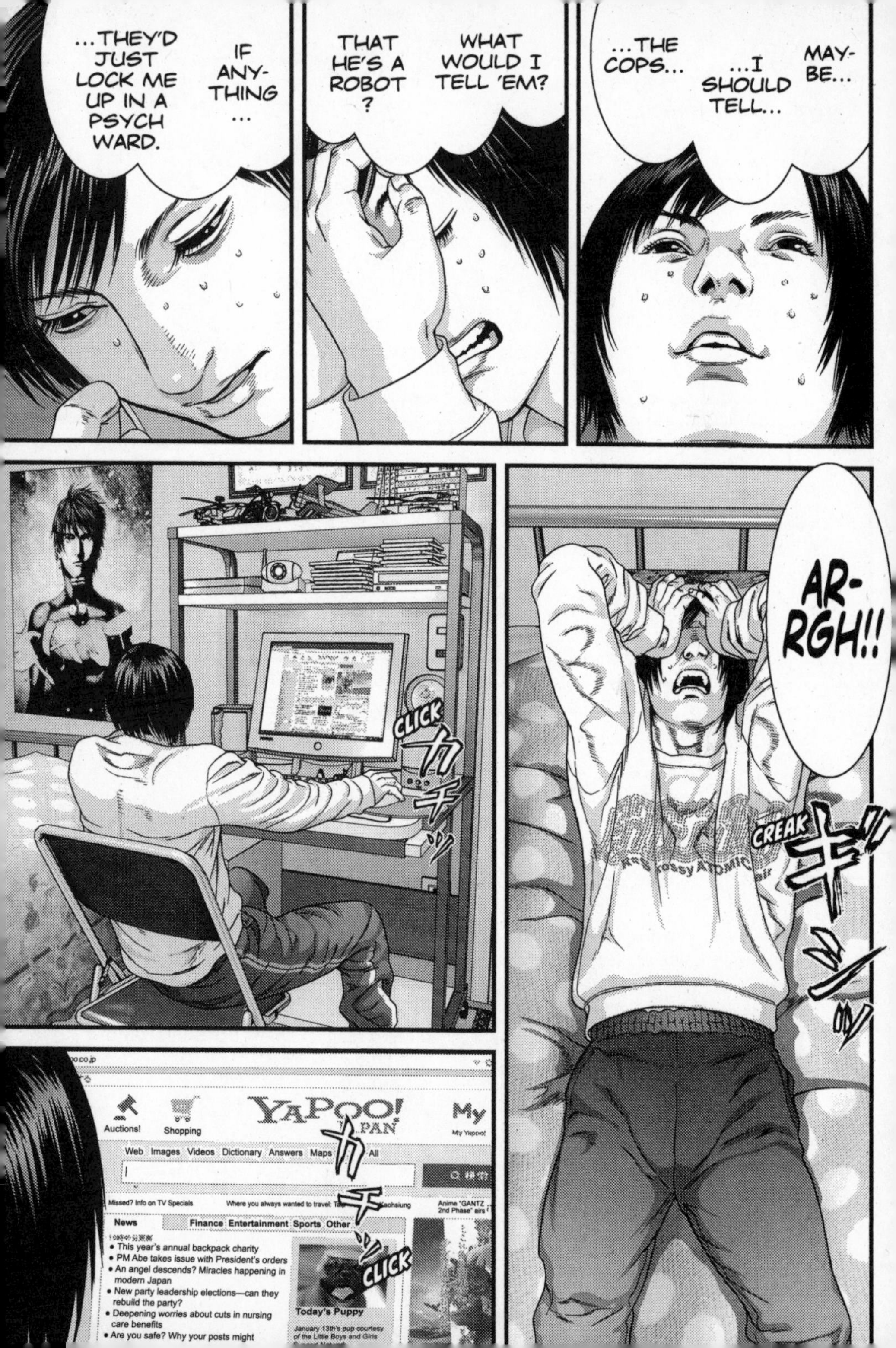
MAY-BE...
...I SHOULD TELL...
...THE COPS...
WHAT WOULD I TELL 'EM?
THAT HE'S A ROBOT?
IF ANY-THING...
...THEY'D JUST LOCK ME UP IN A PSYCH WARD.
AR-RGH!!
CREAK
ギシ
ギシッ
CLICK
カチッ
YAPOO! JAPAN
Auctions!
Shopping
My
My Yapoo!
Web Images Videos Dictionary Answers Maps All
Missed? Info on TV Specials
Where you always wanted to travel:
Kaohsiung
Anime "GANTZ 2nd Phase" airs
News
Finance Entertainment Sports Other
• This year's annual backpack charity
• PM Abe takes issue with President's orders
• An angel descends? Miracles happening in modern Japan
• New party leadership elections—can they rebuild the party?
• Deepening worries about cuts in nursing care benefits
• Are you safe? Why your posts might
Today's Puppy
January 13th's pup courtesy of the Little Boys and Girls
カチッ
CLICK

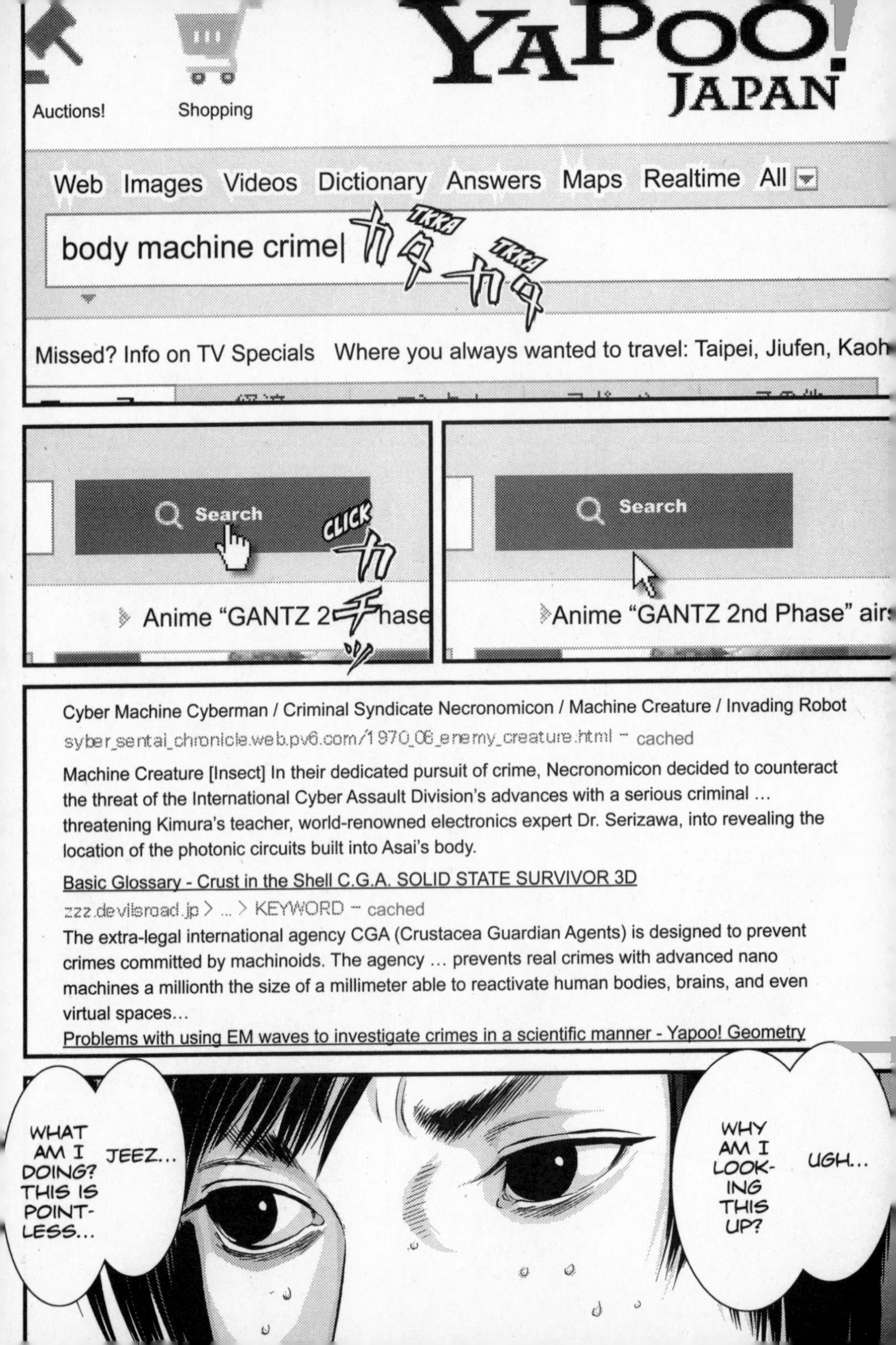

YAPOO! JAPAN
Auctions!
Shopping
Web Images Videos Dictionary Answers Maps Realtime All
body machine crime|
カタ TKKA
カタ TKKA
Missed? Info on TV Specials Where you always wanted to travel: Taipei, Jiufen, Kaoh
Search
Anime "GANTZ 2nd Phase" air
Search
CLICK カチッ
Anime "GANTZ 2 hase
Cyber Machine Cyberman / Criminal Syndicate Necronomicon / Machine Creature / Invading Robot
syber_sentai_chronicle.web.pv6.com/1970_06_enemy_creature.html – cached
Machine Creature [Insect] In their dedicated pursuit of crime, Necronomicon decided to counteract the threat of the International Cyber Assault Division's advances with a serious criminal … threatening Kimura's teacher, world-renowned electronics expert Dr. Serizawa, into revealing the location of the photonic circuits built into Asai's body.
Basic Glossary - Crust in the Shell C.G.A. SOLID STATE SURVIVOR 3D
zzz.devilsroad.jp > … > KEYWORD – cached
The extra-legal international agency CGA (Crustacea Guardian Agents) is designed to prevent crimes committed by machinoids. The agency … prevents real crimes with advanced nano machines a millionth the size of a millimeter able to reactivate human bodies, brains, and even virtual spaces…
Problems with using EM waves to investigate crimes in a scientific manner - Yapoo! Geometry
UGH…
WHY AM I LOOKING THIS UP?
JEEZ…
WHAT AM I DOING? THIS IS POINTLESS…

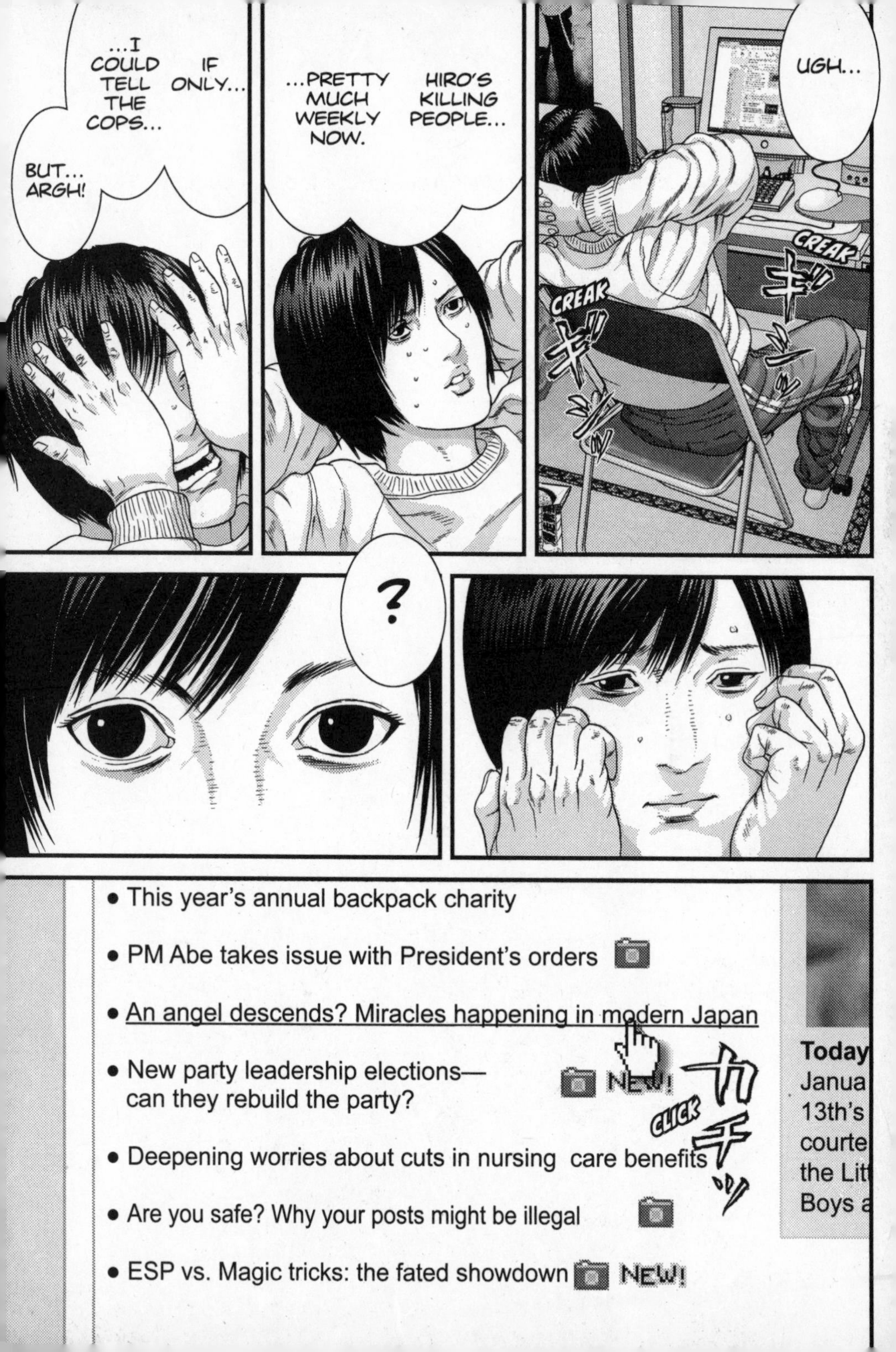
UGH...
CREAK
CREAK
HIRO'S KILLING PEOPLE...
...PRETTY MUCH WEEKLY NOW.
IF ONLY...
...I COULD TELL THE COPS...
BUT... ARGH!
?
• This year's annual backpack charity
• PM Abe takes issue with President's orders
• An angel descends? Miracles happening in modern Japan
• New party leadership elections— can they rebuild the party? NEW!
• Deepening worries about cuts in nursing care benefits
• Are you safe? Why your posts might be illegal
• ESP vs. Magic tricks: the fated showdown NEW!
Today
Janua
13th's
courte
the Litt
Boys a
CLICK
カチ

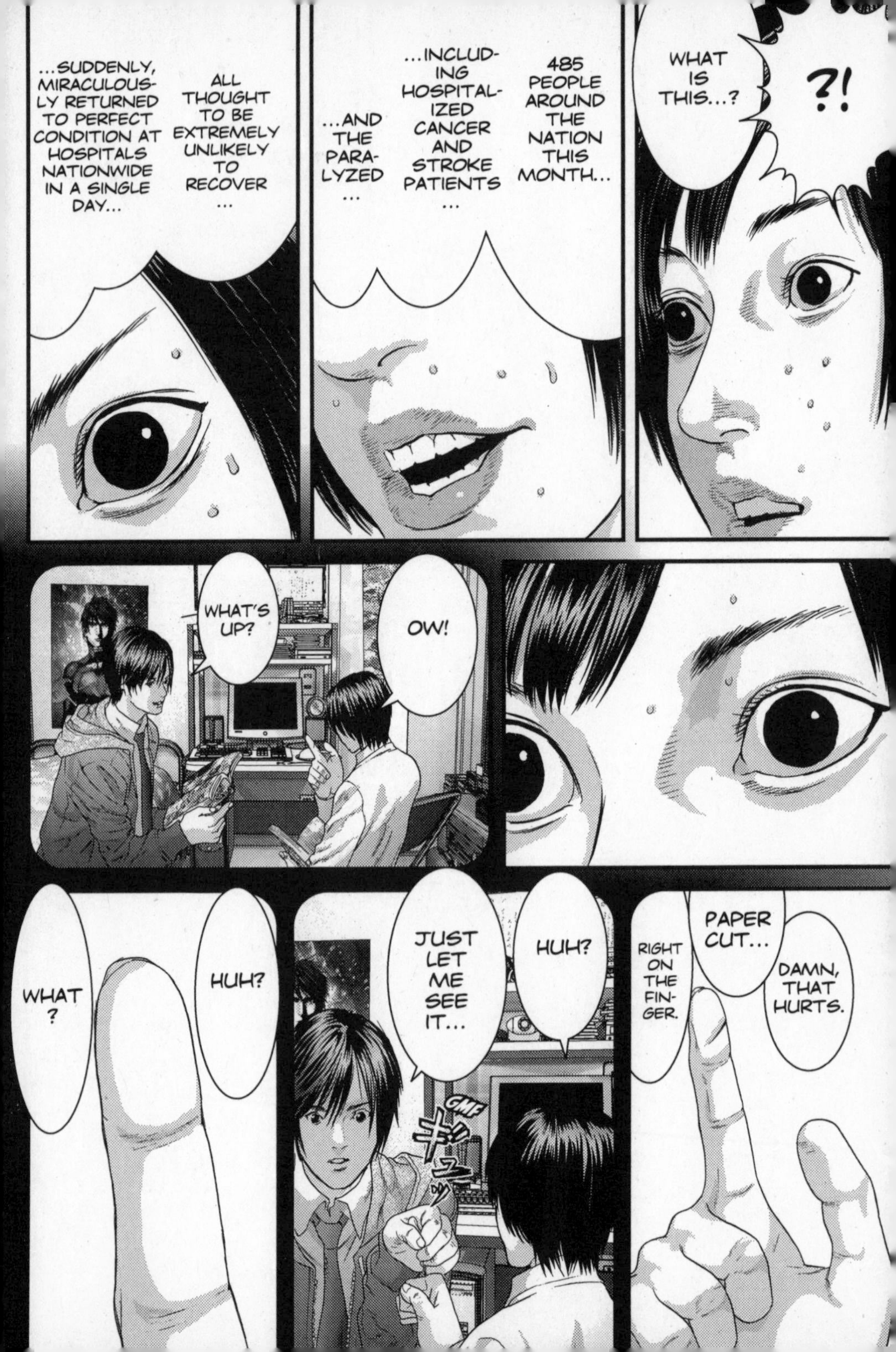
?!
WHAT IS THIS...?
485 PEOPLE AROUND THE NATION THIS MONTH...
...INCLUDING HOSPITALIZED CANCER AND STROKE PATIENTS...
...AND THE PARALYZED...
ALL THOUGHT TO BE EXTREMELY UNLIKELY TO RECOVER...
...SUDDENLY, MIRACULOUSLY RETURNED TO PERFECT CONDITION AT HOSPITALS NATIONWIDE IN A SINGLE DAY...
OW!
WHAT'S UP?
PAPER CUT...
RIGHT ON THE FINGER.
DAMN, THAT HURTS.
HUH?
JUST LET ME SEE IT...
GMF
HUH?
WHAT?

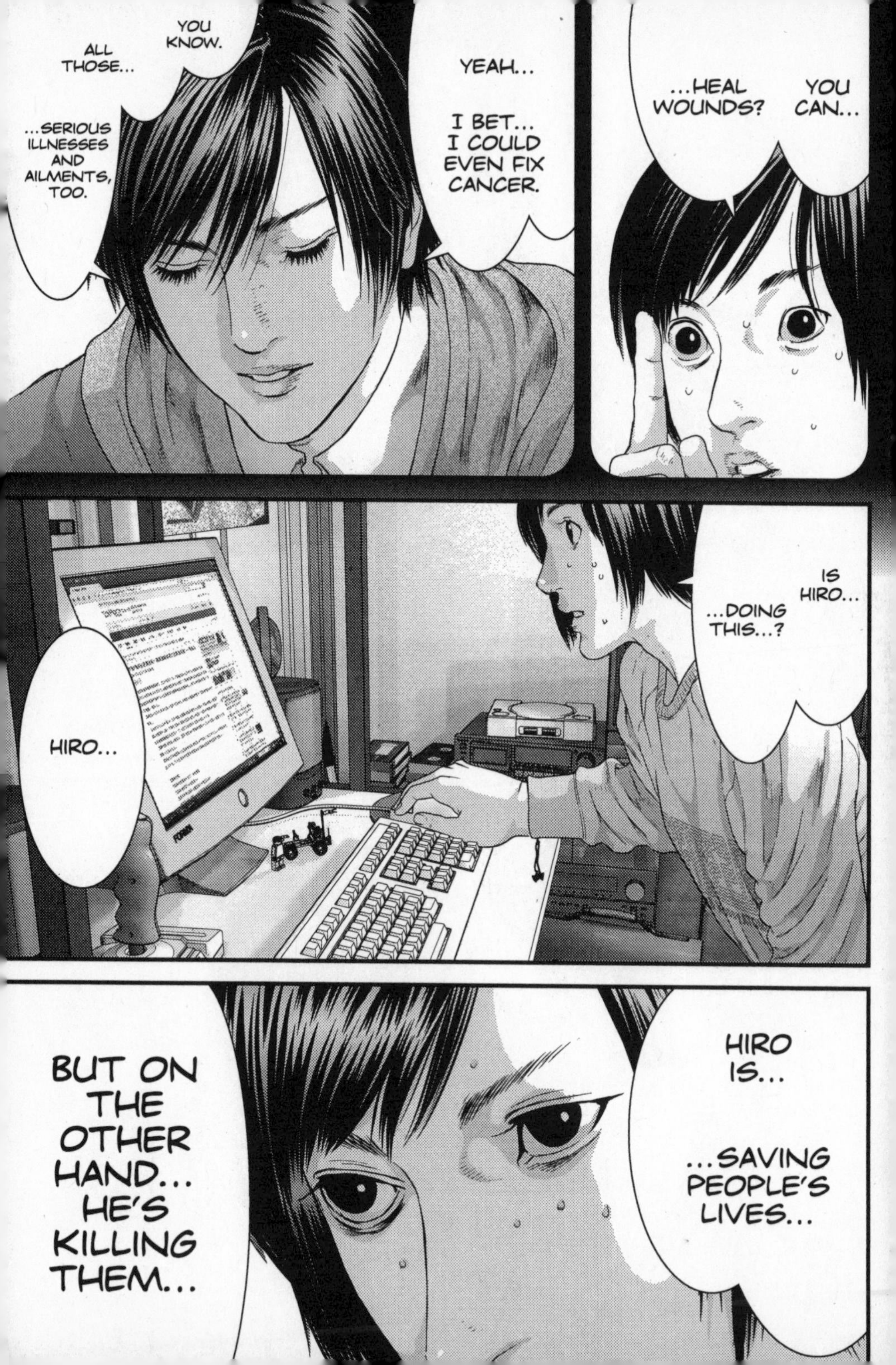
YOU CAN...
...HEAL WOUNDS?
YEAH...
I BET... I COULD EVEN FIX CANCER.
YOU KNOW.
ALL THOSE...
...SERIOUS ILLNESSES AND AILMENTS, TOO.
IS HIRO...
...DOING THIS...?
HIRO...
HIRO IS...
...SAVING PEOPLE'S LIVES...
BUT ON THE OTHER HAND... HE'S KILLING THEM...

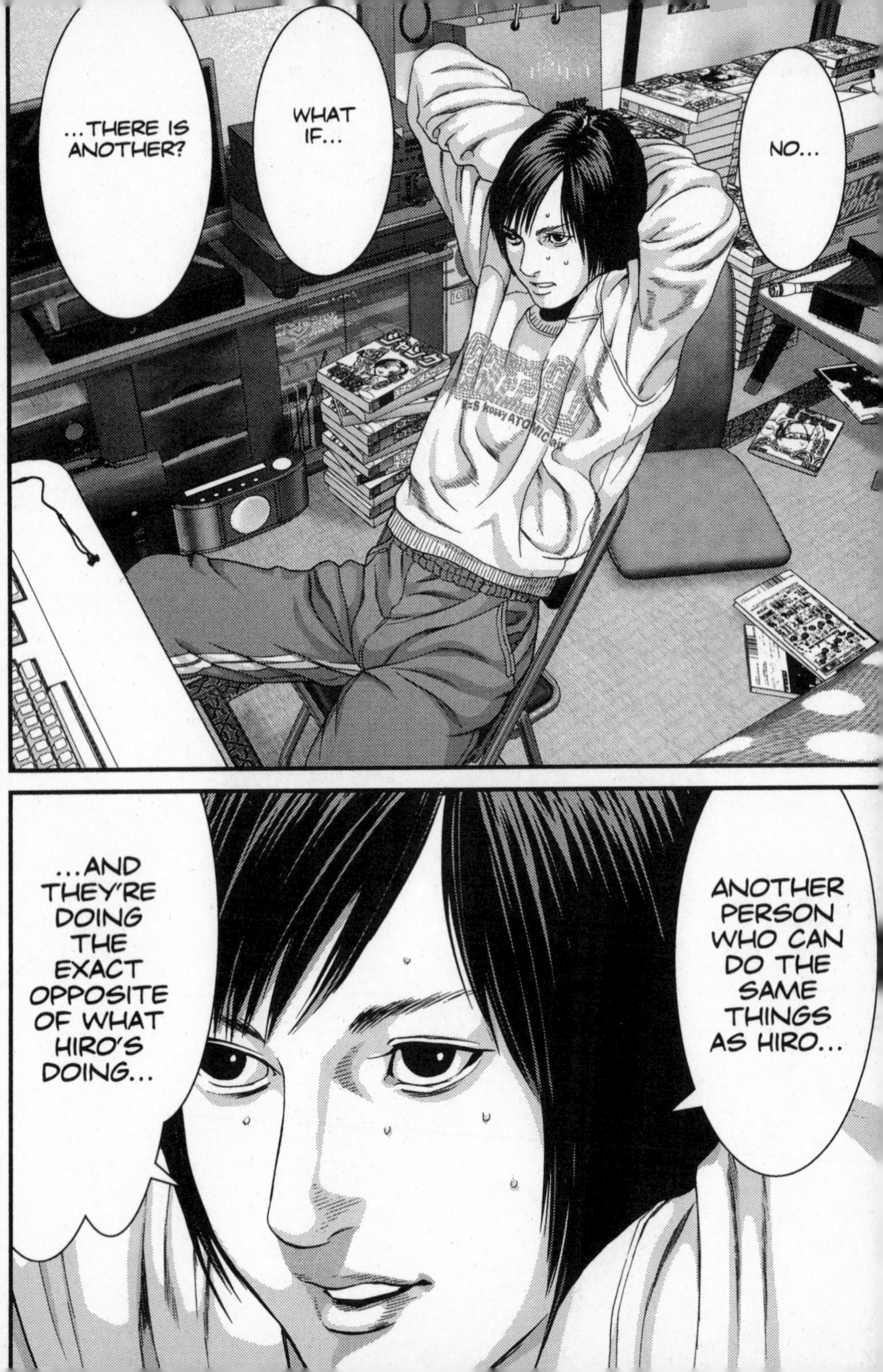
NO...
WHAT IF...
...THERE IS ANOTHER?
ANOTHER PERSON WHO CAN DO THE SAME THINGS AS HIRO...
...AND THEY'RE DOING THE EXACT OPPOSITE OF WHAT HIRO'S DOING...

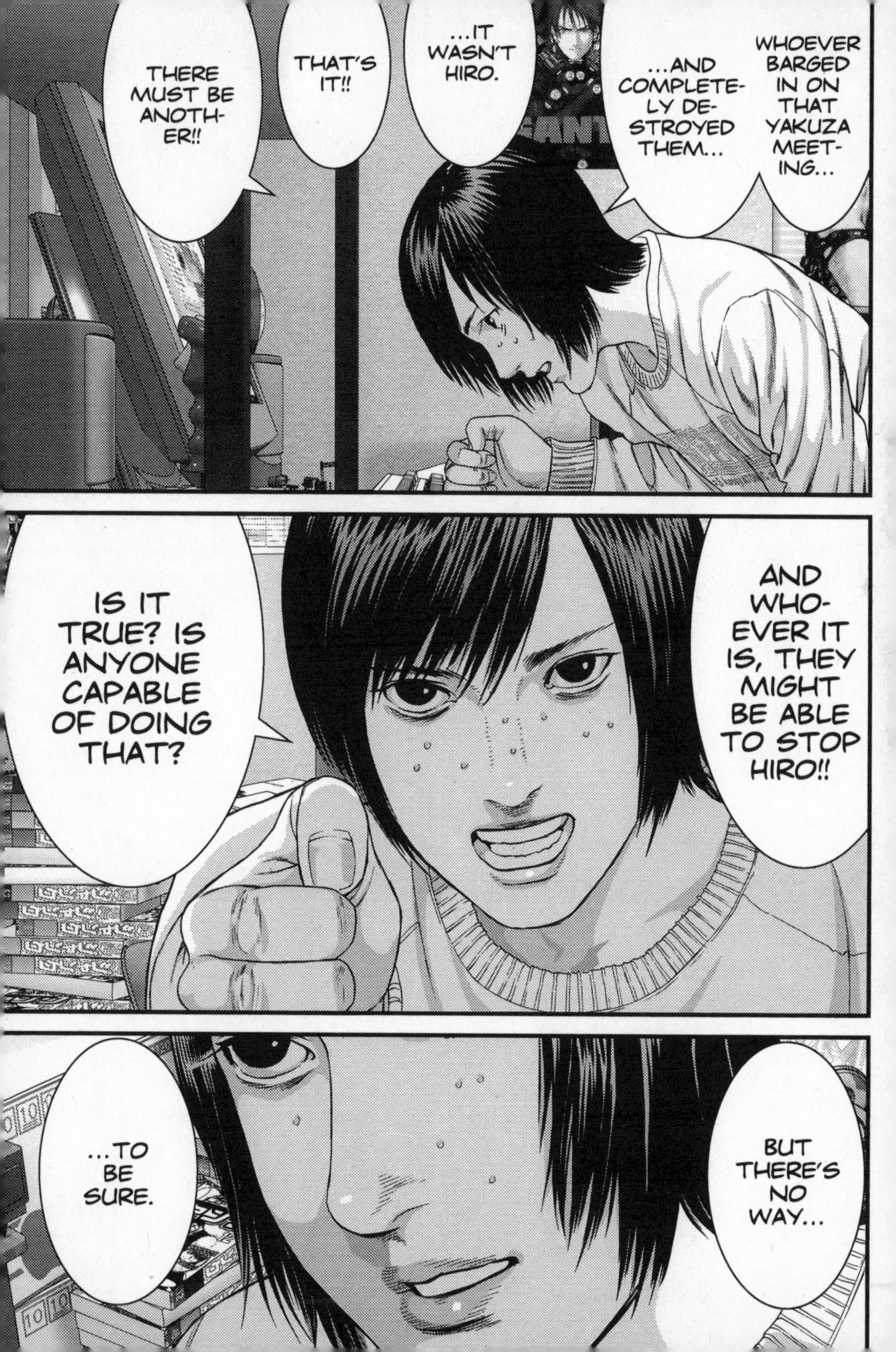

WHOEVER BARGED IN ON THAT YAKUZA MEETING…
…AND COMPLETELY DESTROYED THEM…
…IT WASN'T HIRO.
THAT'S IT!!
THERE MUST BE ANOTHER!!
AND WHOEVER IT IS, THEY MIGHT BE ABLE TO STOP HIRO!!
IS IT TRUE? IS ANYONE CAPABLE OF DOING THAT?
BUT THERE'S NO WAY…
…TO BE SURE.

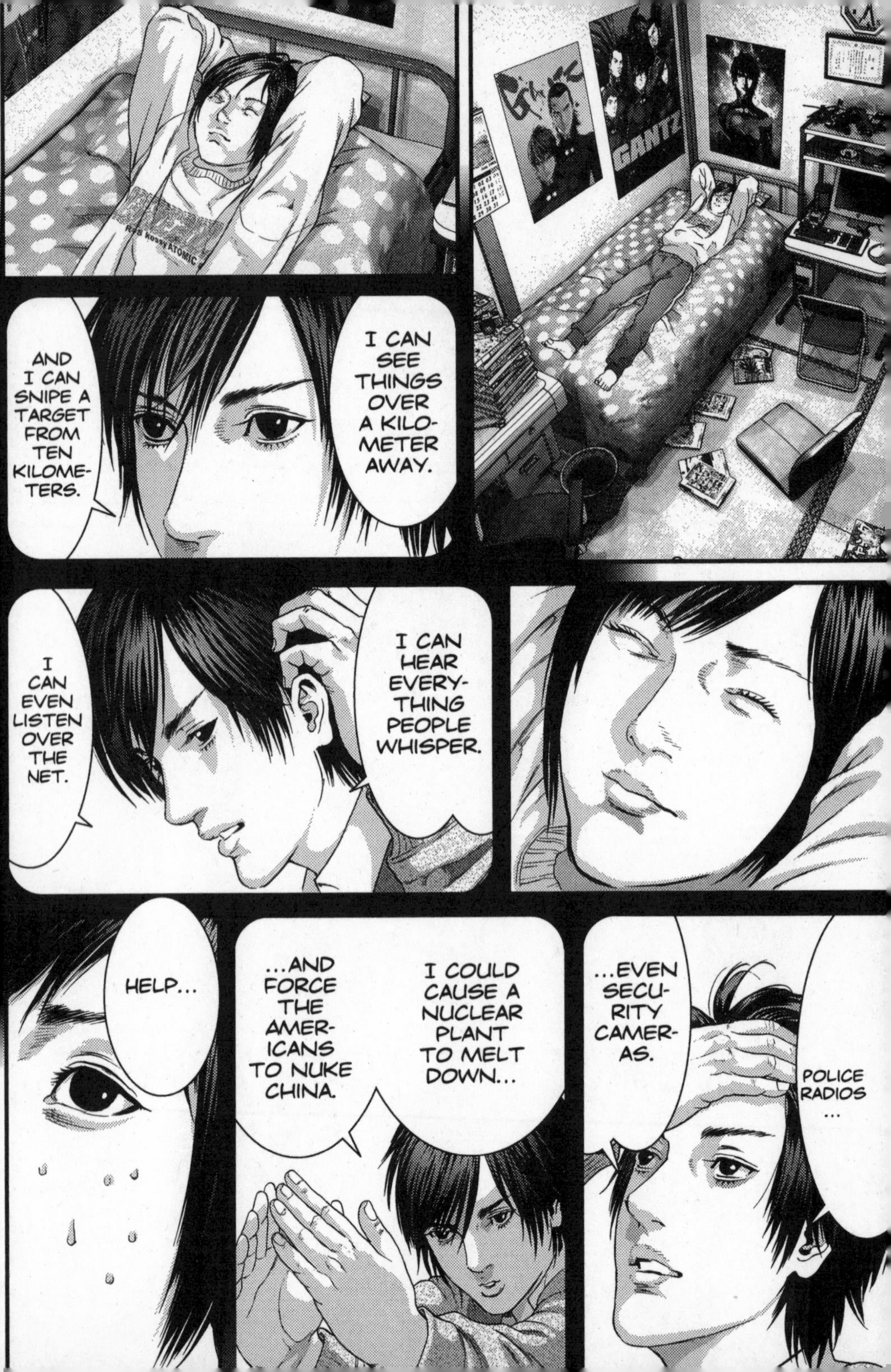
GANTZ
I CAN SEE THINGS OVER A KILOMETER AWAY.
AND I CAN SNIPE A TARGET FROM TEN KILOMETERS.
I CAN HEAR EVERYTHING PEOPLE WHISPER.
I CAN EVEN LISTEN OVER THE NET.
POLICE RADIOS ...
...EVEN SECURITY CAMERAS.
I COULD CAUSE A NUCLEAR PLANT TO MELT DOWN...
...AND FORCE THE AMERICANS TO NUKE CHINA.
HELP...

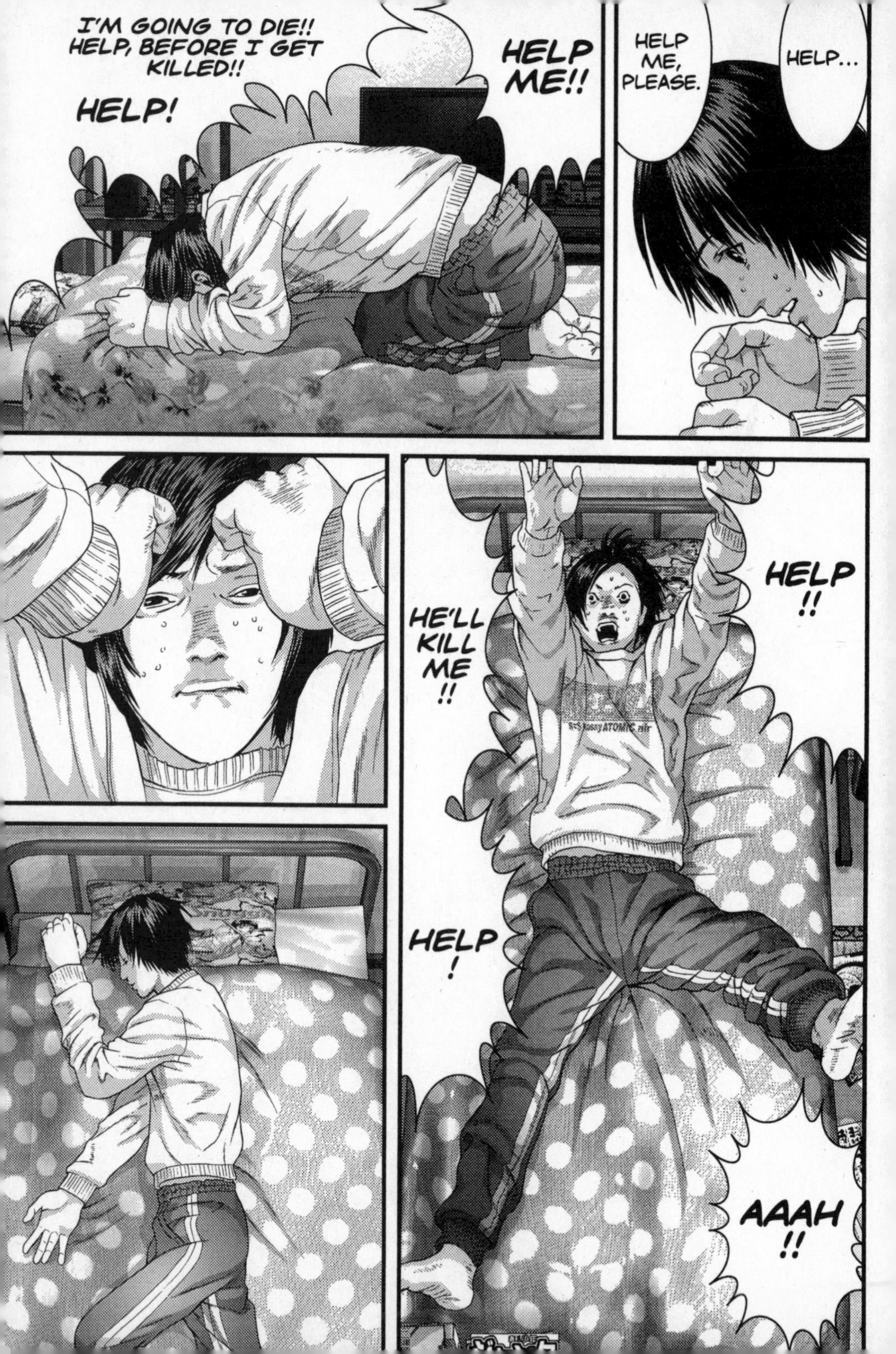
HELP...
HELP ME, PLEASE.
HELP ME!!
I'M GOING TO DIE!! HELP, BEFORE I GET KILLED!!
HELP!
HELP!!
HE'LL KILL ME!!
HELP!
AAAH!!

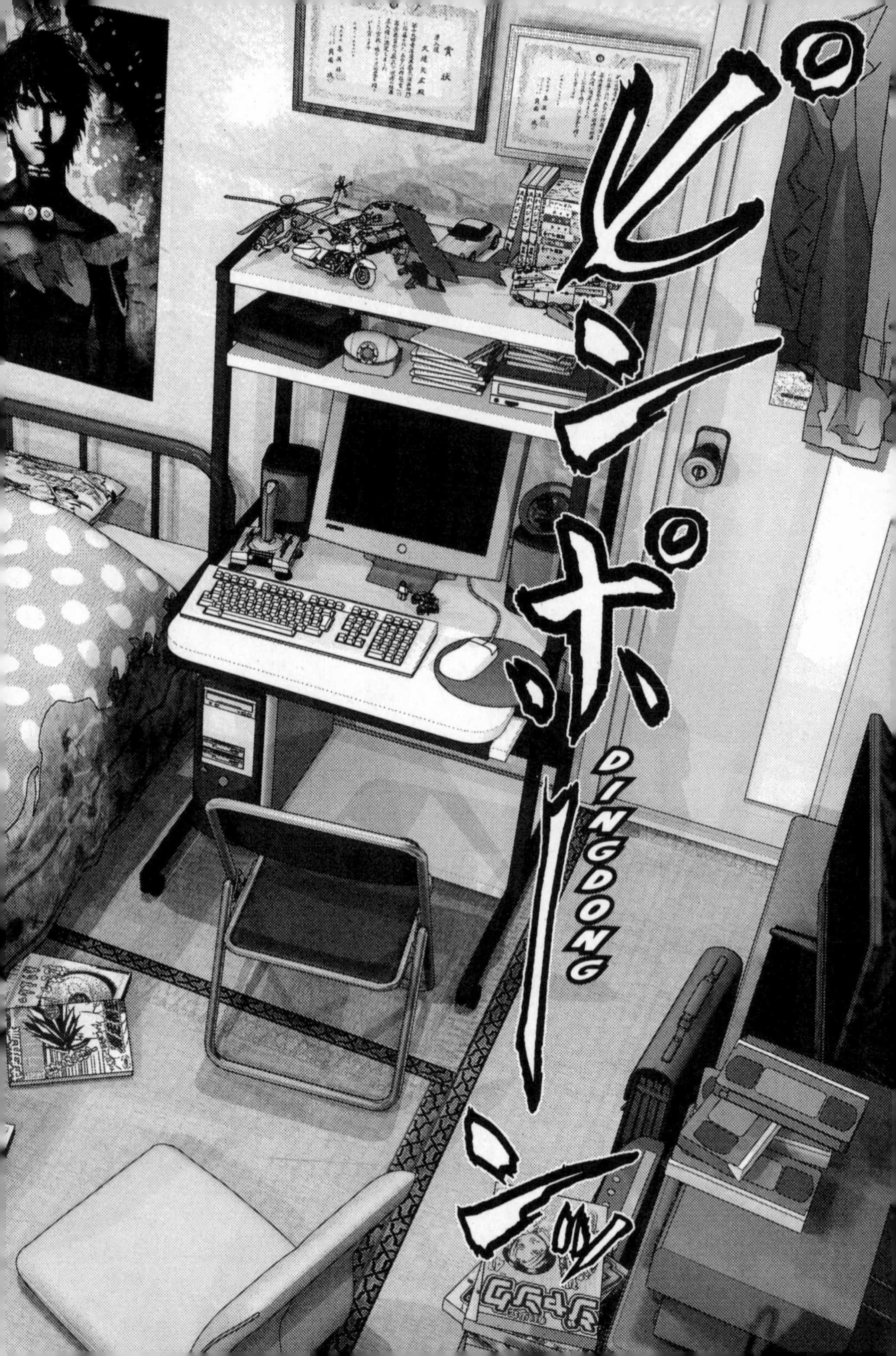
ピンポーン
DINGDONG

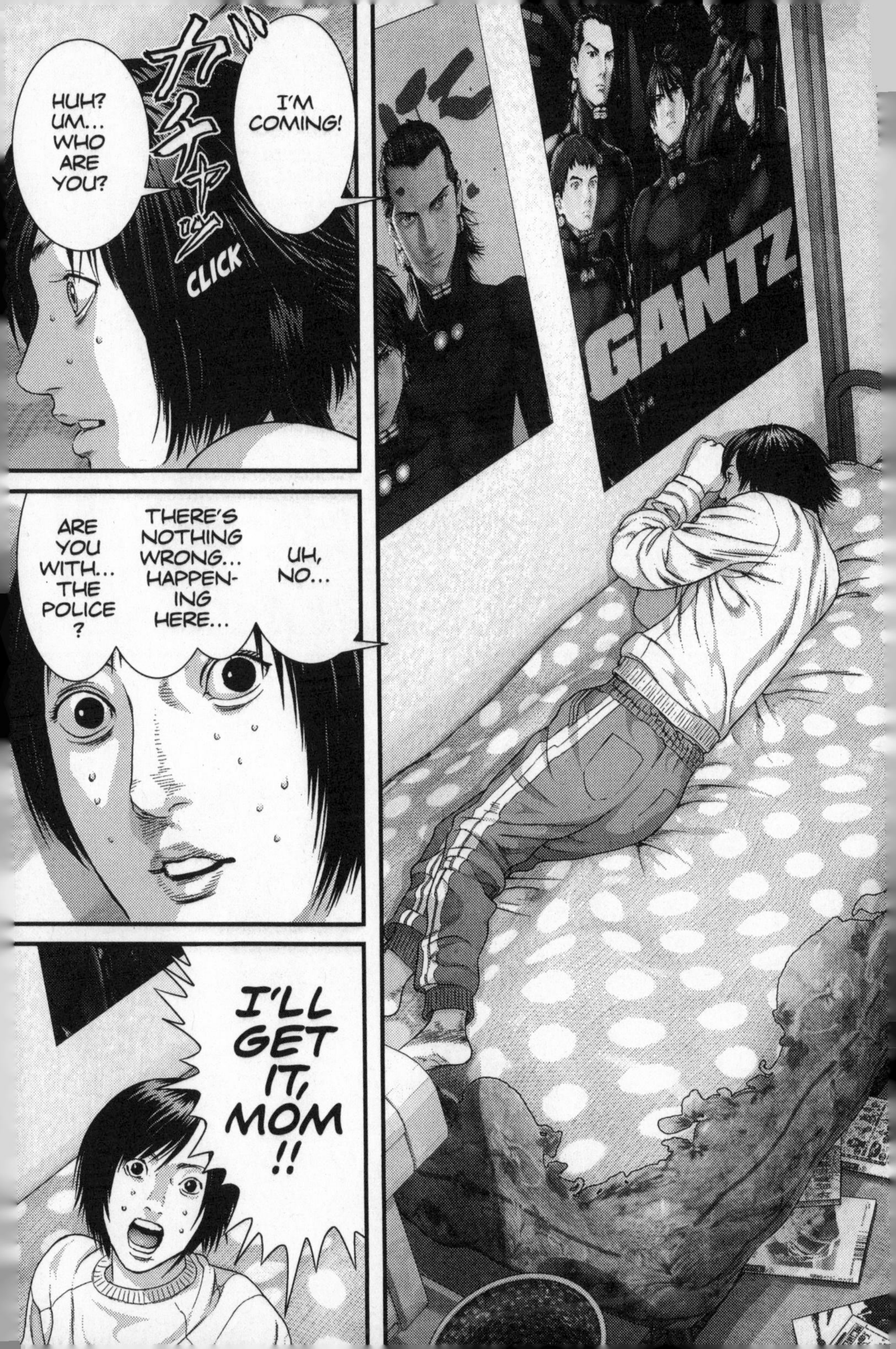
GANTZ
I'M COMING!
ガチャッ
CLICK
HUH? UM... WHO ARE YOU?
UH, NO...
THERE'S NOTHING WRONG... HAPPENING HERE...
ARE YOU WITH... THE POLICE?
I'LL GET IT, MOM!!

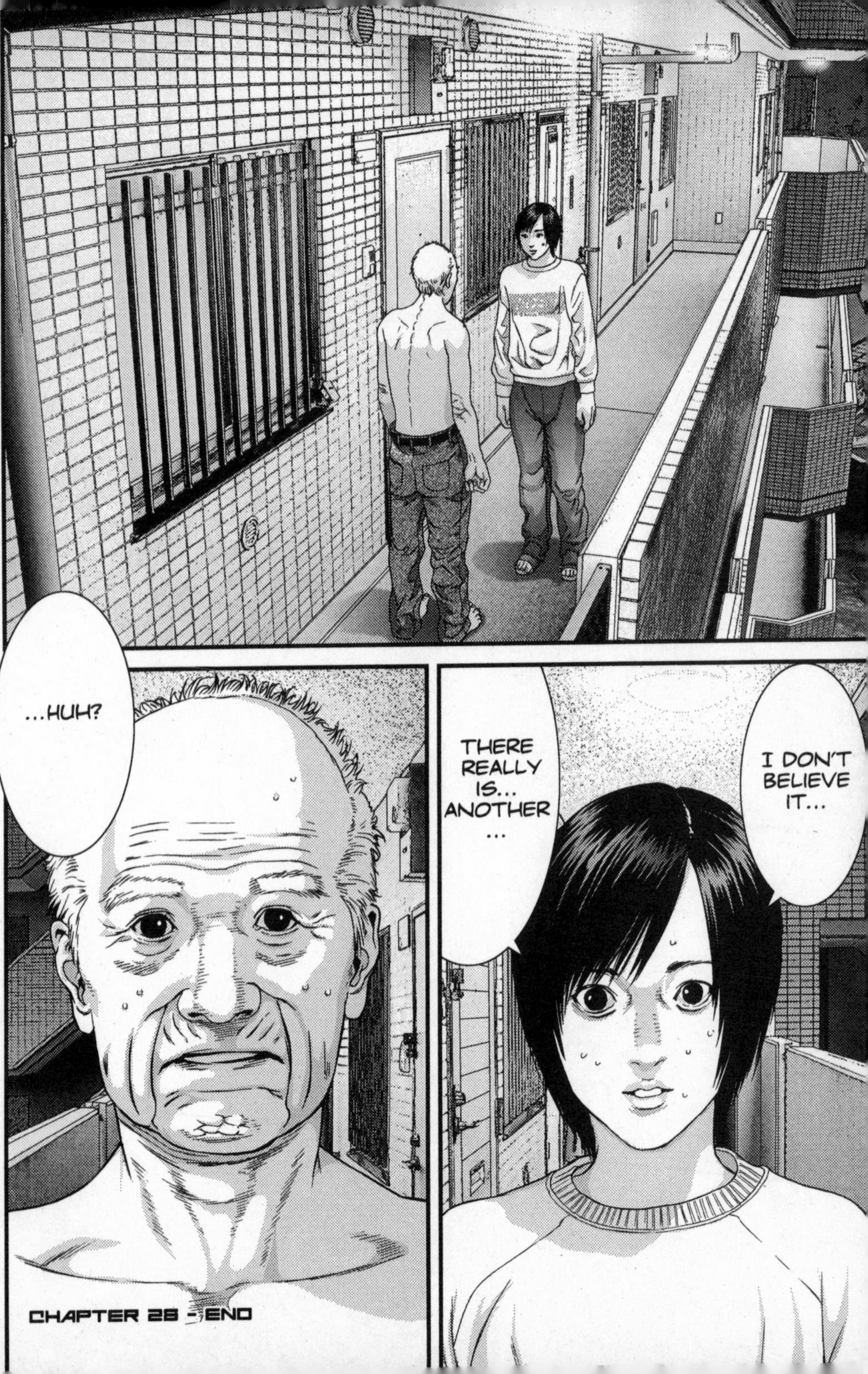
I DON'T BELIEVE IT...
THERE REALLY IS... ANOTHER ...
...HUH?
CHAPTER 28 - END

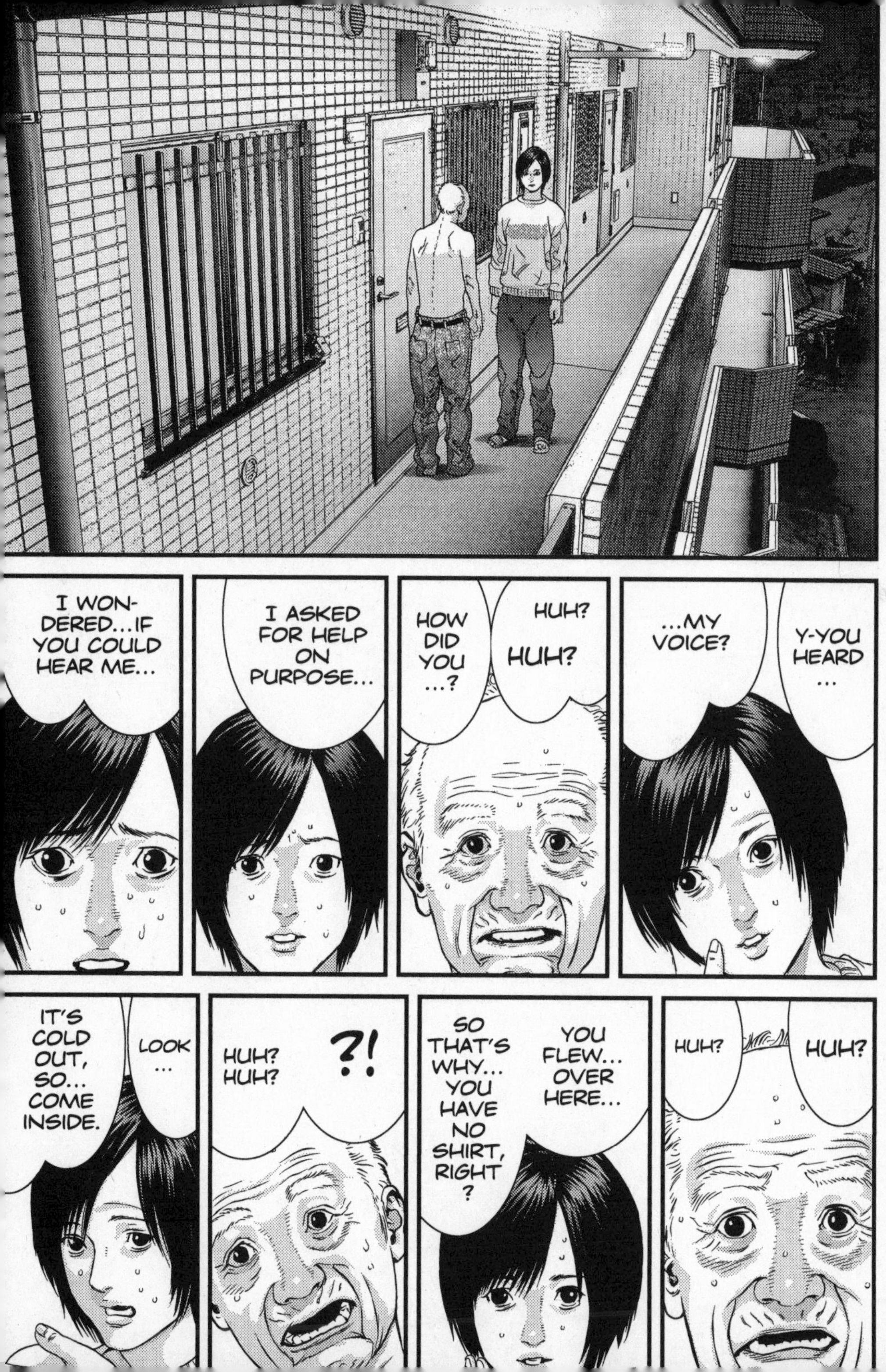
Y-YOU HEARD ...
...MY VOICE?
HUH?
HUH?
HOW DID YOU ...?
I ASKED FOR HELP ON PURPOSE...
I WON-DERED...IF YOU COULD HEAR ME...
HUH?
HUH?
YOU FLEW... OVER HERE...
SO THAT'S WHY... YOU HAVE NO SHIRT, RIGHT?
?!
HUH? HUH?
LOOK ...
IT'S COLD OUT, SO... COME INSIDE.

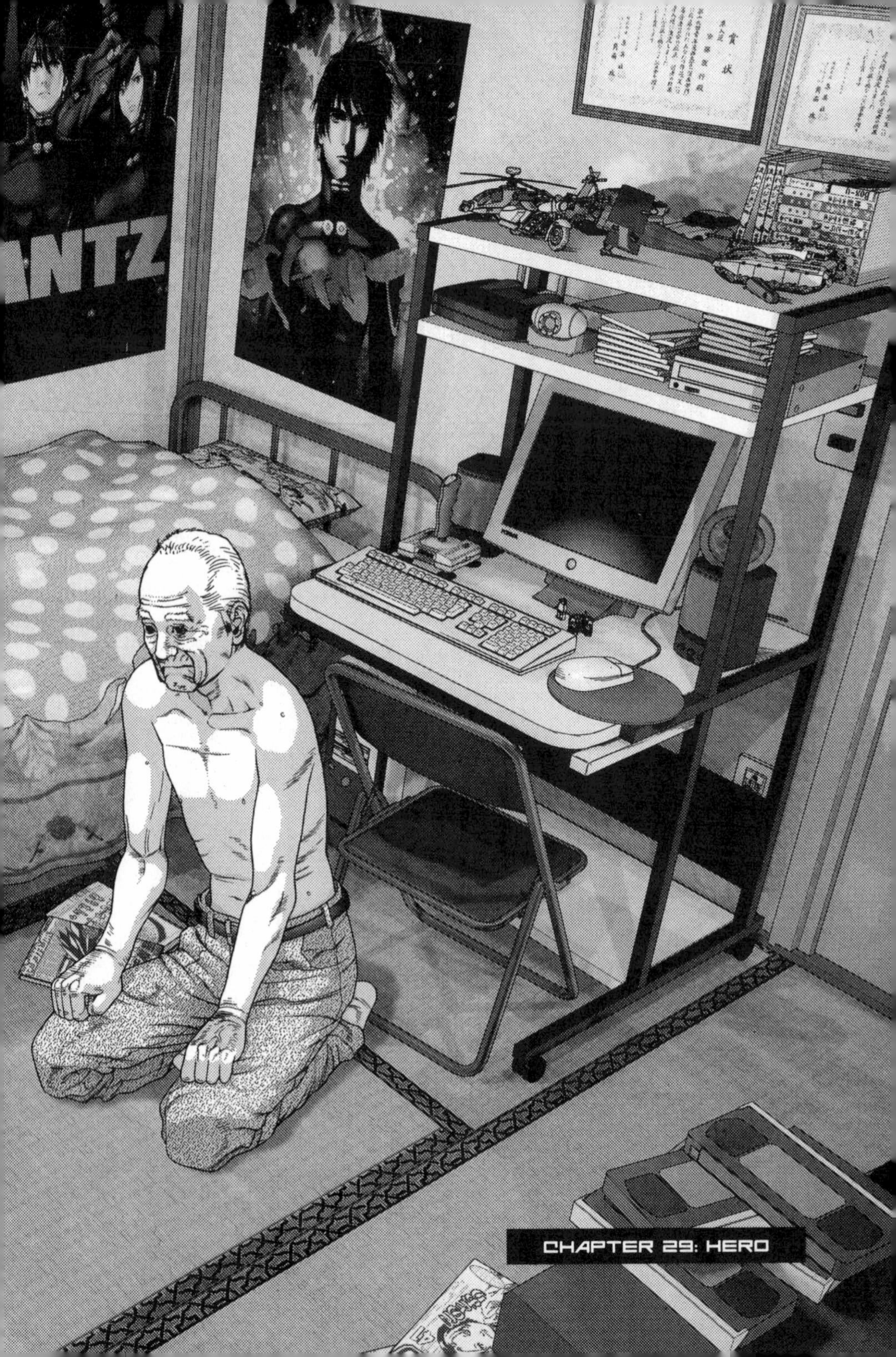
ANTZ
CHAPTER 29: HERO

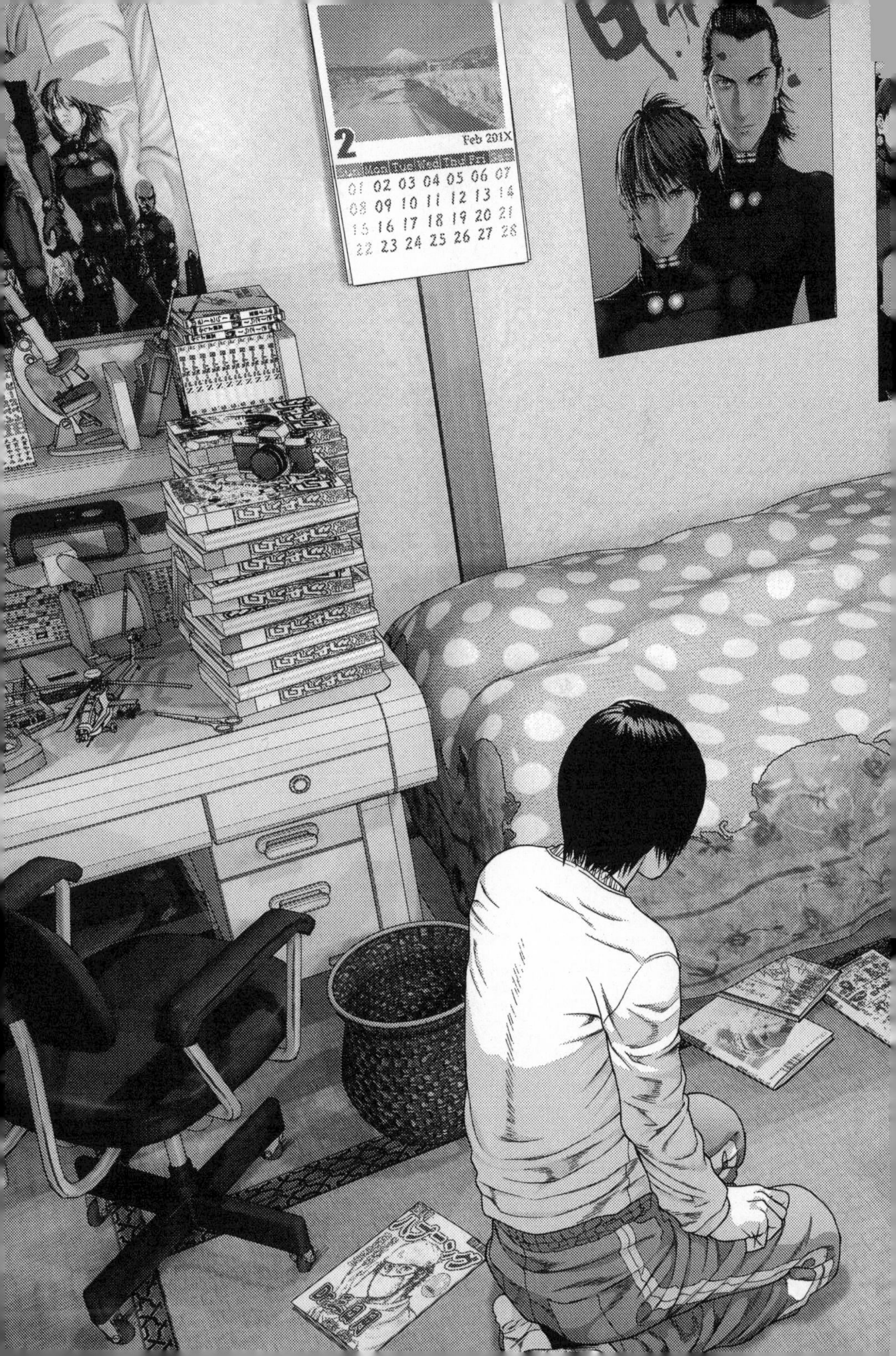
2
Feb 201X
Mon Tue Wed Thu Fri
01 02 03 04 05 06 07
08 09 10 11 12 13 14
15 16 17 18 19 20 21
22 23 24 25 26 27 28

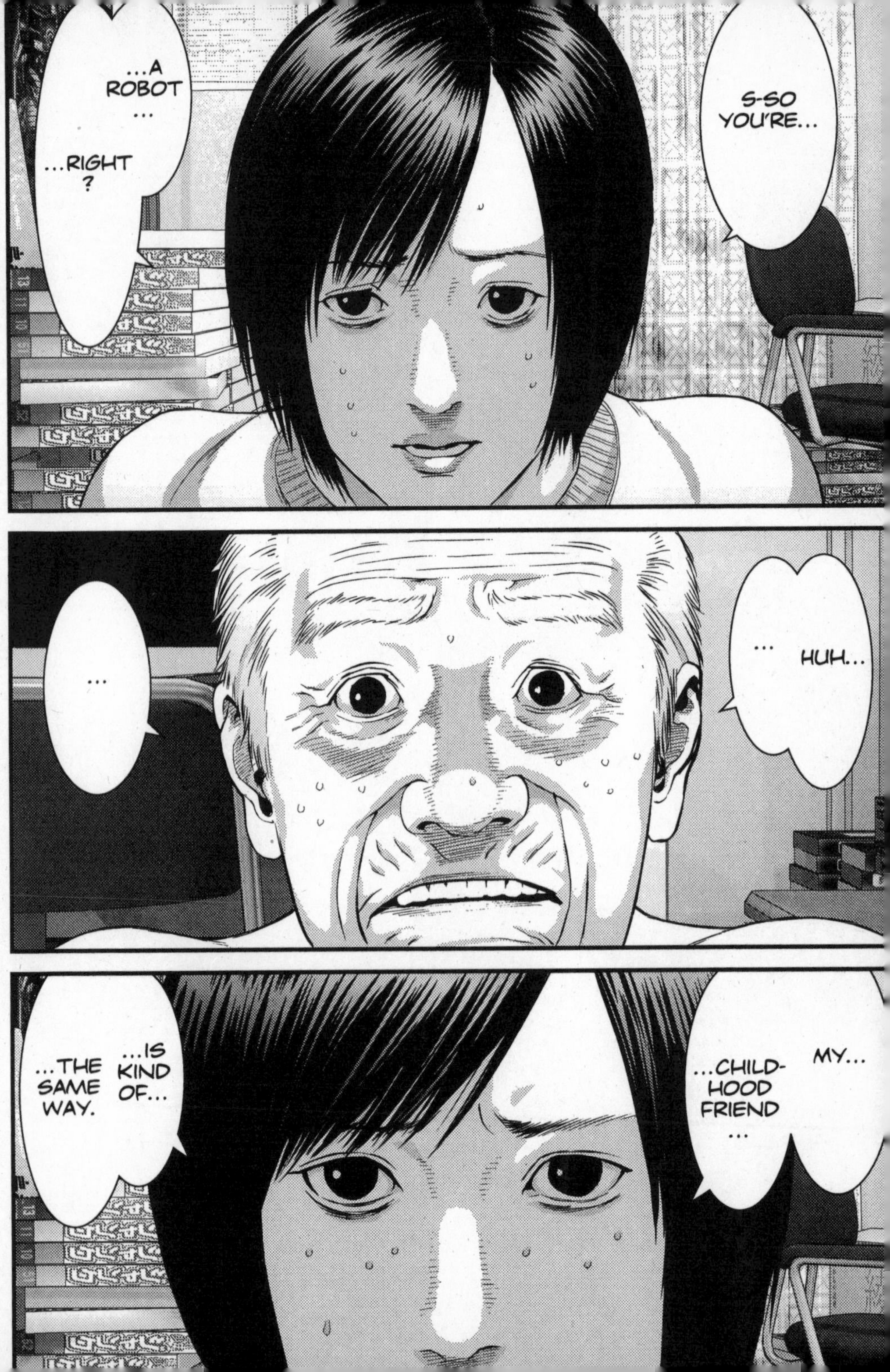
S-SO YOU'RE...
...A ROBOT ... ...RIGHT?
... HUH...
...
MY... ...CHILD-HOOD FRIEND ...
...IS KIND OF... ...THE SAME WAY.

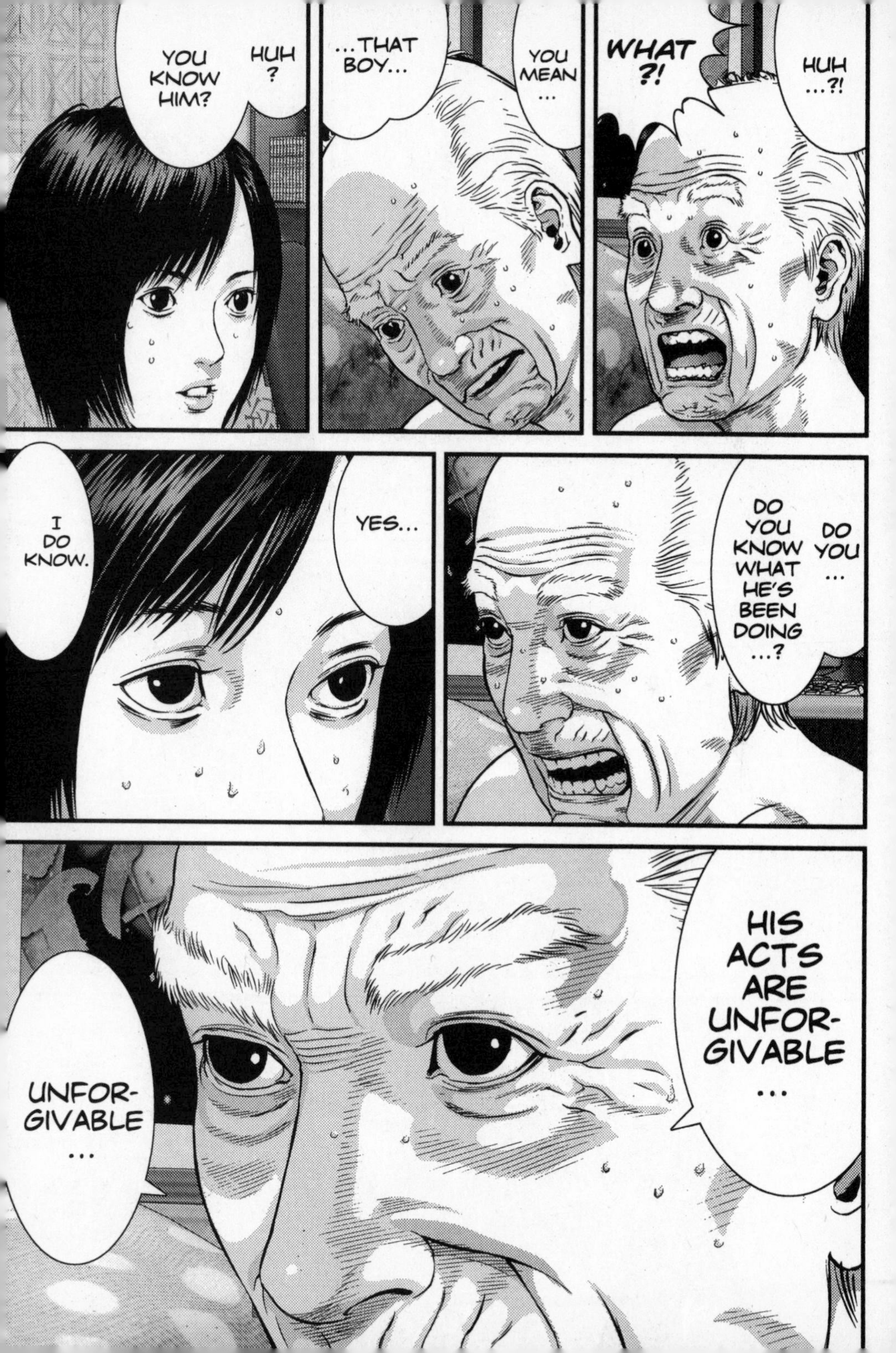
HUH ...?!
WHAT ?!
YOU MEAN ...
...THAT BOY...
HUH ?
YOU KNOW HIM?
DO YOU ...
DO YOU KNOW WHAT HE'S BEEN DOING ...?
YES...
I DO KNOW.
HIS ACTS ARE UNFOR-GIVABLE ...
UNFOR-GIVABLE ...

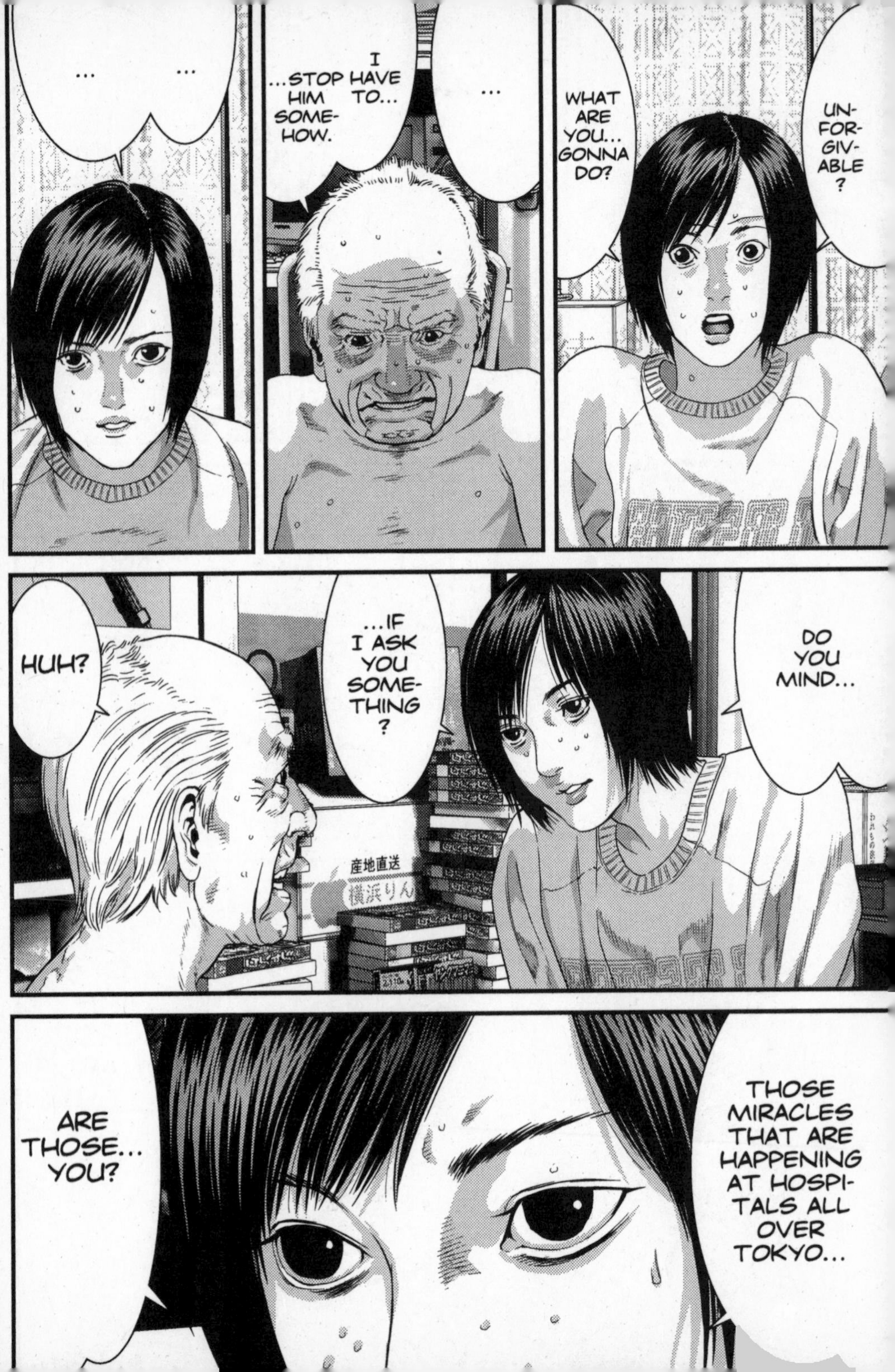
UN-FOR-GIV-ABLE?
WHAT ARE YOU... GONNA DO?
...
I HAVE TO... ...STOP HIM SOMEHOW.
... ...
DO YOU MIND...
...IF I ASK YOU SOMETHING?
HUH?
産地直送
横浜りん
THOSE MIRACLES THAT ARE HAPPENING AT HOSPITALS ALL OVER TOKYO...
ARE THOSE... YOU?

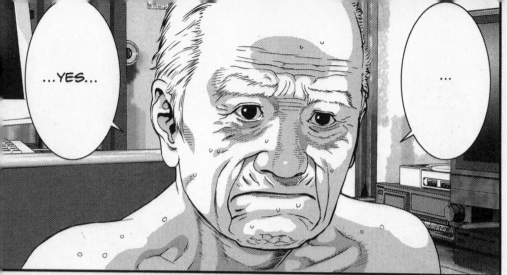

...
...YES...
?!
...
?
AND THE...
...ASSAULT ON THE YAKUZA MEETING YESTER-DAY...
THAT WAS... ALL YOU?

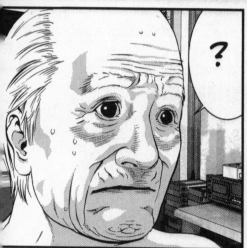

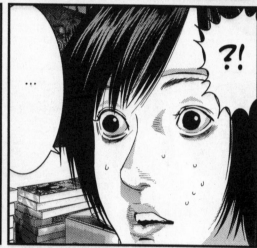

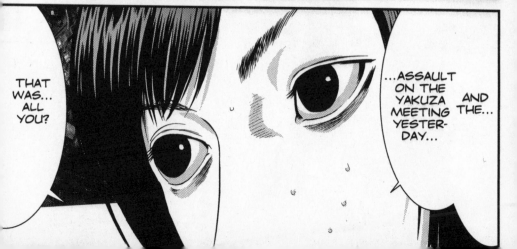

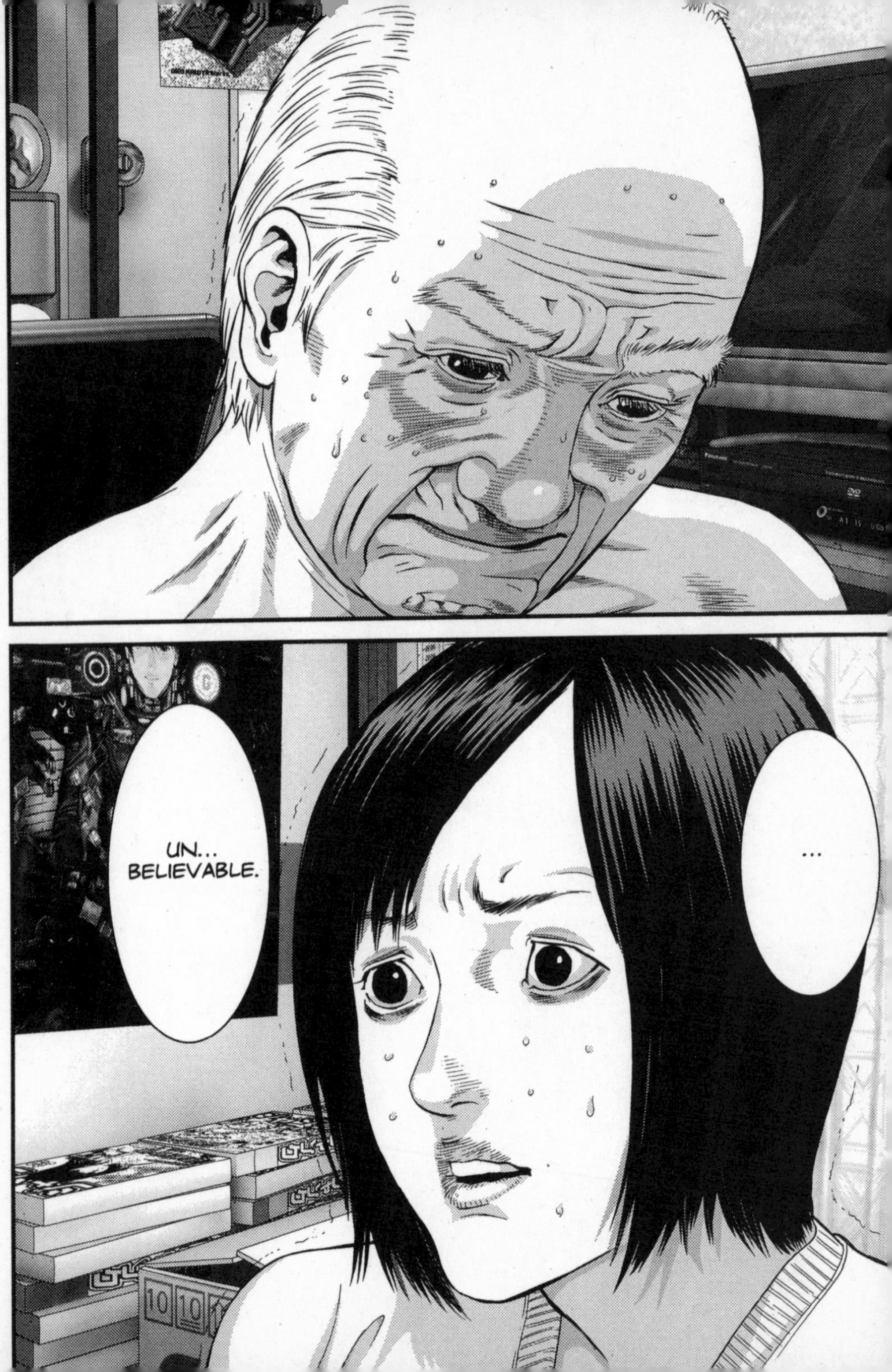
...
UN... BELIEVABLE.

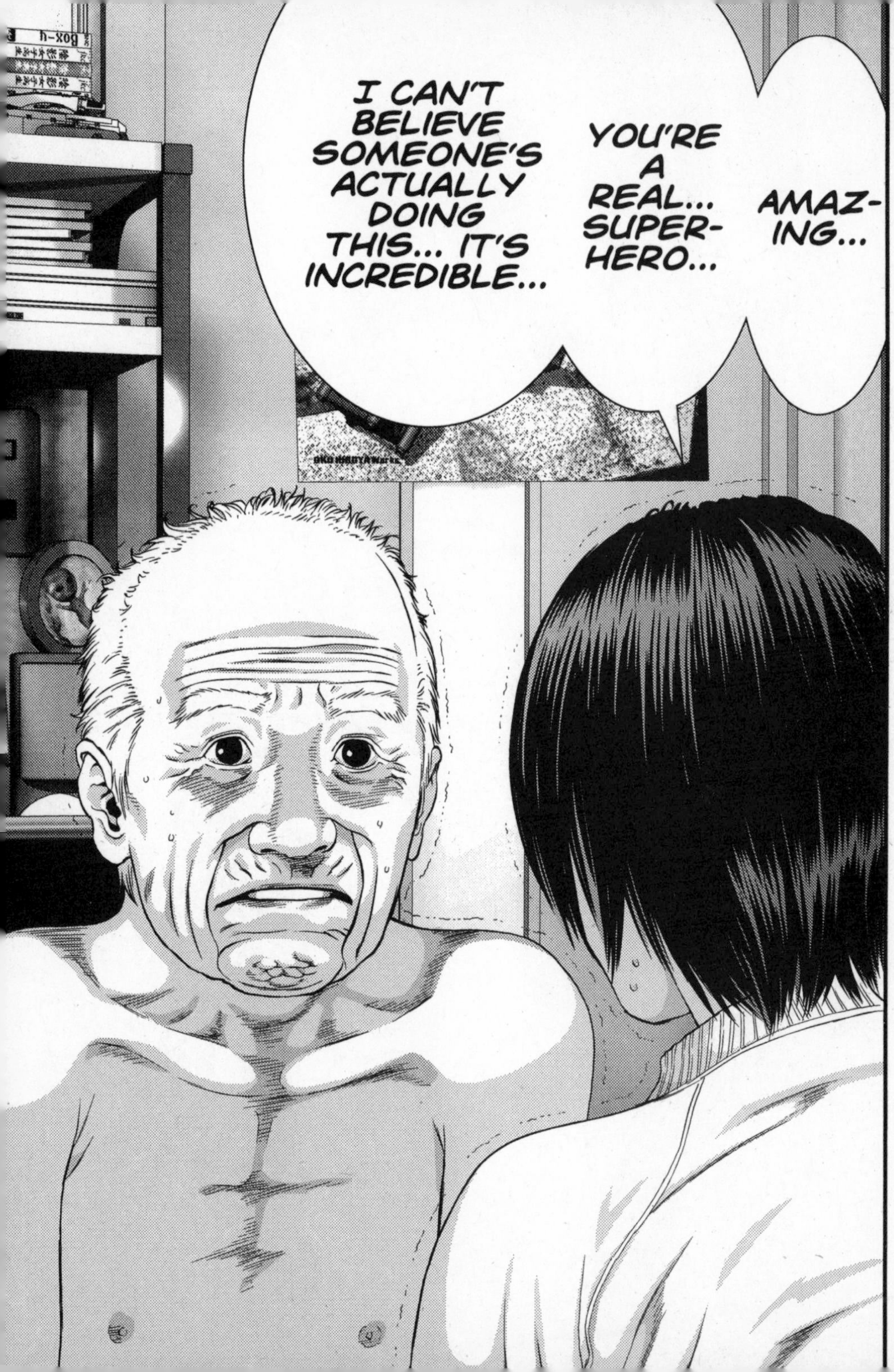
AMAZ-ING...
I CAN'T BELIEVE SOMEONE'S ACTUALLY DOING THIS... IT'S INCREDIBLE...
YOU'RE A REAL... SUPER-HERO...

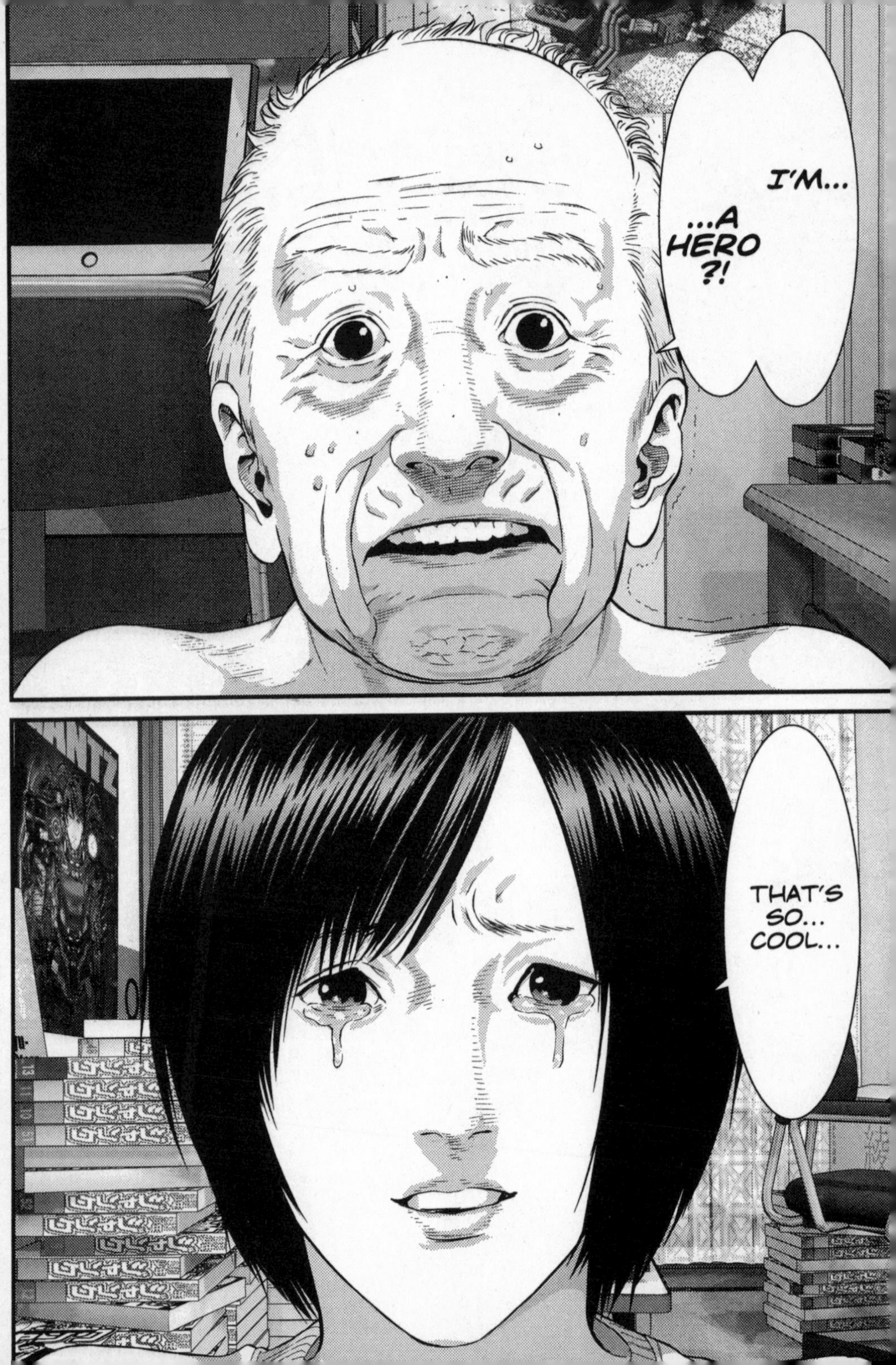
I'M... ...A HERO ?!
THAT'S SO... COOL...

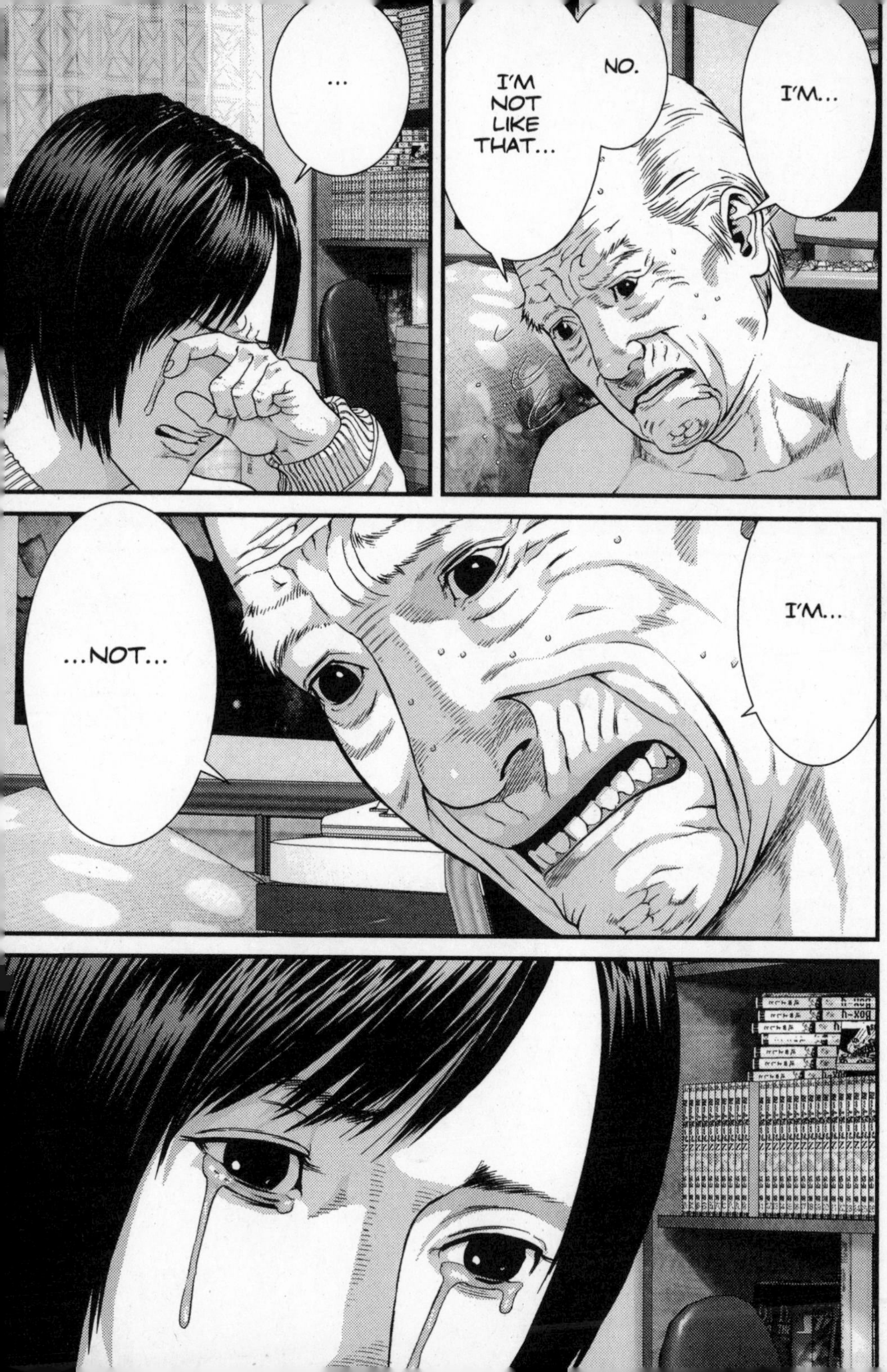
I'M...
NO.
I'M NOT LIKE THAT...
...
I'M...
...NOT...

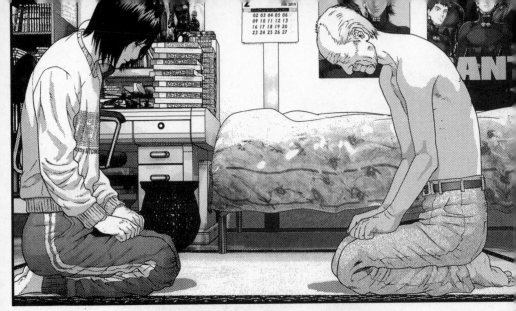

...STOP HIRO...

PLEASE...

YOU HAVE TO...

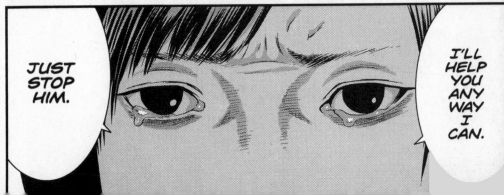

JUST STOP HIM.

I'LL HELP YOU ANY WAY I CAN.

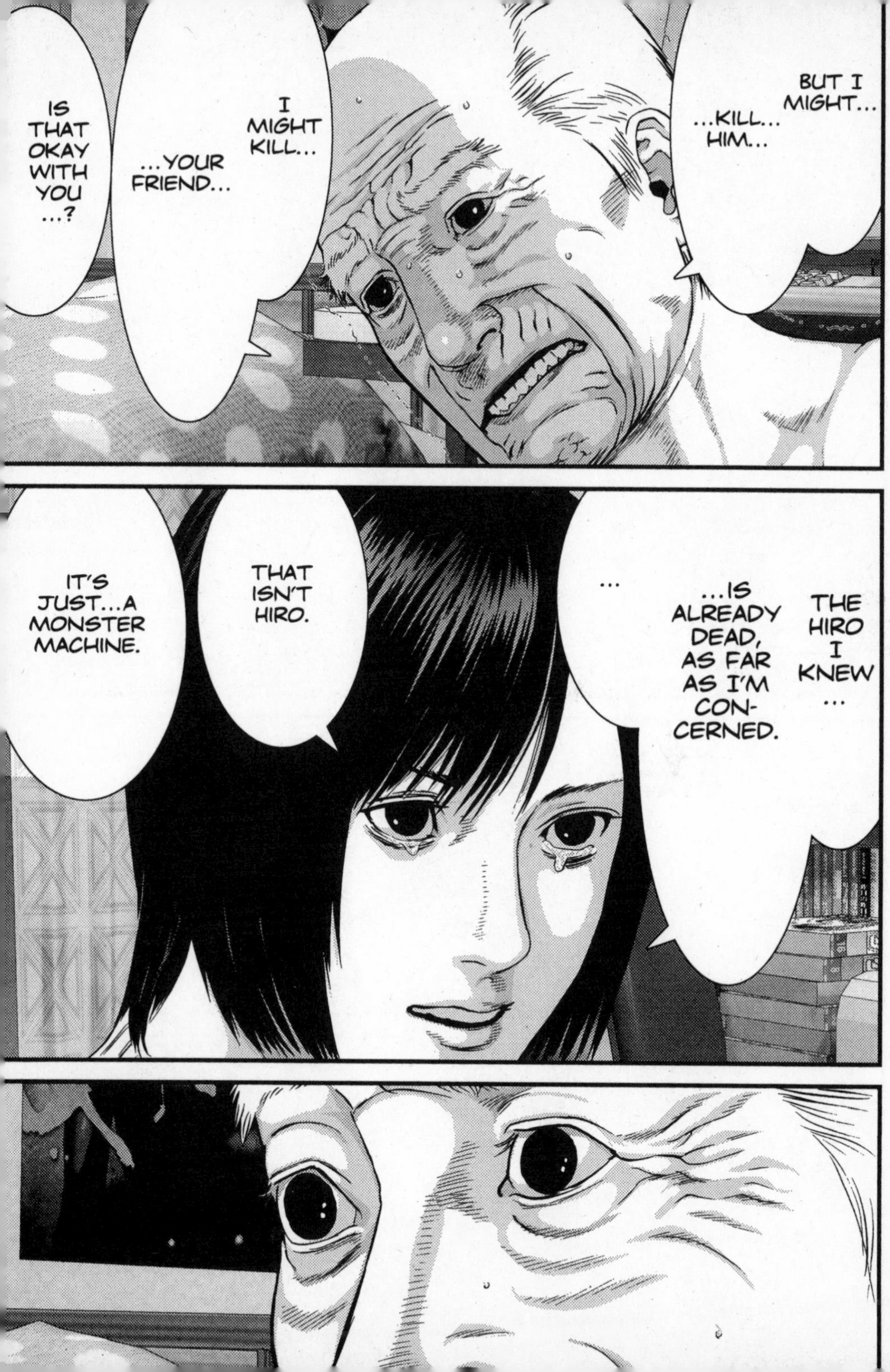
BUT I MIGHT…
…KILL… HIM…
I MIGHT KILL…
…YOUR FRIEND…
IS THAT OKAY WITH YOU …?
THE HIRO I KNEW …
…IS ALREADY DEAD, AS FAR AS I'M CON-CERNED.
…
THAT ISN'T HIRO.
IT'S JUST…A MONSTER MACHINE.

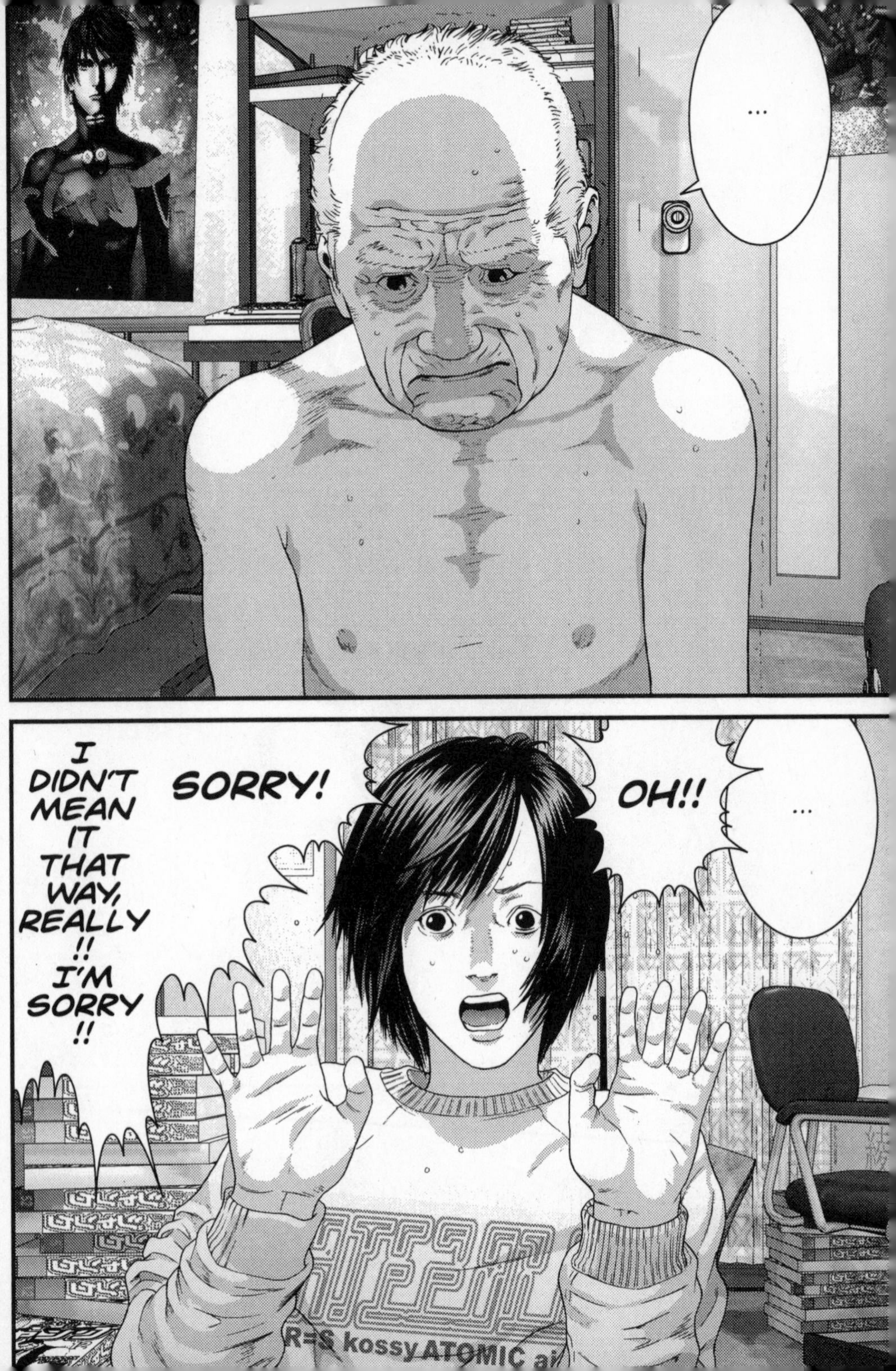
...
...
OH!!
SORRY!
I DIDN'T MEAN IT THAT WAY, REALLY!! I'M SORRY!!

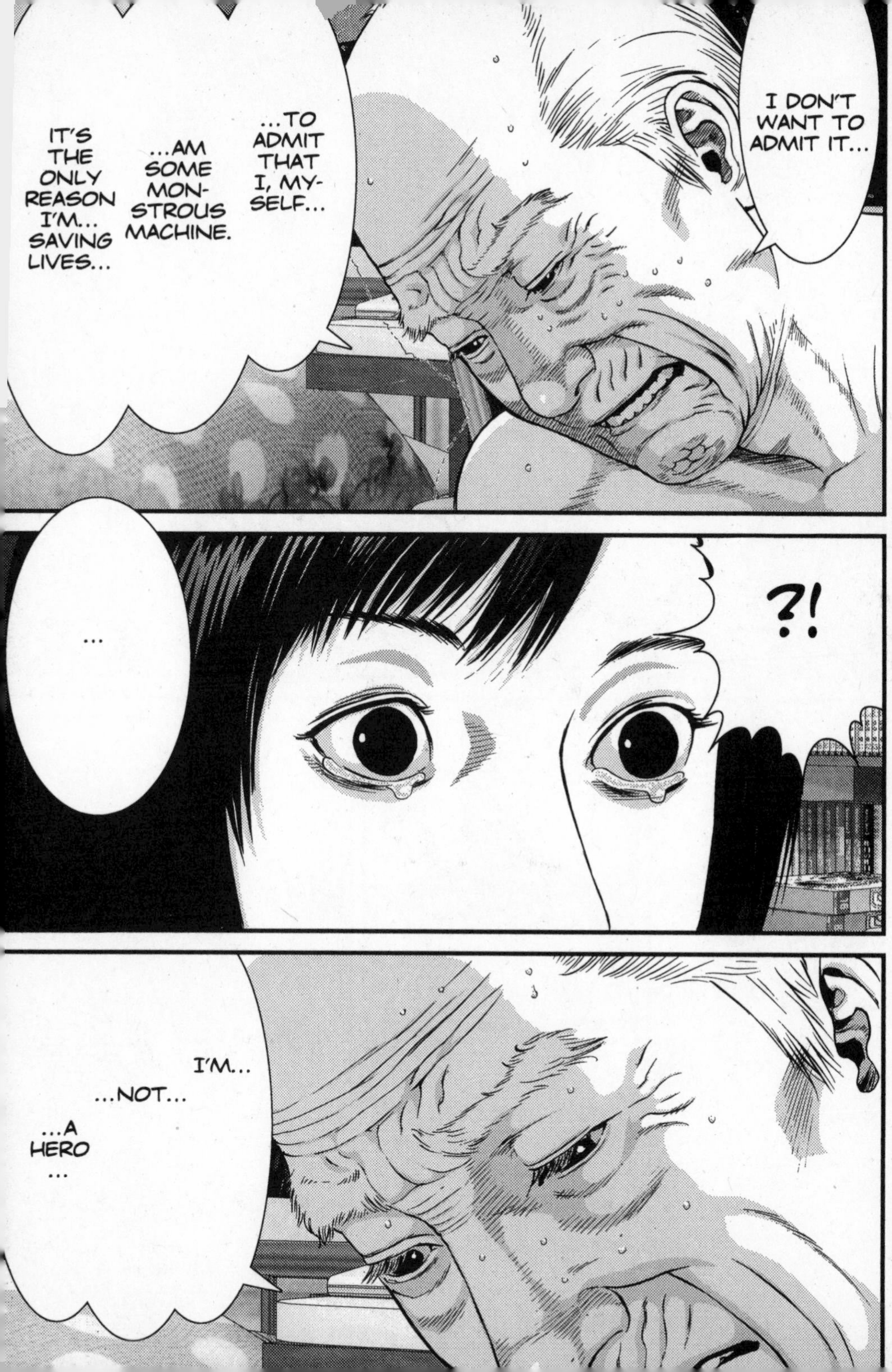
I DON'T WANT TO ADMIT IT...
...TO ADMIT THAT I, MY-SELF...
...AM SOME MON-STROUS MACHINE.
IT'S THE ONLY REASON I'M... SAVING LIVES...
?!
...
I'M...
...NOT...
...A HERO
...

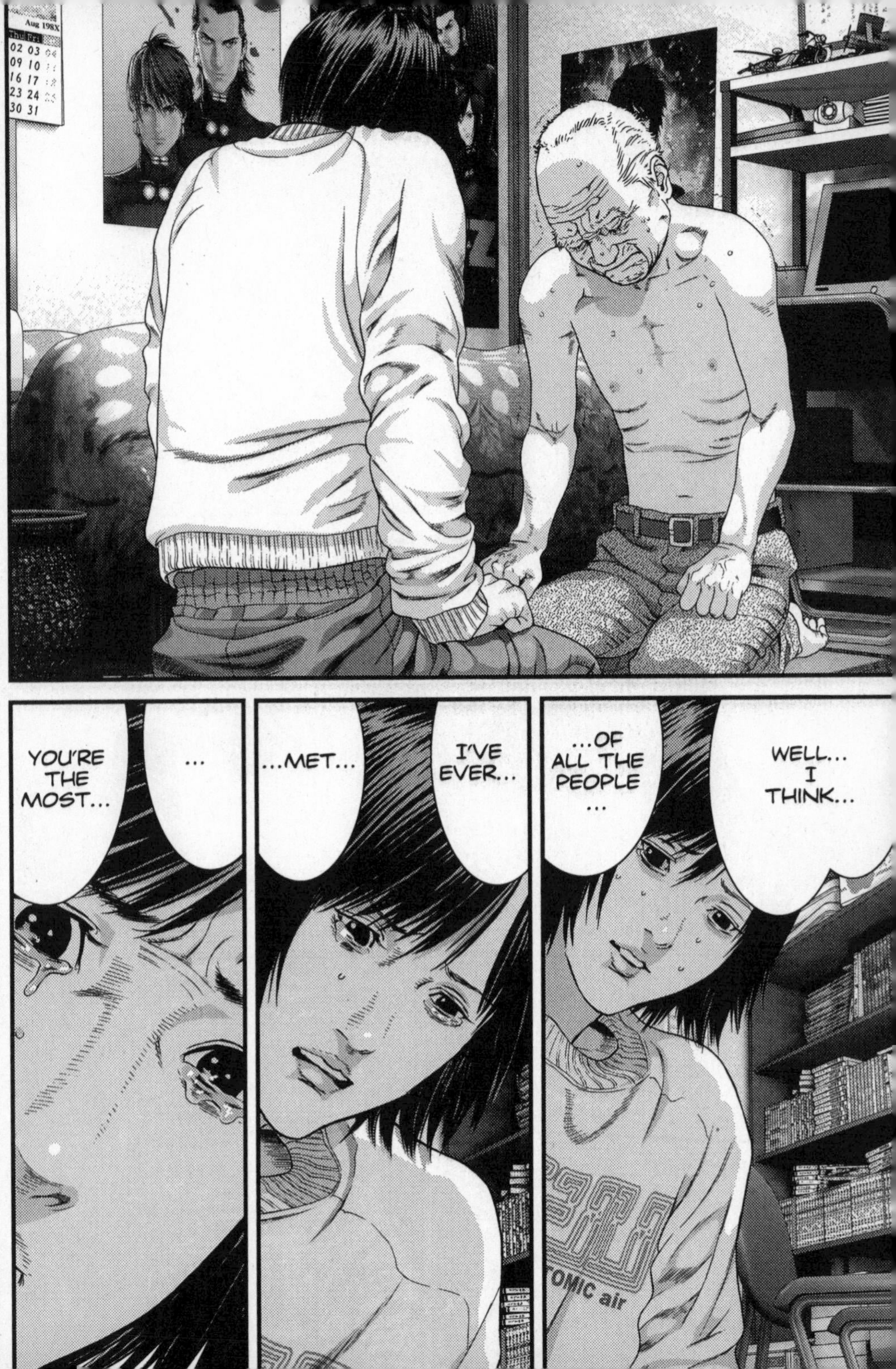
Aug 198X
WELL... I THINK...
...OF ALL THE PEOPLE ...
I'VE EVER...
...MET...
...
YOU'RE THE MOST...
TOMIC air

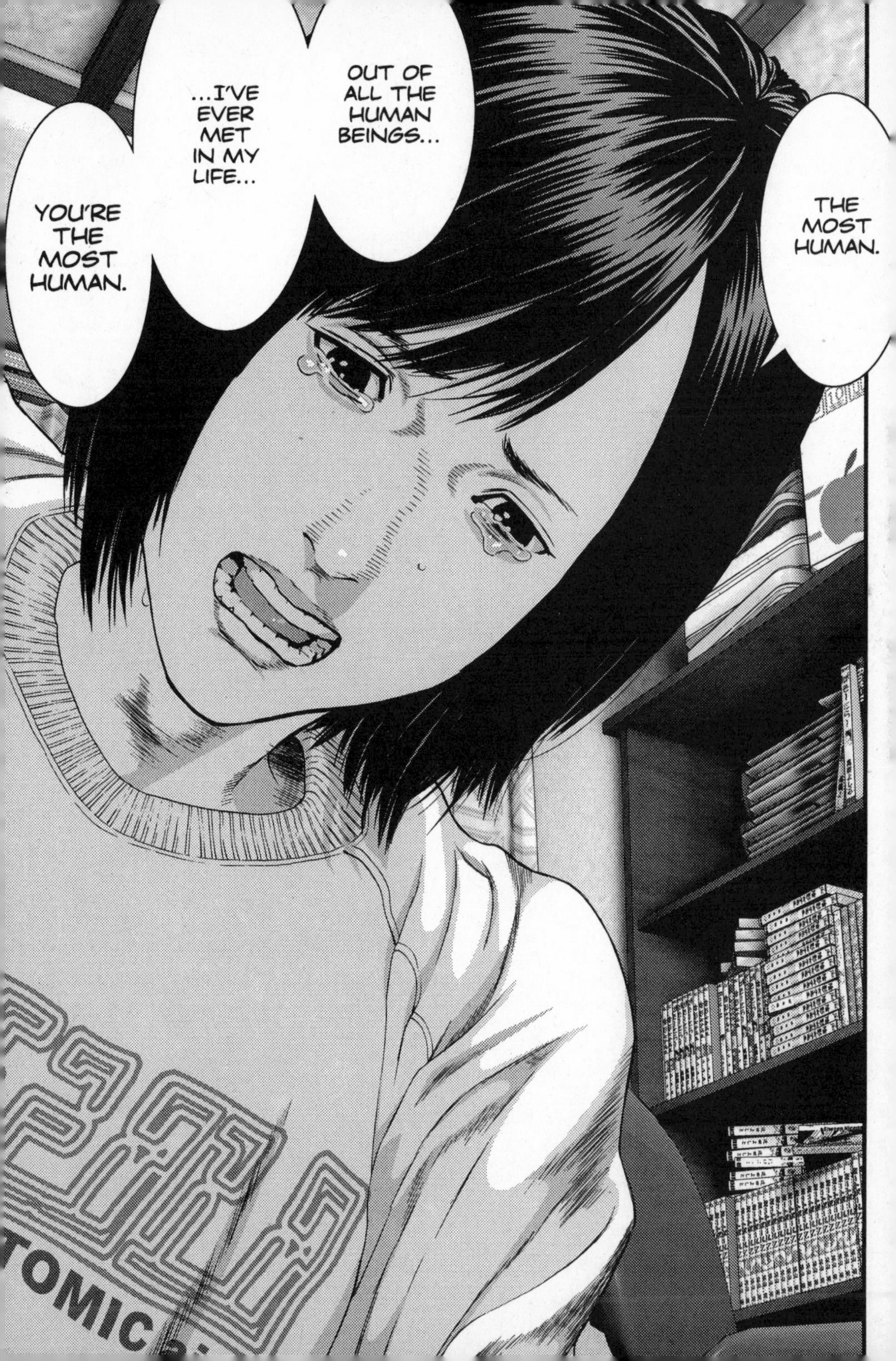
THE MOST HUMAN.
OUT OF ALL THE HUMAN BEINGS...
...I'VE EVER MET IN MY LIFE...
YOU'RE THE MOST HUMAN.

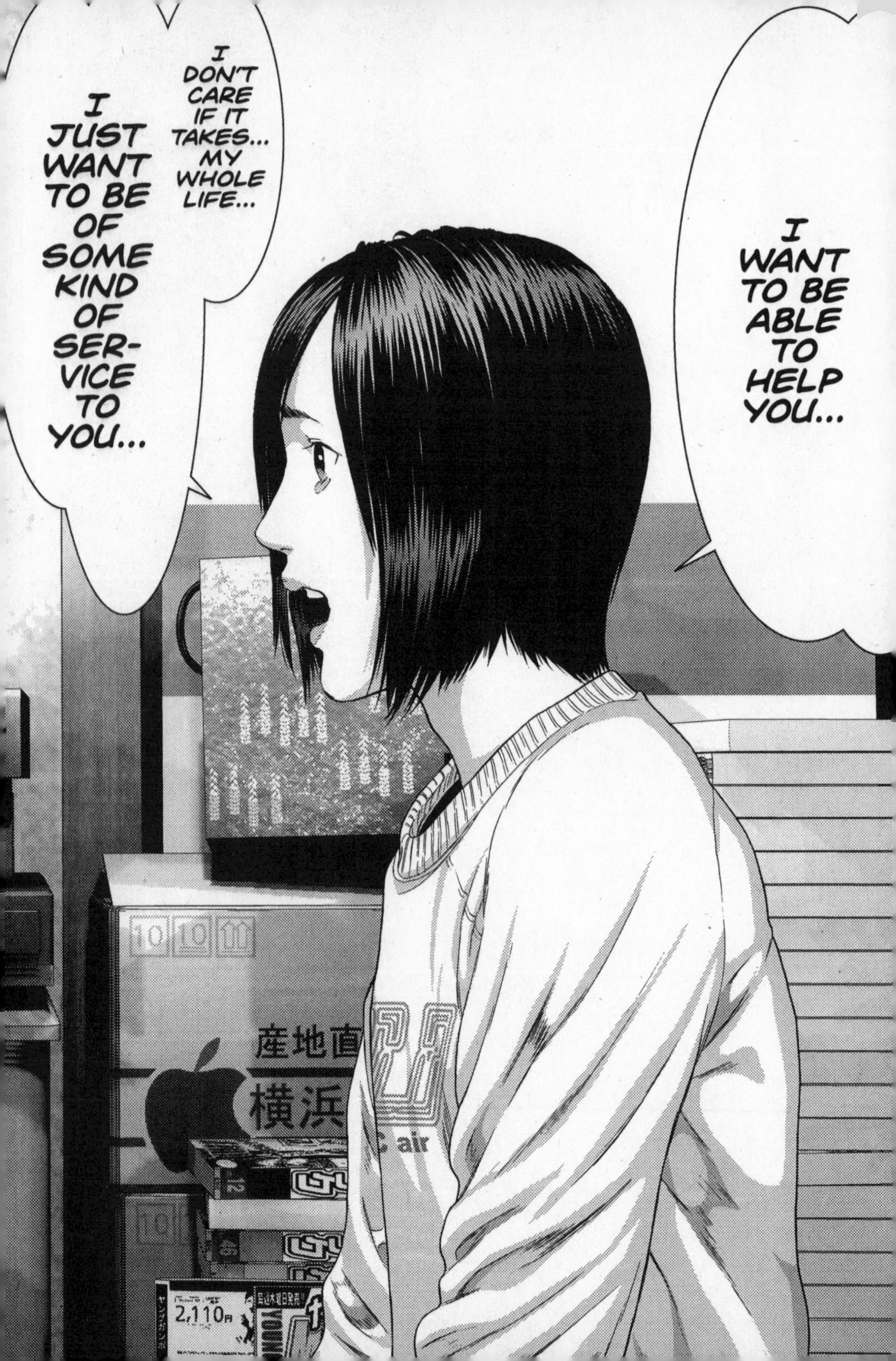
I WANT TO BE ABLE TO HELP YOU...
I DON'T CARE IF IT TAKES... MY WHOLE LIFE...
I JUST WANT TO BE OF SOME KIND OF SER-VICE TO YOU...
産地直
横浜
2,110円

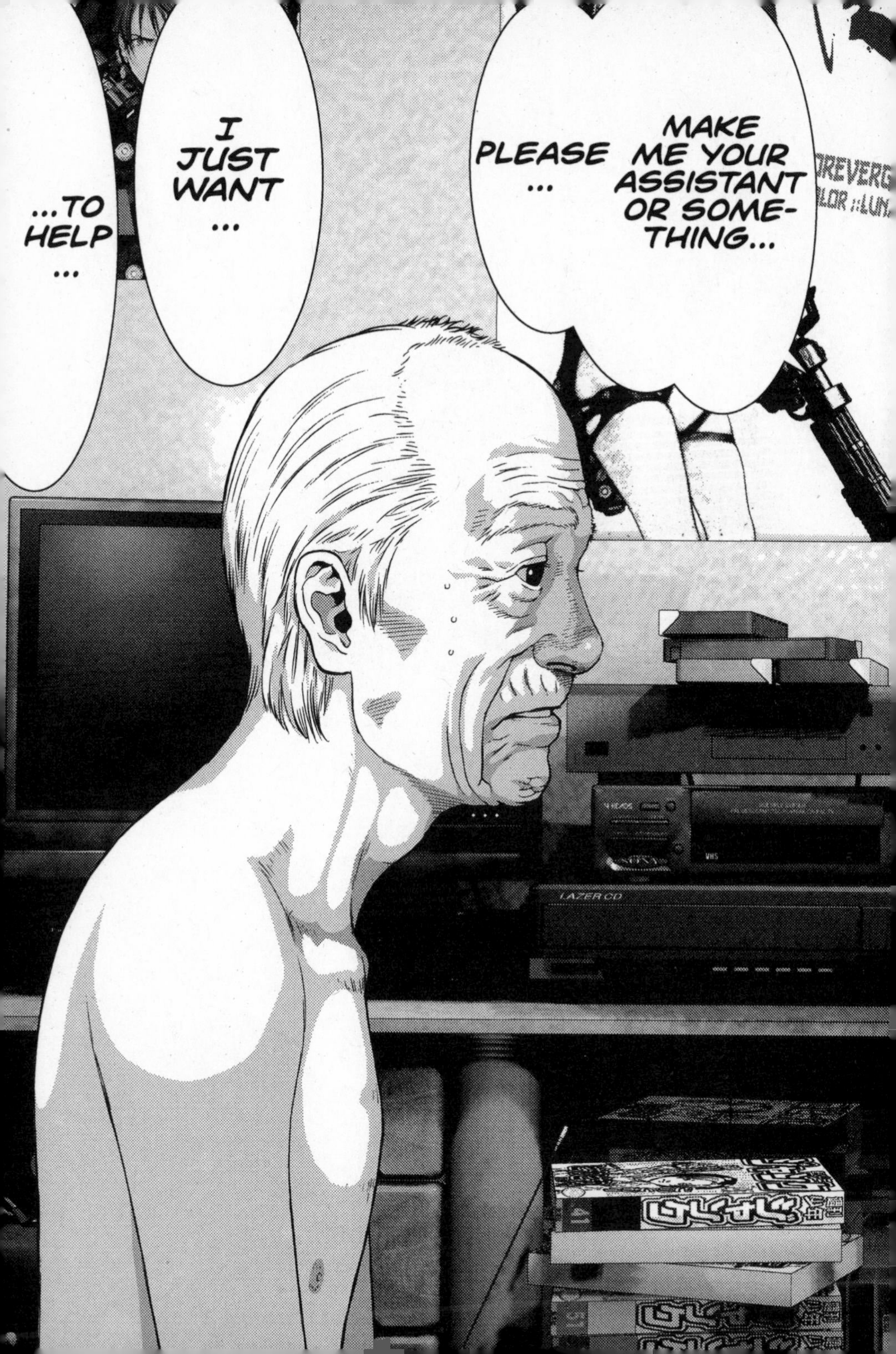
MAKE ME YOUR ASSISTANT OR SOME-THING...
PLEASE ...
I JUST WANT ...
...TO HELP ...
VHS
LAZER CD

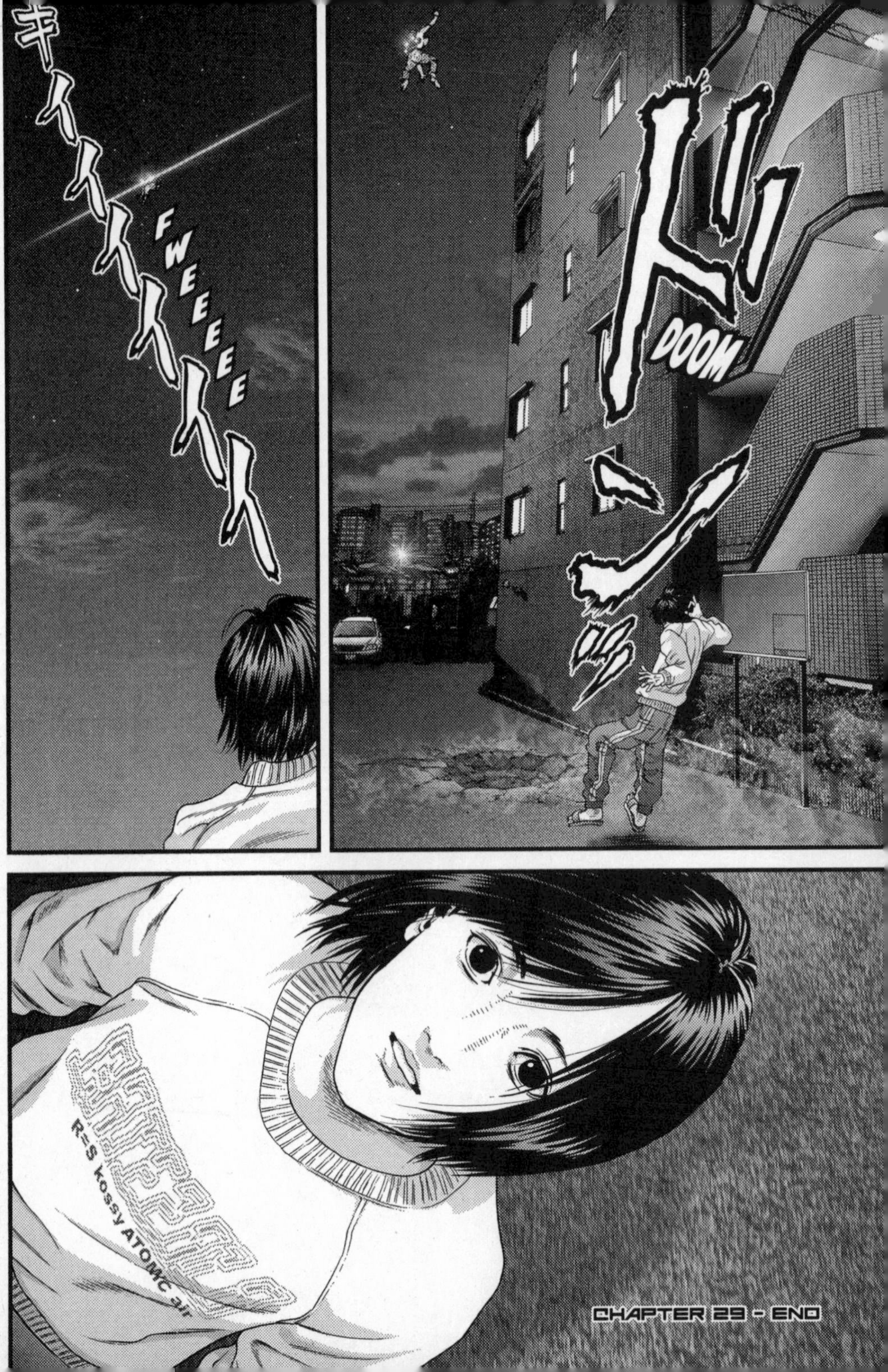
ドーンッ
DOOM
キイイイイイイイイ
FWEEEEE
CHAPTER 29 - END

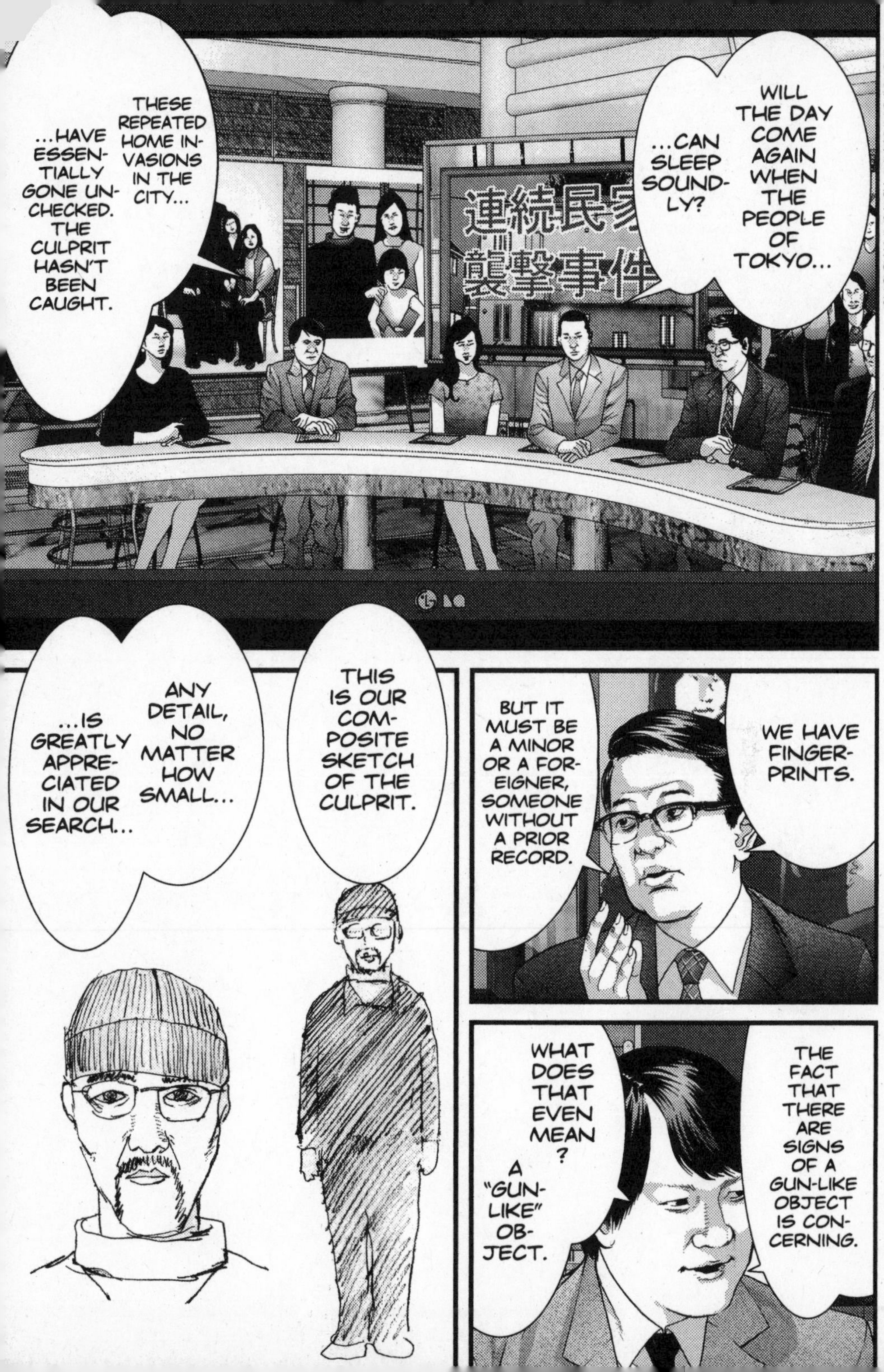
WILL THE DAY COME AGAIN WHEN THE PEOPLE OF TOKYO...
...CAN SLEEP SOUNDLY?
連続民家
襲撃事件
THESE REPEATED HOME INVASIONS IN THE CITY...
...HAVE ESSENTIALLY GONE UNCHECKED. THE CULPRIT HASN'T BEEN CAUGHT.
WE HAVE FINGERPRINTS.
BUT IT MUST BE A MINOR OR A FOREIGNER, SOMEONE WITHOUT A PRIOR RECORD.
THE FACT THAT THERE ARE SIGNS OF A GUN-LIKE OBJECT IS CONCERNING.
WHAT DOES THAT EVEN MEAN? A "GUN-LIKE" OBJECT.
THIS IS OUR COMPOSITE SKETCH OF THE CULPRIT.
ANY DETAIL, NO MATTER HOW SMALL...
...IS GREATLY APPRECIATED IN OUR SEARCH...

BACKDROP: SERIAL HOME INVASIONS

CHAPTER 30: HIRO

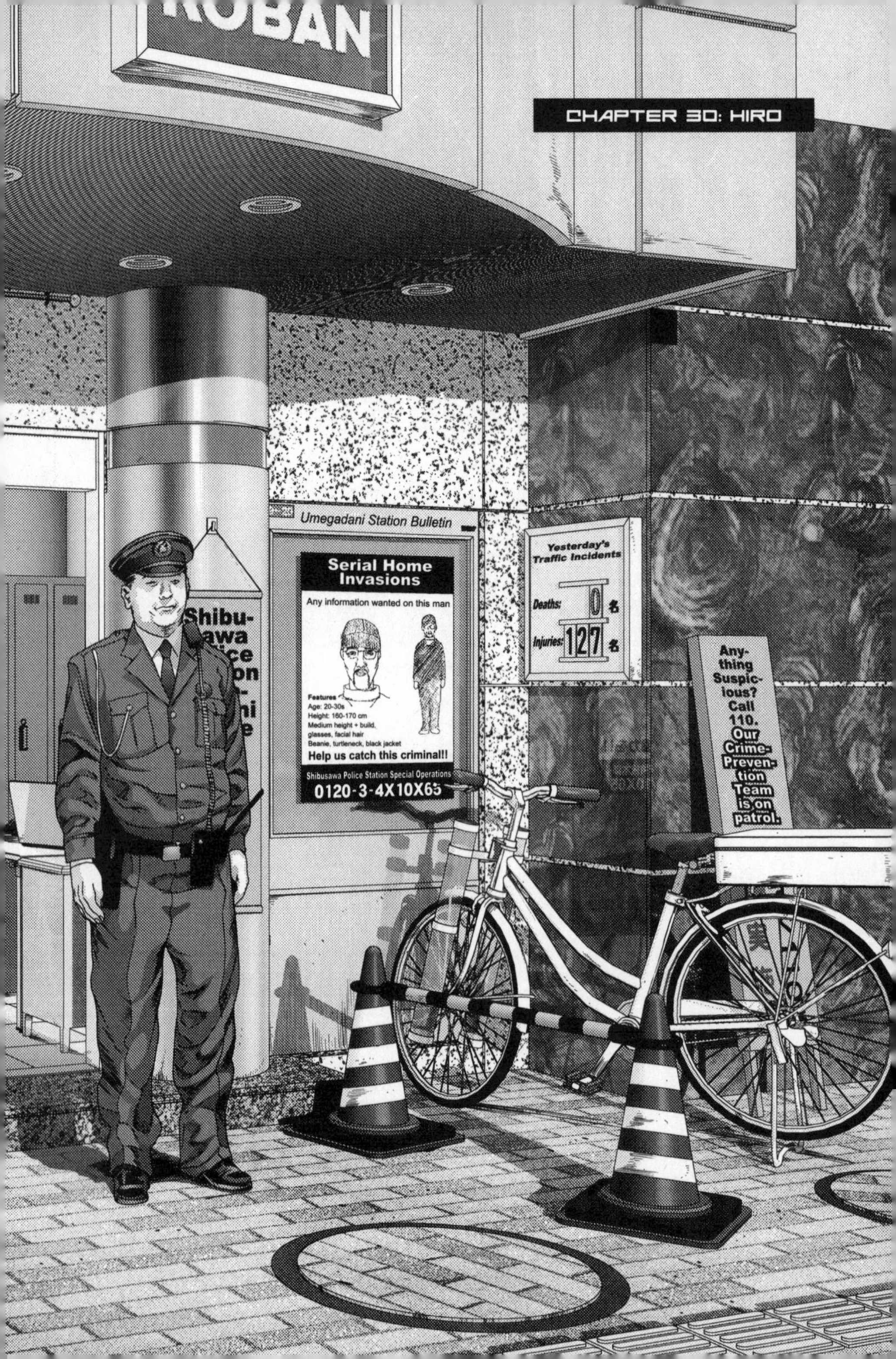
Umegadani Station Bulletin
Serial Home Invasions
Any information wanted on this man
Features
Age: 20-30s
Height: 160-170 cm
Medium height + build,
glasses, facial hair
Beanie, turtleneck, black jacket
Help us catch this criminal!!
Shibusawa Police Station Special Operations
0120-3-4X10X65
Yesterday's Traffic Incidents
Deaths: 0 名
Injuries: 127 名
Any-thing Suspic-ious? Call 110. Our Crime-Preven-tion Team is on patrol.

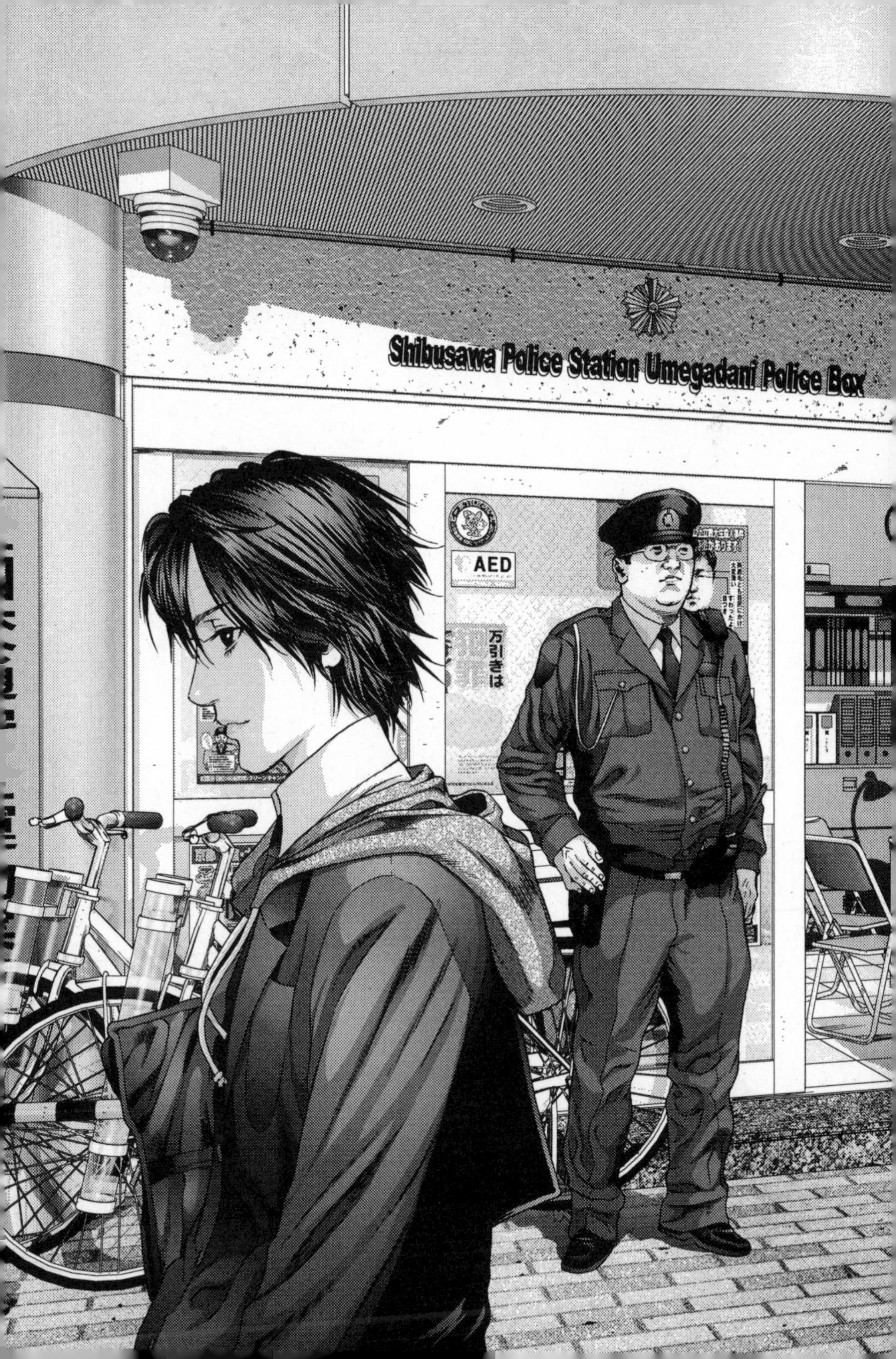
Shibusawa Police Station Umegadani Police Box
AED
万引きは

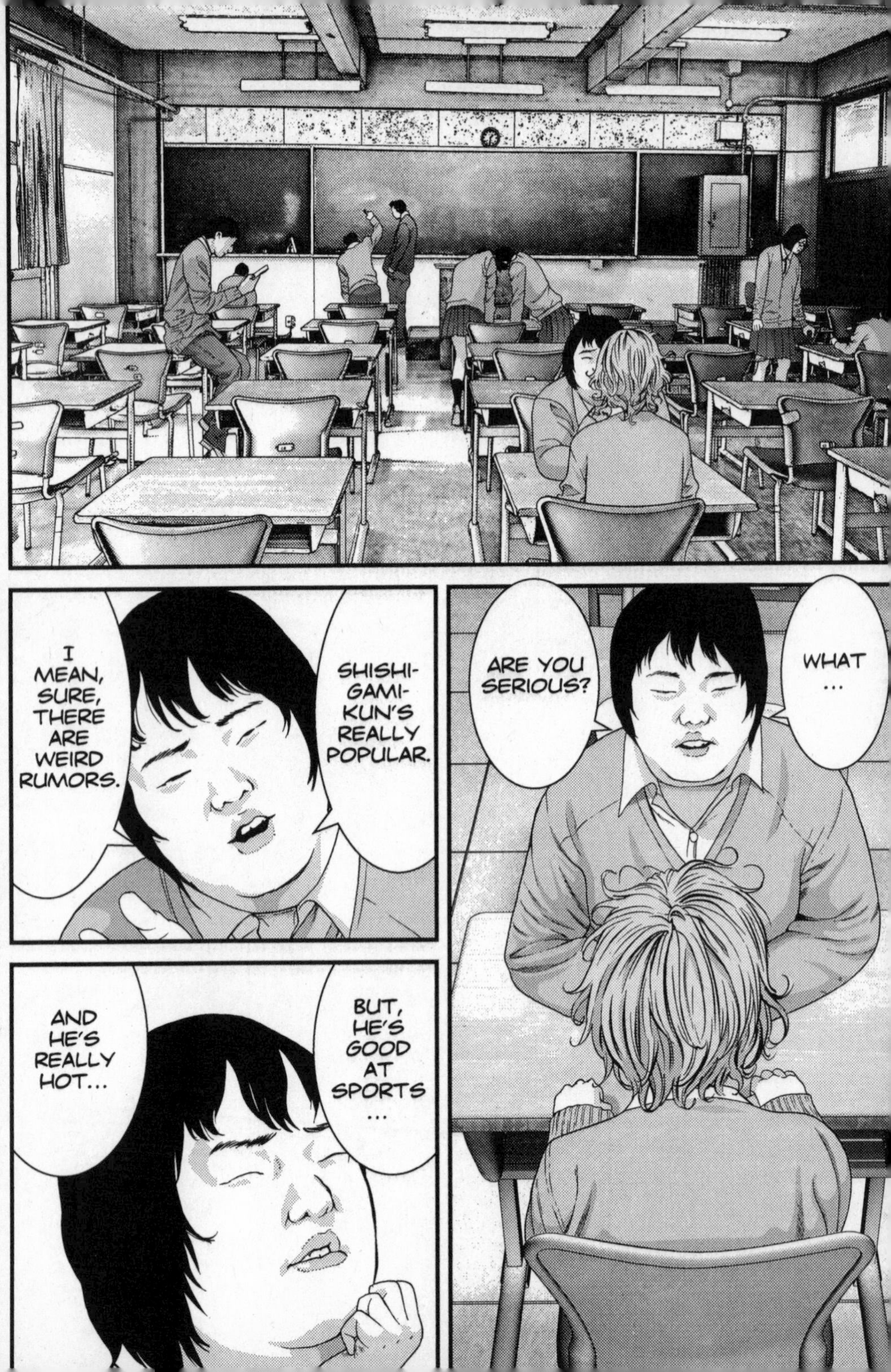
WHAT ...
ARE YOU SERIOUS?
SHISHIGAMI-KUN'S REALLY POPULAR.
I MEAN, SURE, THERE ARE WEIRD RUMORS.
BUT, HE'S GOOD AT SPORTS ...
AND HE'S REALLY HOT...

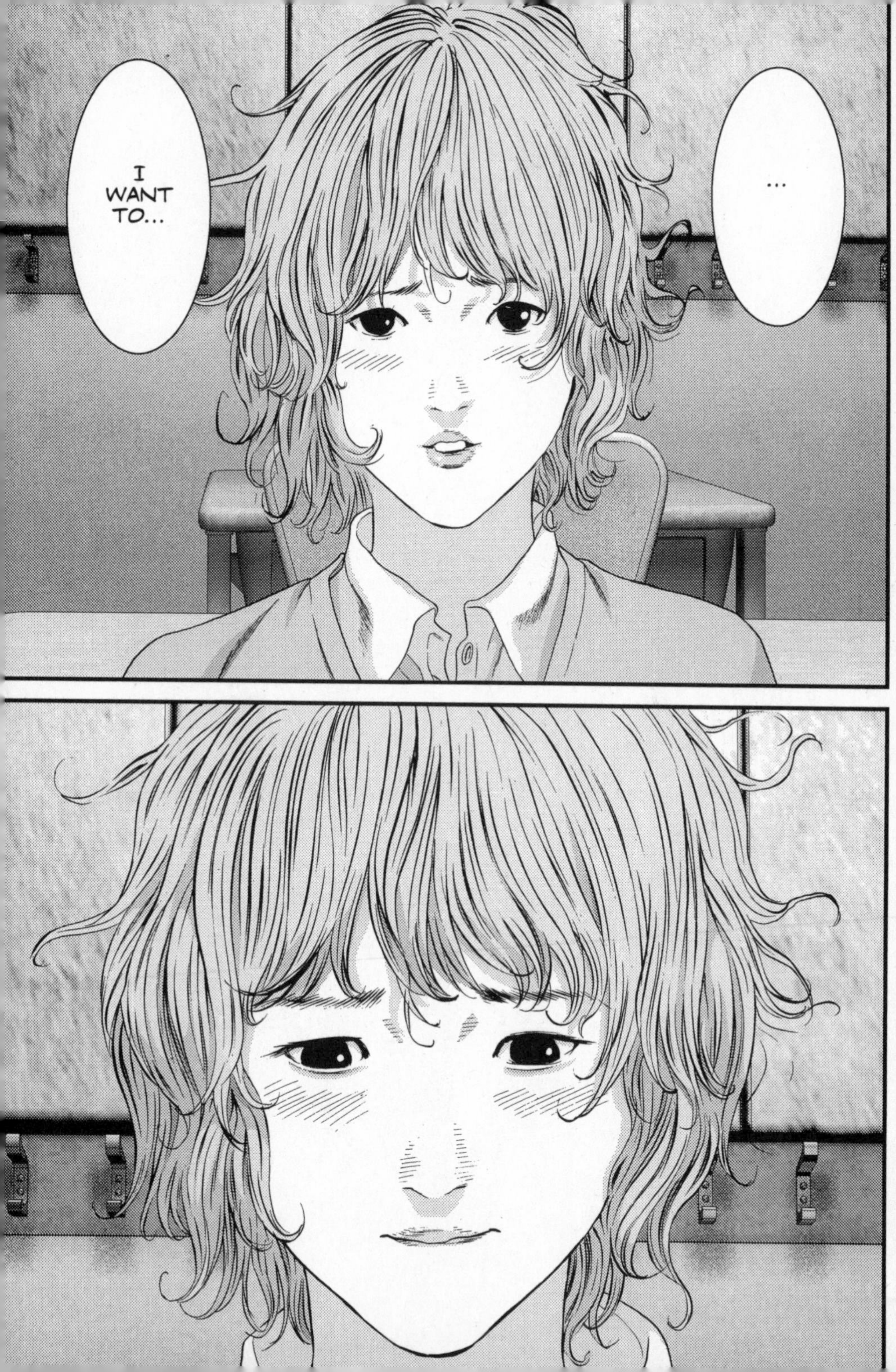
...
I WANT TO...

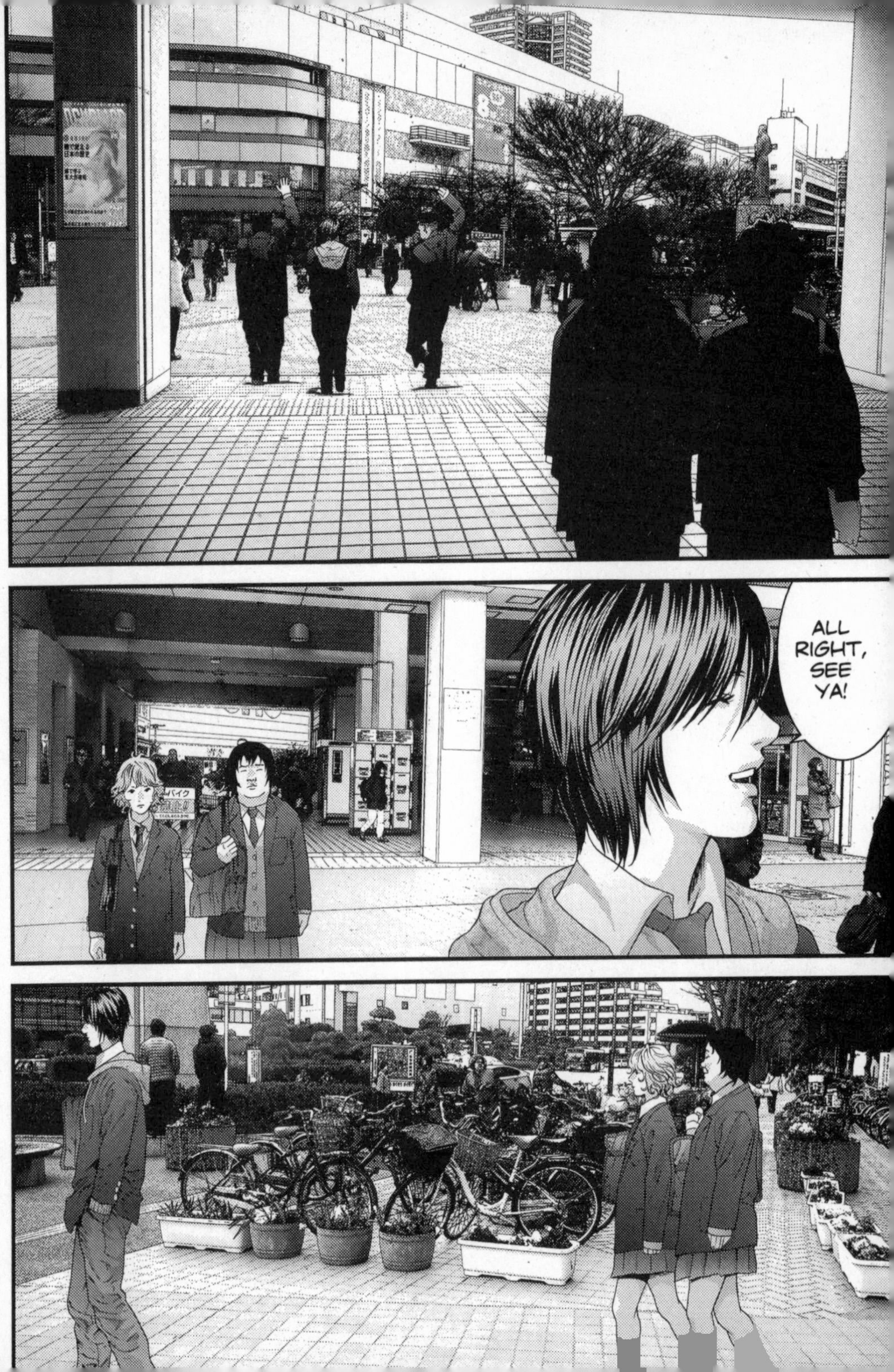
ALL RIGHT, SEE YA!
バイク

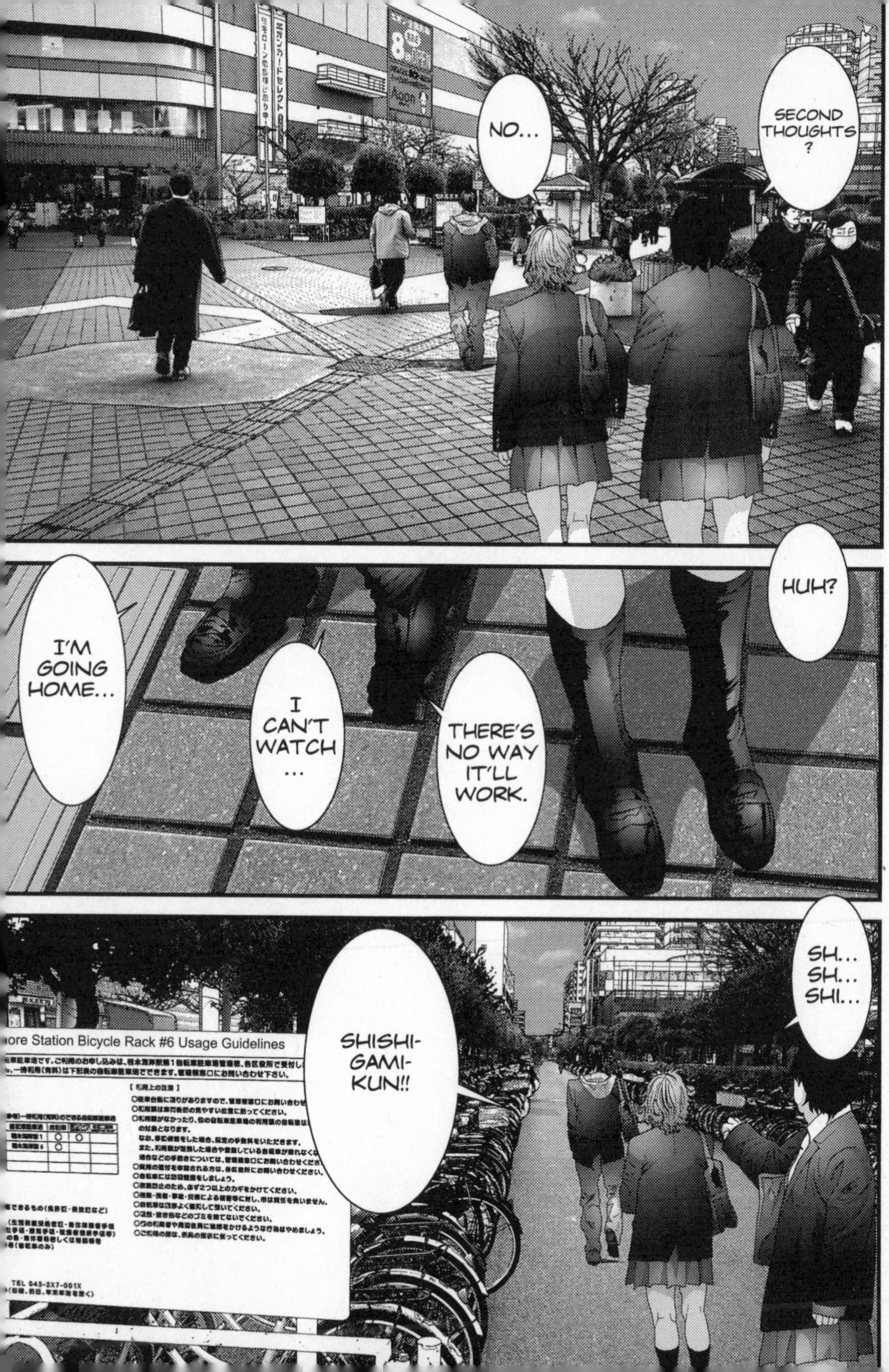
SECOND THOUGHTS ?
NO...
HUH?
THERE'S NO WAY IT'LL WORK.
I CAN'T WATCH ...
I'M GOING HOME...
SH... SH... SHI...
SHISHI-GAMI-KUN!!
ore Station Bicycle Rack #6 Usage Guidelines

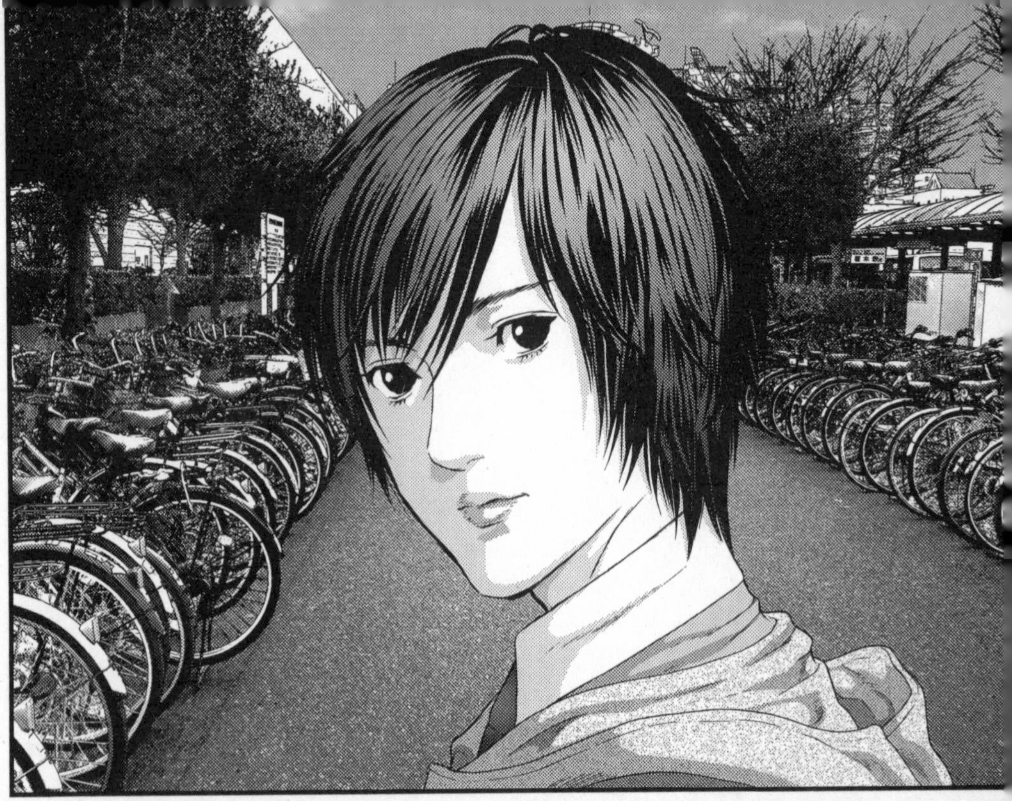

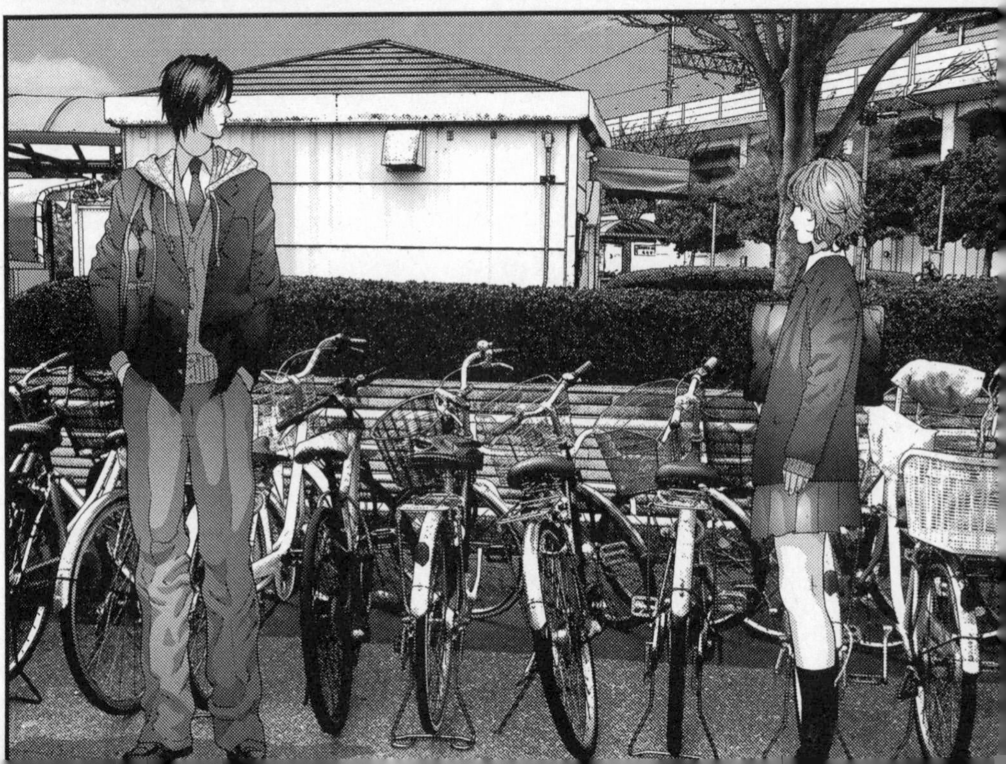

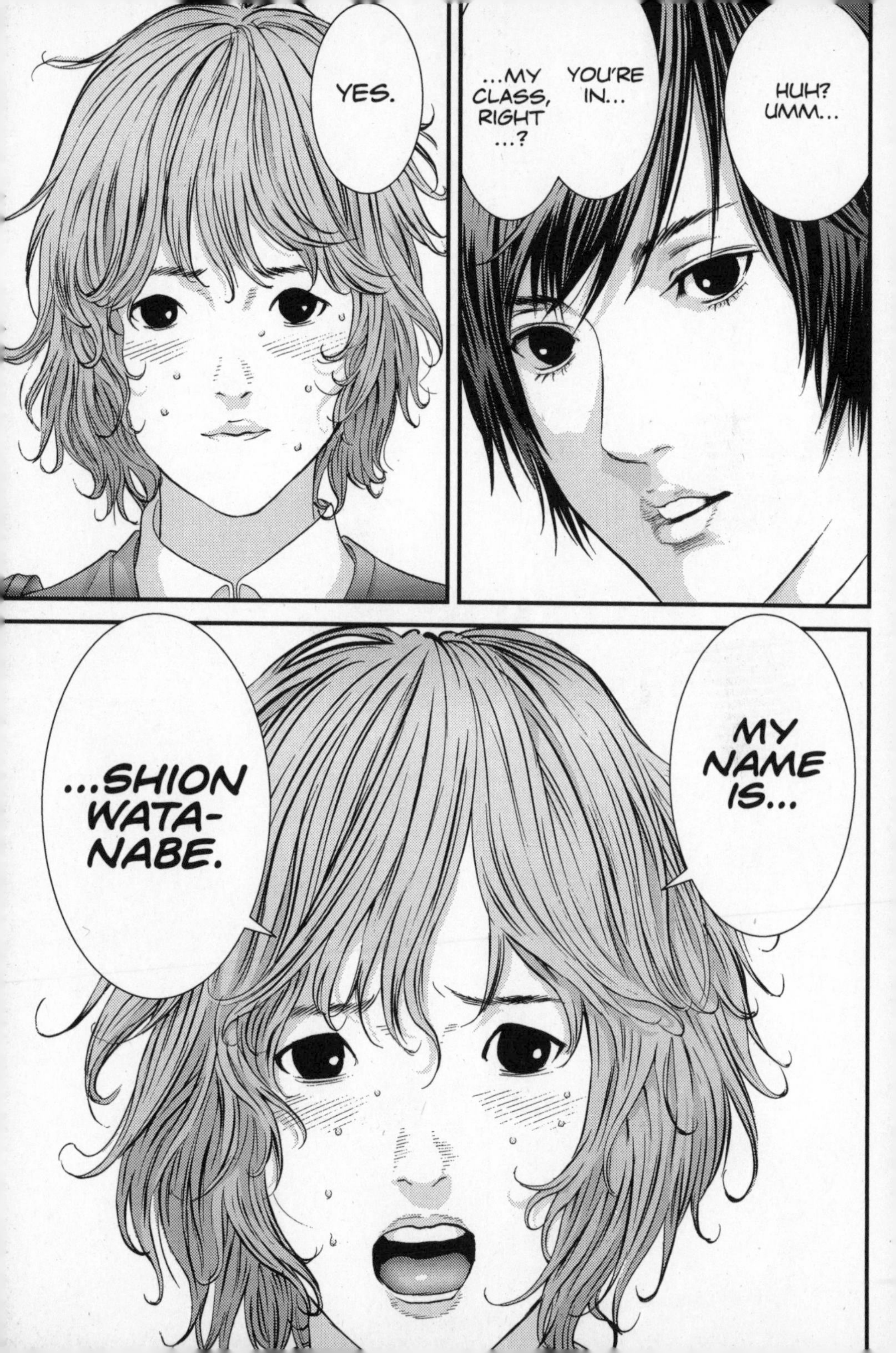
HUH? UMM...
YOU'RE IN...
...MY CLASS, RIGHT ...?
YES.
MY NAME IS...
...SHION WATA-NABE.

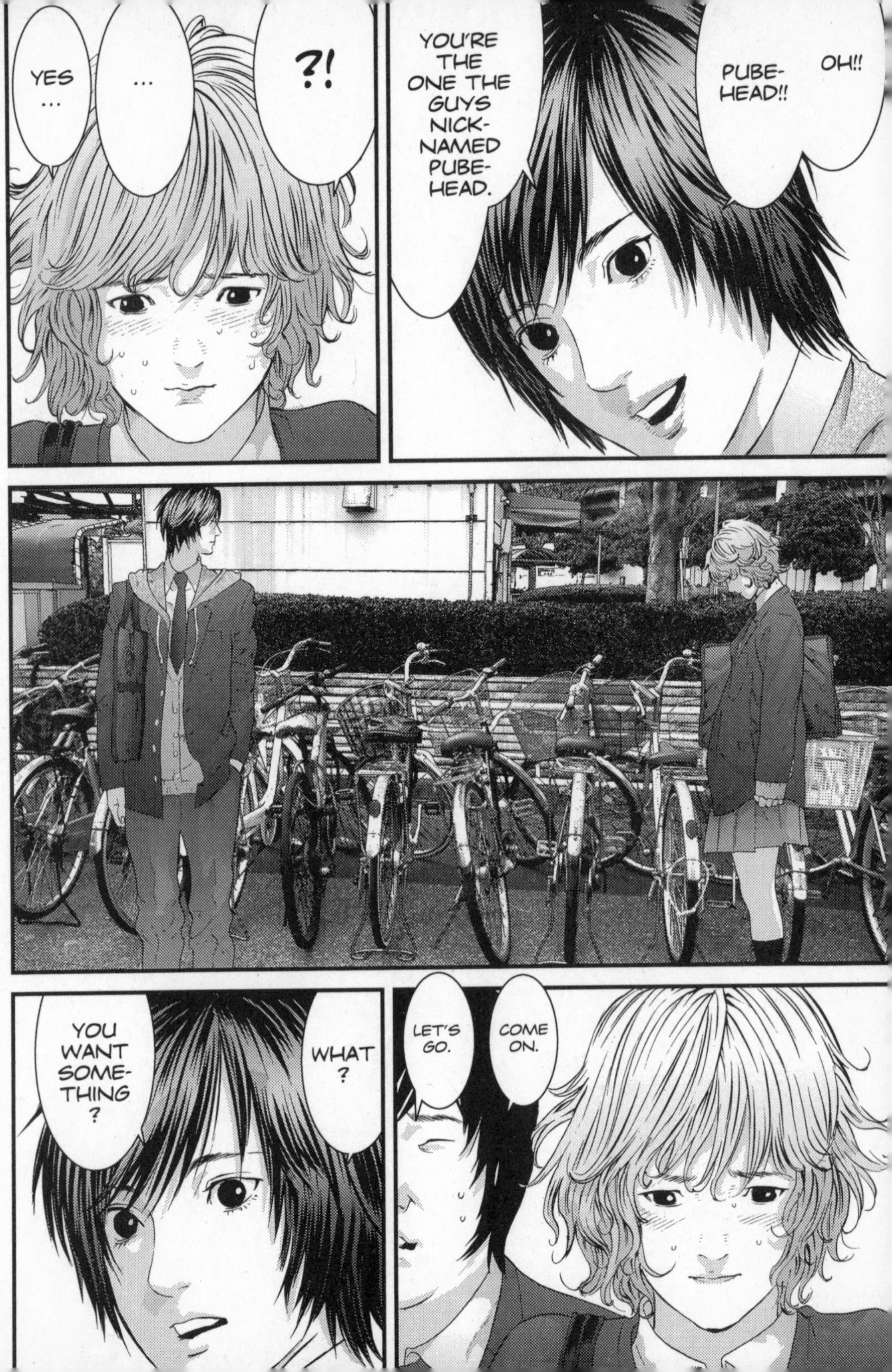
OH!!
PUBE-HEAD!!
YOU'RE THE ONE THE GUYS NICK-NAMED PUBE-HEAD.
?!
...
YES ...
COME ON.
LET'S GO.
WHAT?
YOU WANT SOME-THING?

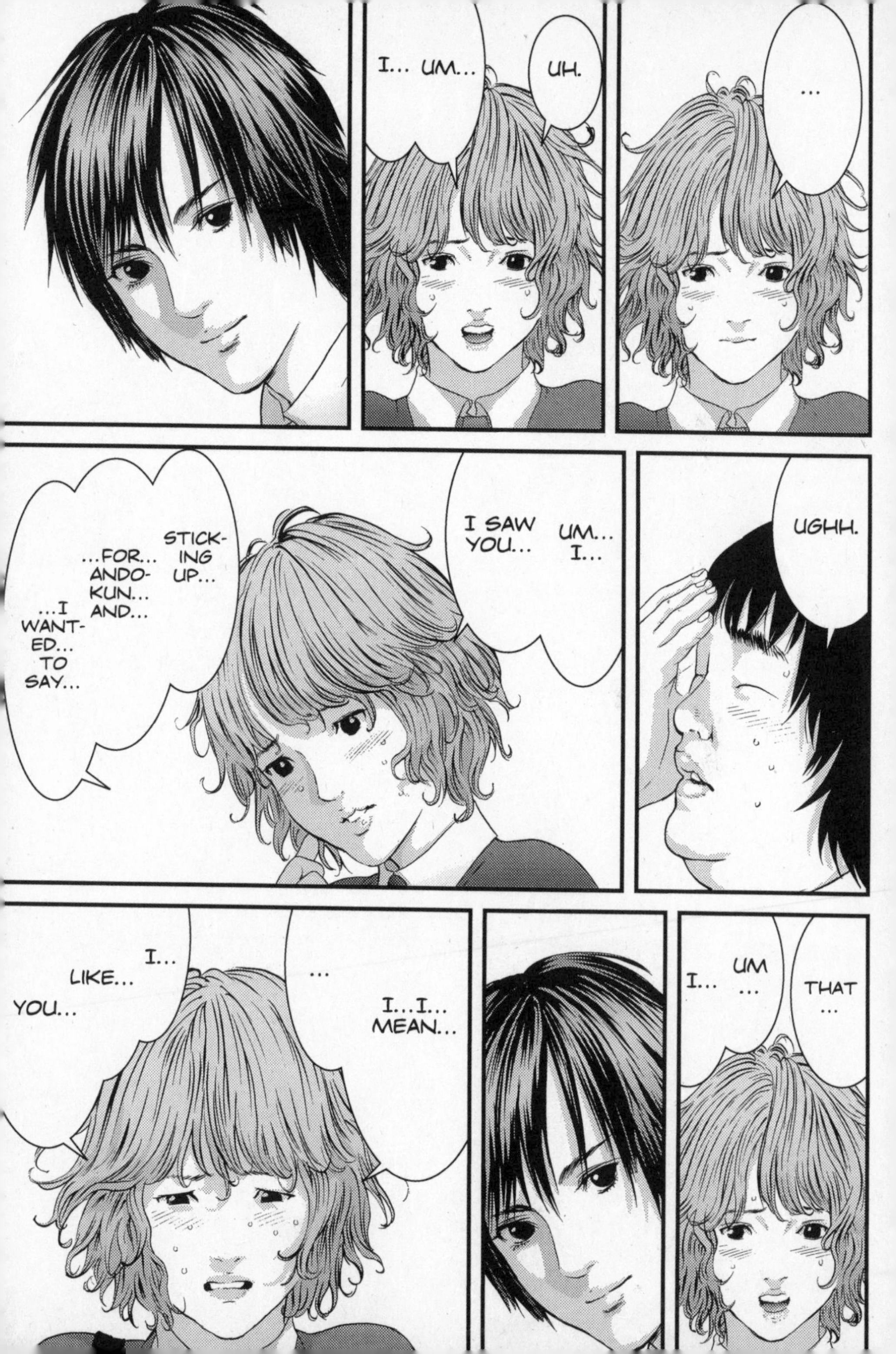
...
UH.
I... UM...
UGHH.
I SAW YOU... UM... I...
STICKING UP... ...FOR... ANDO-KUN... AND... ...I WANTED... TO SAY...
THAT ...
UM ... I...
... I...I... MEAN...
I... LIKE... YOU...

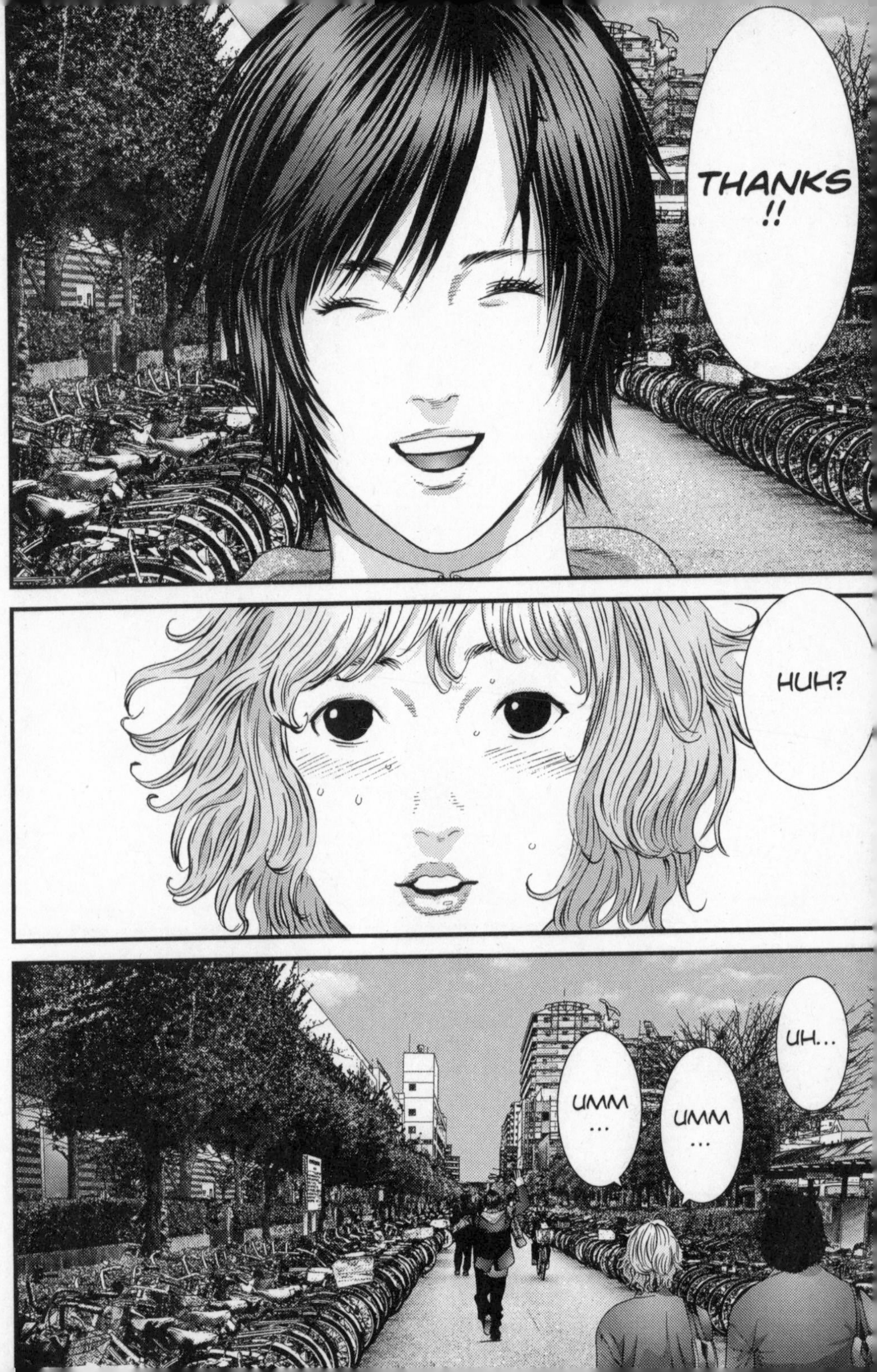
THANKS !!
HUH?
UH...
UMM ...
UMM ...

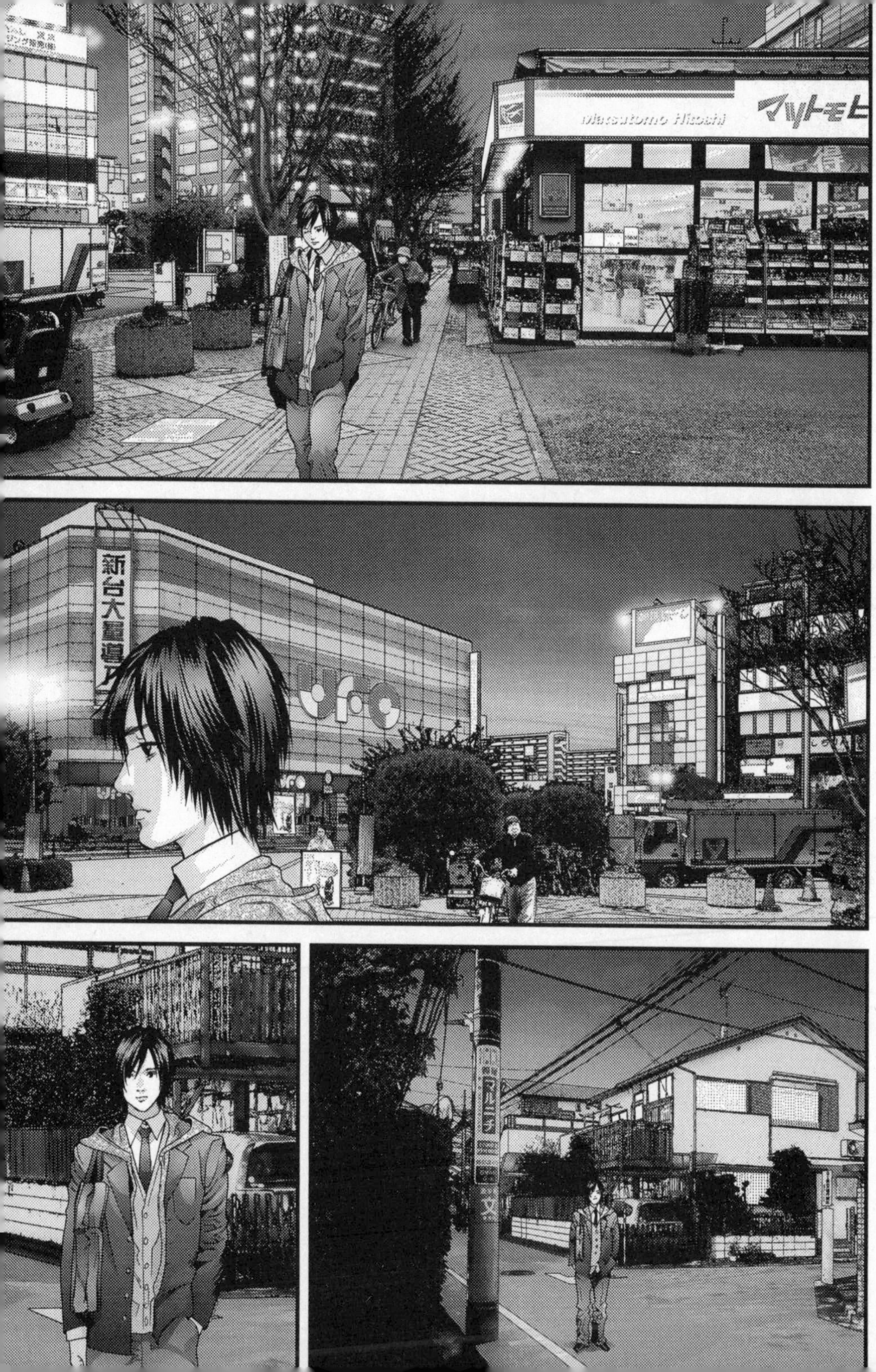

マツトモヒ
Matsutomo Hitoshi
新台大量導

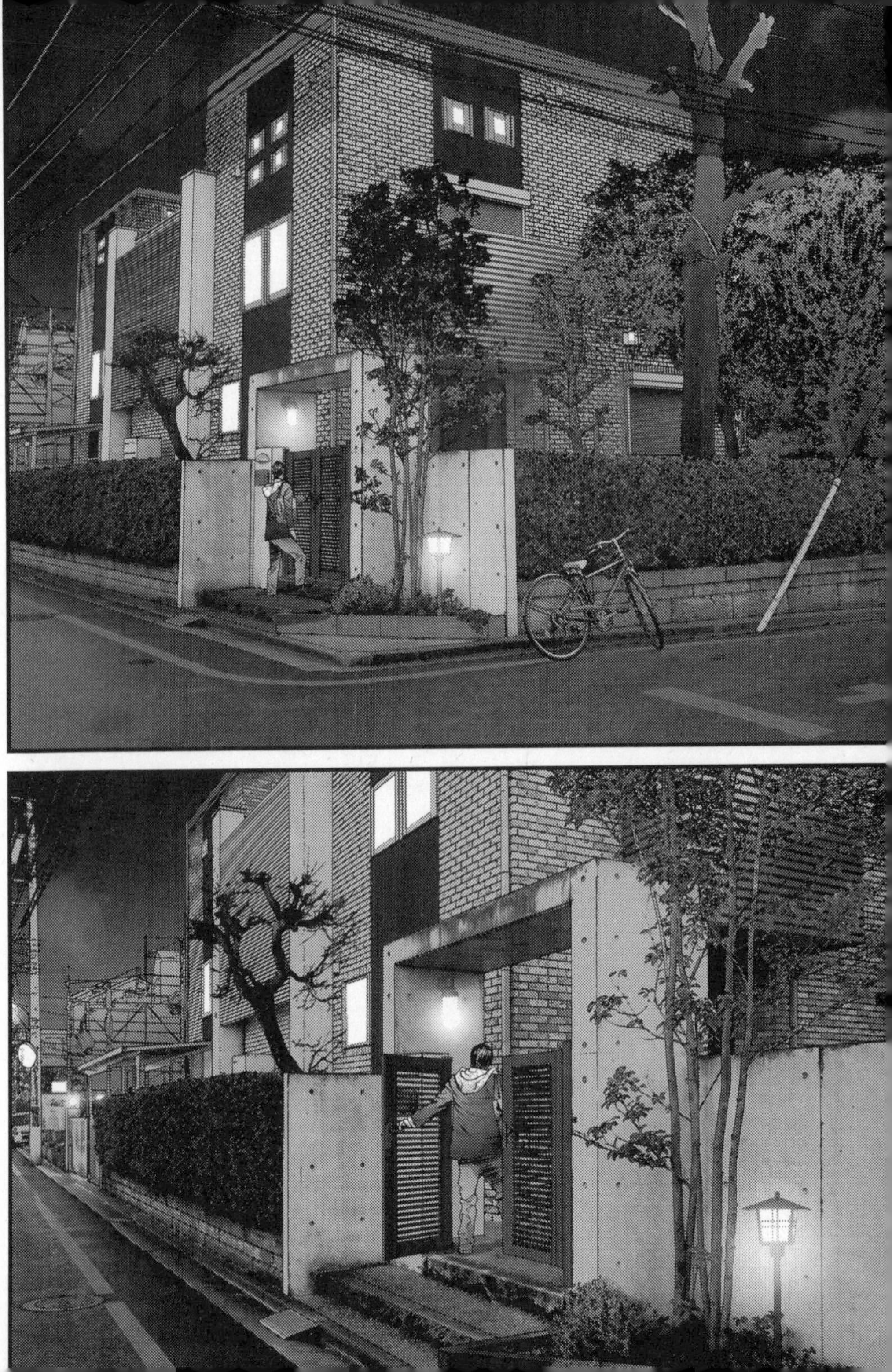

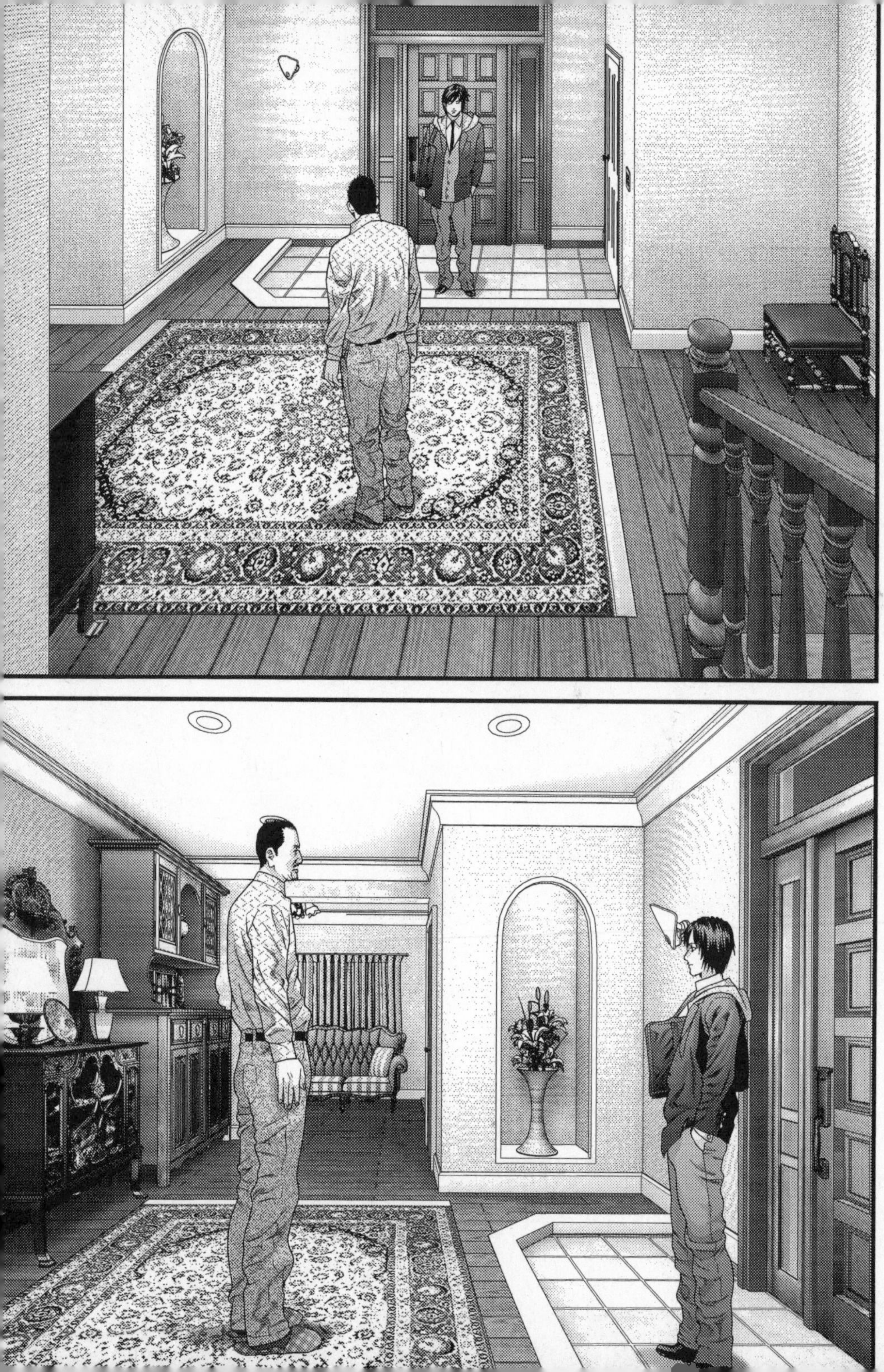

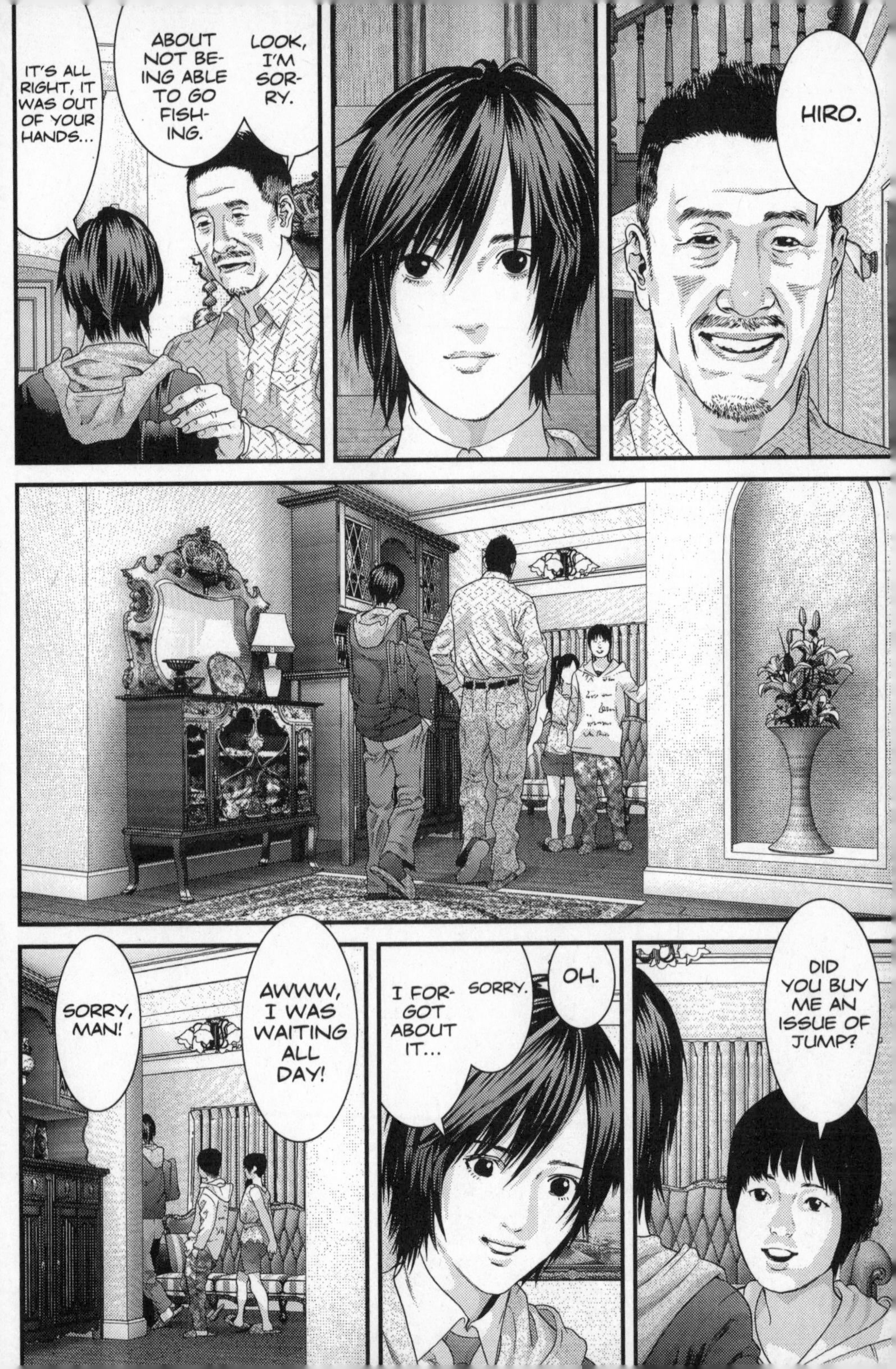
HIRO.
LOOK, I'M SORRY.
ABOUT NOT BEING ABLE TO GO FISHING.
IT'S ALL RIGHT, IT WAS OUT OF YOUR HANDS...
DID YOU BUY ME AN ISSUE OF JUMP?
OH.
SORRY.
I FORGOT ABOUT IT...
AWWW, I WAS WAITING ALL DAY!
SORRY, MAN!

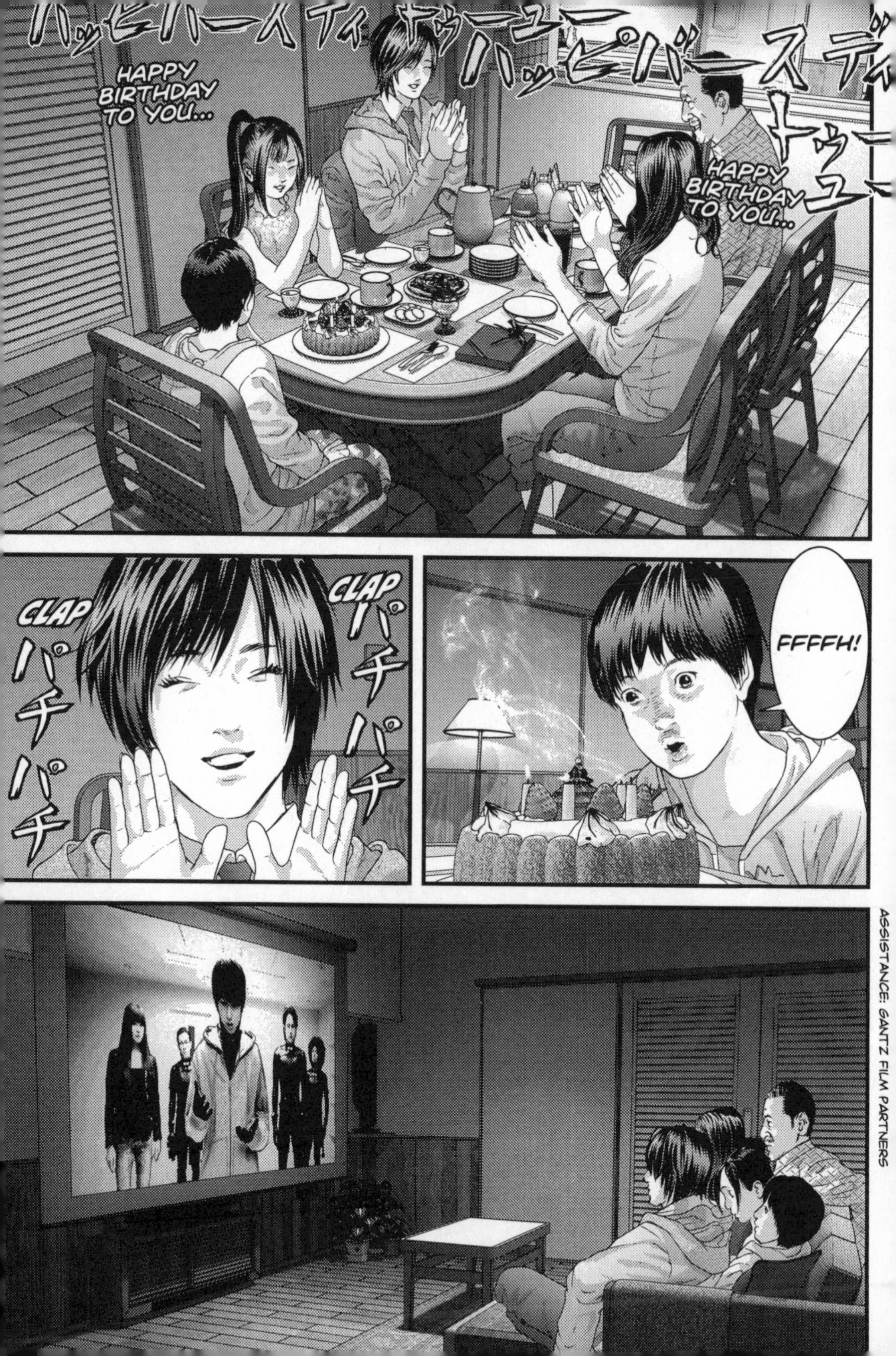

ハッピバースディトゥーユー
HAPPY BIRTHDAY TO YOU...
ハッピバースディトゥーユー
HAPPY BIRTHDAY TO YOU...
FFFFH!
CLAP
パチパチ
CLAP
パチパチ

ASSISTANCE: GANTZ FILM PARTNERS

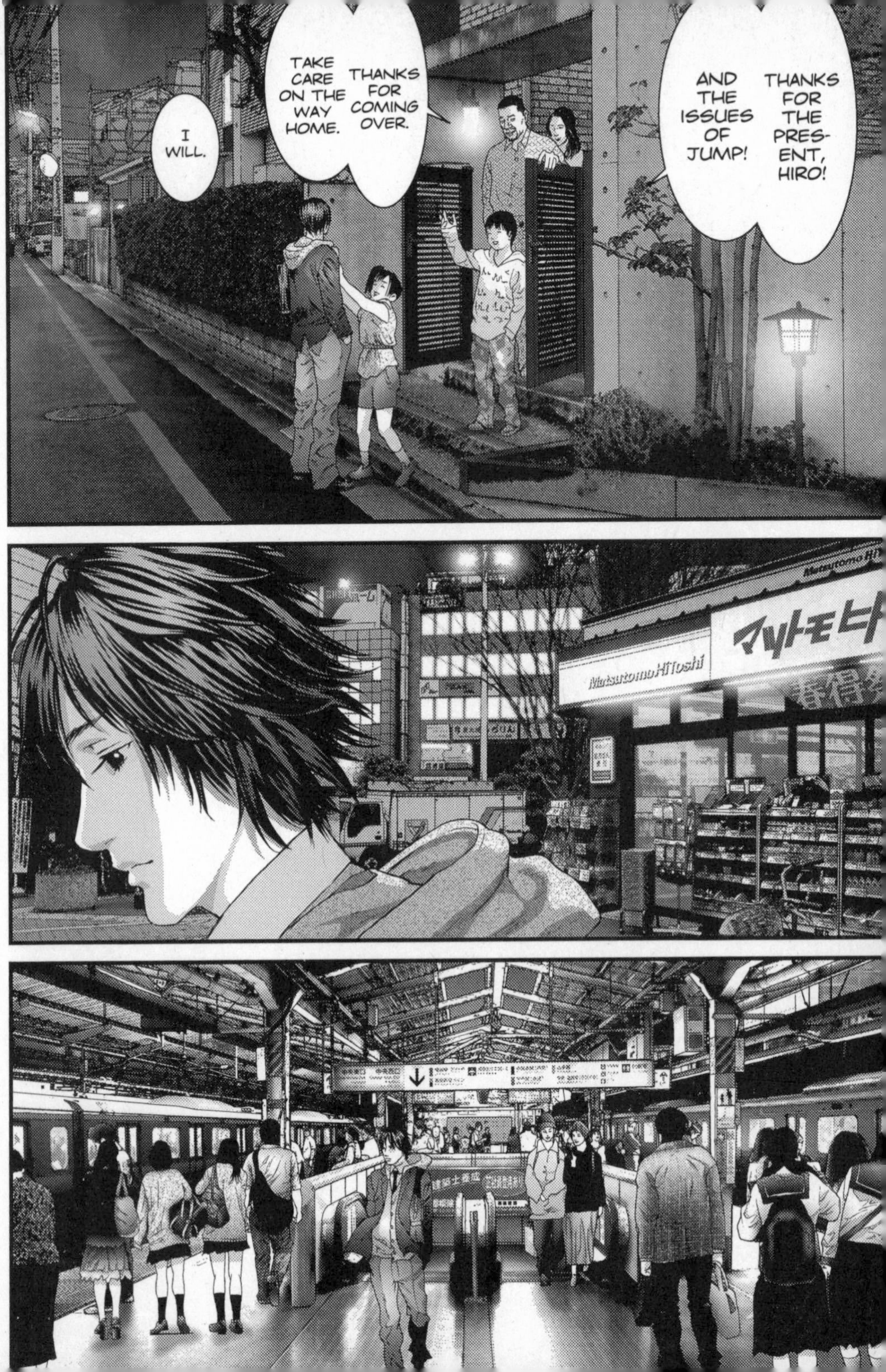
THANKS FOR THE PRESENT, HIRO!
AND THE ISSUES OF JUMP!
THANKS FOR COMING OVER.
TAKE CARE ON THE WAY HOME.
I WILL.
Matsutomo HiToshi

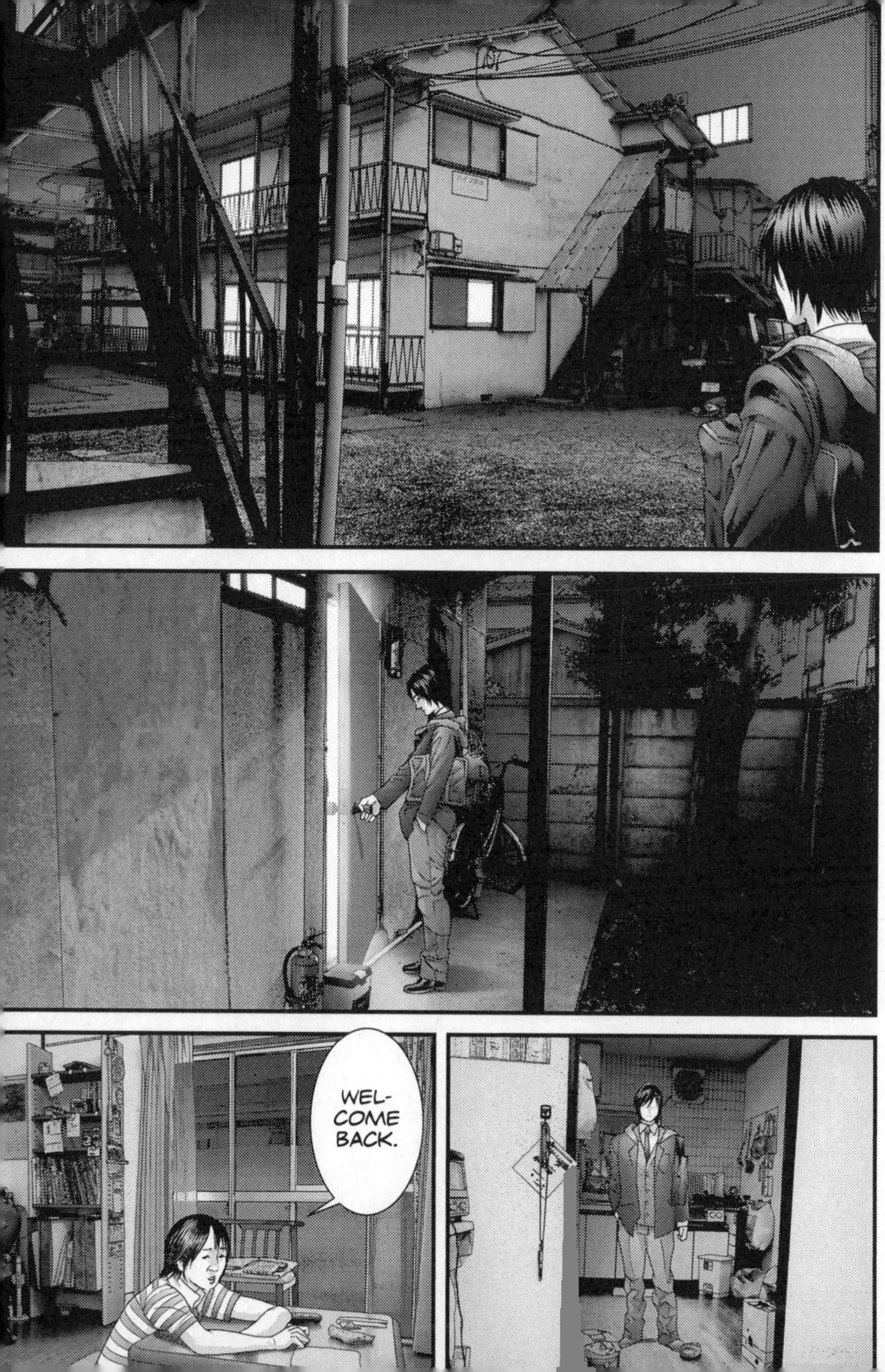
WEL-
COME
BACK.

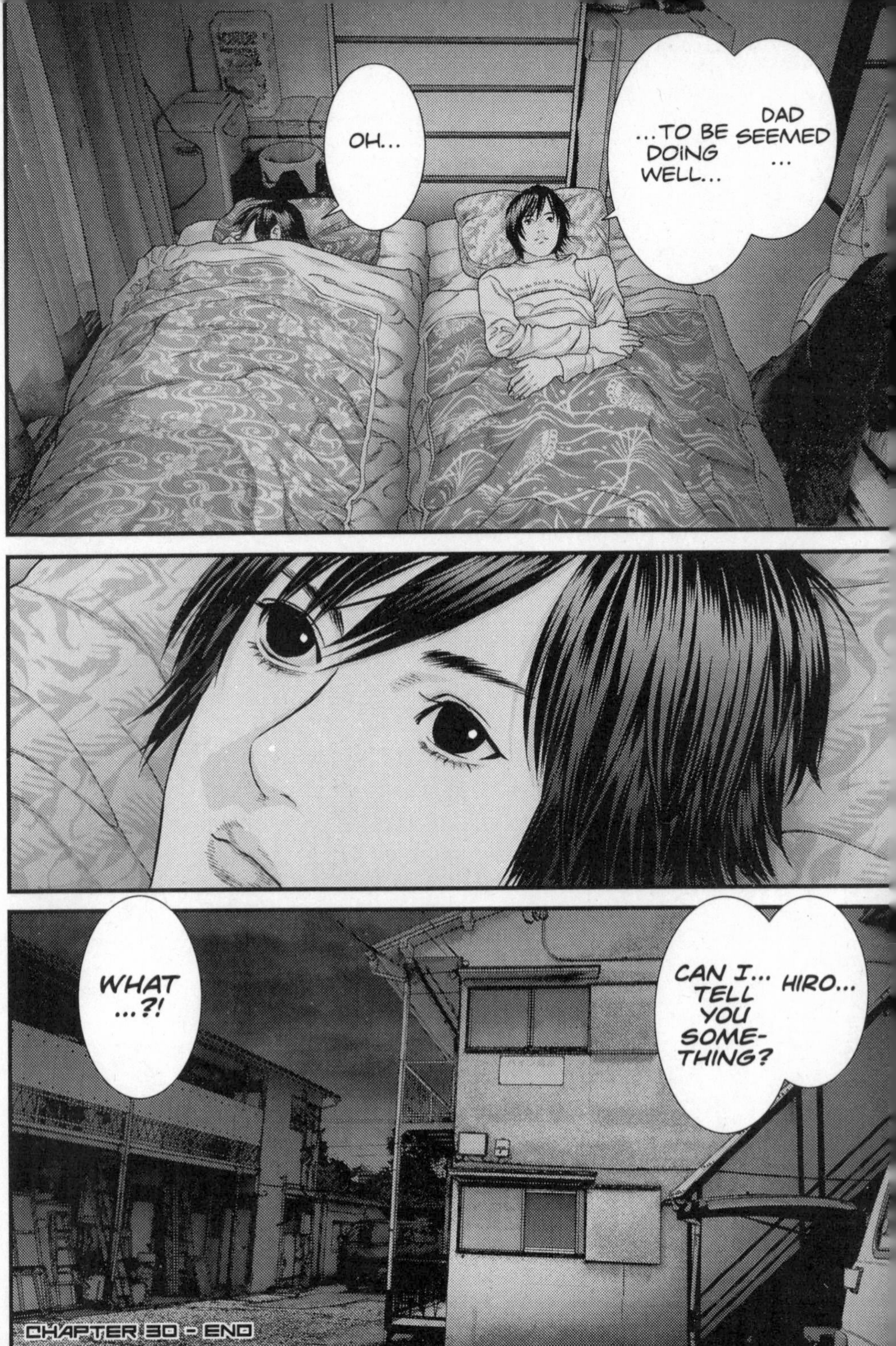
DAD SEEMED ...
...TO BE DOING WELL...
OH...
HIRO...
CAN I... TELL YOU SOME-THING?
WHAT ...?!
CHAPTER 30 - END

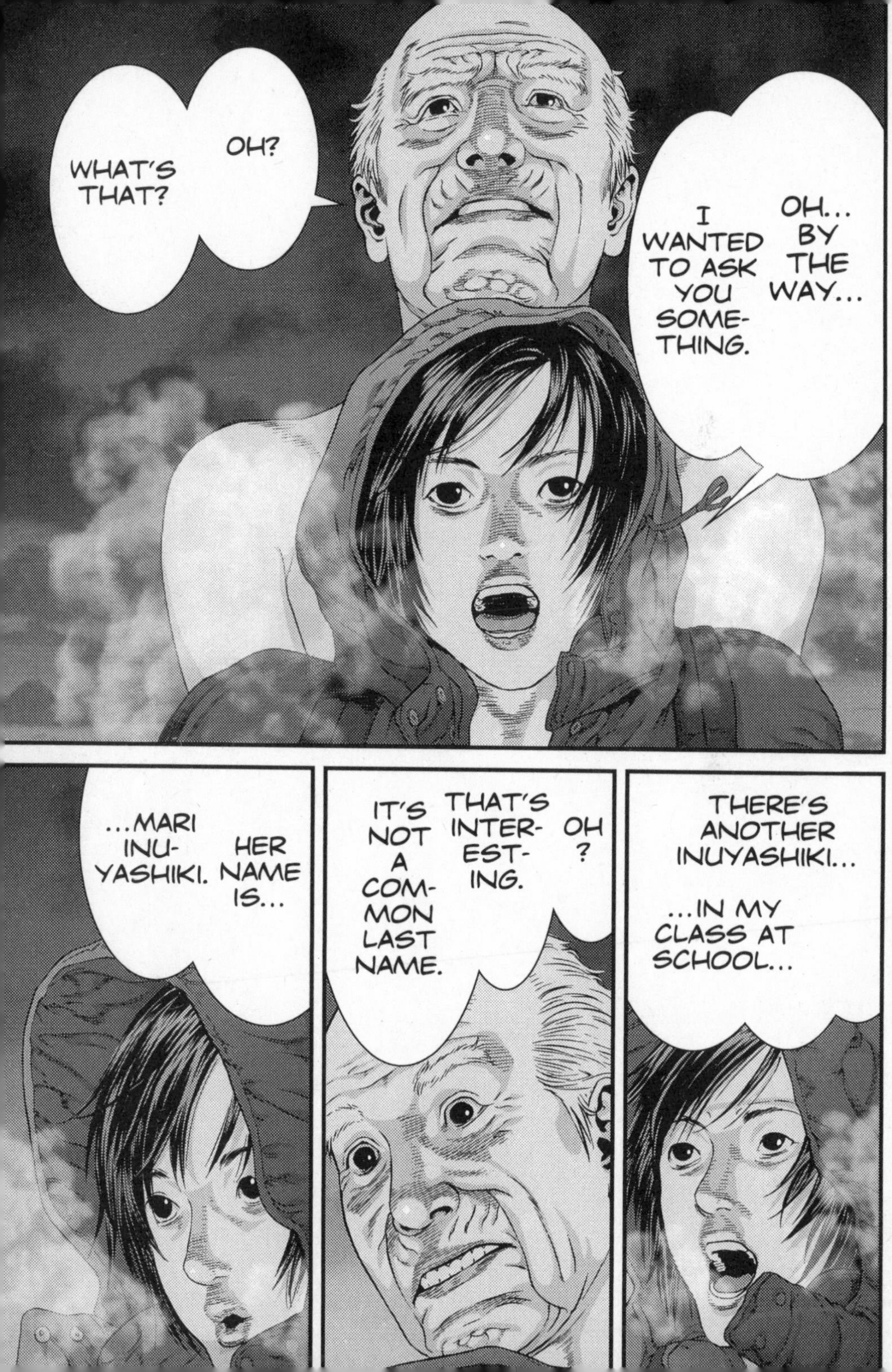
OH... BY THE WAY... I WANTED TO ASK YOU SOME-THING.
OH? WHAT'S THAT?
THERE'S ANOTHER INUYASHIKI...
...IN MY CLASS AT SCHOOL...
OH?
THAT'S INTER-EST-ING.
IT'S NOT A COM-MON LAST NAME.
HER NAME IS...
...MARI INU-YASHIKI.

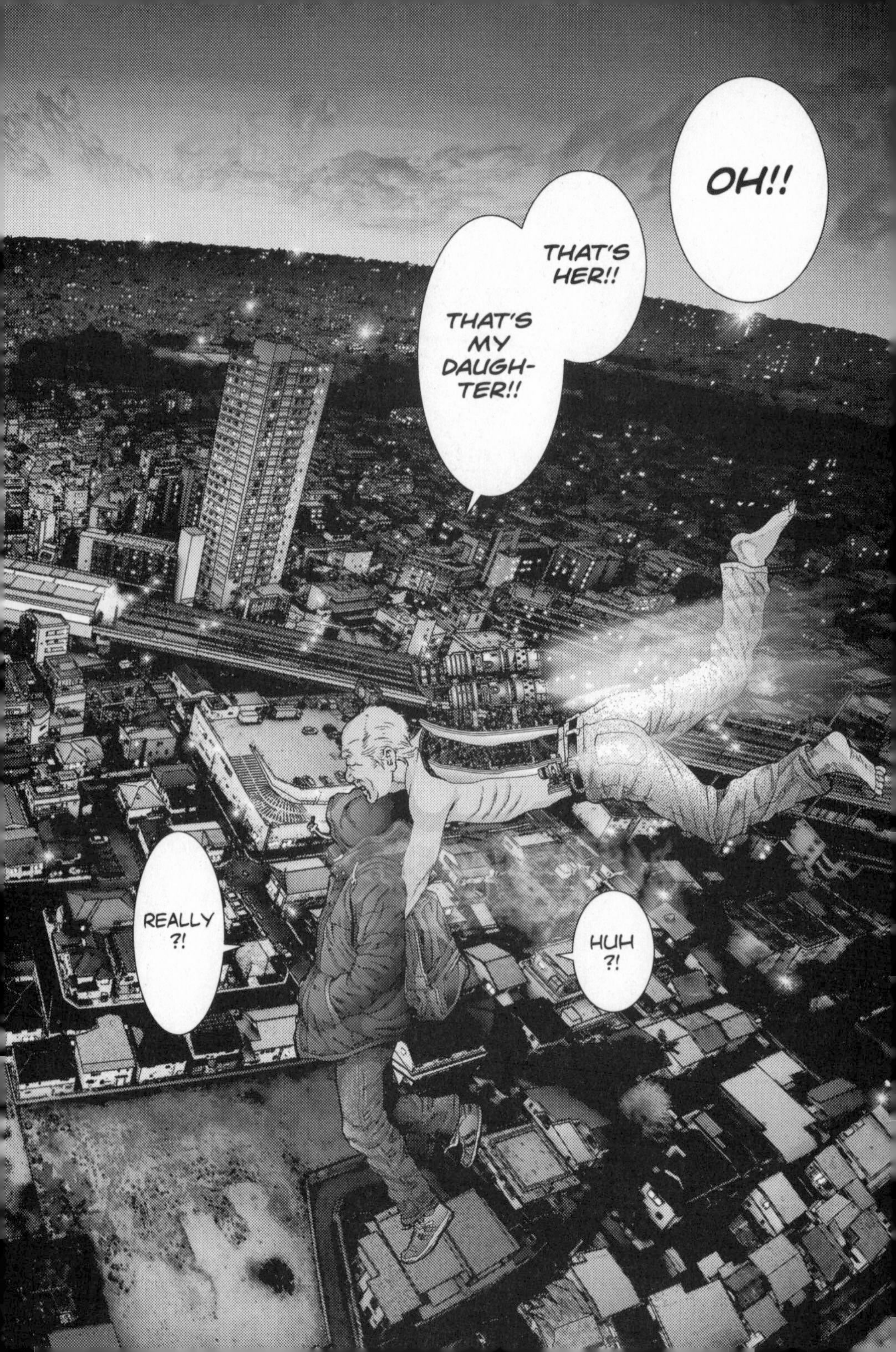
OH!!
THAT'S HER!!
THAT'S MY DAUGH-TER!!
HUH ?!
REALLY ?!

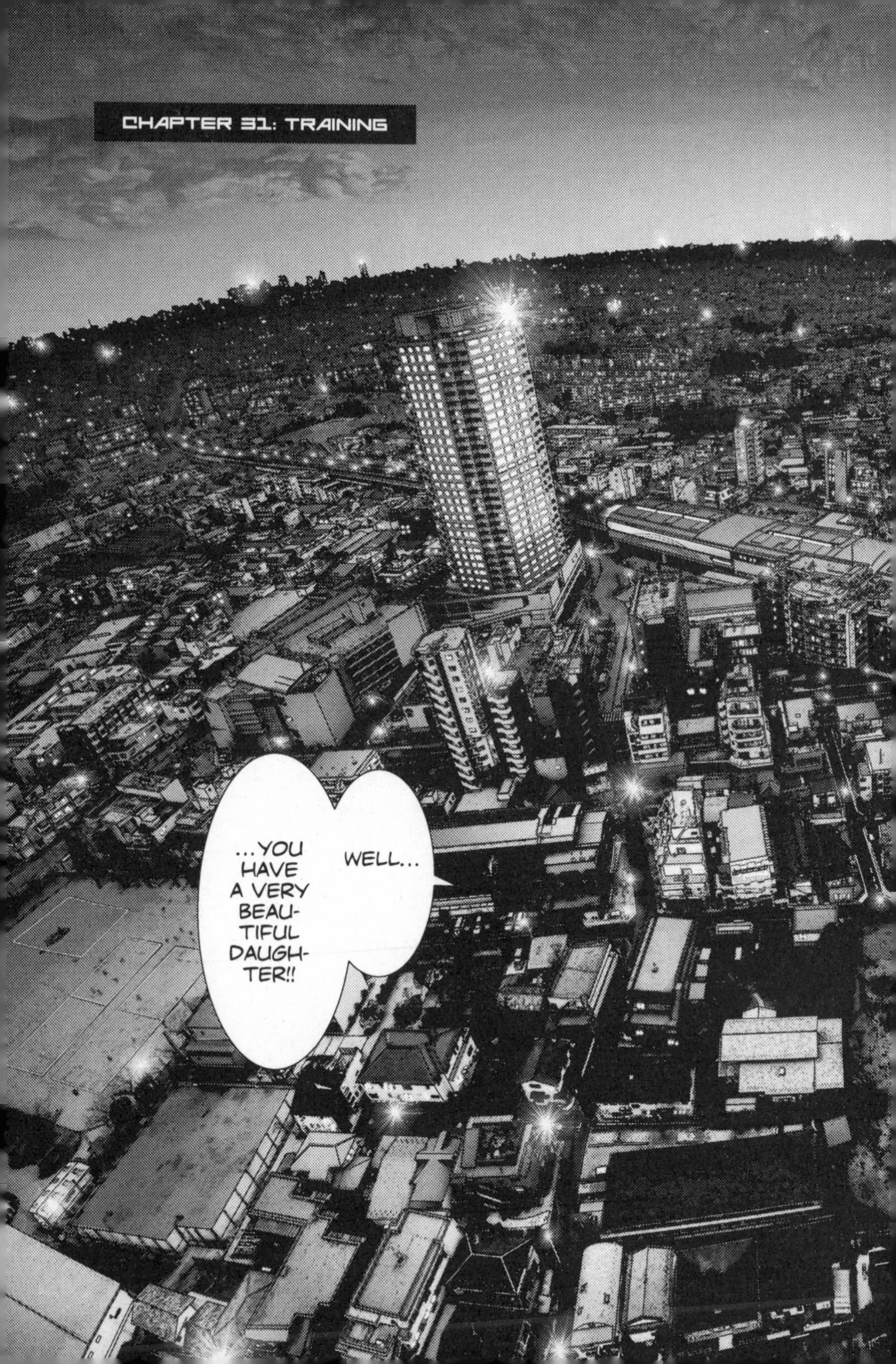
CHAPTER 31: TRAINING
WELL...
...YOU HAVE A VERY BEAUTIFUL DAUGHTER!!

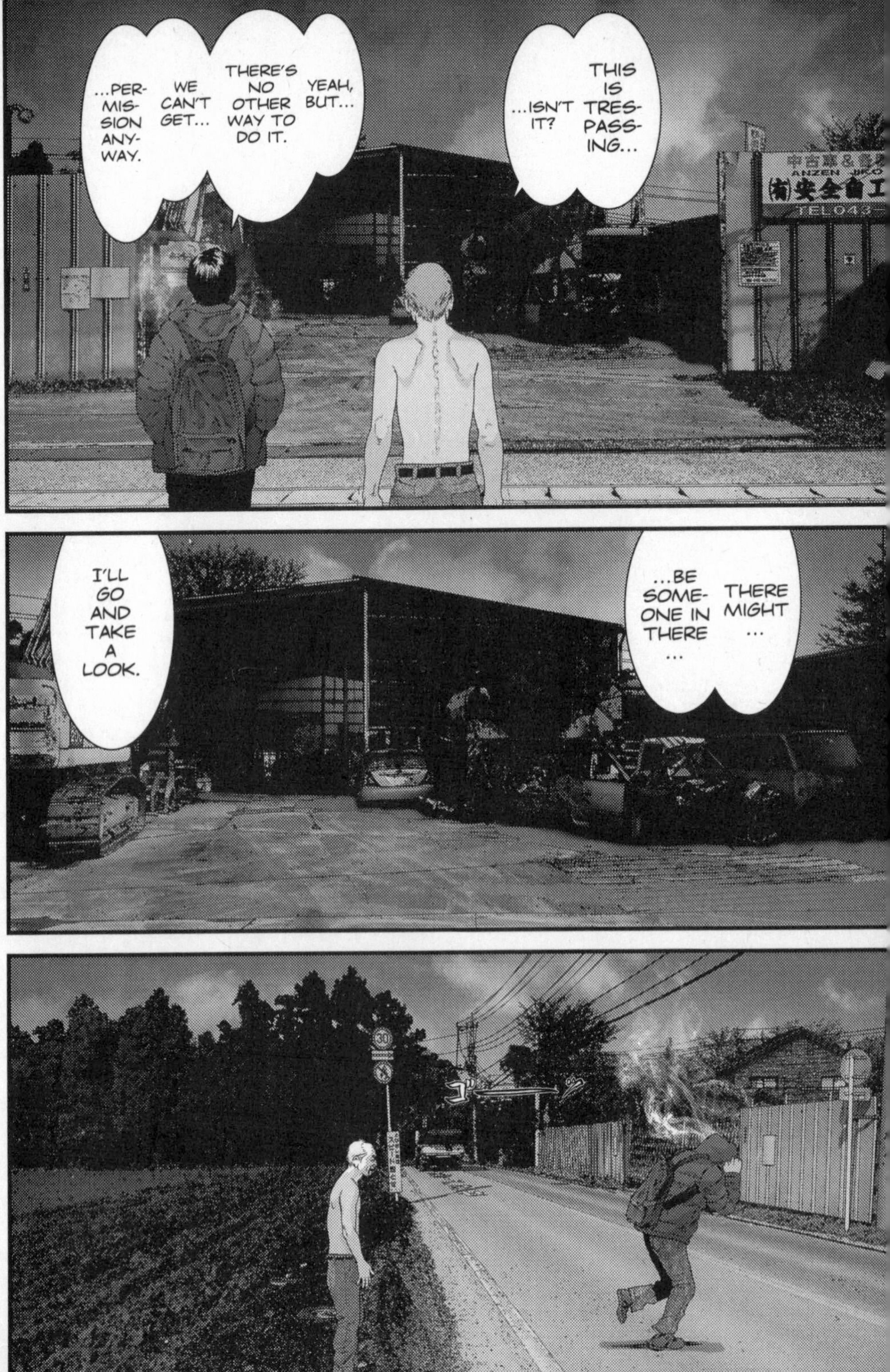
THIS IS TRESPASSING... ...ISN'T IT?
YEAH, BUT... THERE'S NO OTHER WAY TO DO IT.
WE CAN'T GET... ...PERMISSION ANYWAY.
THERE MIGHT... ...BE SOMEONE IN THERE...
I'LL GO AND TAKE A LOOK.
ゴ

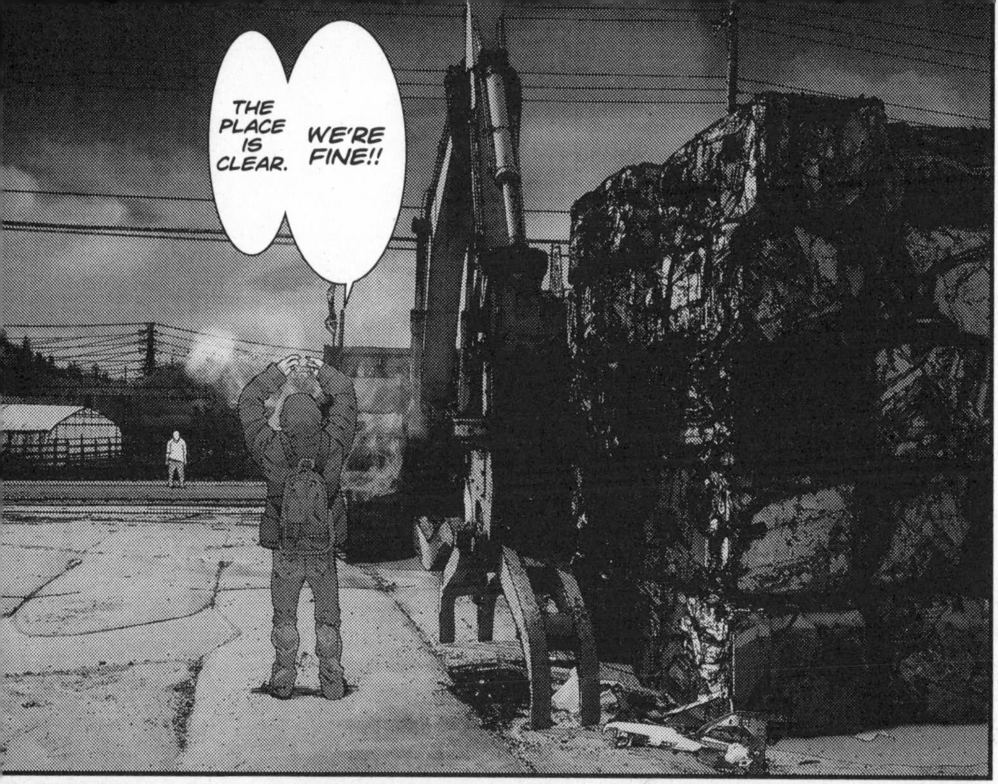
WE'RE FINE!!
THE PLACE IS CLEAR.

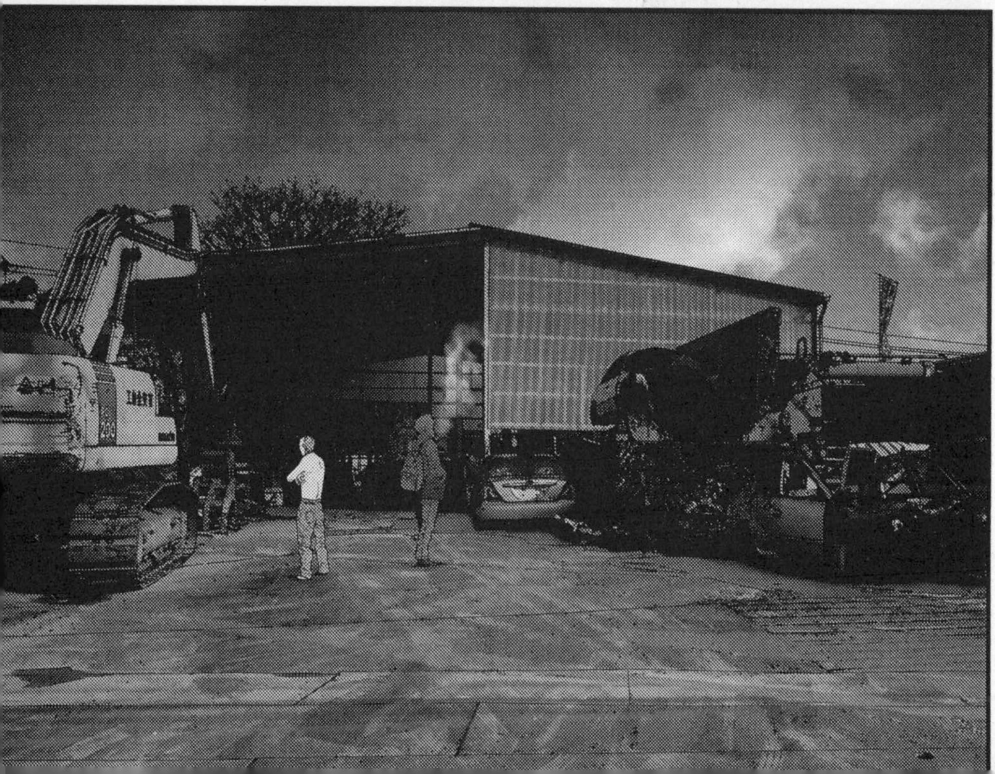

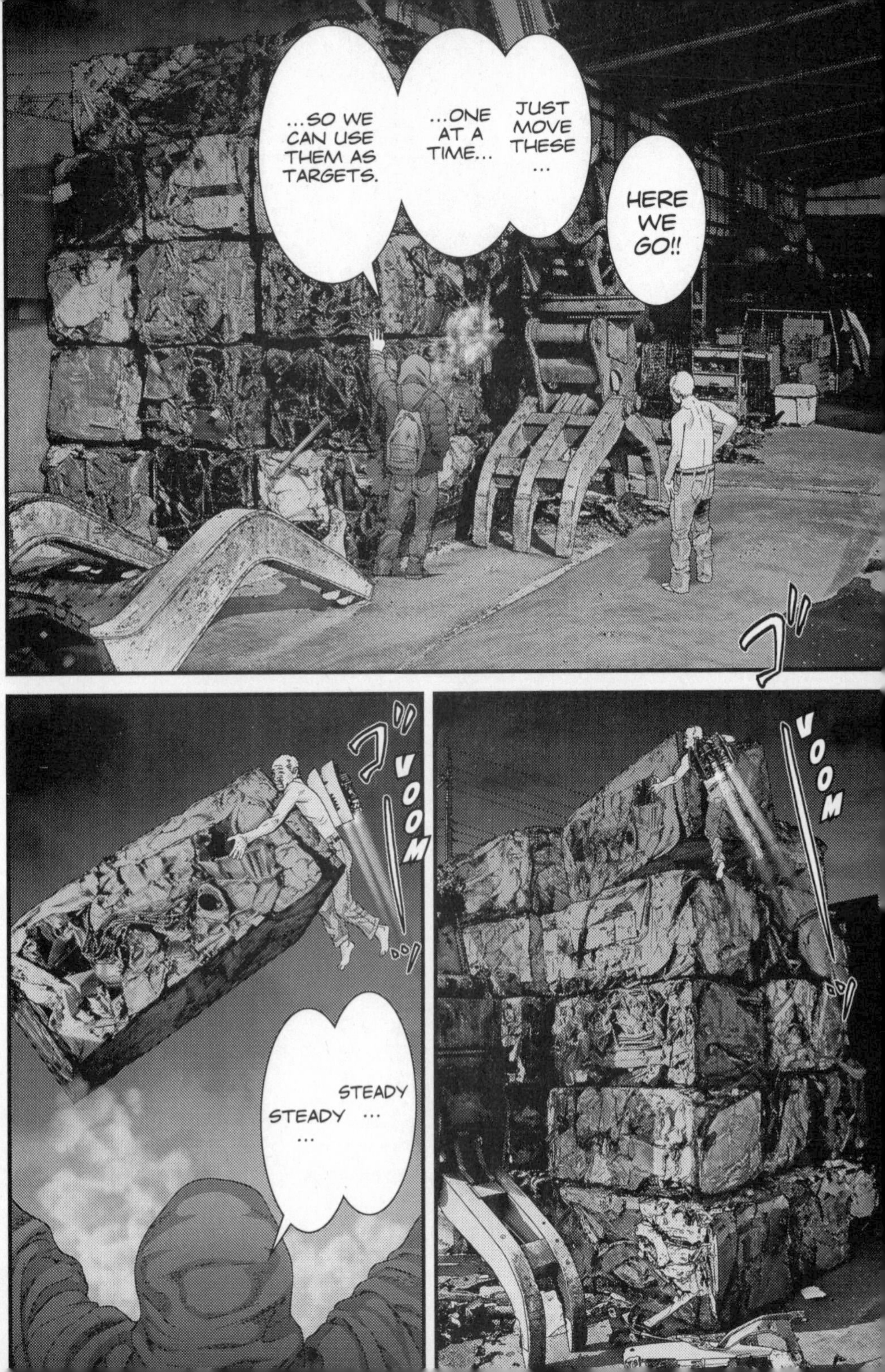
HERE WE GO!!
JUST MOVE THESE ...
...ONE AT A TIME...
...SO WE CAN USE THEM AS TARGETS.
ゴ
VOOM
ゴ
VOOM
STEADY ... STEADY ...

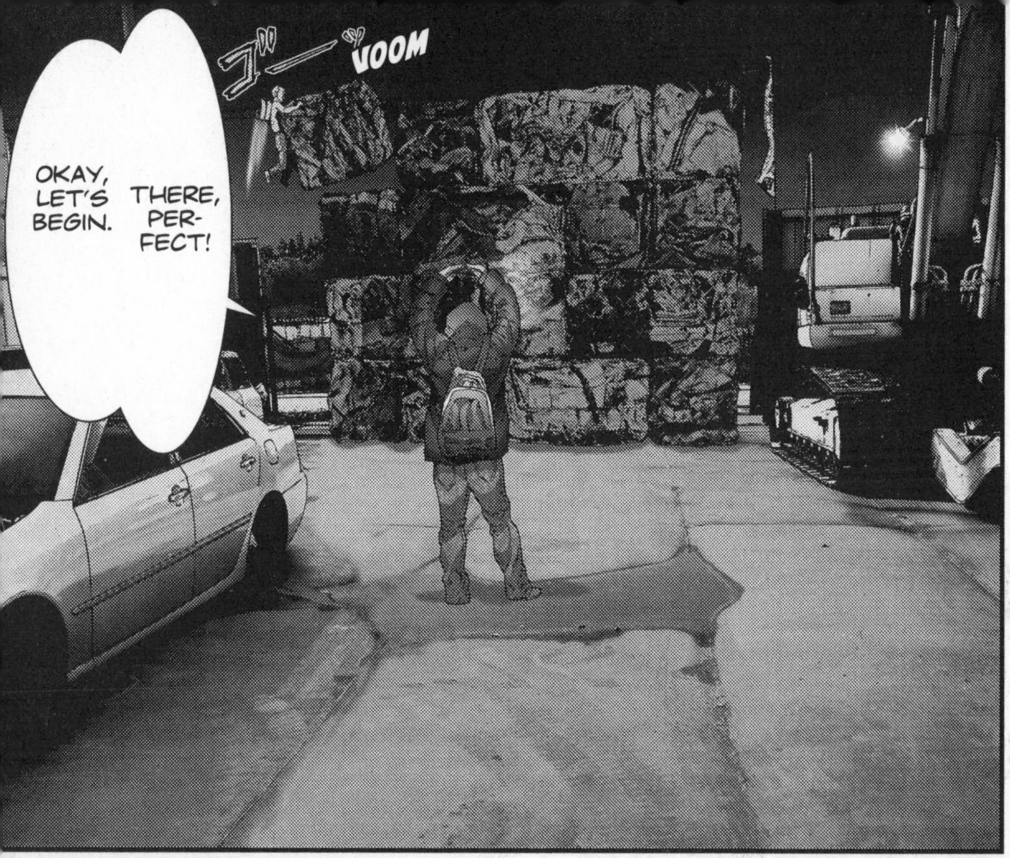
ゴー VOOM
THERE, PER-FECT!
OKAY, LET'S BEGIN.

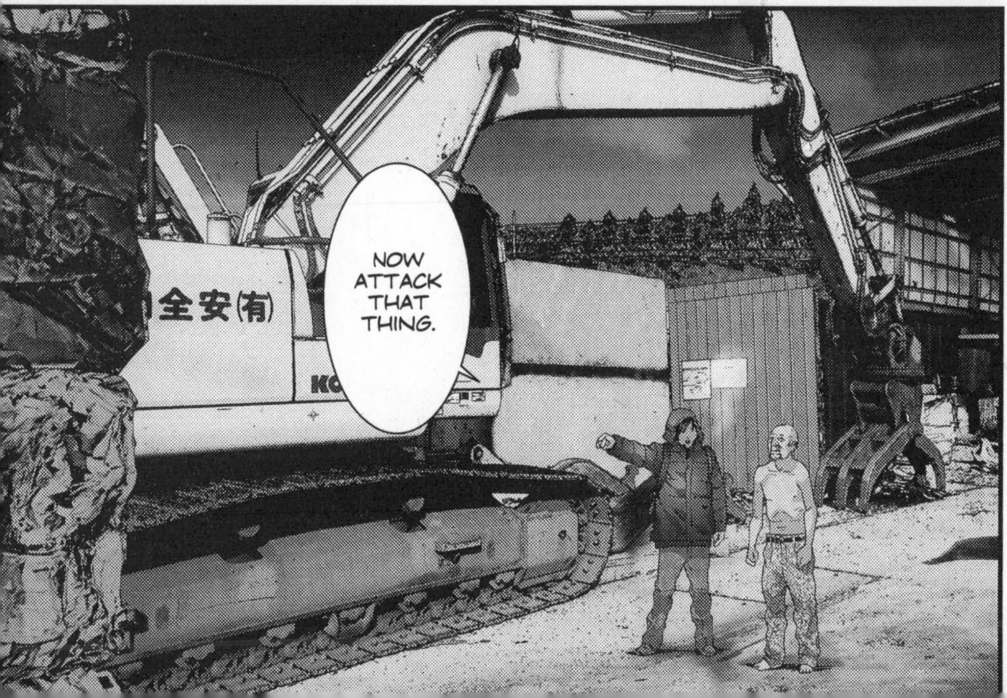
NOW ATTACK THAT THING.
全安(有)

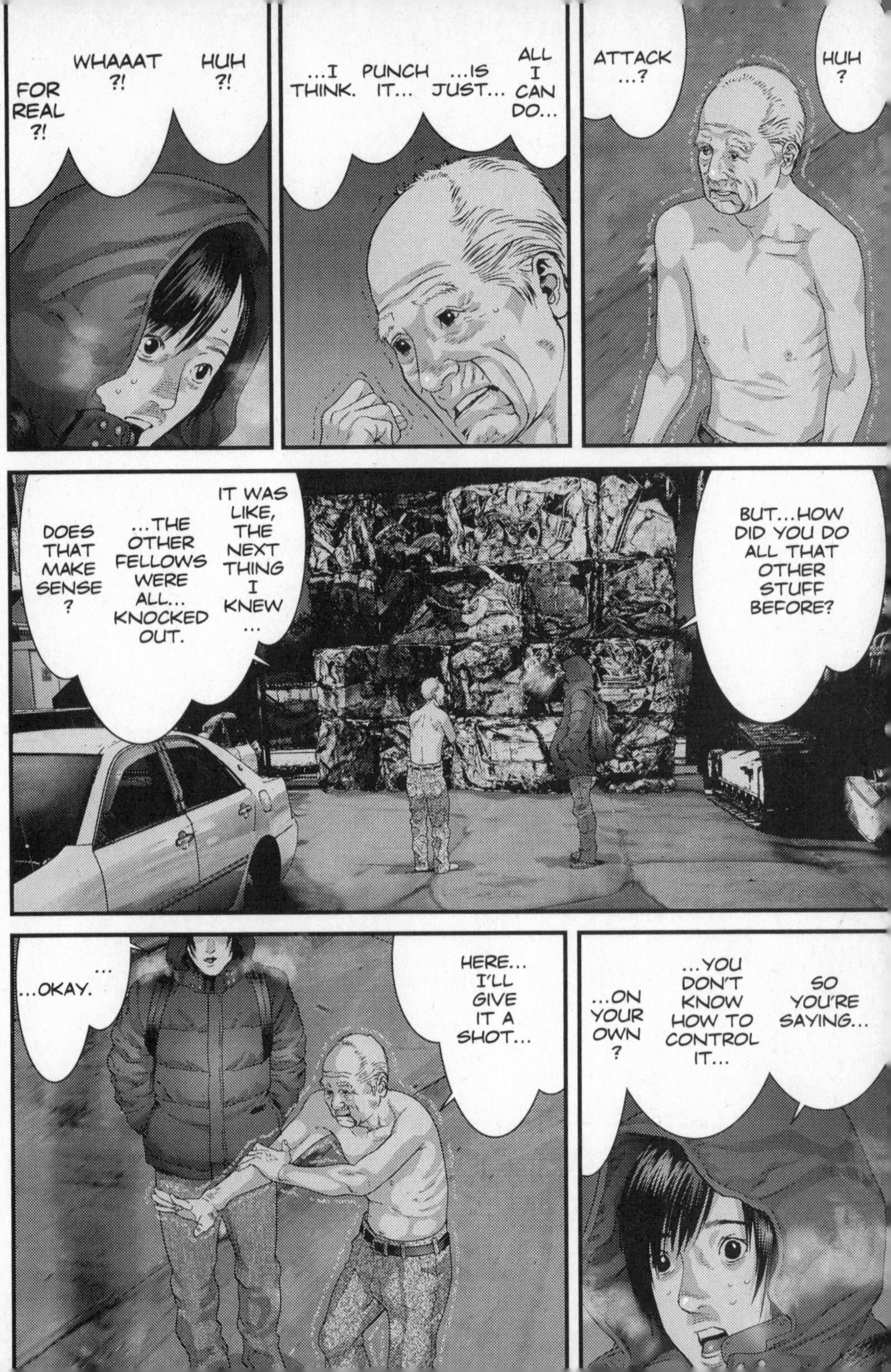
HUH ?
ATTACK ...?
ALL I CAN DO...
...IS JUST...
PUNCH IT...
...I THINK.
HUH ?!
WHAAAT ?!
FOR REAL ?!
BUT...HOW DID YOU DO ALL THAT OTHER STUFF BEFORE?
IT WAS LIKE, THE NEXT THING I KNEW ...
...THE OTHER FELLOWS WERE ALL... KNOCKED OUT.
DOES THAT MAKE SENSE ?
SO YOU'RE SAYING...
...YOU DON'T KNOW HOW TO CONTROL IT...
...ON YOUR OWN ?
HERE... I'LL GIVE IT A SHOT...
... ...OKAY.

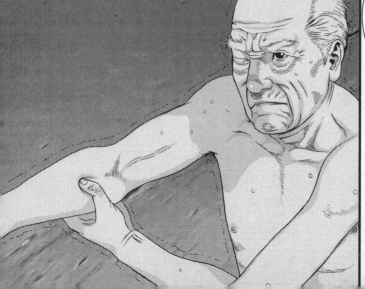

MM!

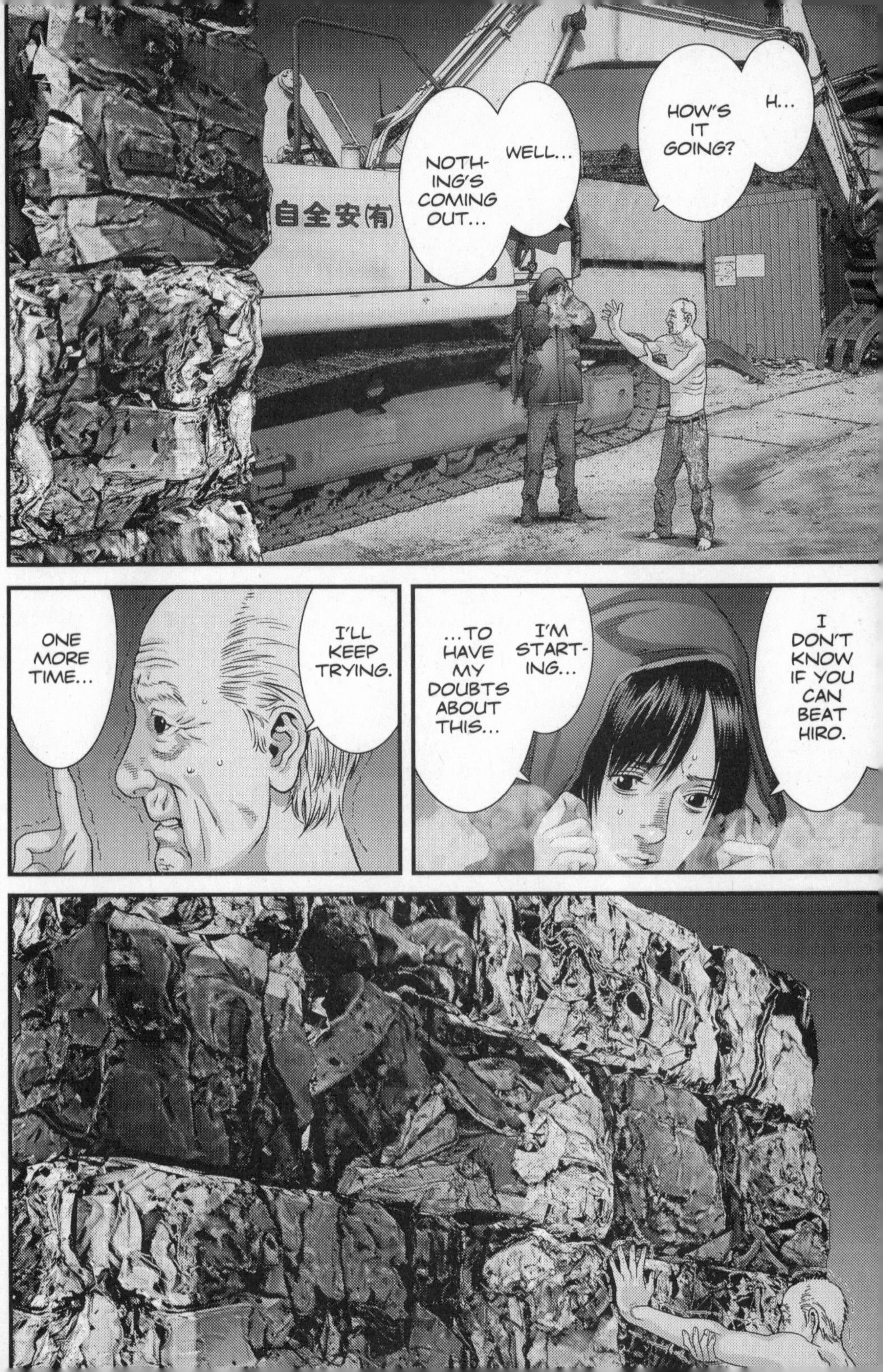
H…
HOW'S IT GOING?
WELL…
NOTH-ING'S COMING OUT…
自全安(有)
I DON'T KNOW IF YOU CAN BEAT HIRO.
I'M START-ING…
…TO HAVE MY DOUBTS ABOUT THIS…
I'LL KEEP TRYING.
ONE MORE TIME…

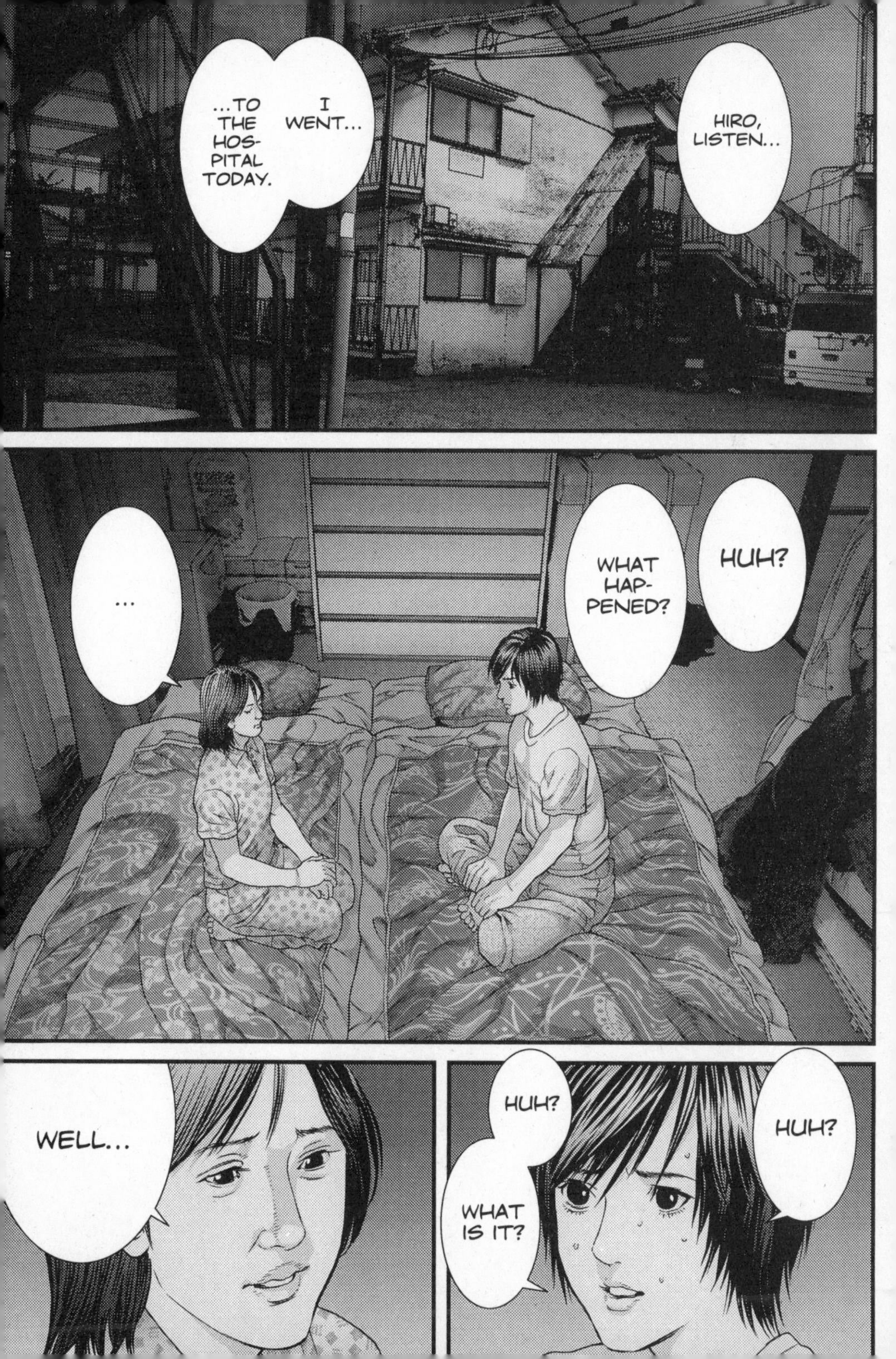
HIRO, LISTEN...
I WENT...
...TO THE HOSPITAL TODAY.
HUH?
WHAT HAPPENED?
...
HUH?
HUH?
WHAT IS IT?
WELL...

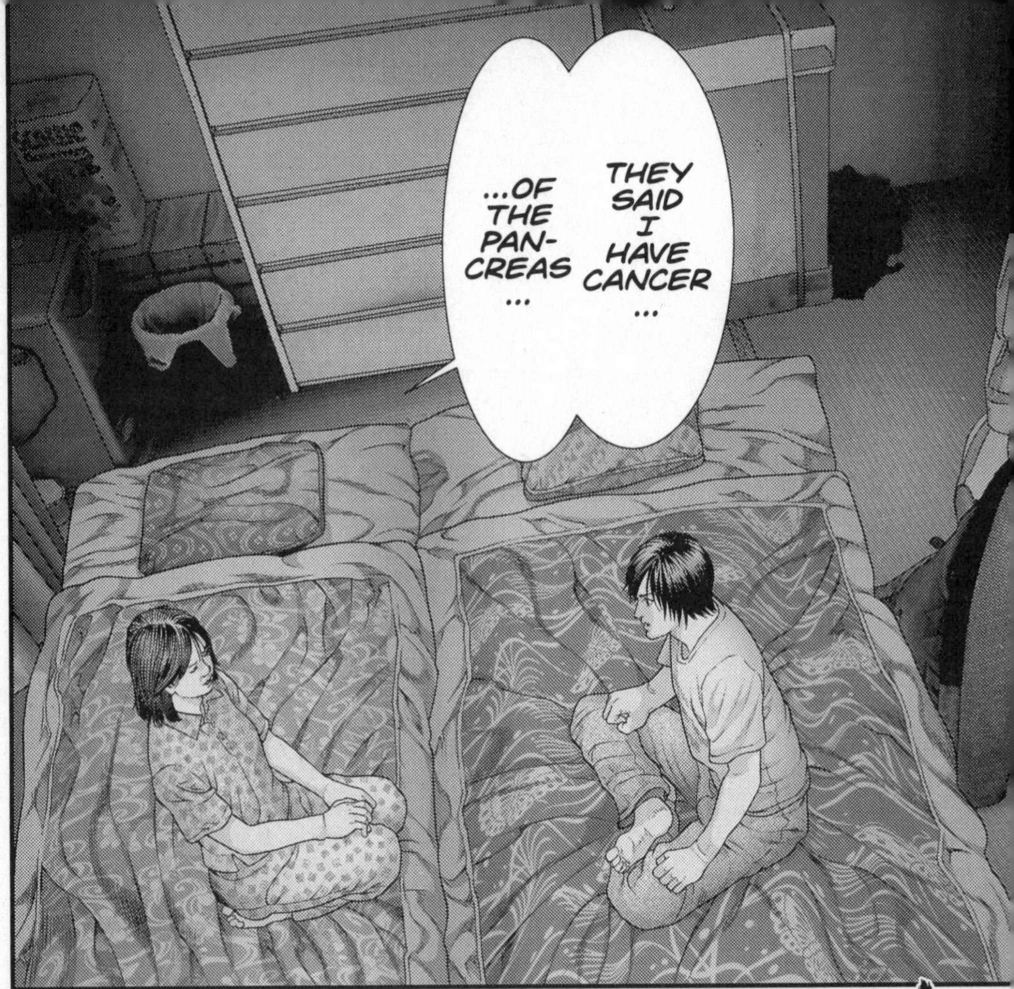
THEY SAID I HAVE CANCER...
...OF THE PAN-CREAS...

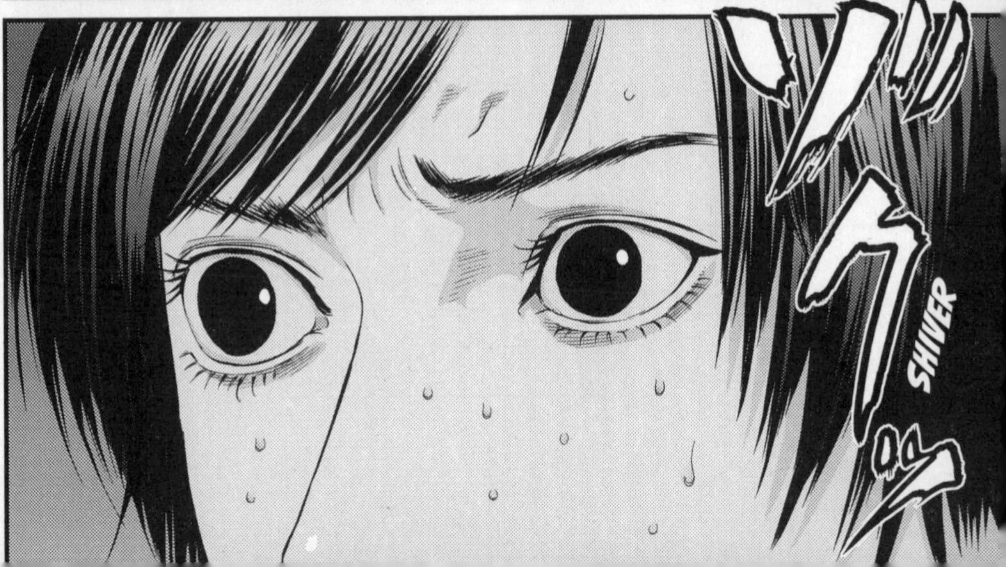
SHIVER

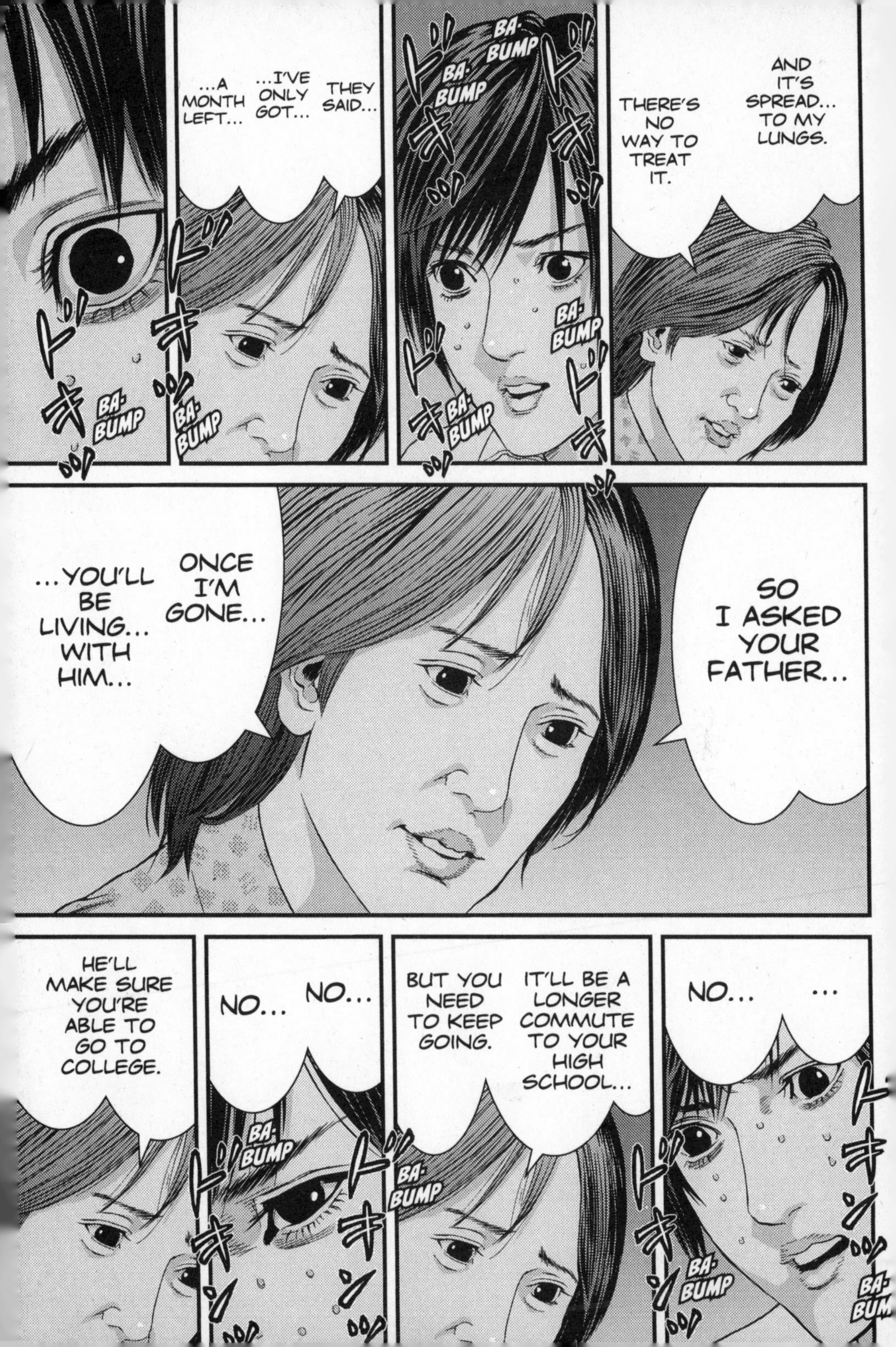
AND IT'S SPREAD... TO MY LUNGS.
THERE'S NO WAY TO TREAT IT.
BA-BUMP
BA-BUMP
BA-BUMP
BA-BUMP
THEY SAID...
...I'VE ONLY GOT...
...A MONTH LEFT...
BA-BUMP
BA-BUMP
SO I ASKED YOUR FATHER...
ONCE I'M GONE...
...YOU'LL BE LIVING... WITH HIM...
...
NO...
BA-BUMP
BA-BUM
IT'LL BE A LONGER COMMUTE TO YOUR HIGH SCHOOL...
BUT YOU NEED TO KEEP GOING.
BA-BUMP
NO...
NO...
BA-BUMP
HE'LL MAKE SURE YOU'RE ABLE TO GO TO COLLEGE.

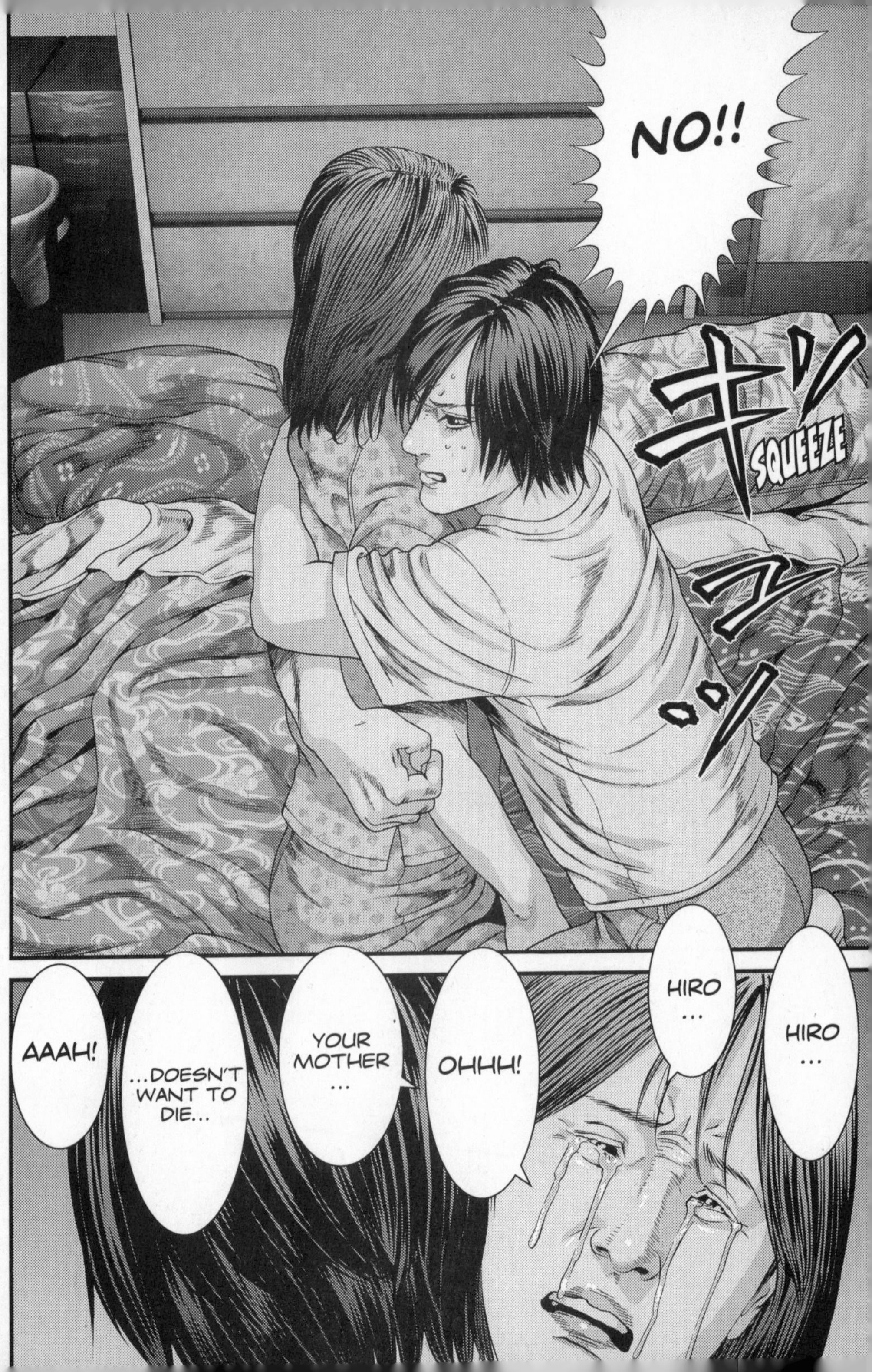
NO!!
キュッ
SQUEEZE
HIRO …
HIRO …
OHHH!
YOUR MOTHER …
…DOESN'T WANT TO DIE…
AAAH!

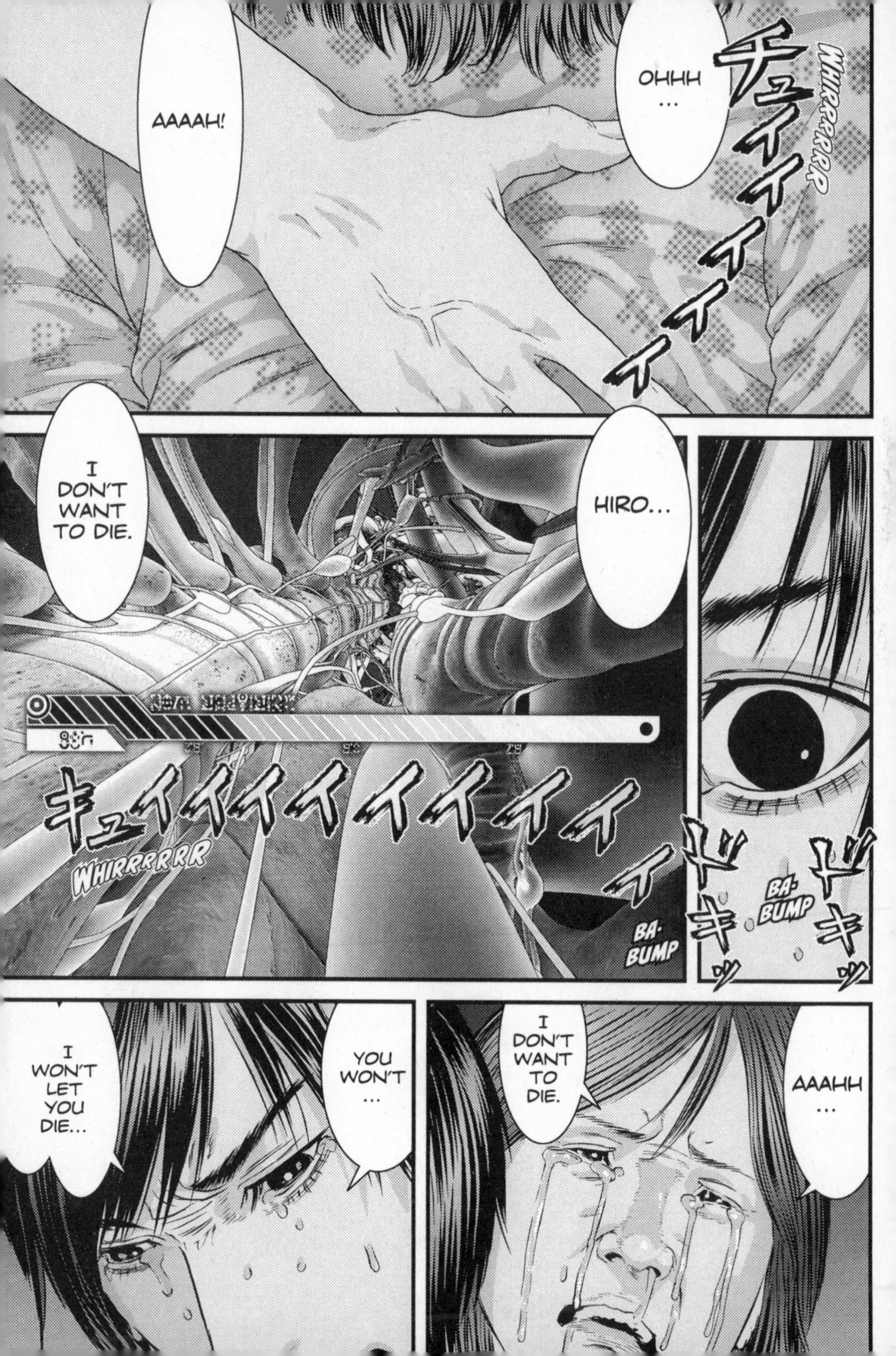

チュイイイイイ
WHIRRRRRR
OHHH ...
AAAAH!
ドキッ
BA-BUMP
ドキッ
BA-BUMP
HIRO...
I DON'T WANT TO DIE.
キュイイイイイイイイイ
WHIRRRRRR
AAAHH ...
I DON'T WANT TO DIE.
YOU WON'T ...
I WON'T LET YOU DIE...

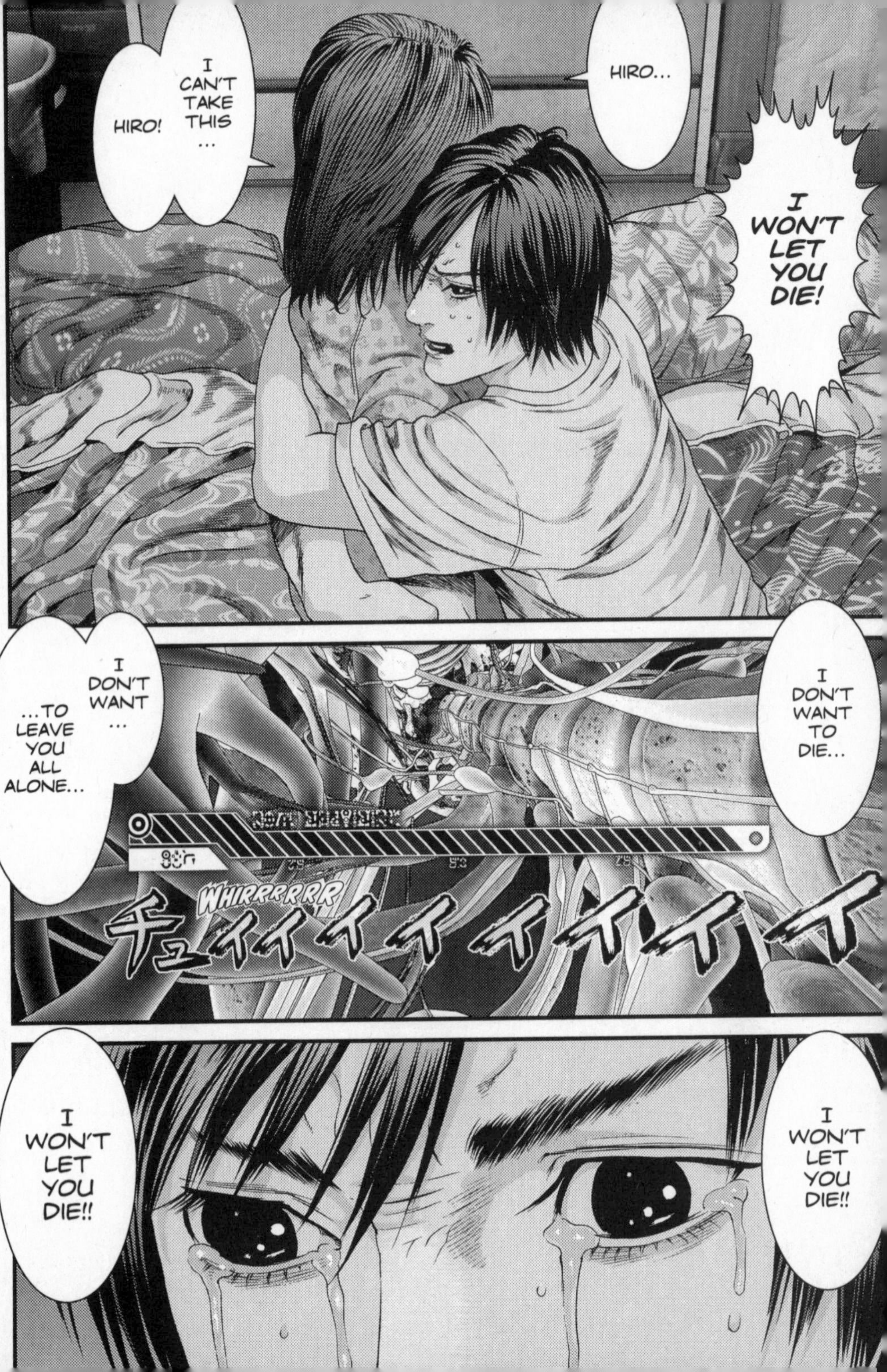
HIRO...
I WON'T LET YOU DIE!
I CAN'T TAKE THIS ...
HIRO!
I DON'T WANT TO DIE...
I DON'T WANT ...
...TO LEAVE YOU ALL ALONE...
WHIRRRRRRR
チュイイイイイイイ
I WON'T LET YOU DIE!!
I WON'T LET YOU DIE!!

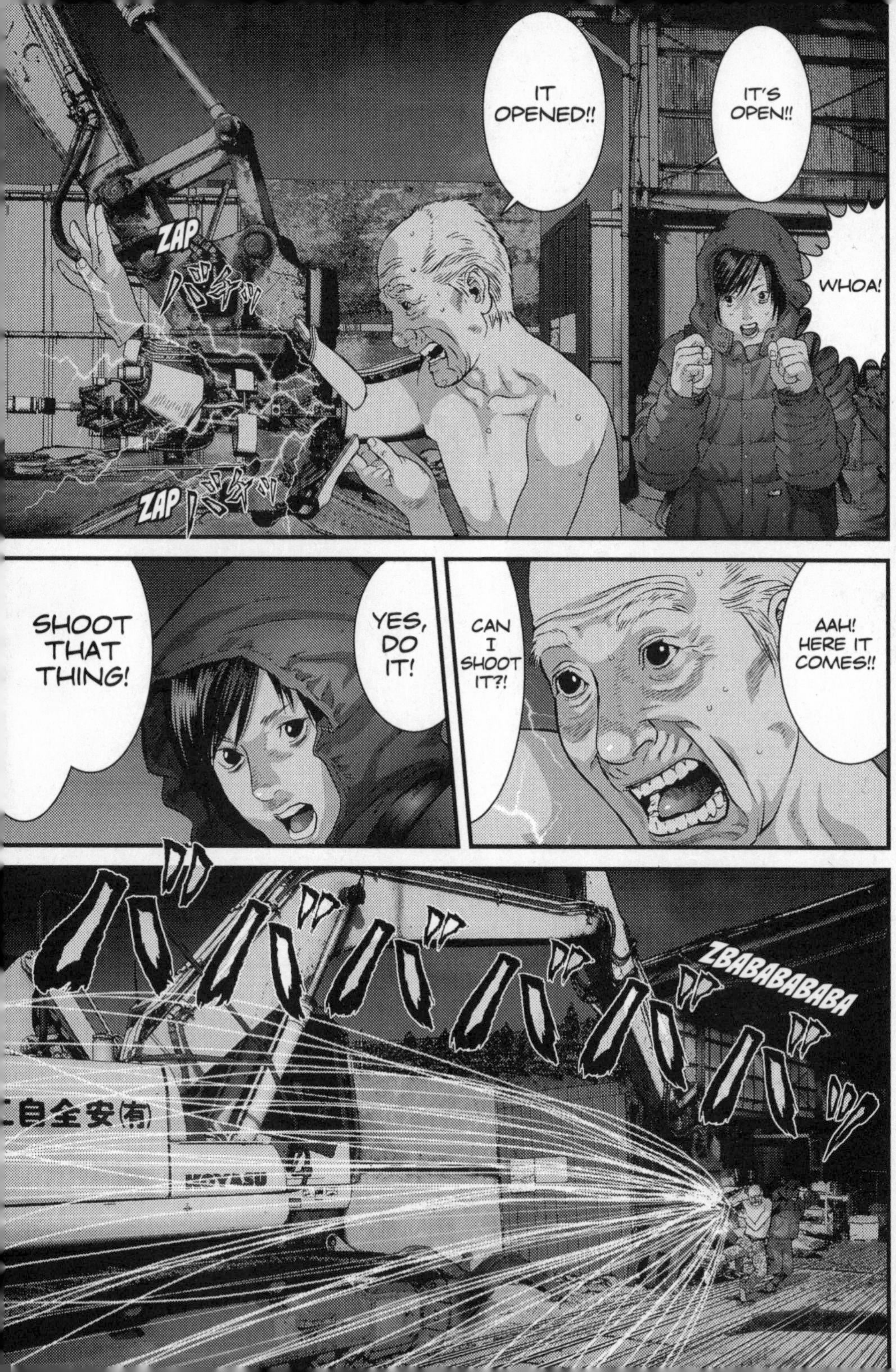
IT'S OPEN!!
IT OPENED!!
WHOA!
ZAP
ZAP
AAH! HERE IT COMES!!
CAN I SHOOT IT?!
YES, DO IT!
SHOOT THAT THING!
ZBABABABABA

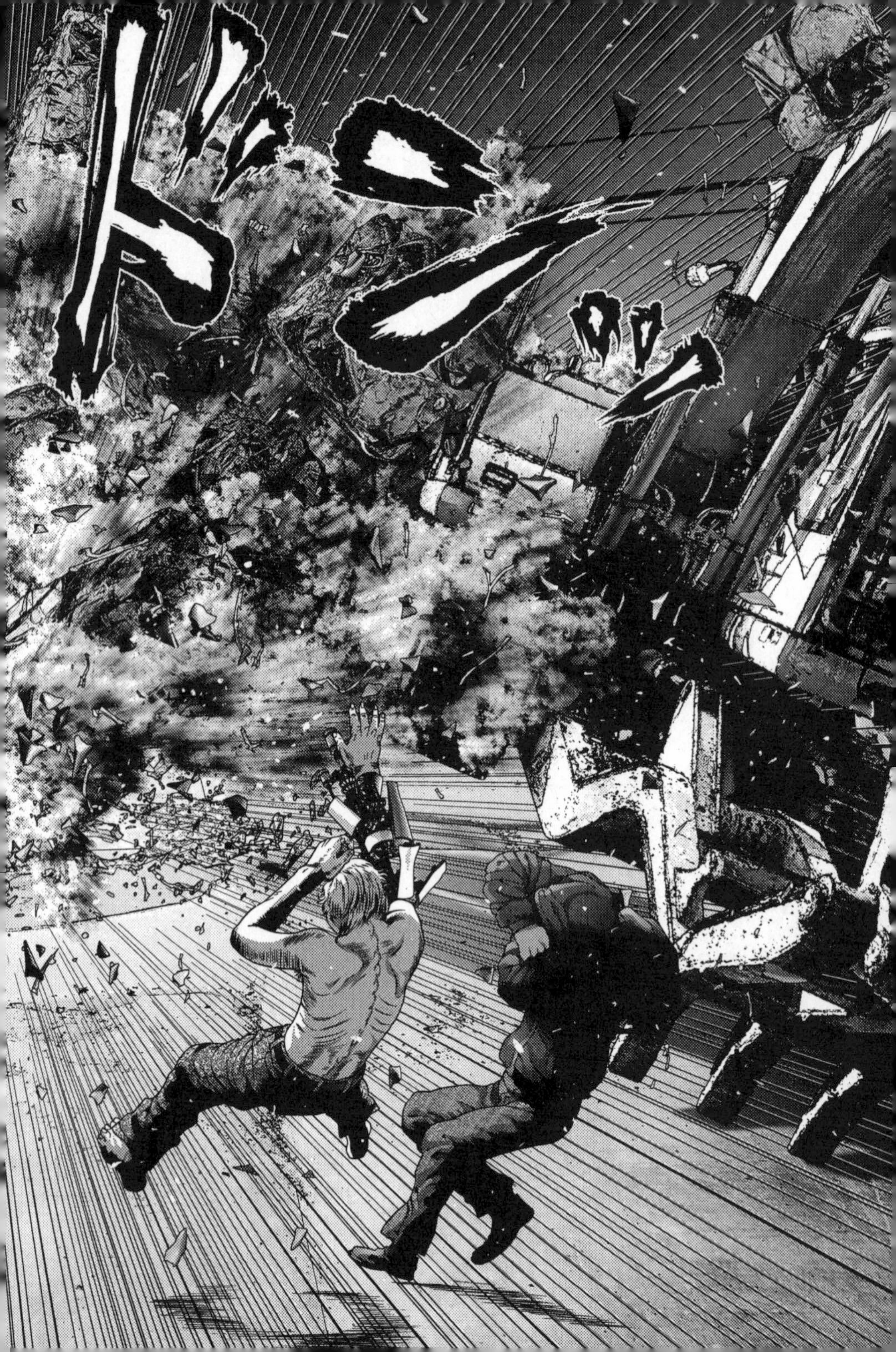

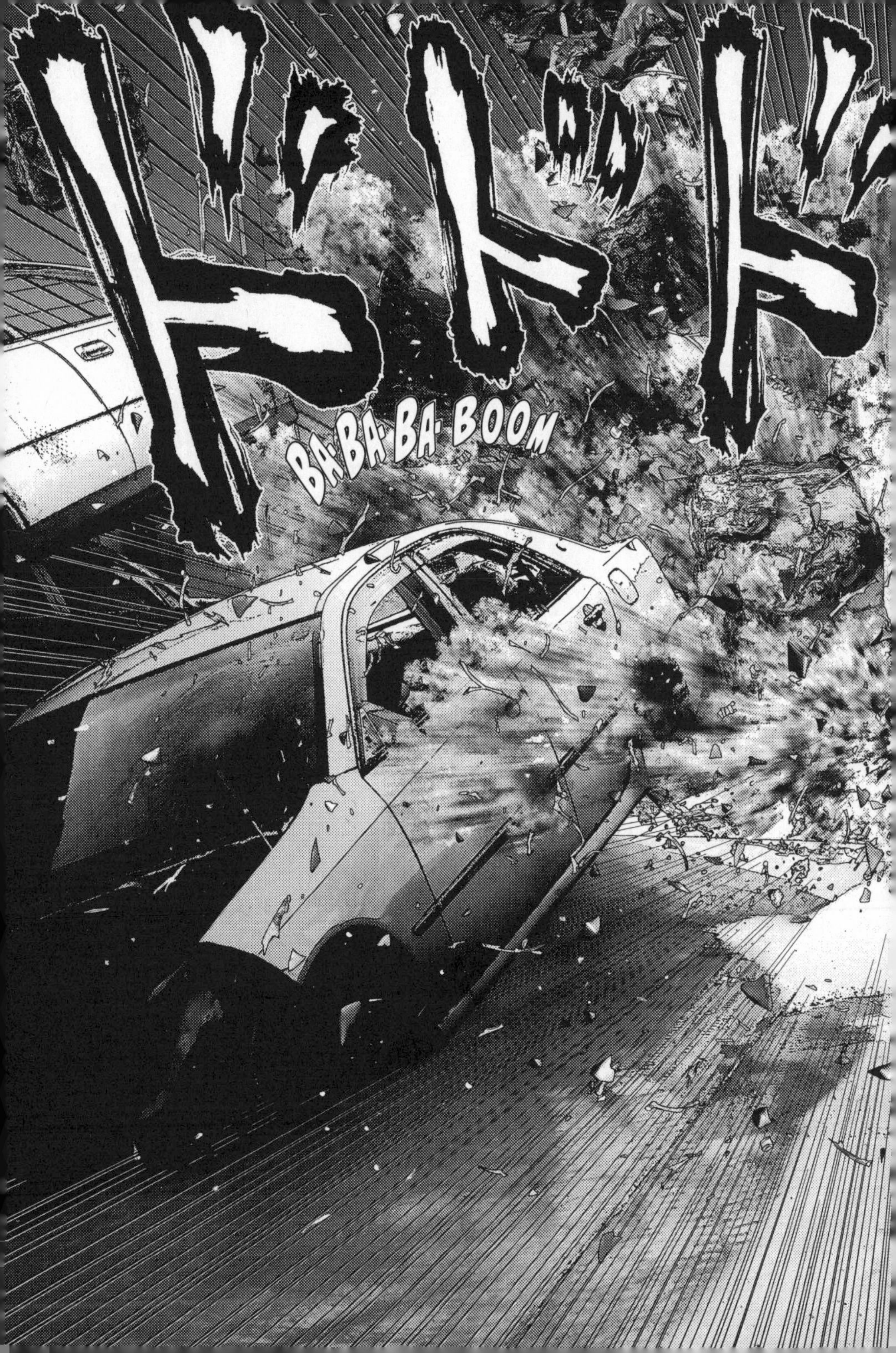
BA-BA-BA-BOOM

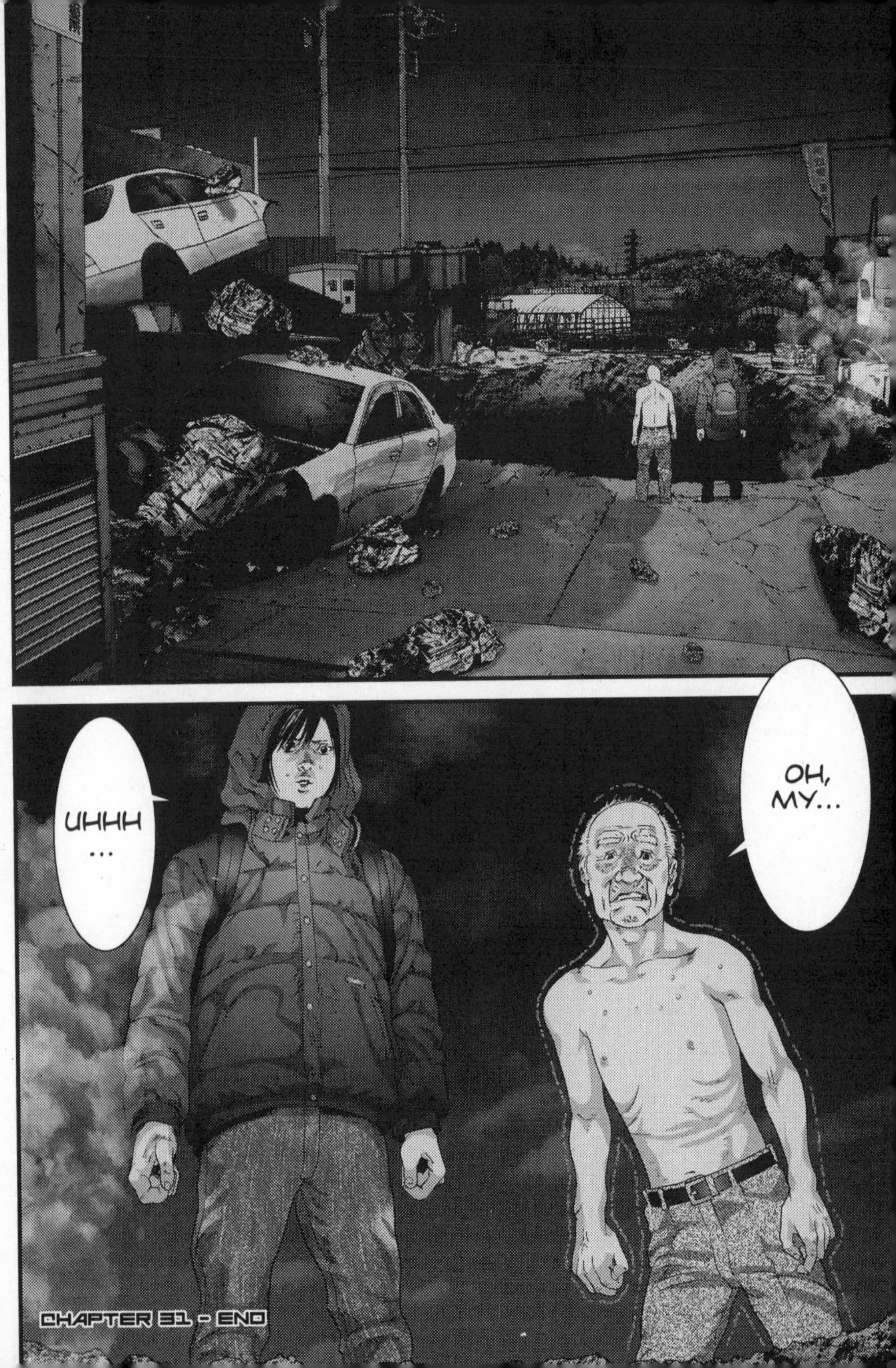
OH, MY...
UHHH ...
CHAPTER 31 - END

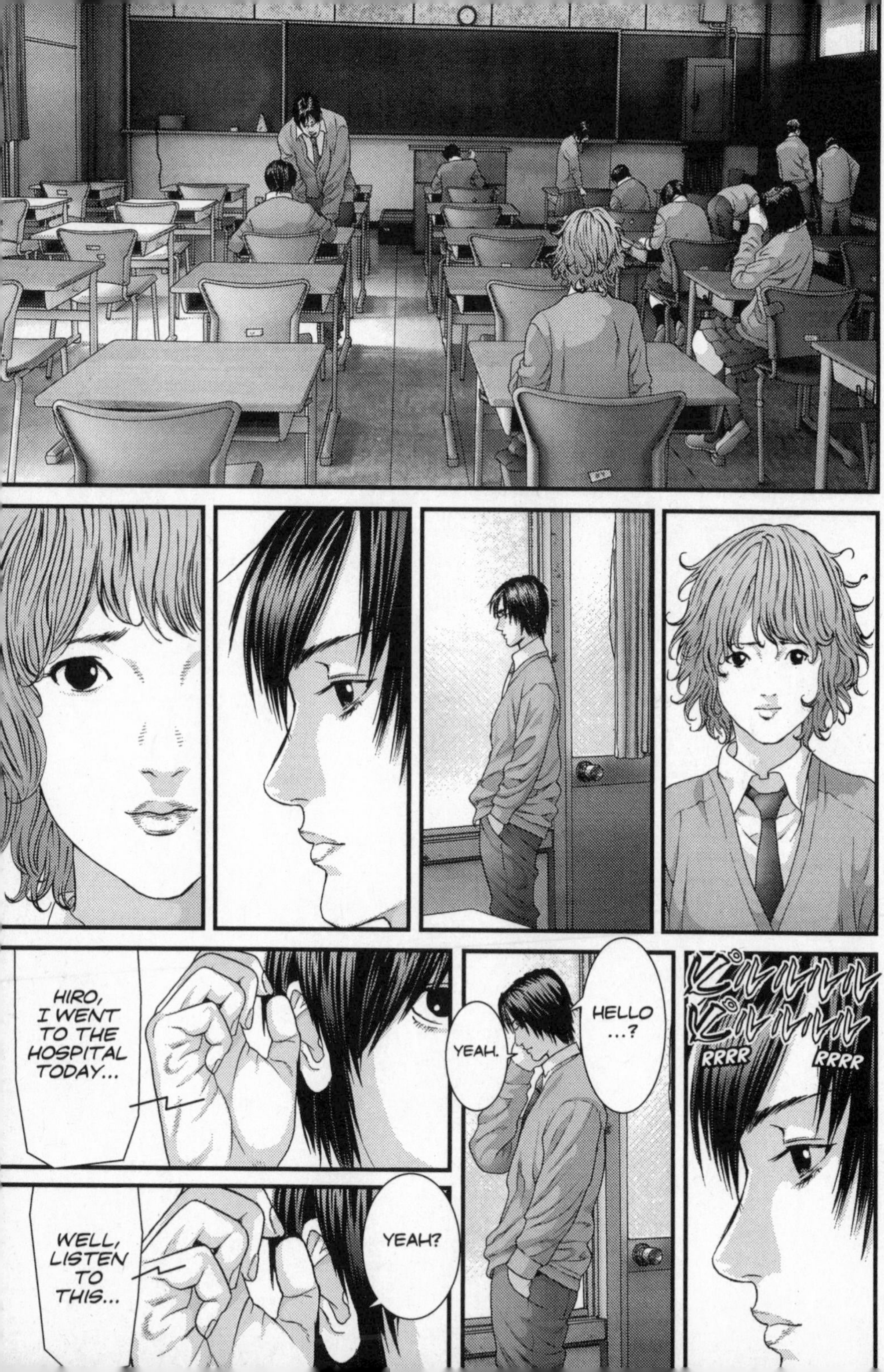
ピルルルル
ピルルルル
RRRR
RRRR
HELLO ...?
YEAH.
HIRO, I WENT TO THE HOSPITAL TODAY...
YEAH?
WELL, LISTEN TO THIS...

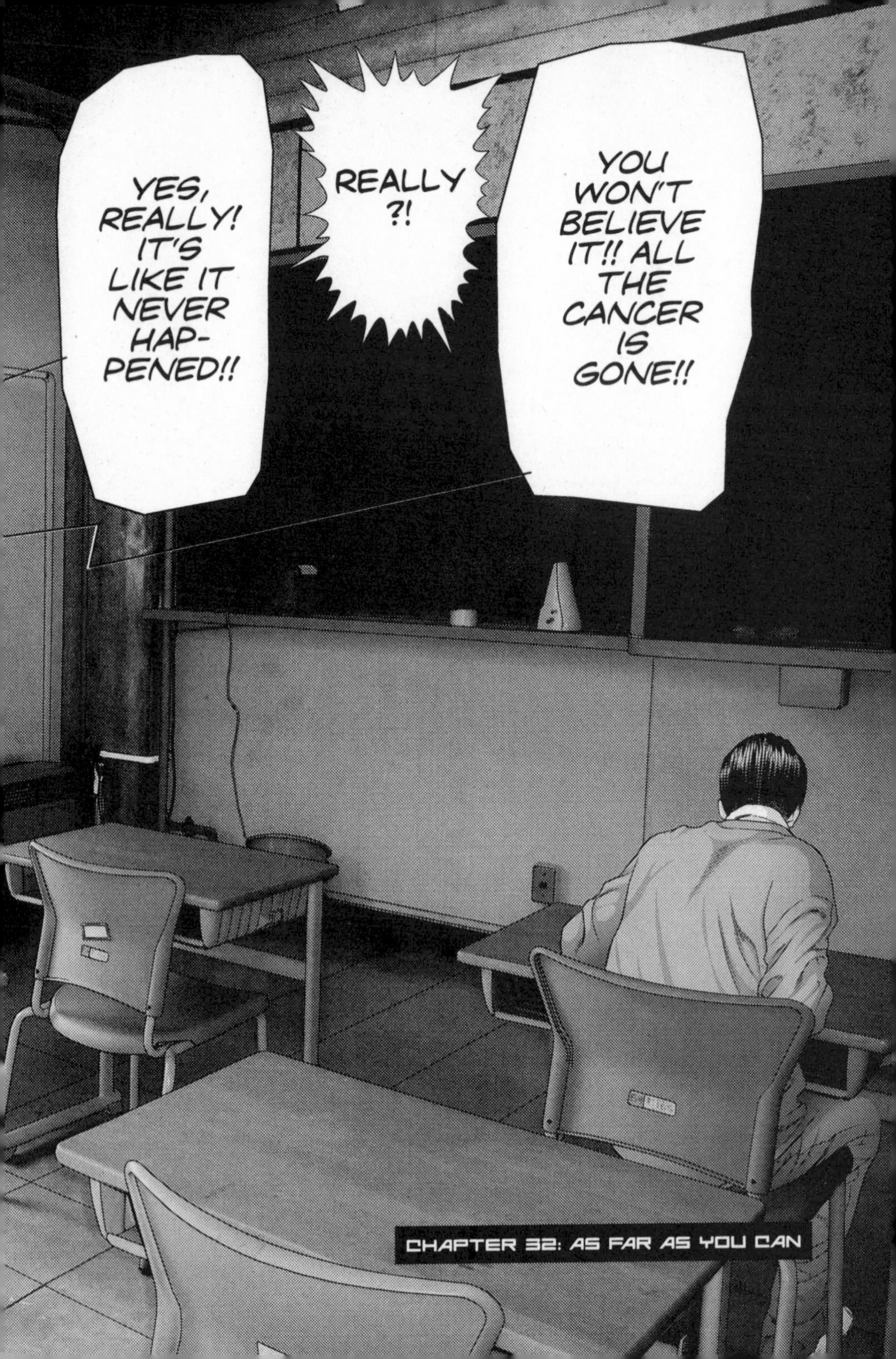
YOU WON'T BELIEVE IT!! ALL THE CANCER IS GONE!!
REALLY ?!
YES, REALLY! IT'S LIKE IT NEVER HAP-PENED!!
CHAPTER 32: AS FAR AS YOU CAN

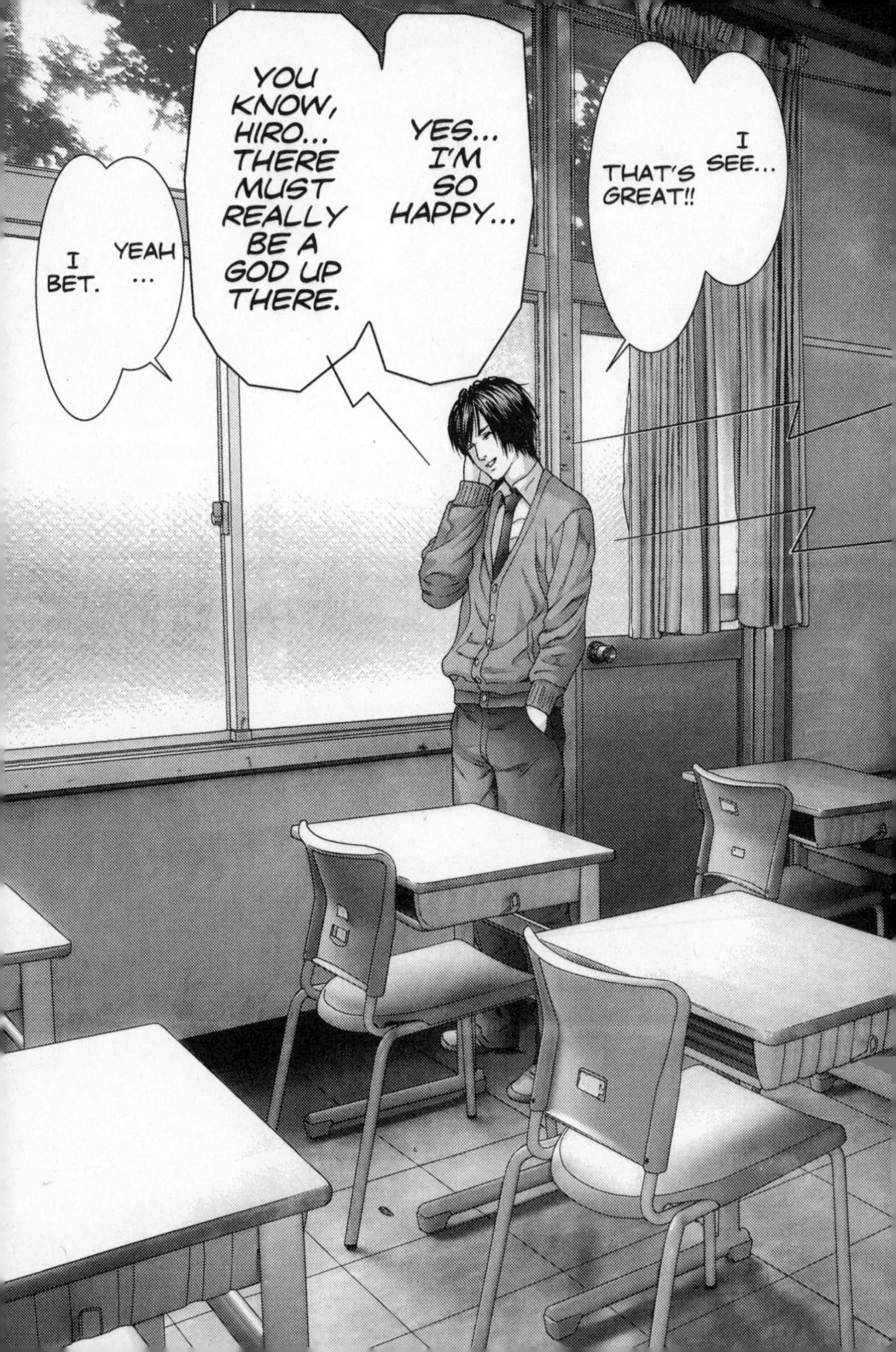
I SEE...
THAT'S GREAT!!
YES... I'M SO HAPPY...
YOU KNOW, HIRO... THERE MUST REALLY BE A GOD UP THERE.
YEAH...
I BET.

HUH?

HERE, THIS IS IT...

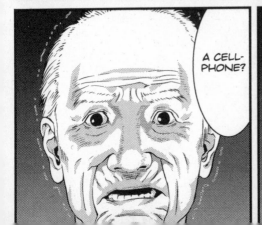

A CELL-PHONE?

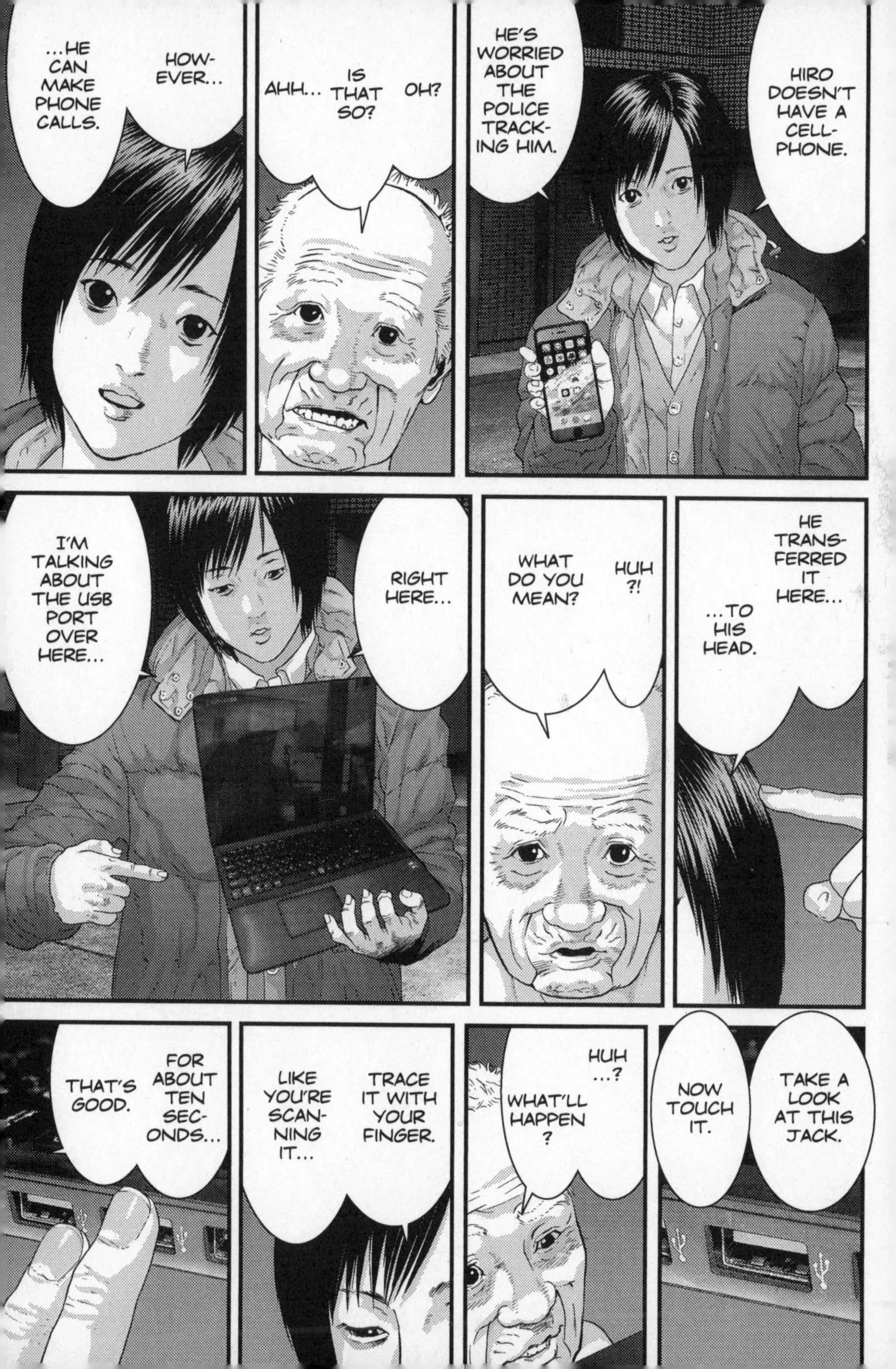
HIRO DOESN'T HAVE A CELL-PHONE.
HE'S WORRIED ABOUT THE POLICE TRACKING HIM.
OH?
IS THAT SO?
AHH...
HOW-EVER...
...HE CAN MAKE PHONE CALLS.
HE TRANSFERRED IT HERE...
...TO HIS HEAD.
HUH ?!
WHAT DO YOU MEAN?
RIGHT HERE...
I'M TALKING ABOUT THE USB PORT OVER HERE...
TAKE A LOOK AT THIS JACK.
NOW TOUCH IT.
HUH ...?
WHAT'LL HAPPEN ?
TRACE IT WITH YOUR FINGER.
LIKE YOU'RE SCANNING IT...
FOR ABOUT TEN SECONDS...
THAT'S GOOD.

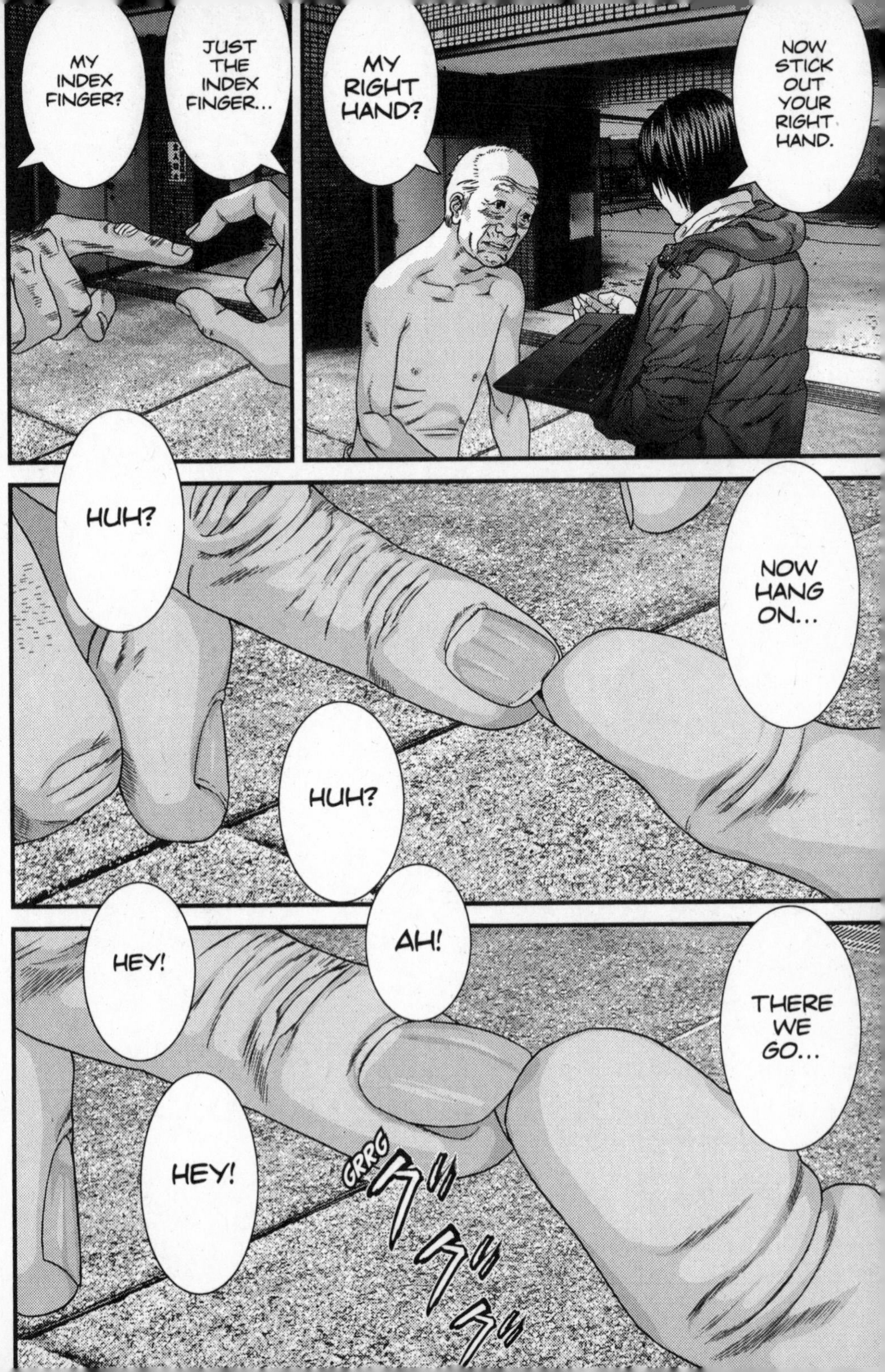
NOW STICK OUT YOUR RIGHT HAND.
MY RIGHT HAND?
JUST THE INDEX FINGER...
MY INDEX FINGER?
NOW HANG ON...
HUH?
HUH?
THERE WE GO...
AH!
HEY!
HEY!
GRRG

WH-WH-WHAT THE-?!

AH!

SHUP

AH!

TINK

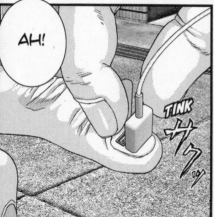

NOW I'LL PLUG YOU IN...

HUH?

YOU SHOULD ALREADY BE ABLE TO SEE IT.

LET ME GUESS...

IT'S THERE...
RIGHT IN FRONT OF YOUR EYES...
...ISN'T IT?
Call
Mine
Pixy
Mail
28
Date
Photos
Video
Weather
Time
Maps
Movies
Memo
Reminders
Forex
Games
News
Music Store
AppalWatch
Books
App Store
Passbook
Music
Safari
Settings
Messages
Y-YOU'RE RIGHT! THIS IS INCREDIBLE!!
GREAT! THEN...
LET'S SET UP A PHONE NUMBER.
PHONE NUMBER?

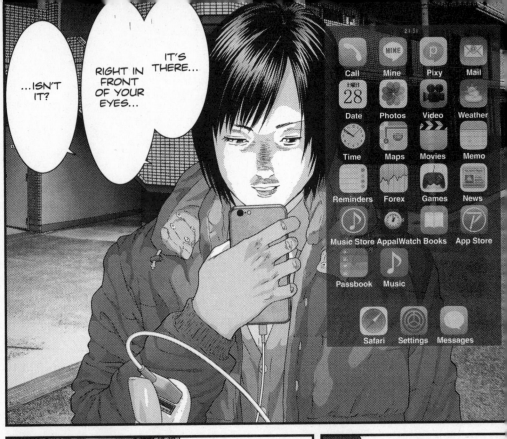

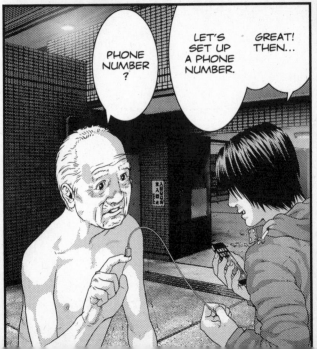

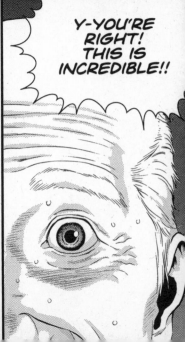

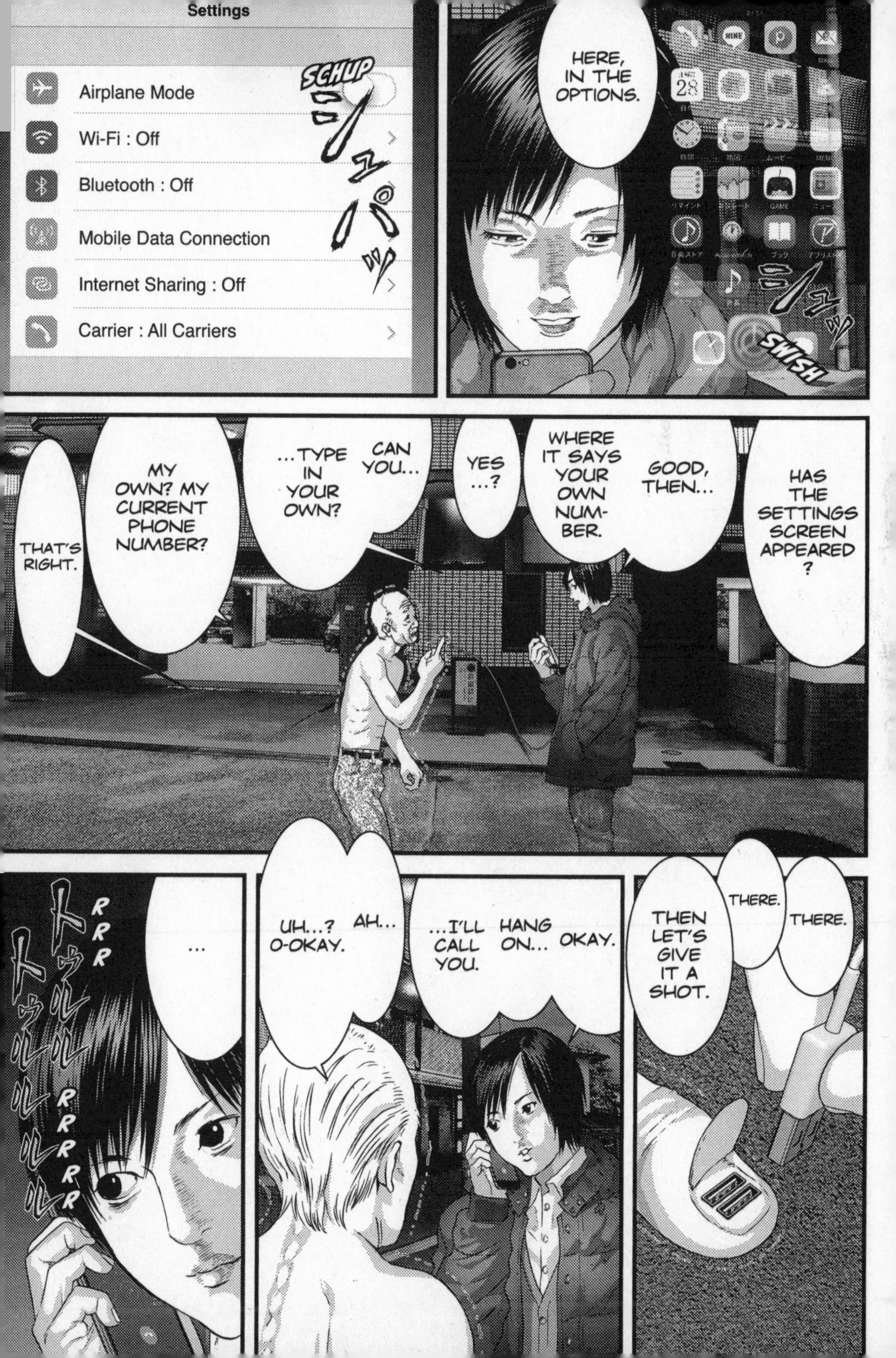
HERE, IN THE OPTIONS.
SWISH
Settings
Airplane Mode
Wi-Fi : Off
Bluetooth : Off
Mobile Data Connection
Internet Sharing : Off
Carrier : All Carriers
SCHUP
HAS THE SETTINGS SCREEN APPEARED?
GOOD, THEN...
WHERE IT SAYS YOUR OWN NUM-BER.
YES ...?
CAN YOU...
...TYPE IN YOUR OWN?
MY OWN? MY CURRENT PHONE NUMBER?
THAT'S RIGHT.
THERE.
THERE.
THEN LET'S GIVE IT A SHOT.
OKAY.
HANG ON...
...I'LL CALL YOU.
AH...
UH...? O-OKAY.
...
RRR
RRRR

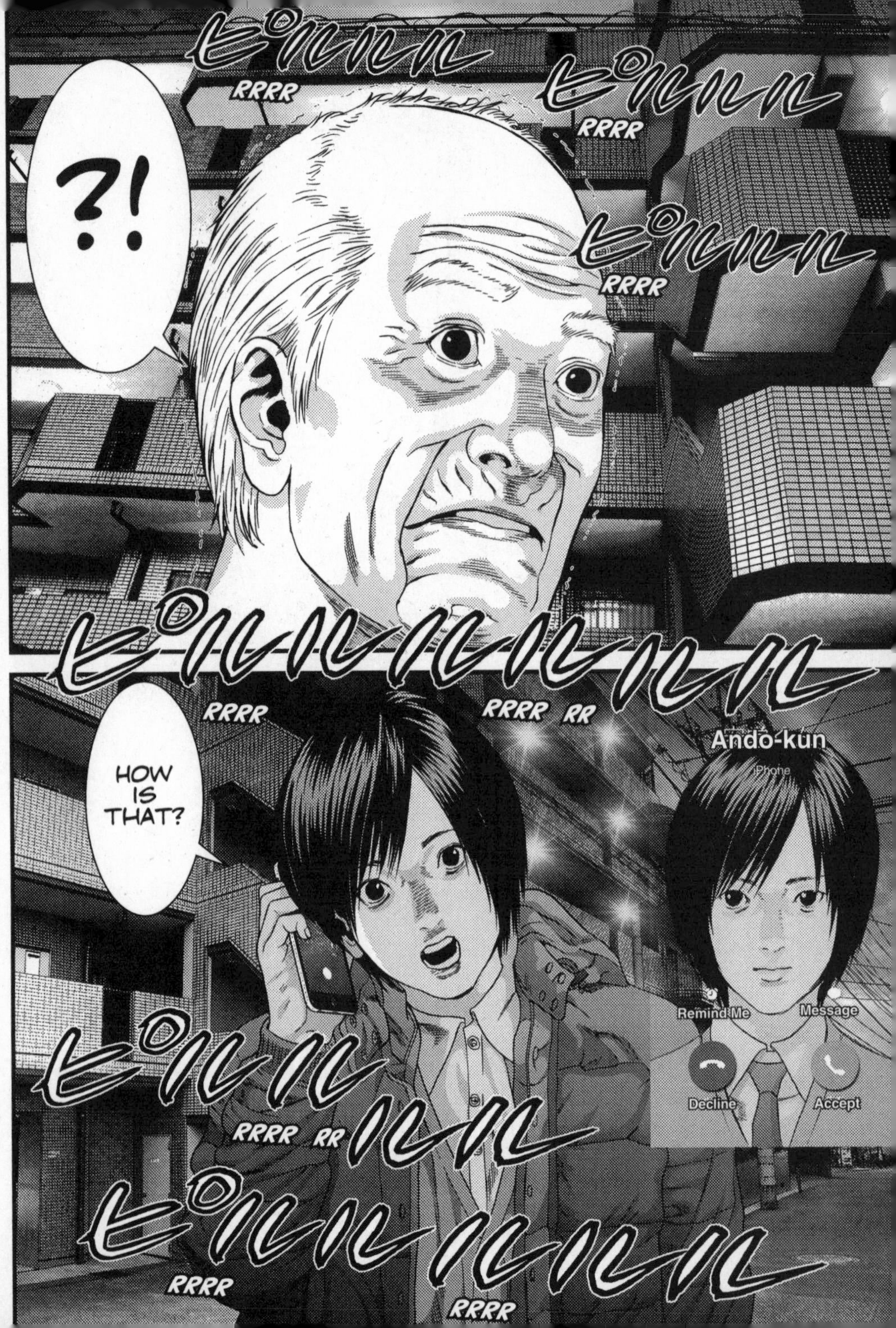
RRRR
RRRR
RRRR
?!
RRRR
RRRR RR
RRRR
Ando-kun
iPhone
Remind Me
Message
Decline
Accept
HOW IS THAT?
RRRR RR
RRRR
RRRR

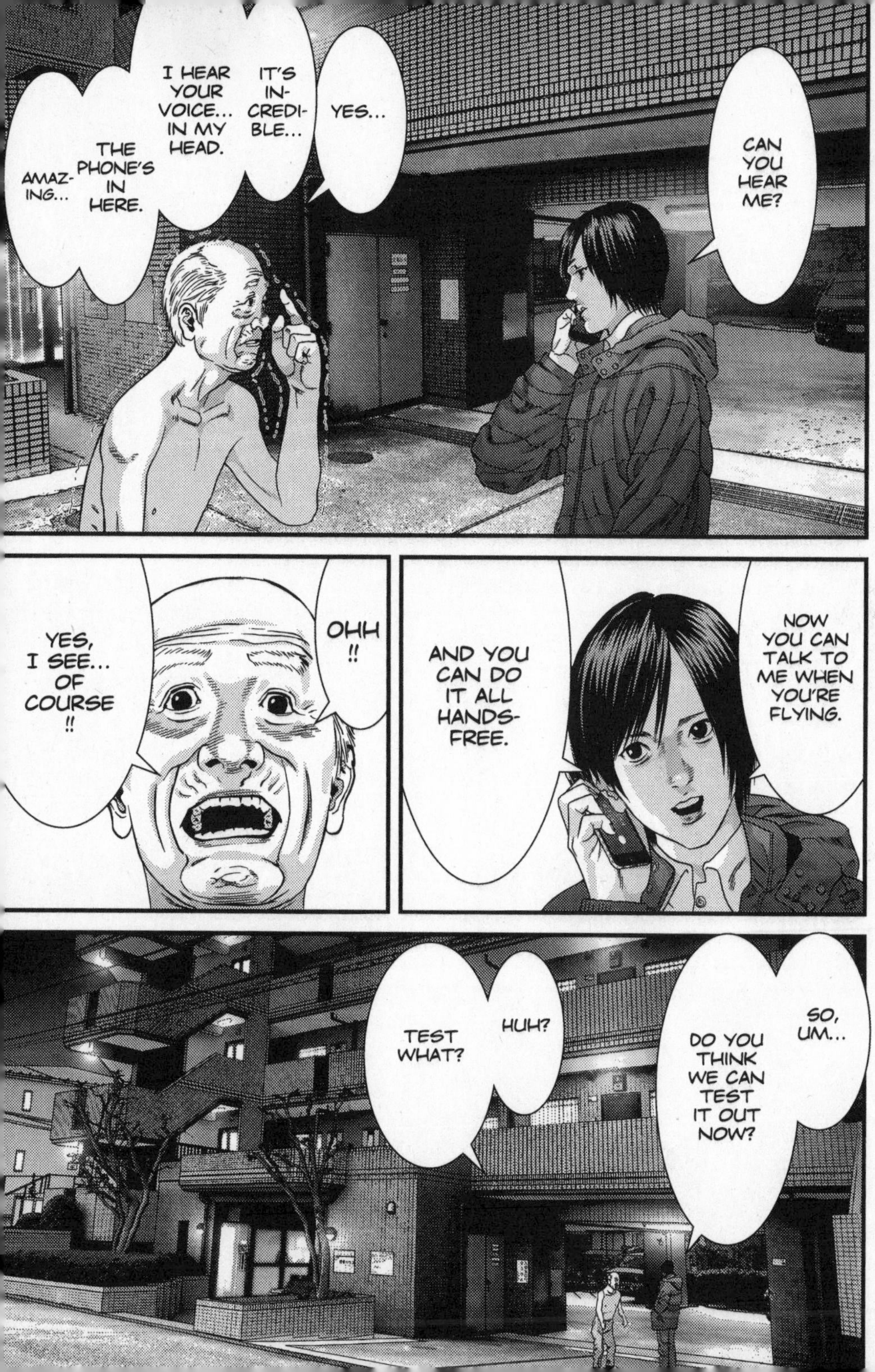
CAN YOU HEAR ME?
YES...
IT'S INCREDIBLE...
I HEAR YOUR VOICE... IN MY HEAD.
THE PHONE'S IN HERE.
AMAZING...
NOW YOU CAN TALK TO ME WHEN YOU'RE FLYING.
AND YOU CAN DO IT ALL HANDS-FREE.
OHH !!
YES, I SEE... OF COURSE !!
SO, UM...
DO YOU THINK WE CAN TEST IT OUT NOW?
HUH?
TEST WHAT?

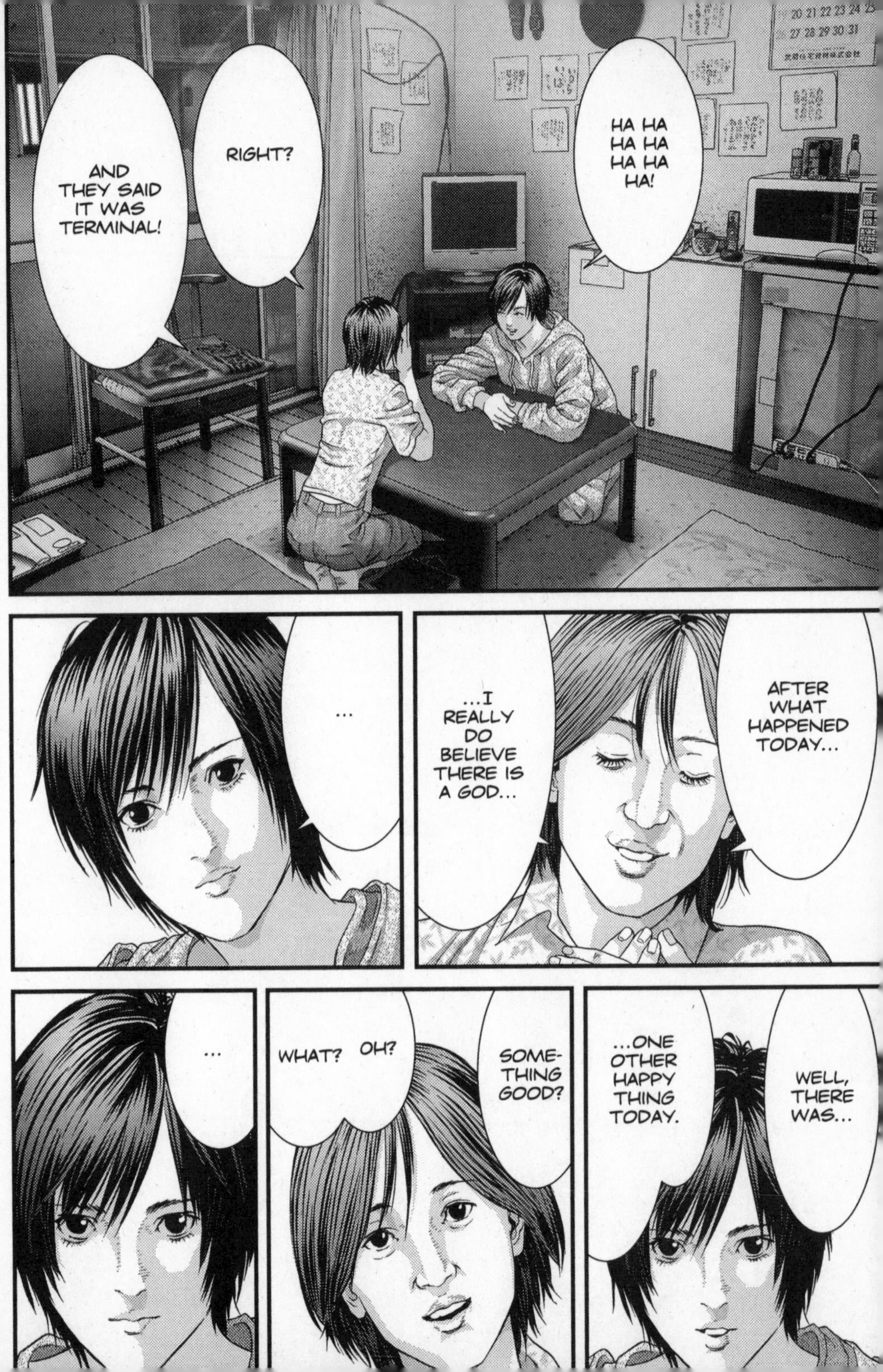
HA HA HA HA HA HA HA!
RIGHT?
AND THEY SAID IT WAS TERMINAL!
AFTER WHAT HAPPENED TODAY...
...I REALLY DO BELIEVE THERE IS A GOD...
...
WELL, THERE WAS...
...ONE OTHER HAPPY THING TODAY.
SOME-THING GOOD?
OH?
WHAT?
...

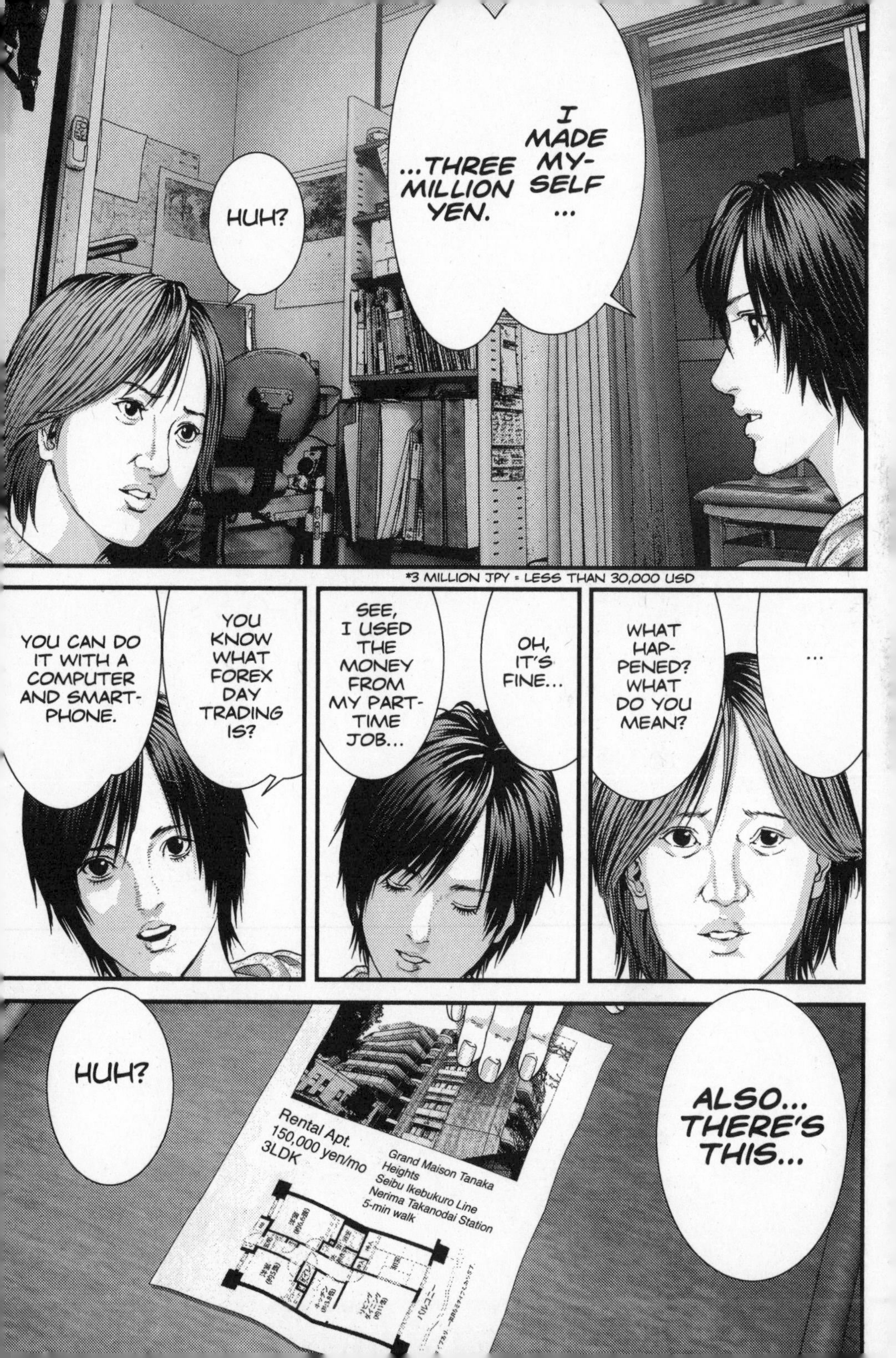
I MADE MYSELF...
...THREE MILLION YEN.
HUH?
*3 MILLION JPY = LESS THAN 30,000 USD
...
WHAT HAPPENED? WHAT DO YOU MEAN?
OH, IT'S FINE...
SEE, I USED THE MONEY FROM MY PART-TIME JOB...
YOU KNOW WHAT FOREX DAY TRADING IS?
YOU CAN DO IT WITH A COMPUTER AND SMARTPHONE.
ALSO... THERE'S THIS...
Rental Apt.
150,000 yen/mo
3LDK
Grand Maison Tanaka Heights
Seibu Ikebukuro Line
Nerima Takanodai Station
5-min walk
HUH?

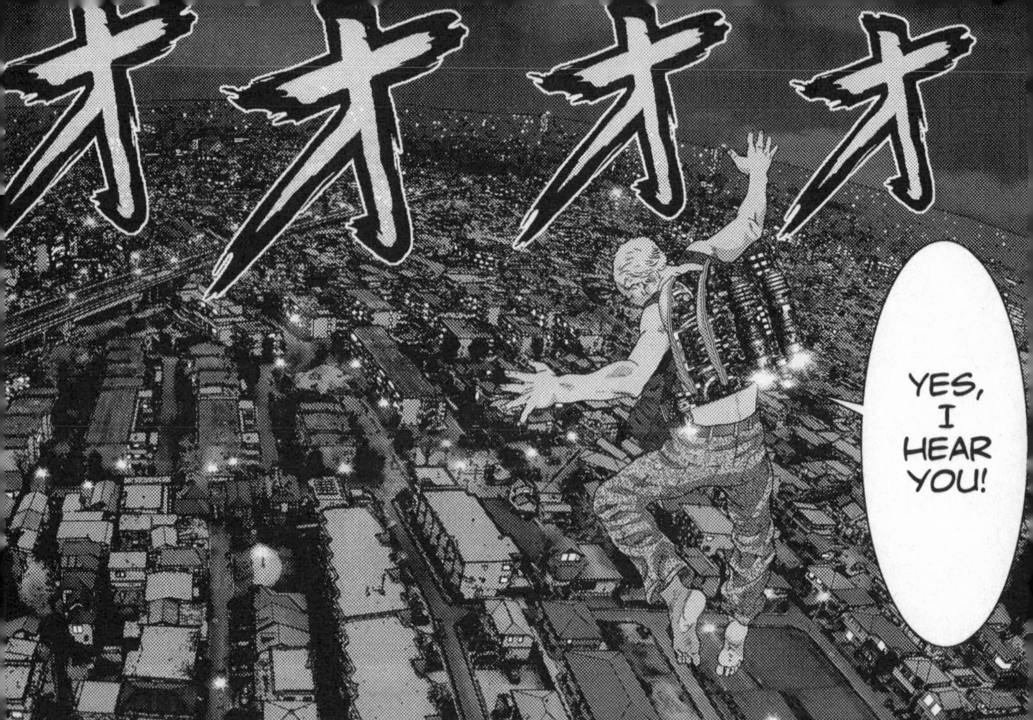
オオオオ
YES, I HEAR YOU!
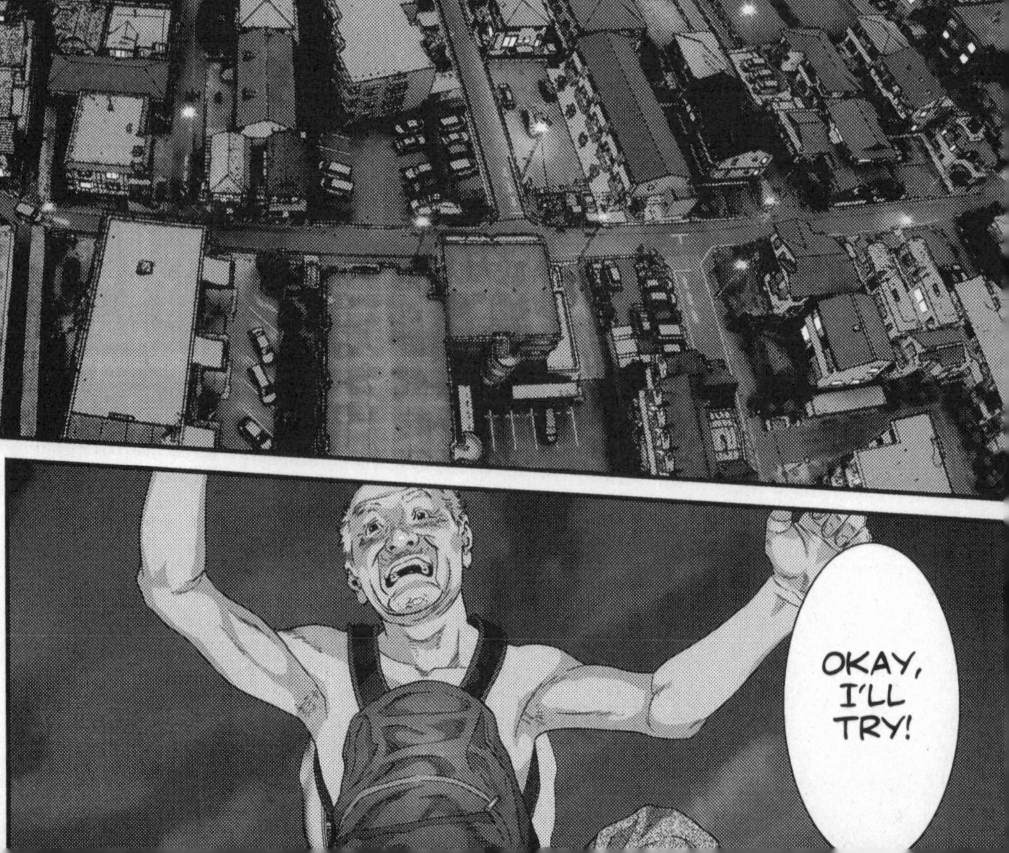
OKAY, I'LL TRY!

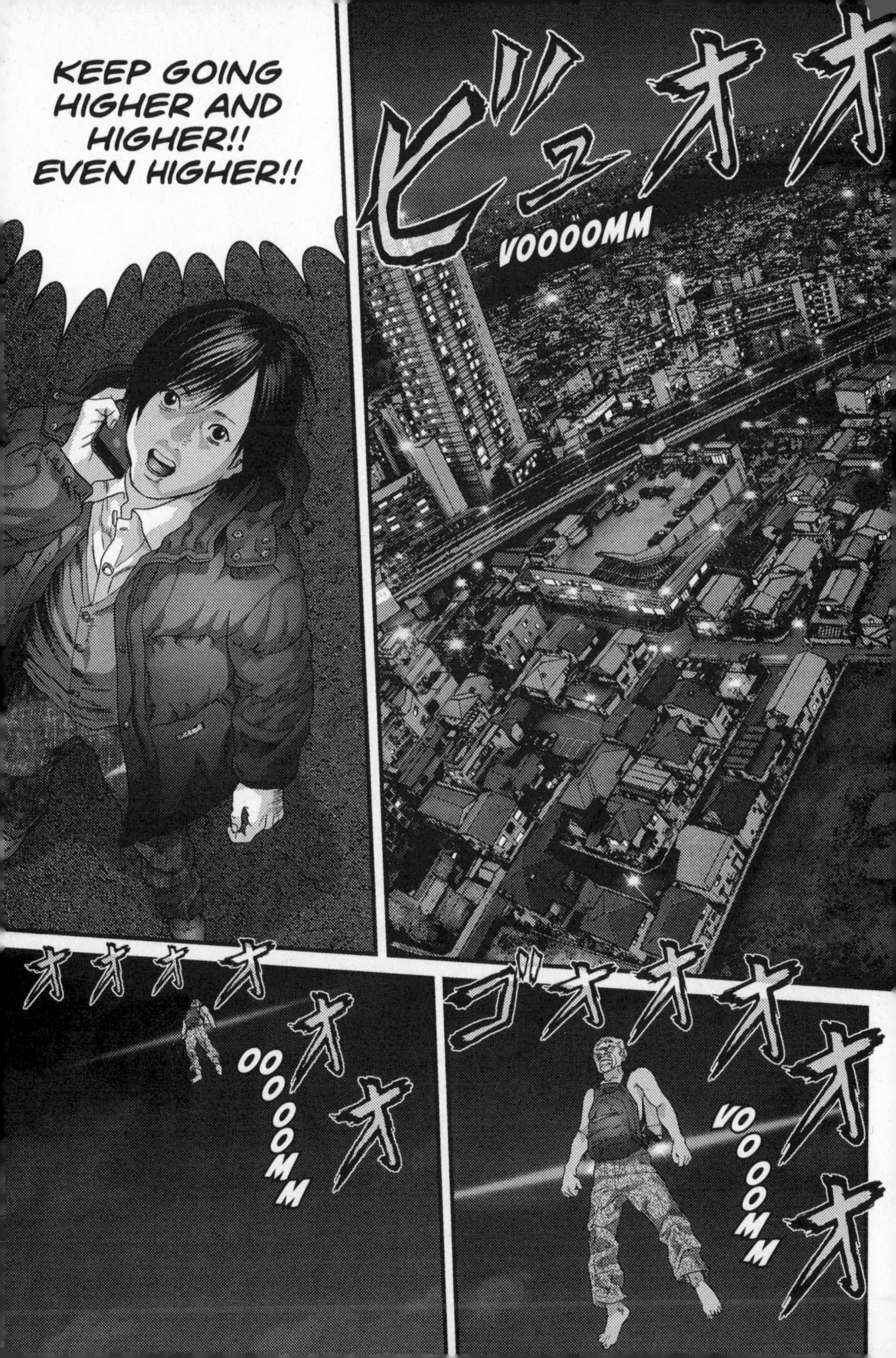
ビュオオ
VOOOOMM
KEEP GOING HIGHER AND HIGHER!! EVEN HIGHER!!
ゴオオオオオ
VOOOOMM
オオオオオオ
OOOOOMM

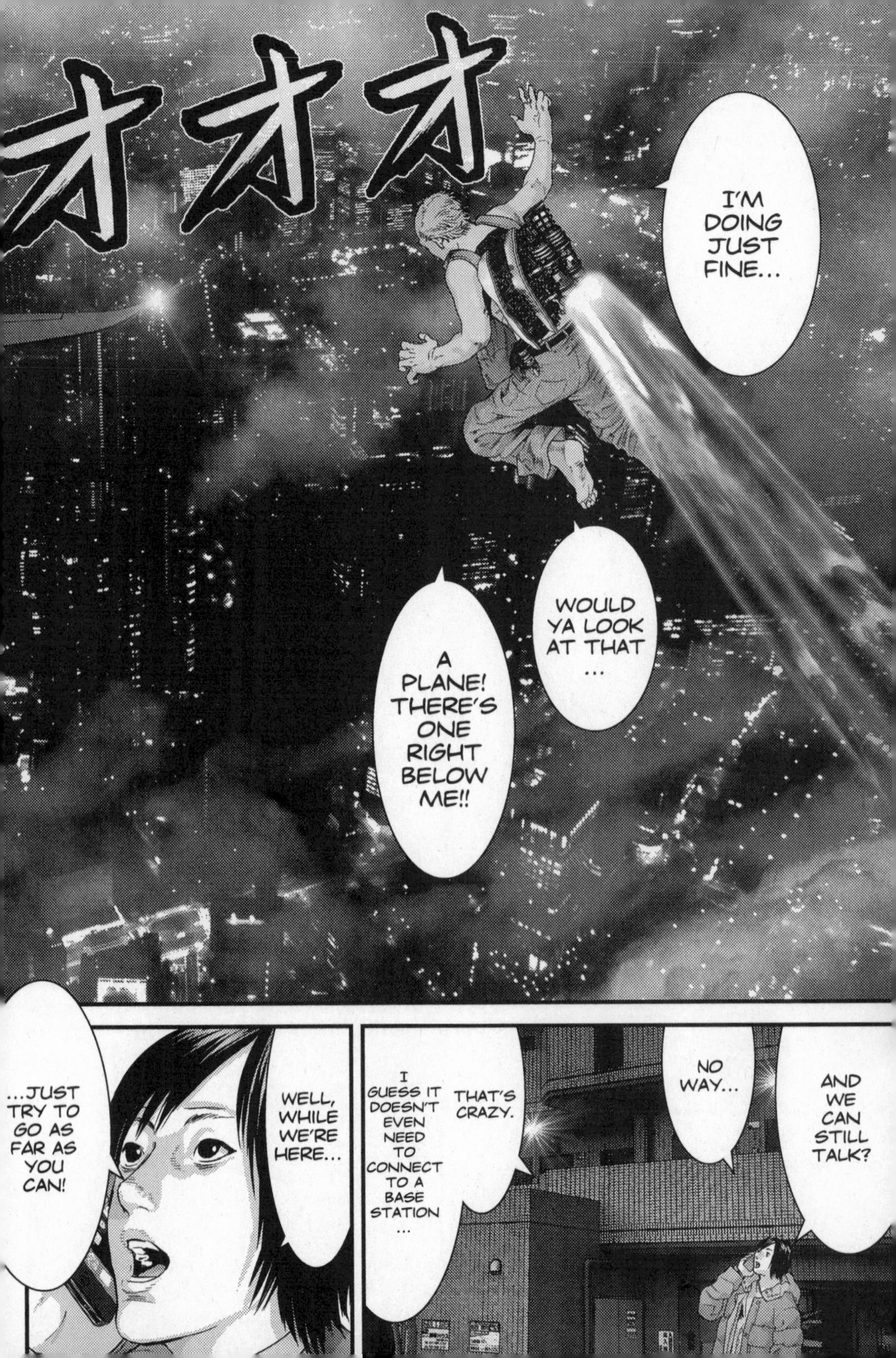
I'M DOING JUST FINE...
オオオ
WOULD YA LOOK AT THAT ...
A PLANE! THERE'S ONE RIGHT BELOW ME!!
AND WE CAN STILL TALK?
NO WAY...
THAT'S CRAZY.
I GUESS IT DOESN'T EVEN NEED TO CONNECT TO A BASE STATION ...
WELL, WHILE WE'RE HERE...
...JUST TRY TO GO AS FAR AS YOU CAN!

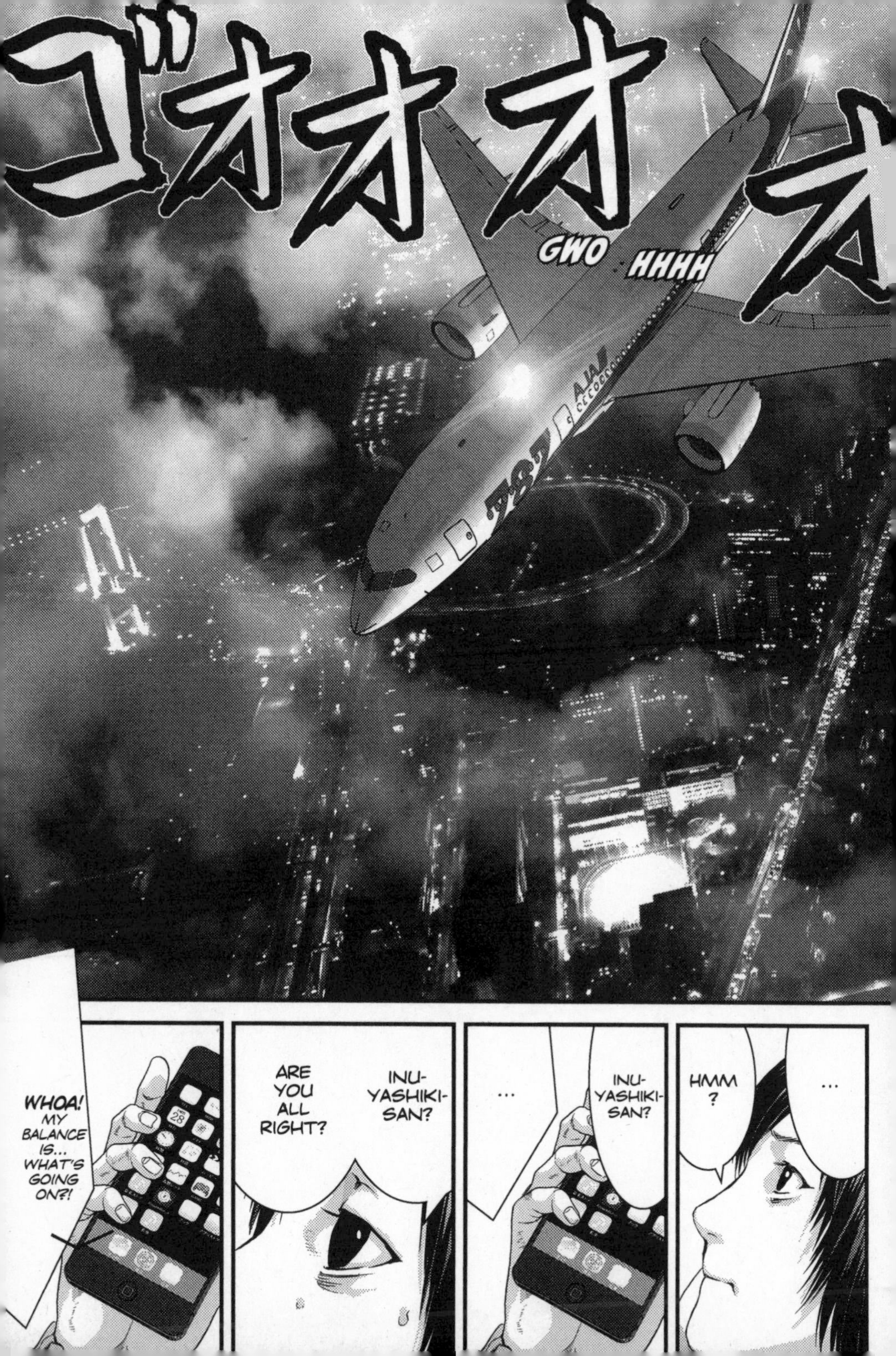
ゴオオオ
GWO HHHH
...
HMM?
INU-YASHIKI-SAN?
...
INU-YASHIKI-SAN?
ARE YOU ALL RIGHT?
WHOA! MY BALANCE IS... WHAT'S GOING ON?!

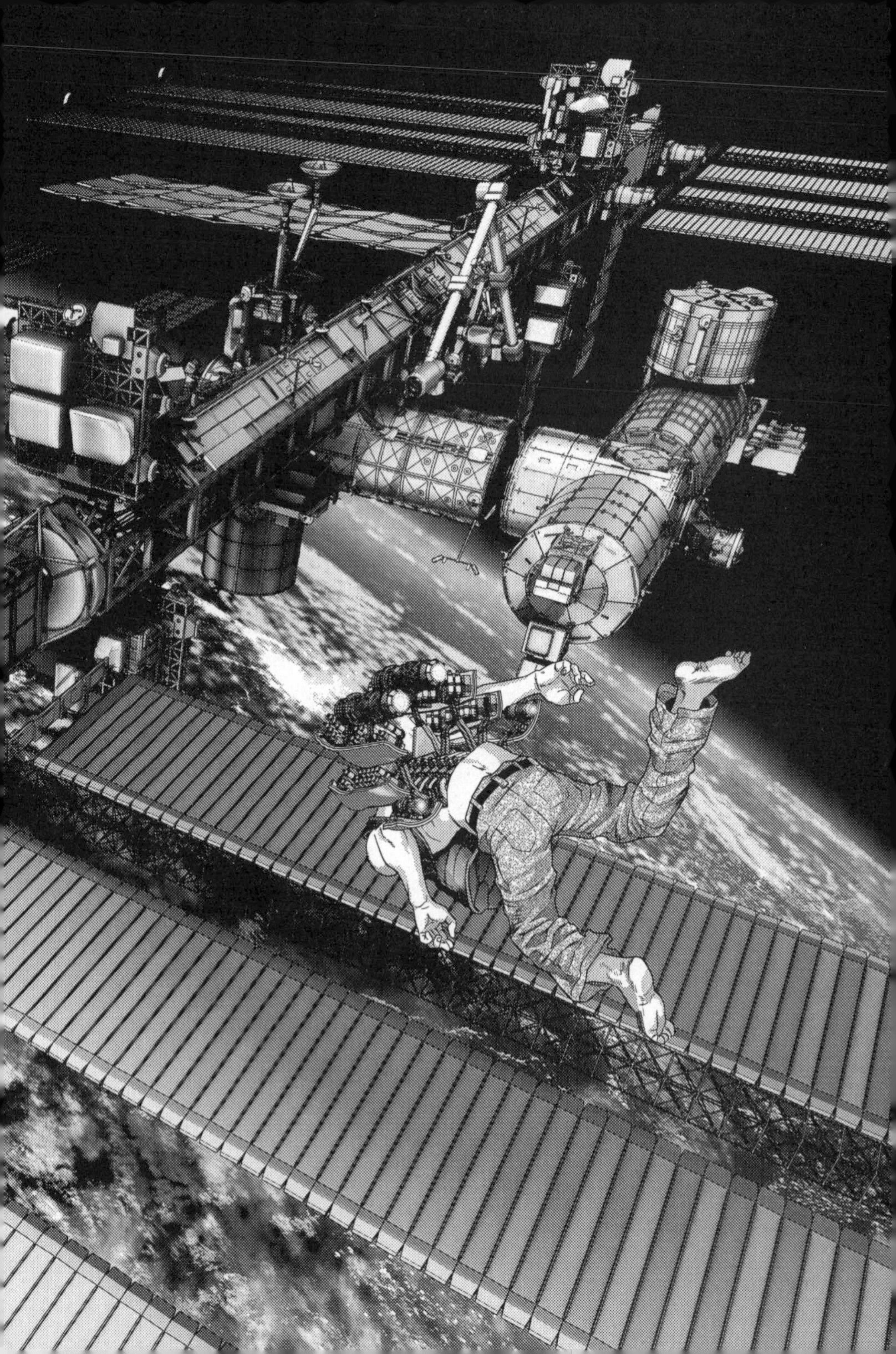

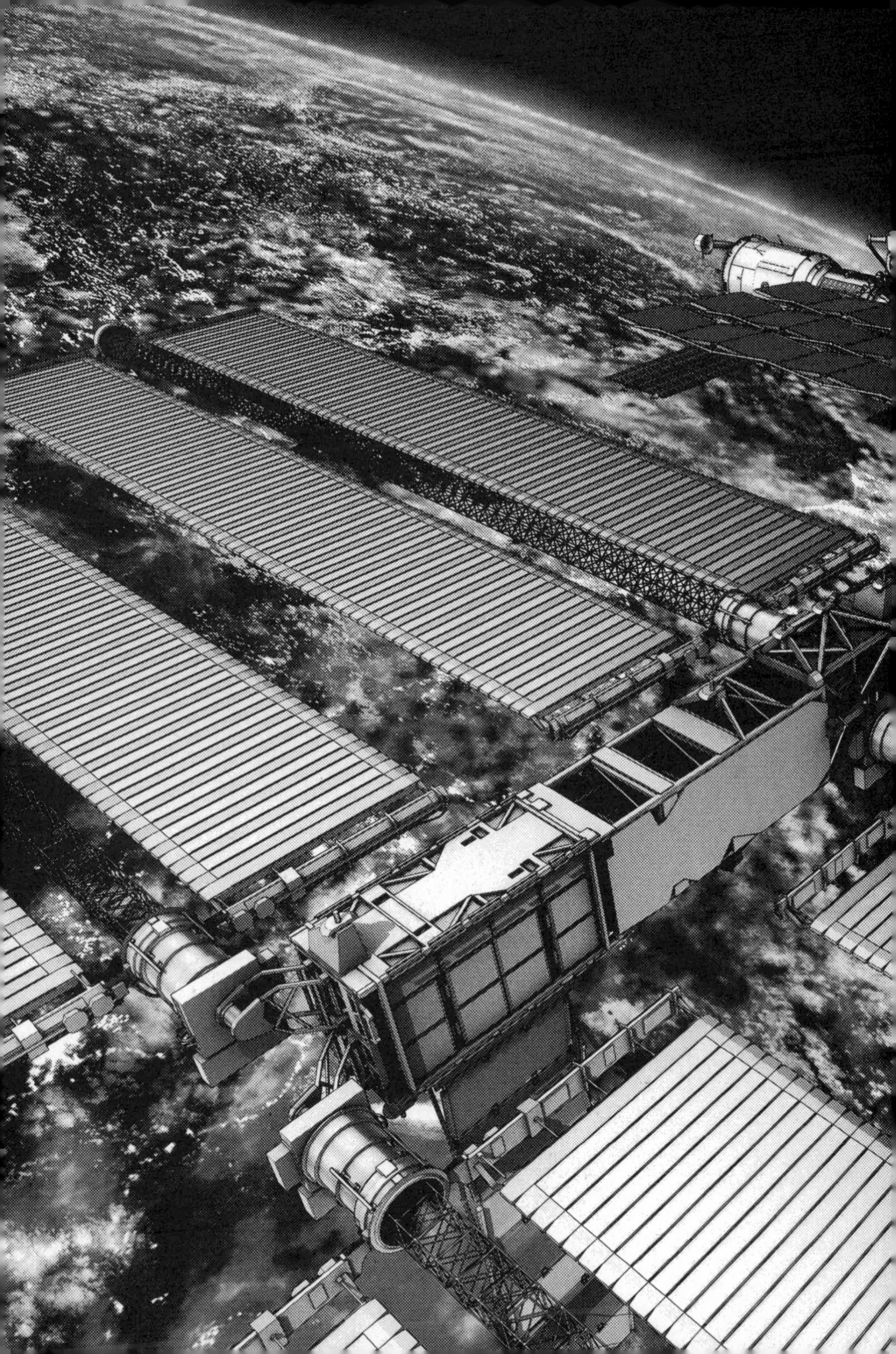

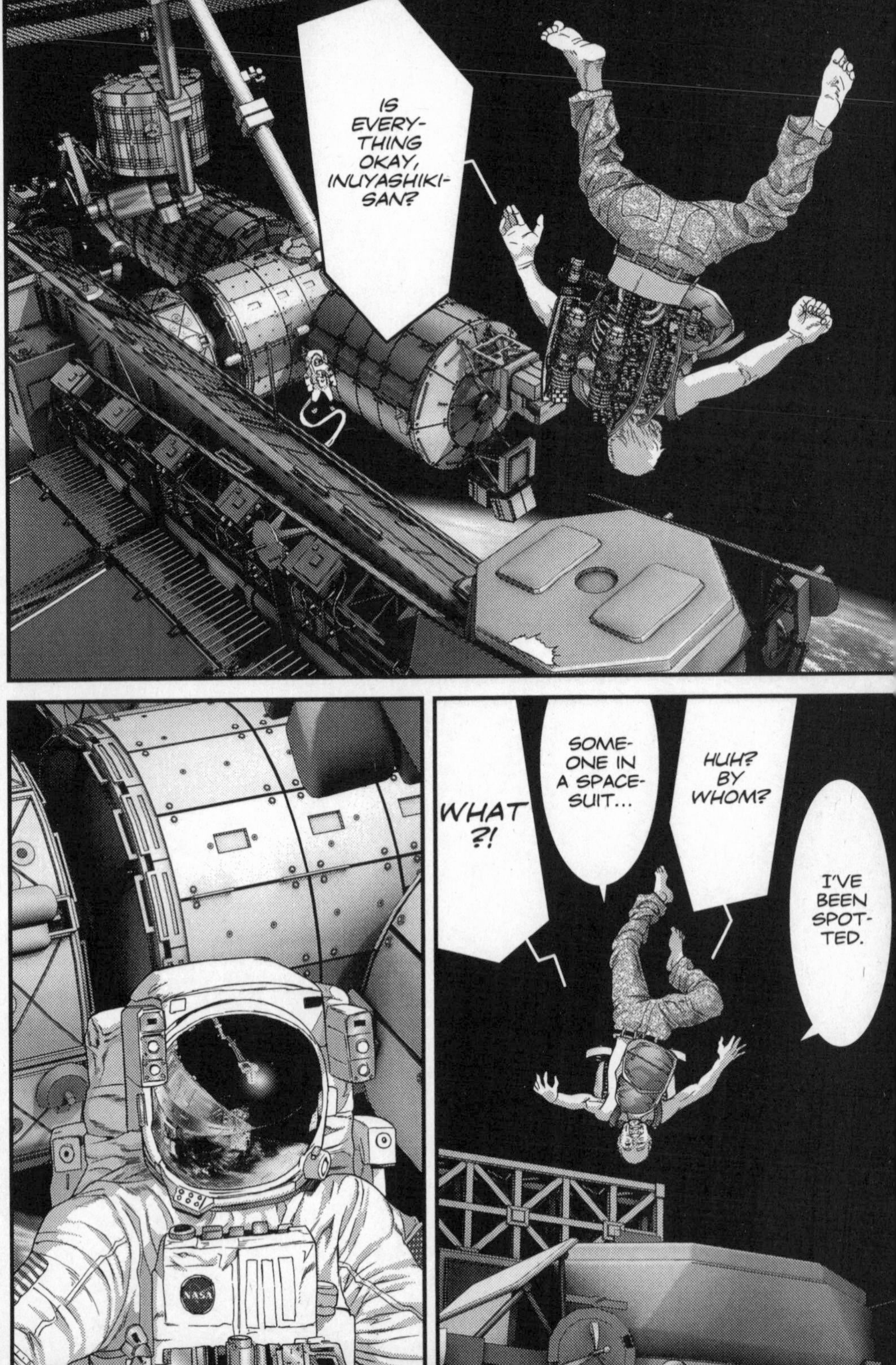
IS EVERYTHING OKAY, INUYASHIKI-SAN?
I'VE BEEN SPOTTED.
HUH? BY WHOM?
SOMEONE IN A SPACESUIT...
WHAT?!

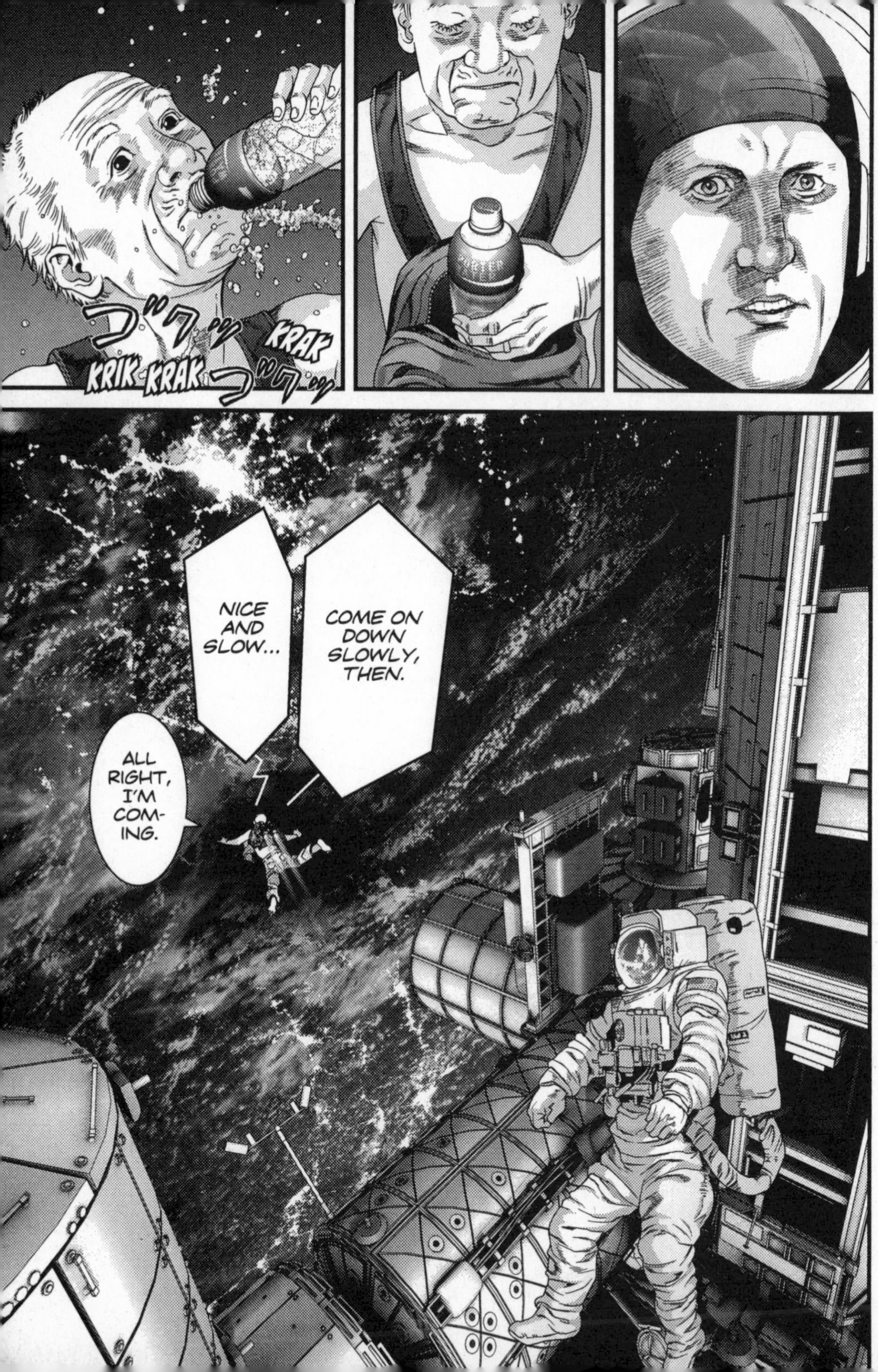

KRAK
ゴクッ
KRIK KRAK
ゴクッ
COME ON DOWN SLOWLY, THEN.
NICE AND SLOW...
ALL RIGHT, I'M COMING.

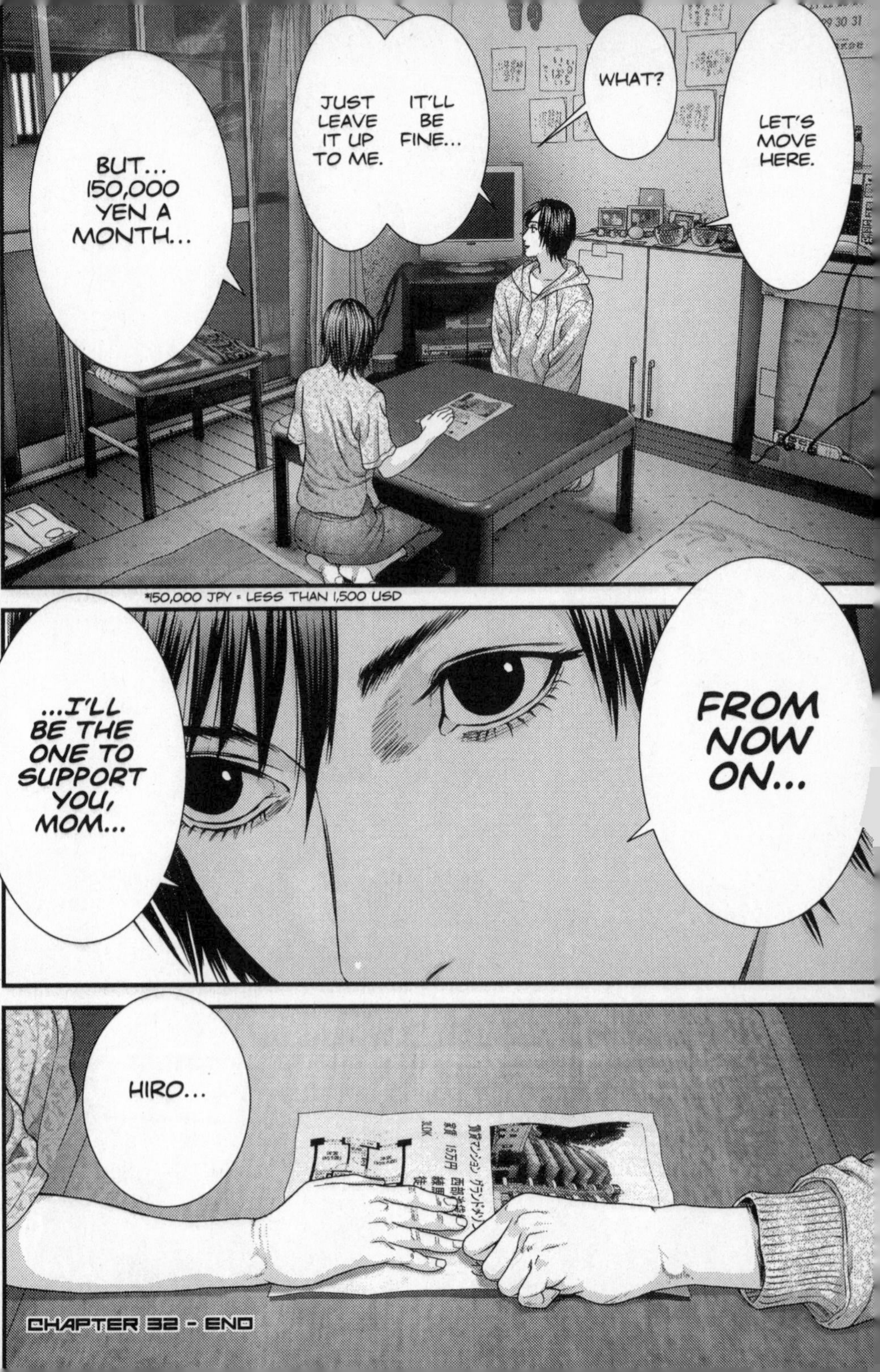
LET'S MOVE HERE.
WHAT?
IT'LL BE FINE...
JUST LEAVE IT UP TO ME.
BUT... 150,000 YEN A MONTH...
*150,000 JPY = LESS THAN 1,500 USD
FROM NOW ON...
...I'LL BE THE ONE TO SUPPORT YOU, MOM...
HIRO...
CHAPTER 32 - END

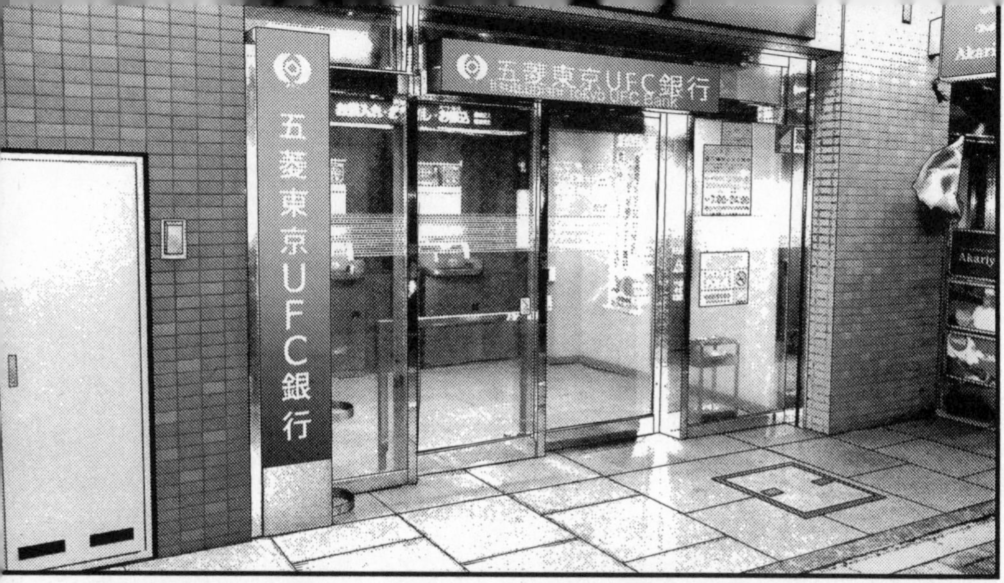
五菱東京UFC銀行
五菱東京UFC銀行
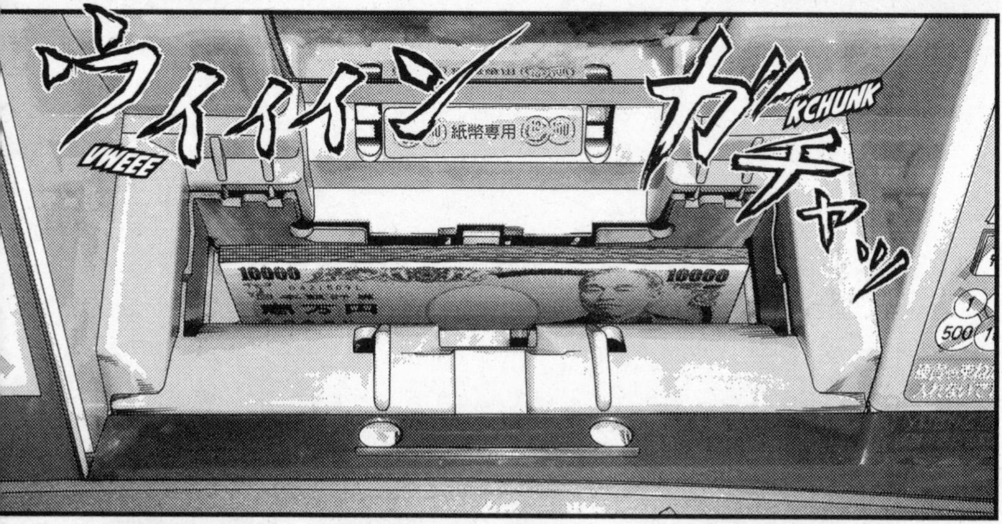
ウィイイン
VWEEE
紙幣専用
ガチャッ
KCHUNK
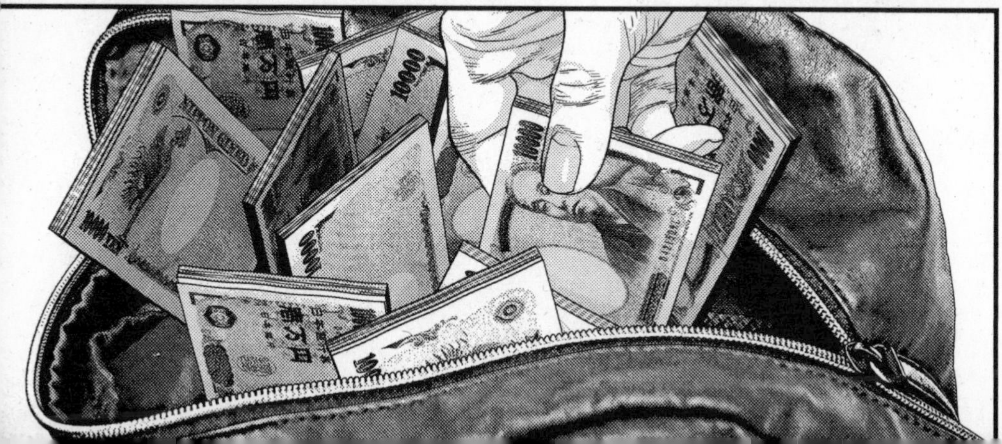

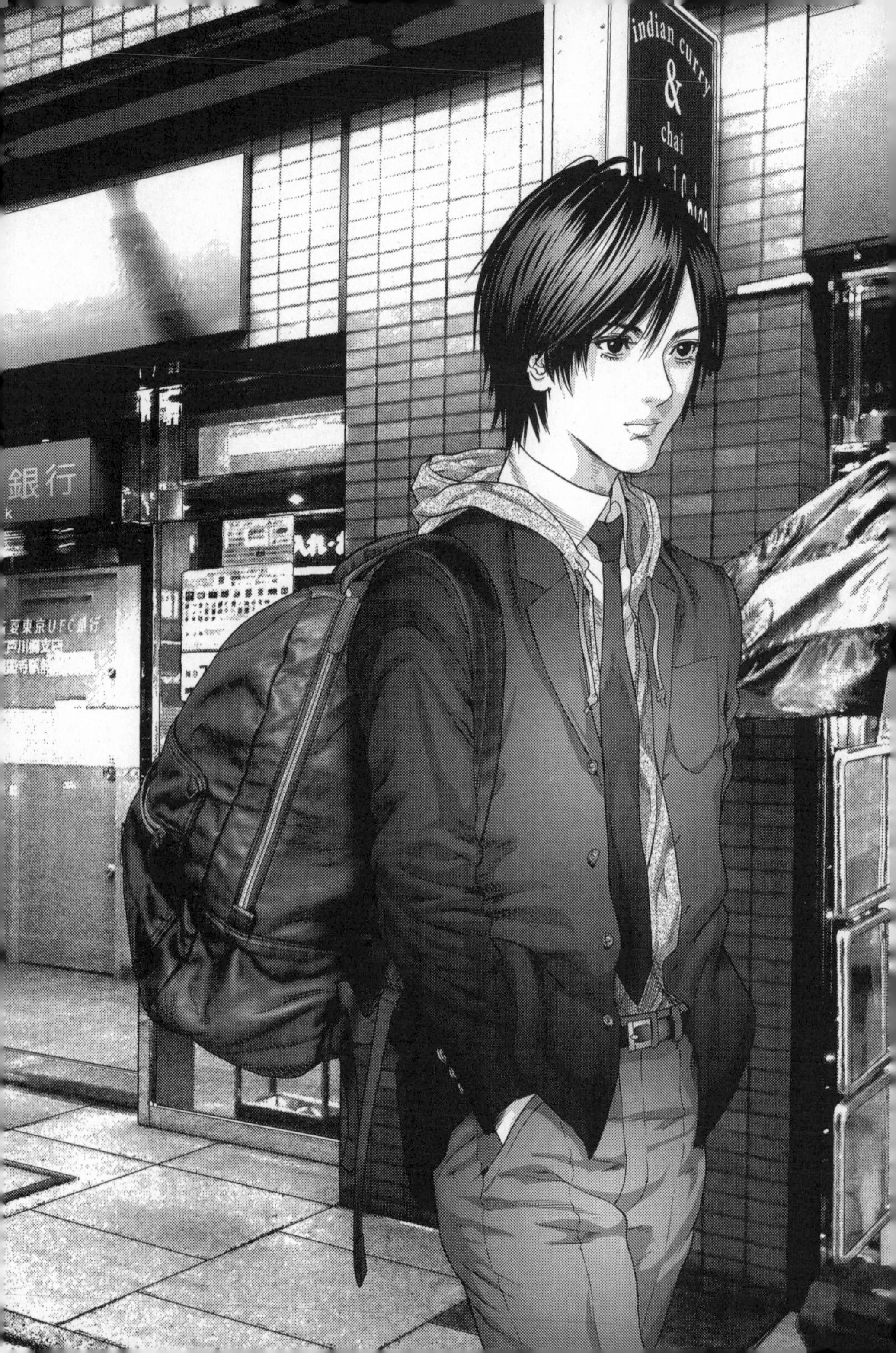
indian curry
&
chai
銀行

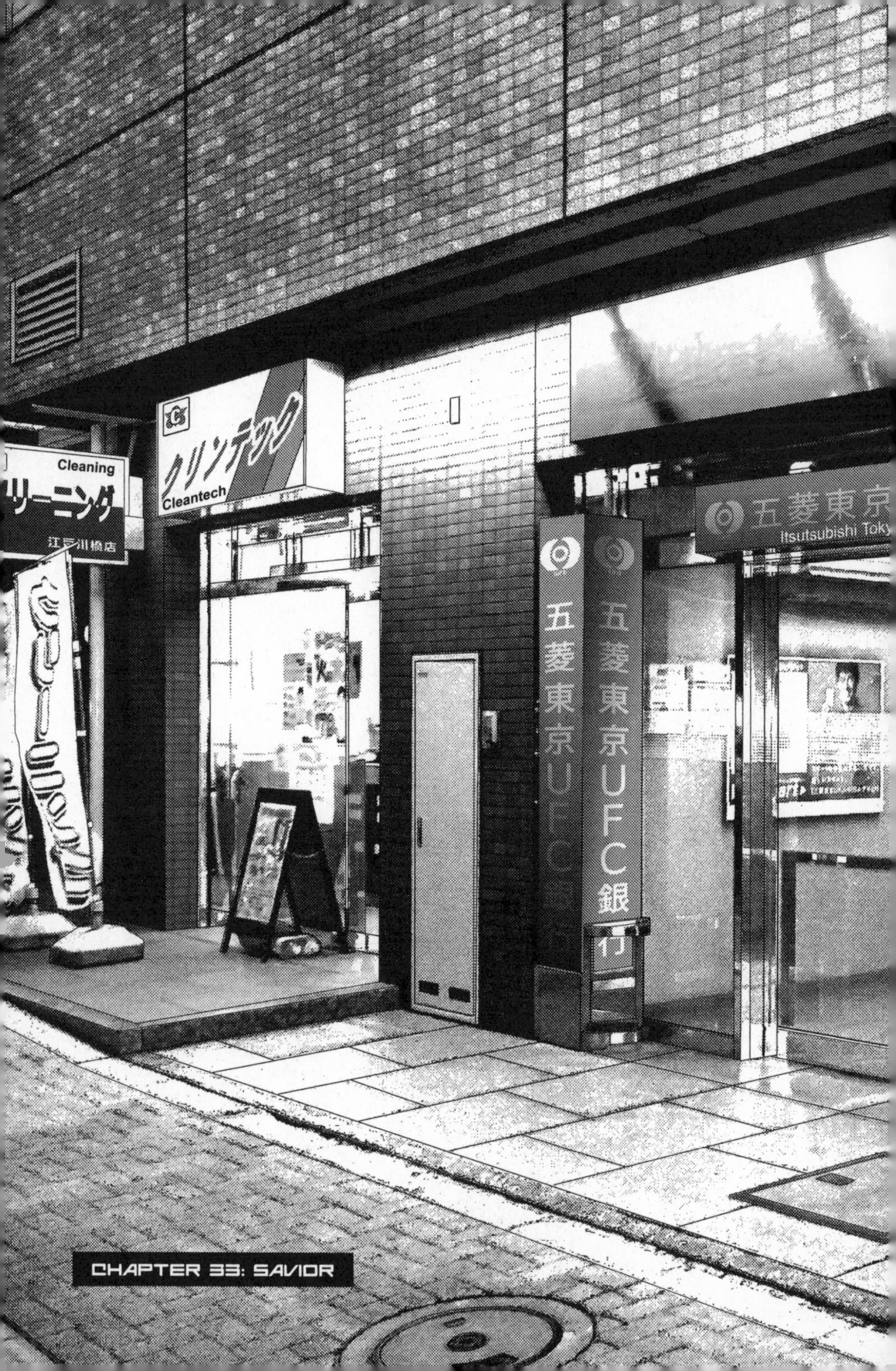
Cleaning
クリンテック
Cleantech
五菱東京UFC銀行
CHAPTER 33: SAVIOR

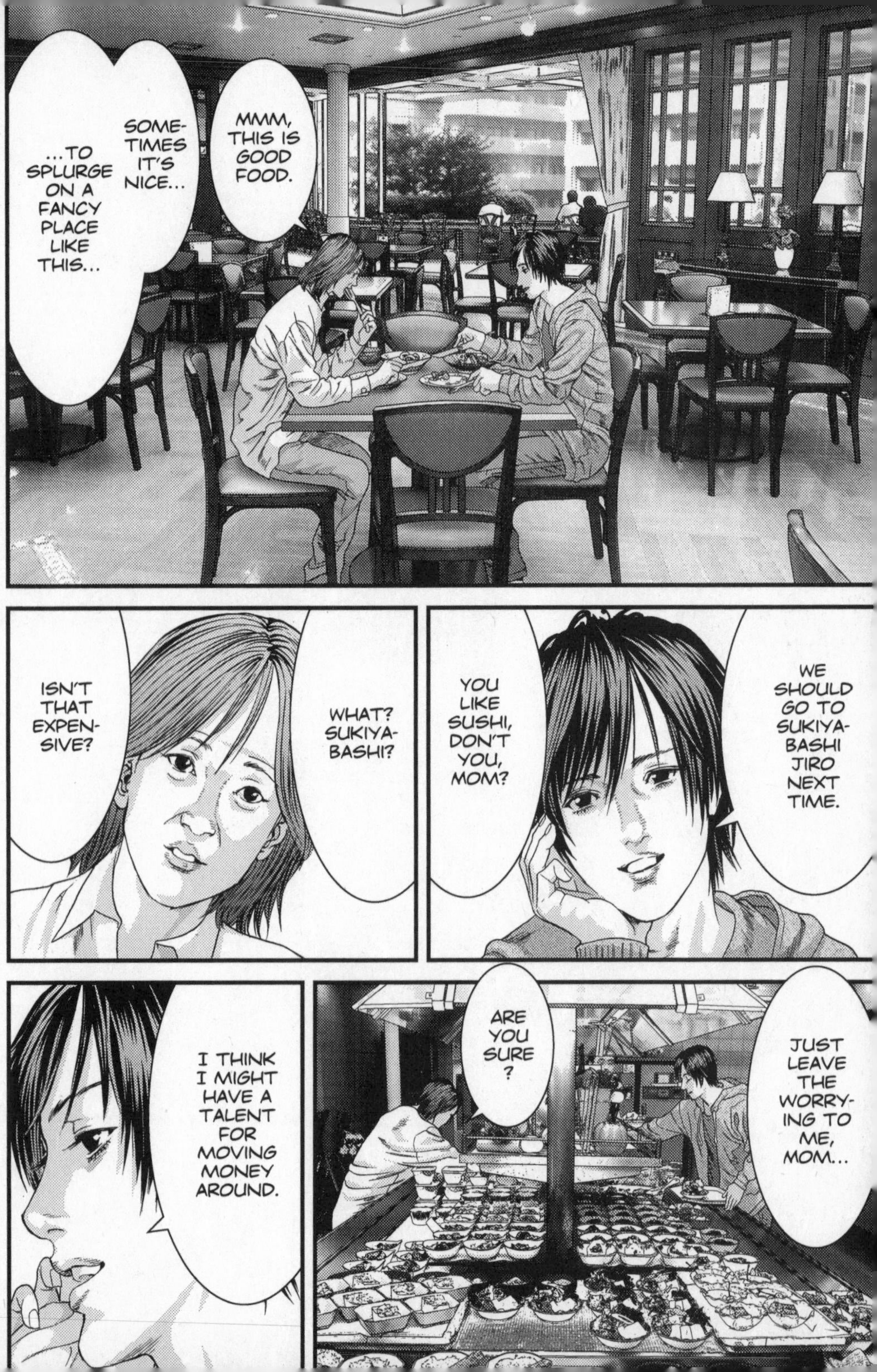
MMM, THIS IS GOOD FOOD.
SOMETIMES IT'S NICE...
...TO SPLURGE ON A FANCY PLACE LIKE THIS...
WE SHOULD GO TO SUKIYABASHI JIRO NEXT TIME.
YOU LIKE SUSHI, DON'T YOU, MOM?
WHAT? SUKIYABASHI?
ISN'T THAT EXPENSIVE?
JUST LEAVE THE WORRYING TO ME, MOM...
ARE YOU SURE?
I THINK I MIGHT HAVE A TALENT FOR MOVING MONEY AROUND.

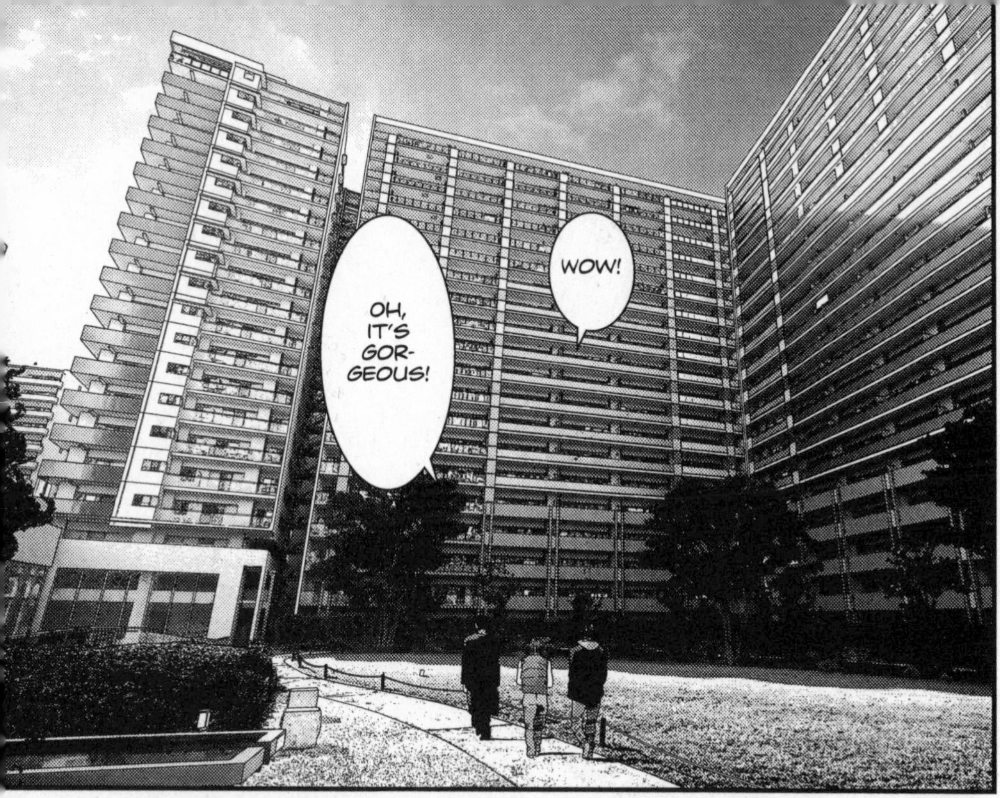
WOW!
OH, IT'S GORGEOUS!

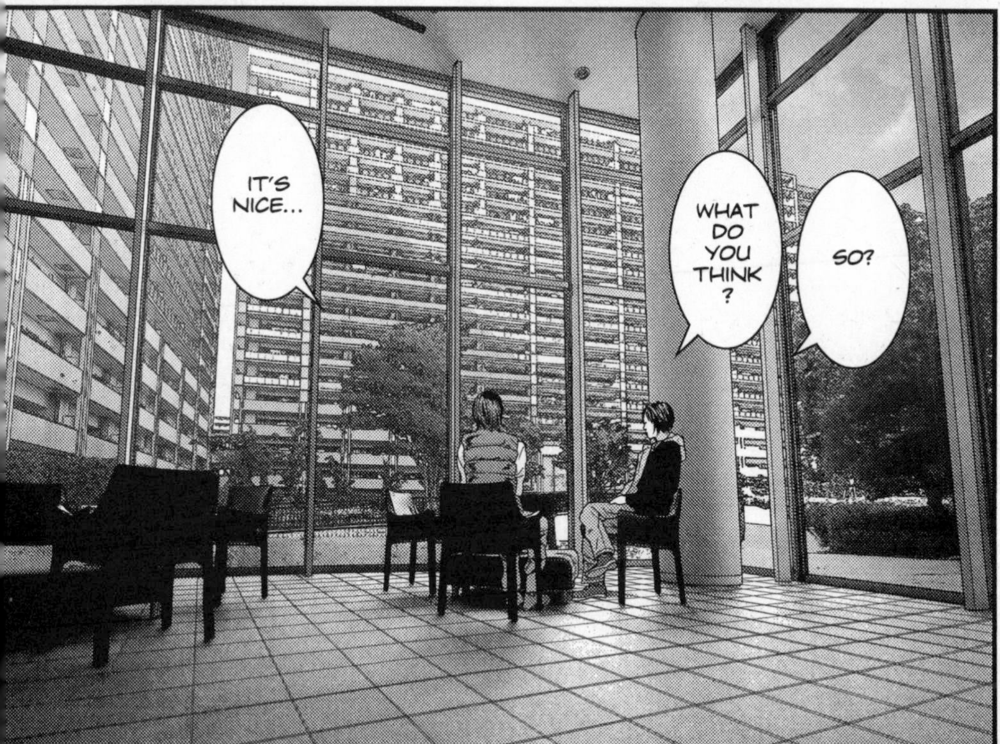
SO?
WHAT DO YOU THINK?
IT'S NICE...

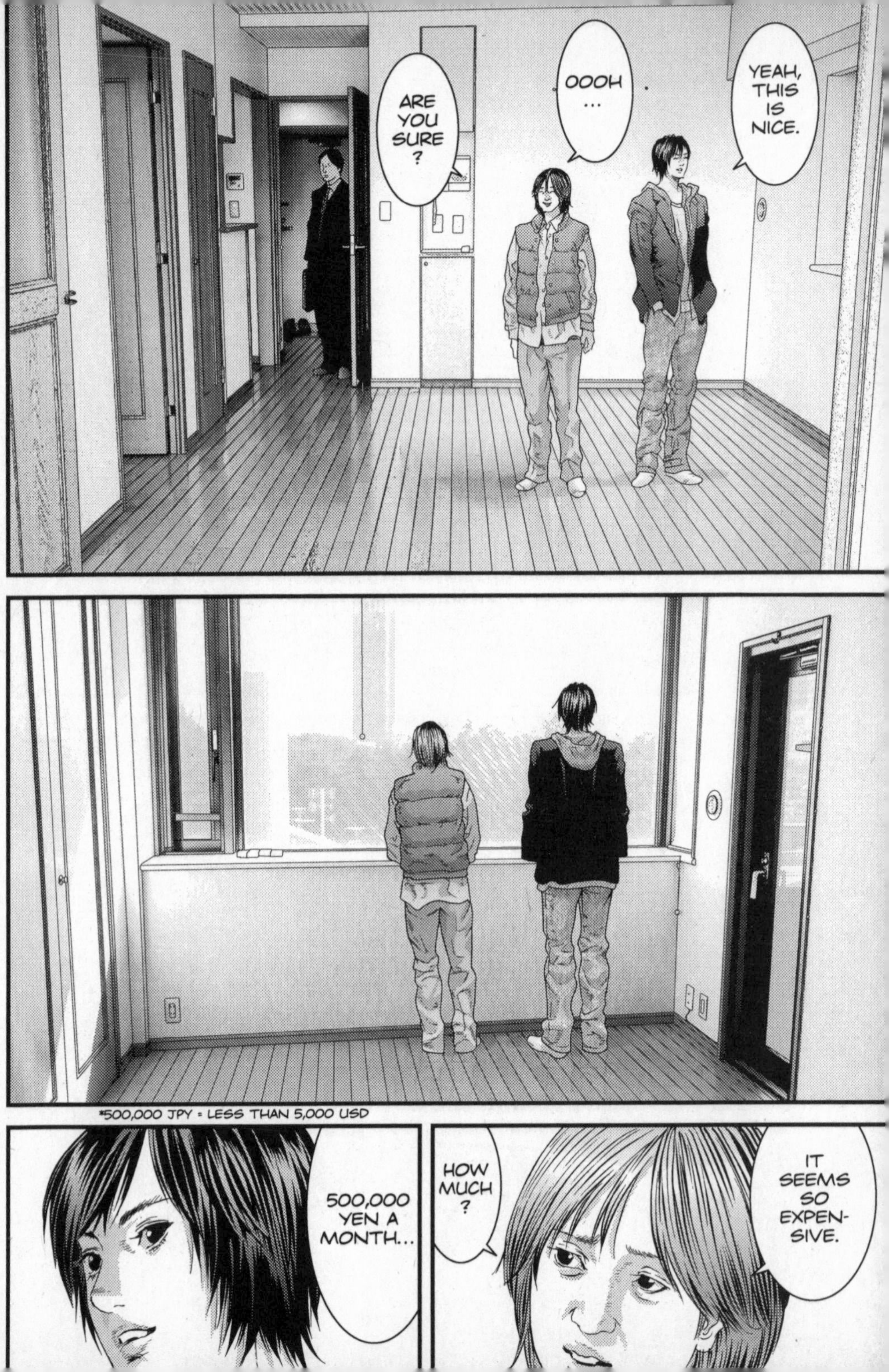
YEAH, THIS IS NICE.
OOOH...
ARE YOU SURE?
*500,000 JPY = LESS THAN 5,000 USD
IT SEEMS SO EXPEN-SIVE.
HOW MUCH?
500,000 YEN A MONTH...

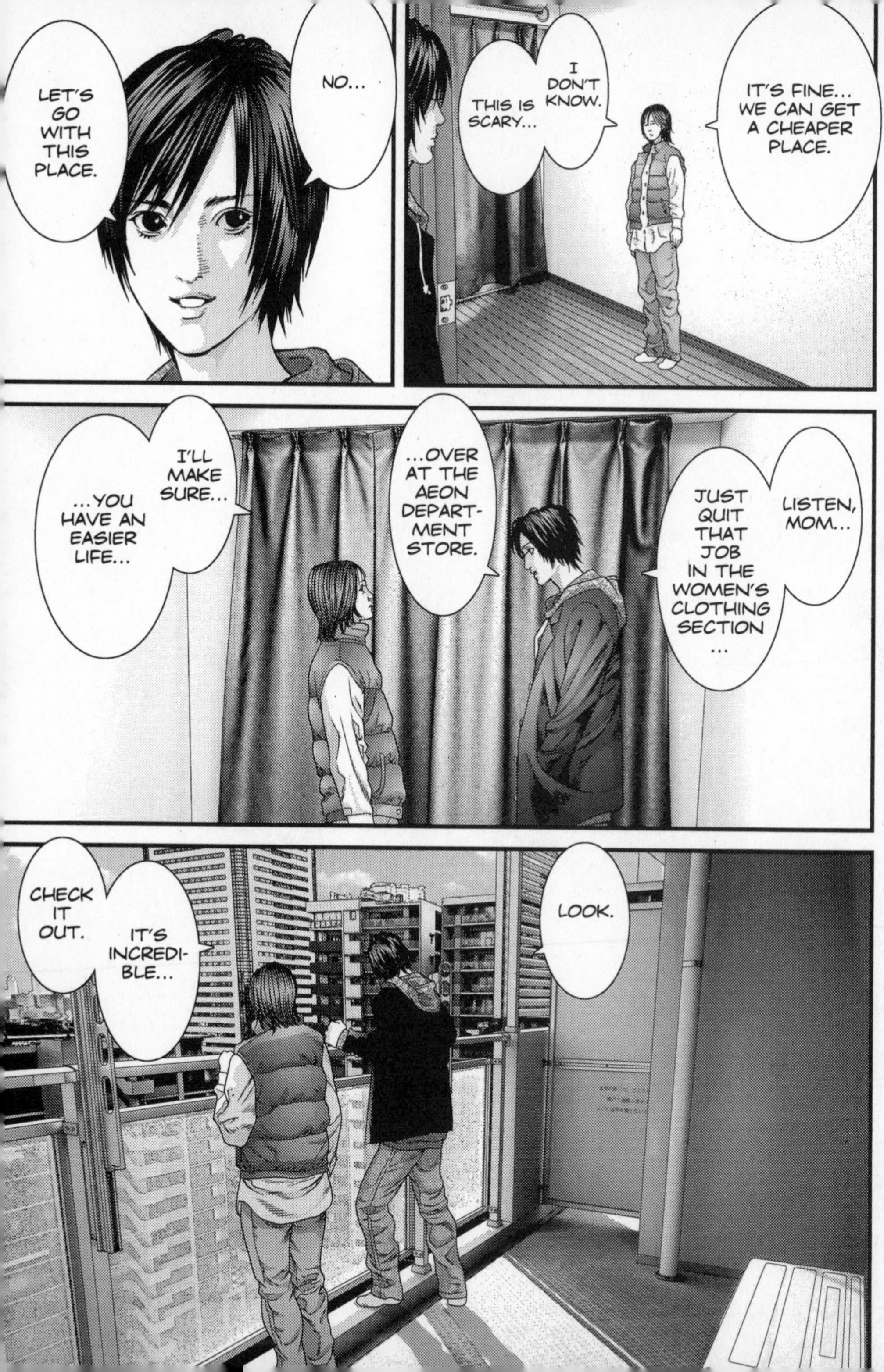
IT'S FINE... WE CAN GET A CHEAPER PLACE.
I DON'T KNOW.
THIS IS SCARY...
NO...
LET'S GO WITH THIS PLACE.
LISTEN, MOM...
JUST QUIT THAT JOB IN THE WOMEN'S CLOTHING SECTION ...
...OVER AT THE AEON DEPARTMENT STORE.
I'LL MAKE SURE...
...YOU HAVE AN EASIER LIFE...
LOOK.
IT'S INCREDIBLE...
CHECK IT OUT.

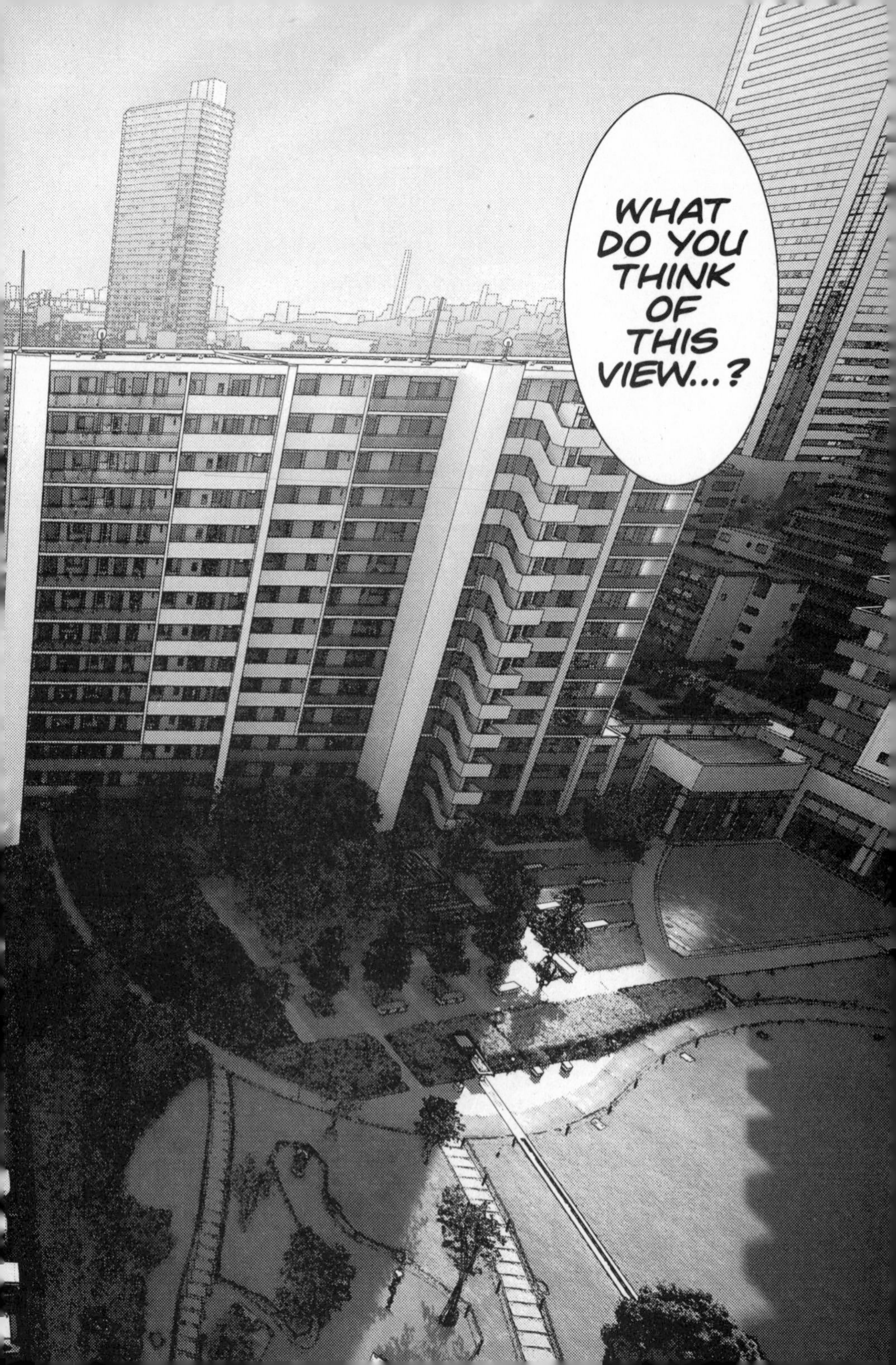
WHAT DO YOU THINK OF THIS VIEW...?

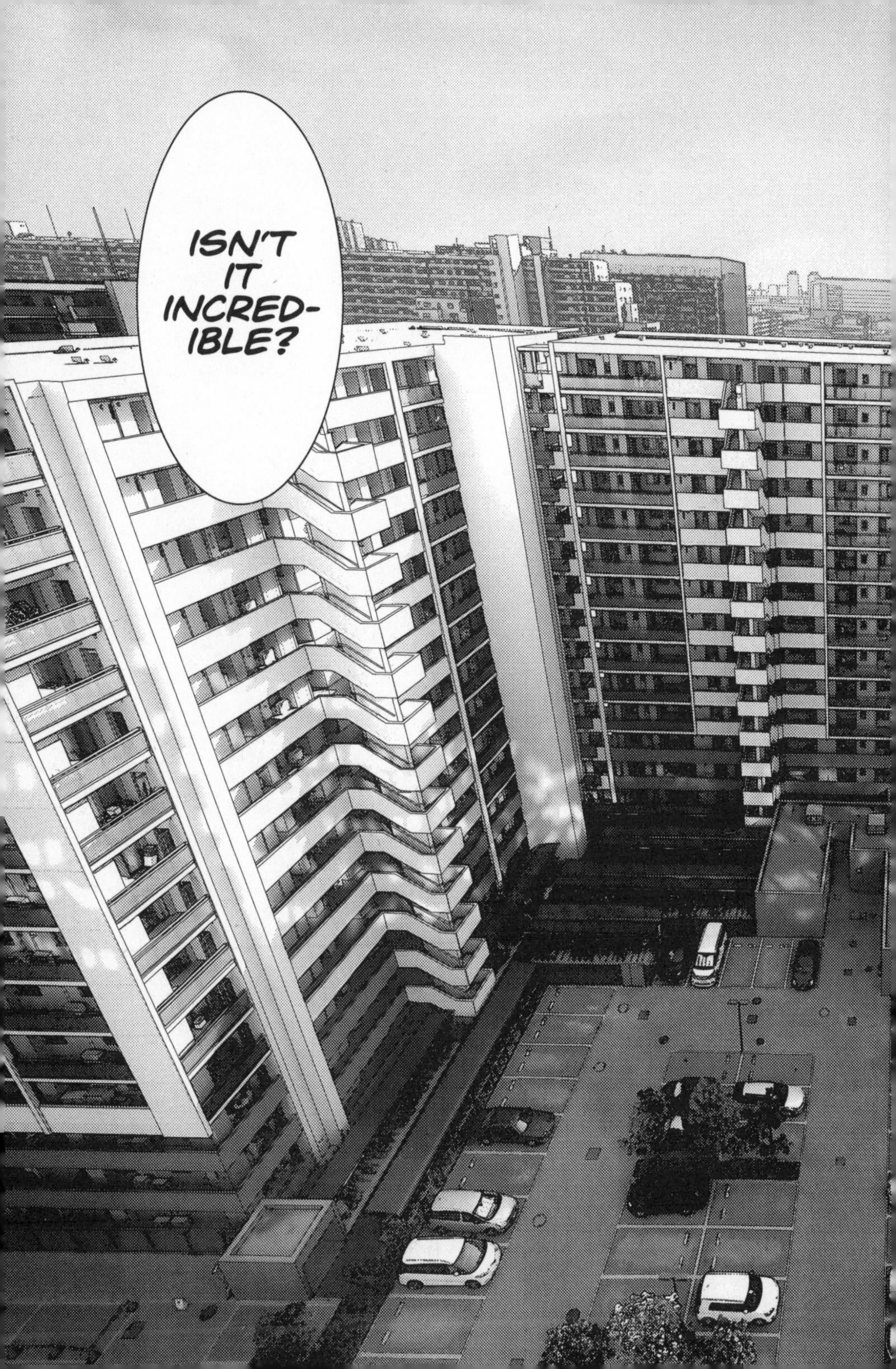
ISN'T IT INCRED-IBLE?

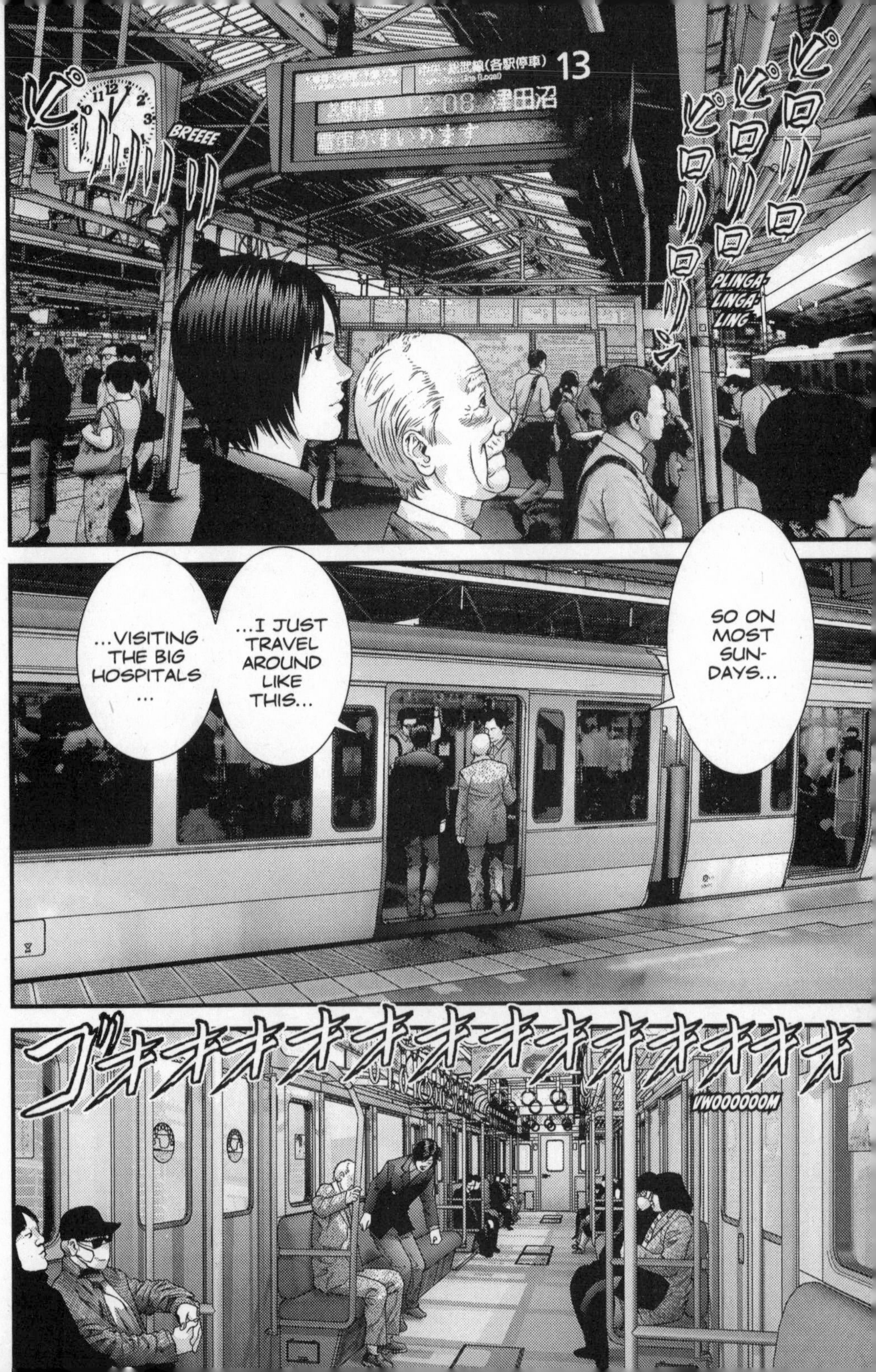
13
PLINGA-LINGA-LING
BREEEE
SO ON MOST SUN-DAYS...
...I JUST TRAVEL AROUND LIKE THIS...
...VISITING THE BIG HOSPITALS ...
VWOOOOOOM

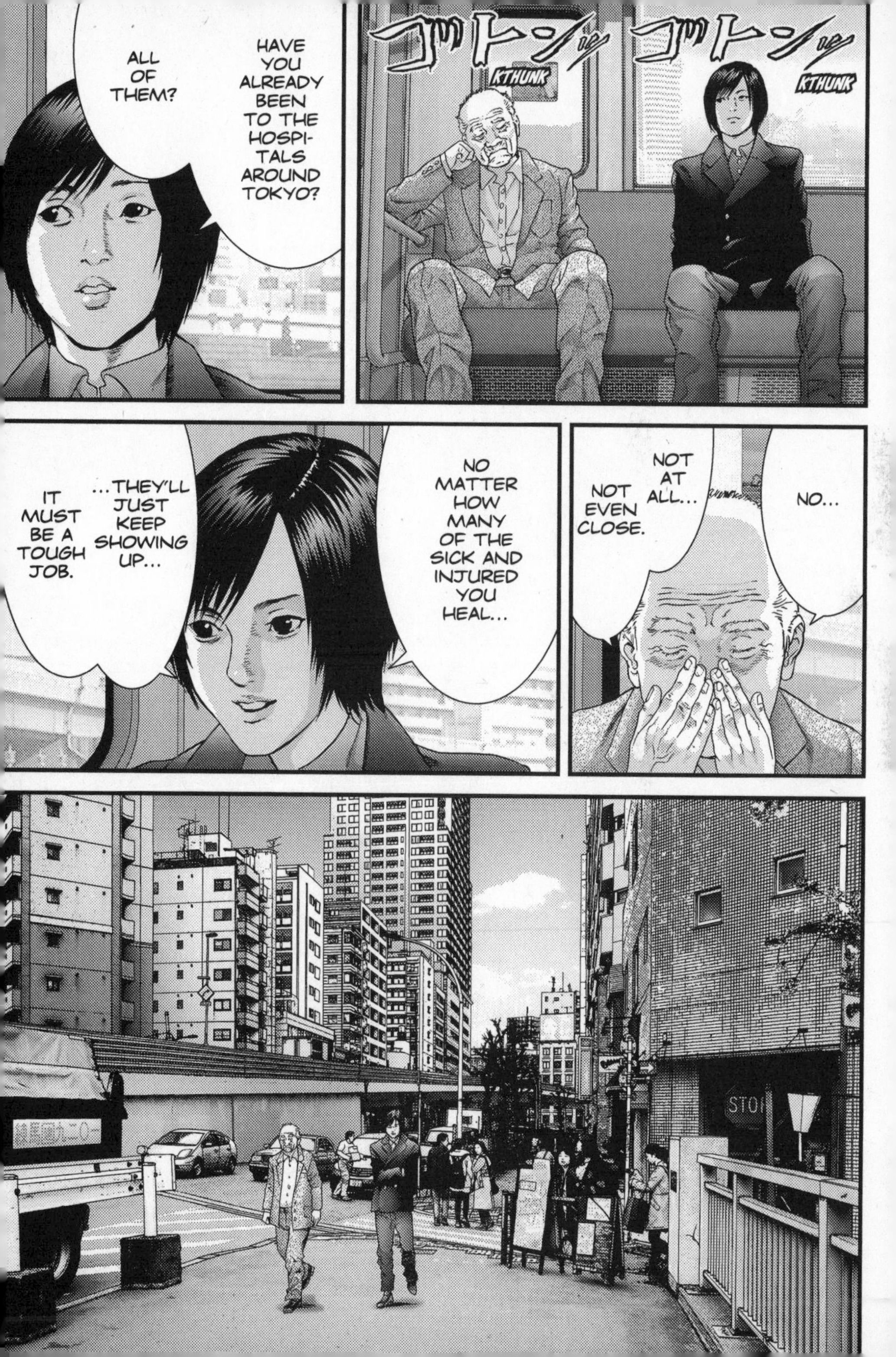
ゴトンッ
KTHUNK
ゴトンッ
KTHUNK
HAVE YOU ALREADY BEEN TO THE HOSPITALS AROUND TOKYO?
ALL OF THEM?
NO...
NOT AT ALL...
NOT EVEN CLOSE.
NO MATTER HOW MANY OF THE SICK AND INJURED YOU HEAL...
...THEY'LL JUST KEEP SHOWING UP...
IT MUST BE A TOUGH JOB.
STOP

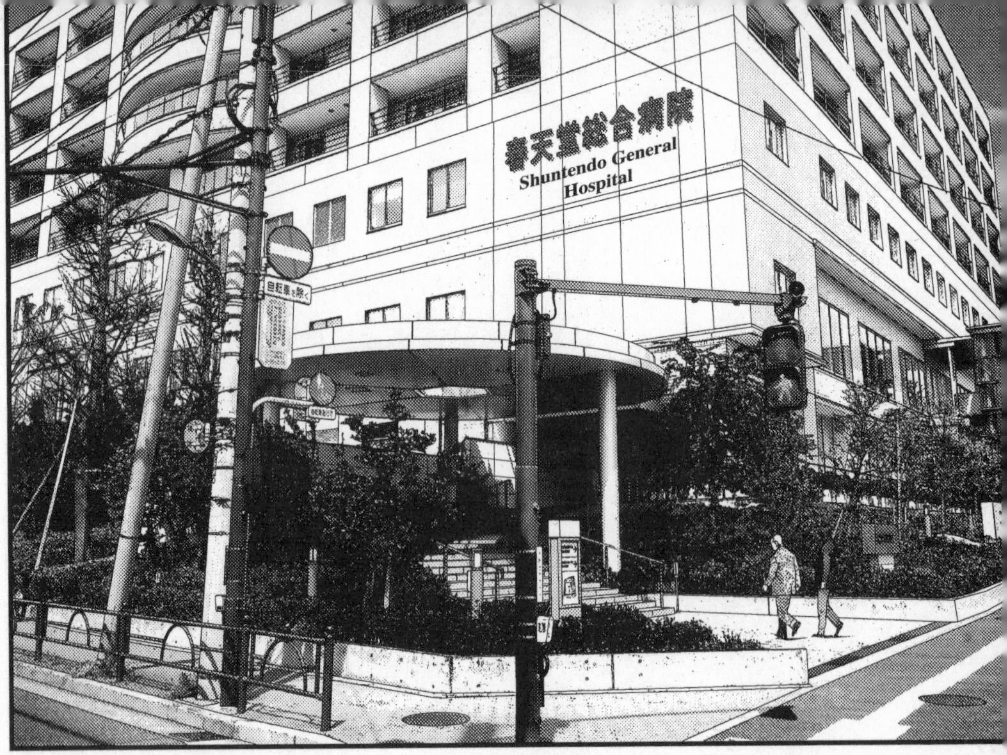
春天堂総合病院
Shuntendo General
Hospital
自転車を除く
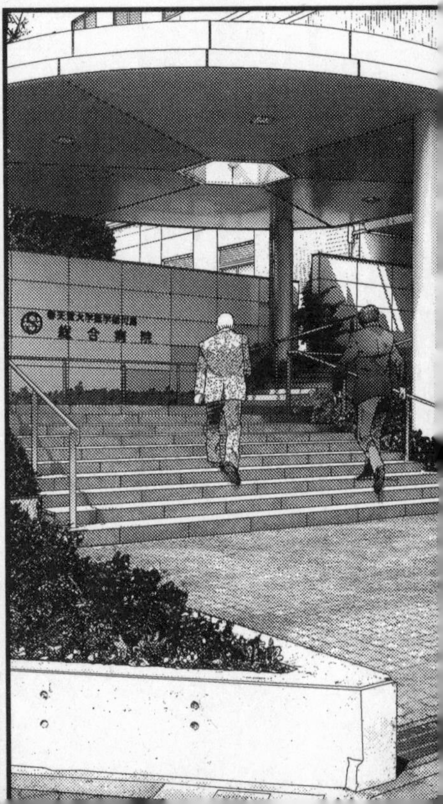
総合病院
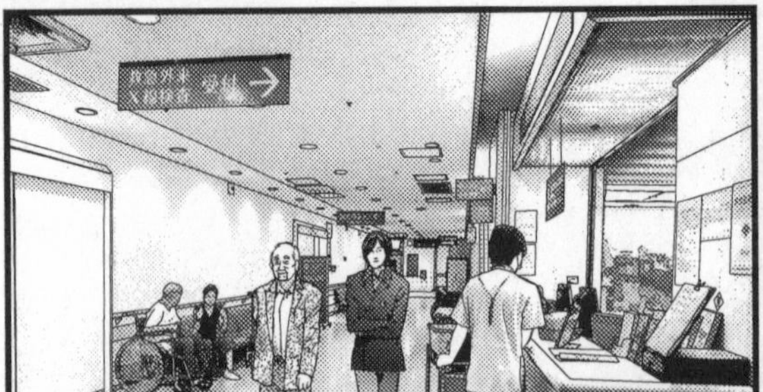
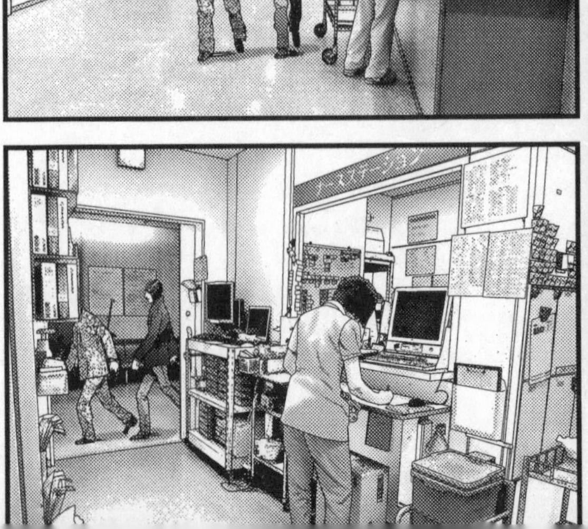

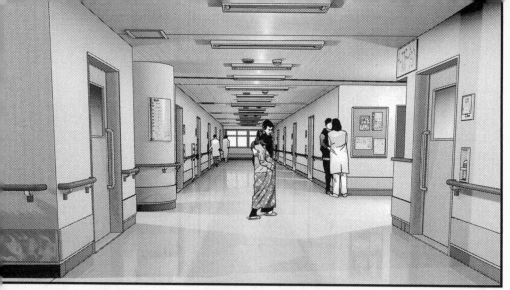

SURE.

WILL YOU KEEP A LOOKOUT FOR ME?

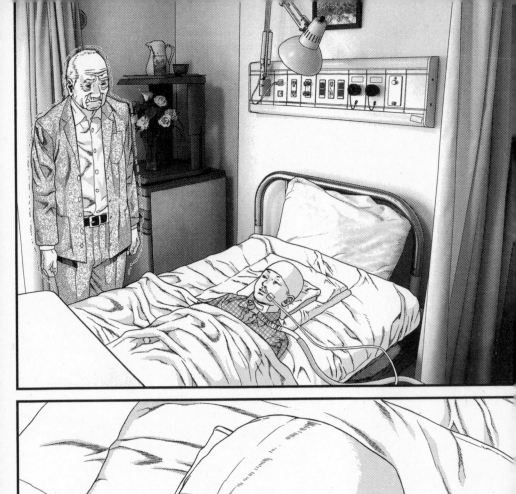
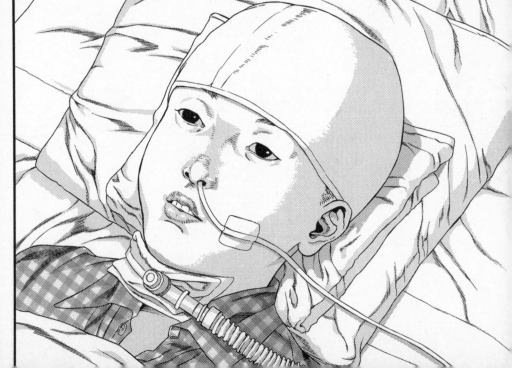

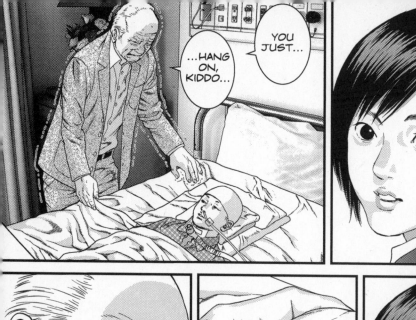

...HANG ON, KIDDO...

YOU JUST...

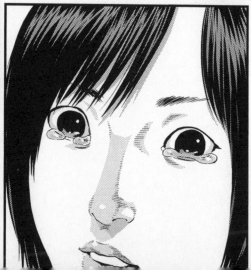

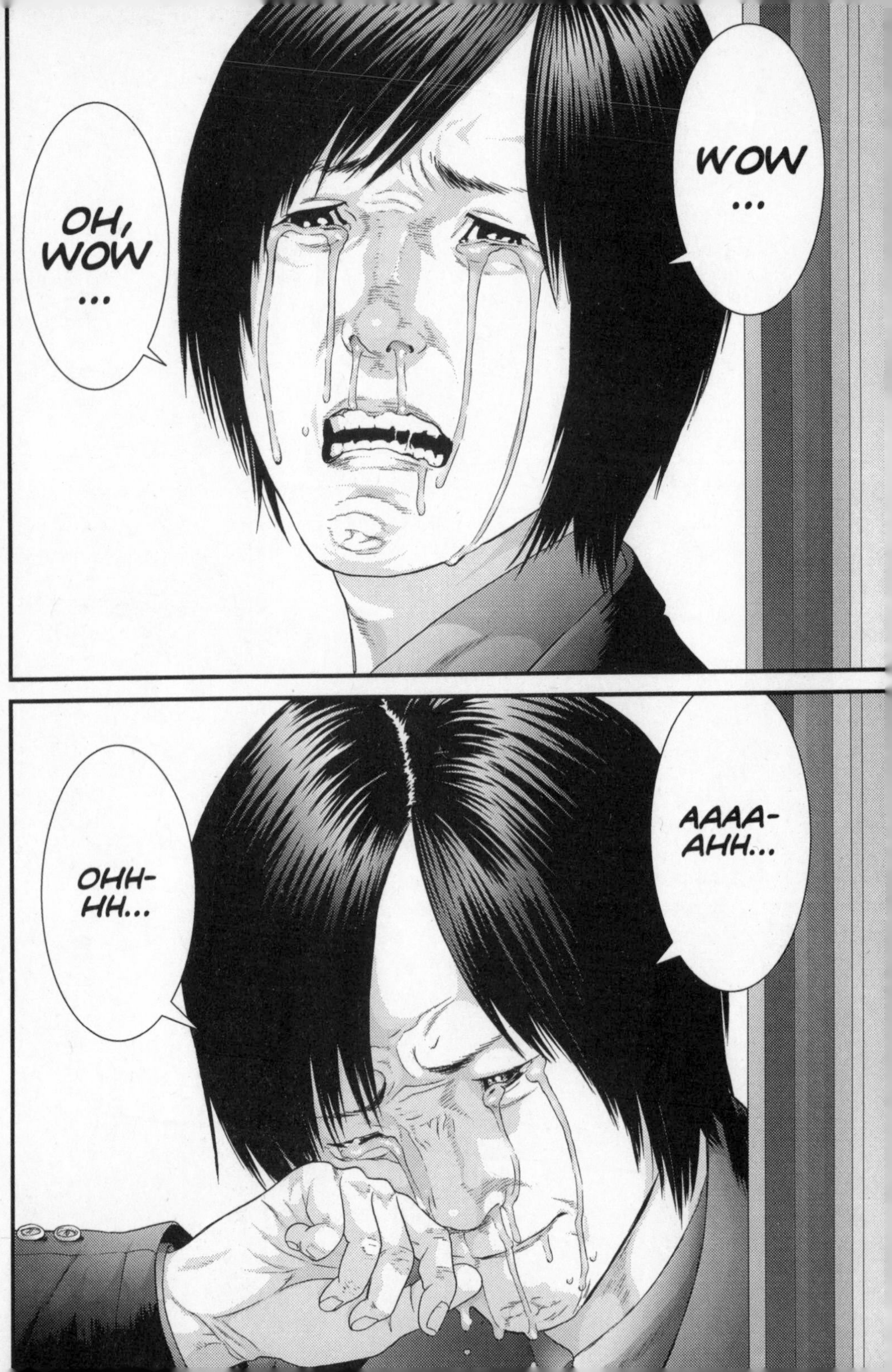
WOW ...
OH, WOW ...
AAAA-AHH...
OHH-HH...

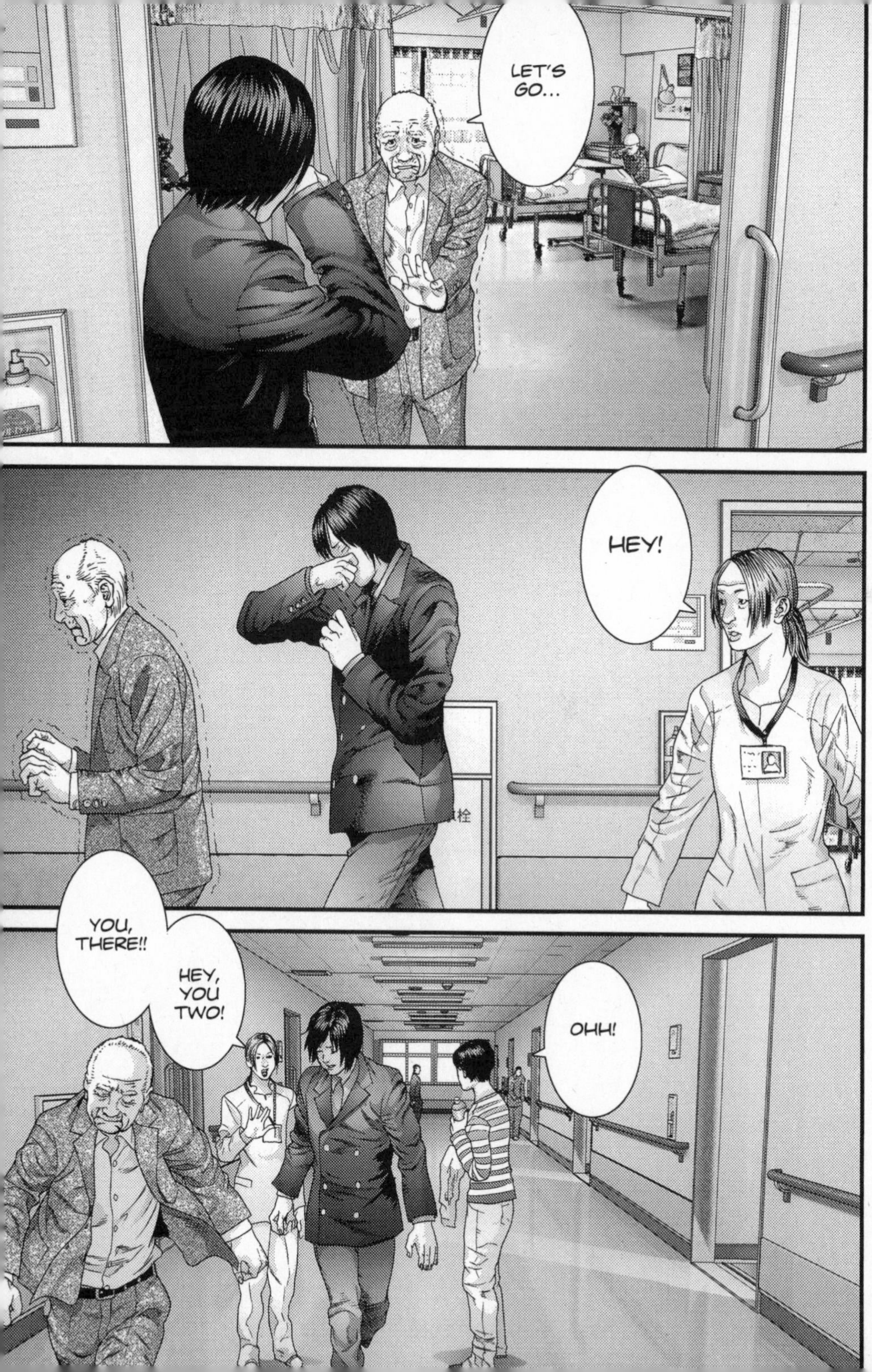
LET'S GO...
HEY!
YOU, THERE!!
HEY, YOU TWO!
OHH!

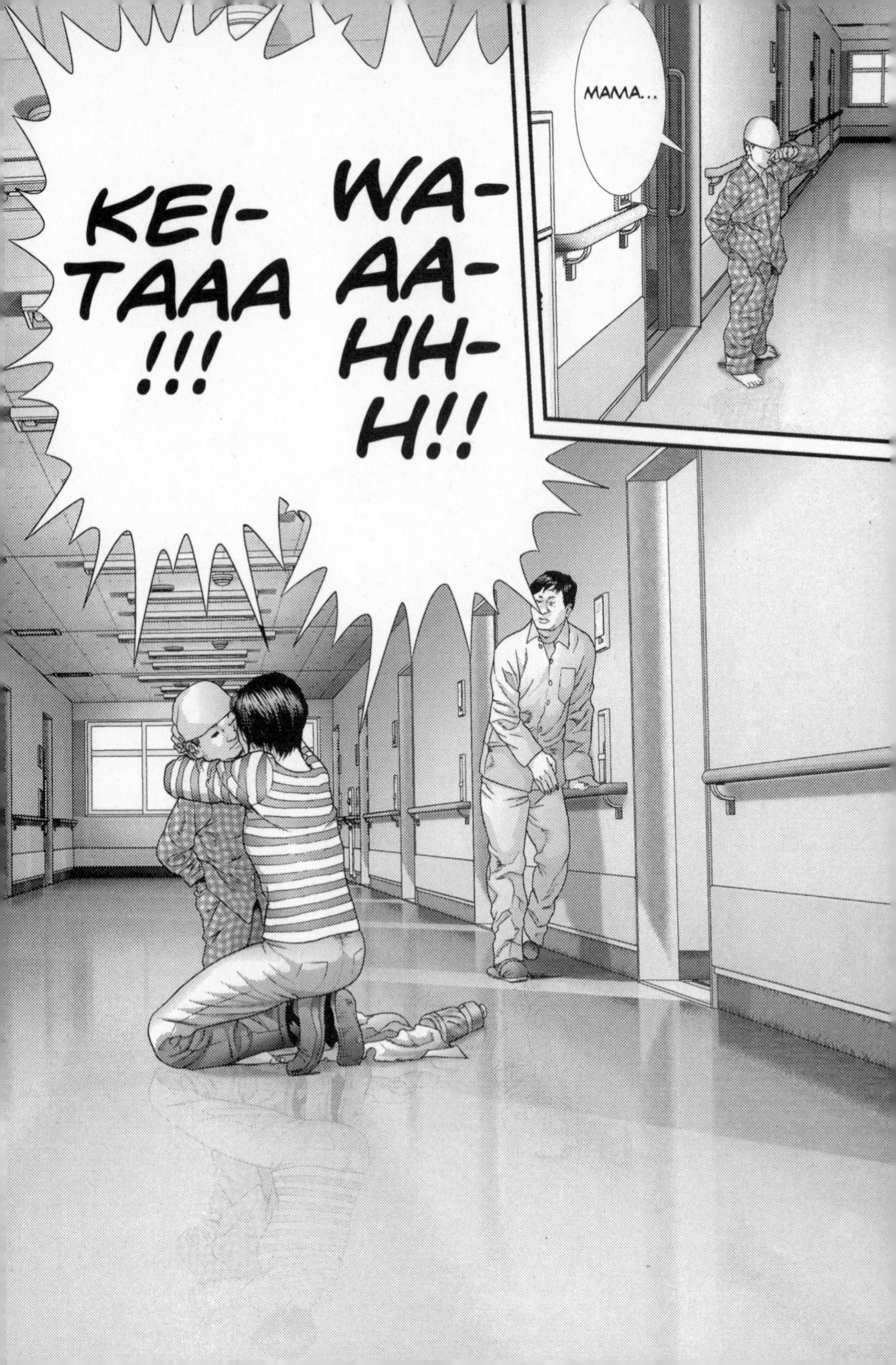
MAMA...
WA-AA-HH-H!!
KEI-TAAA!!!

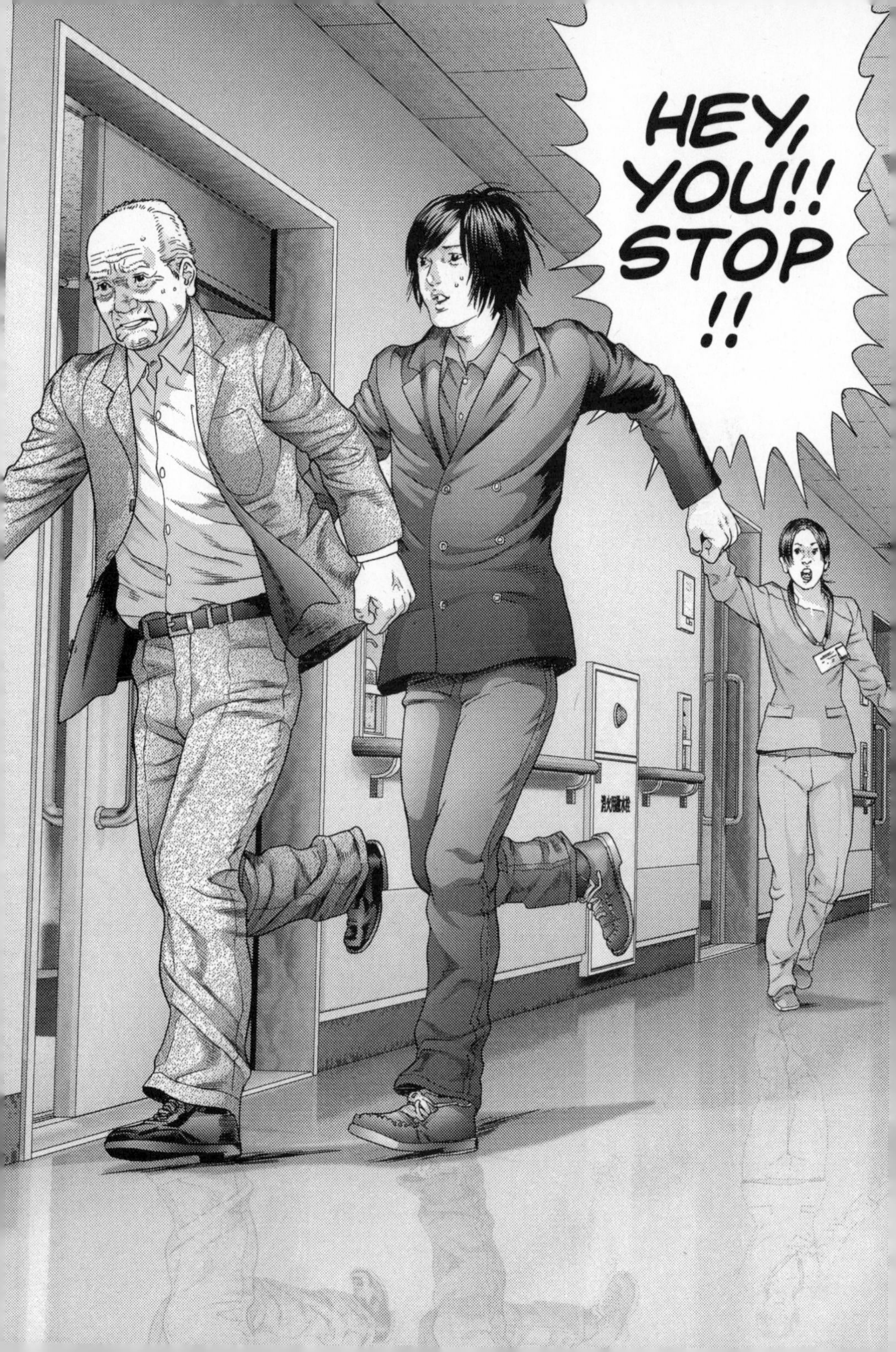
HEY, YOU!! STOP !!

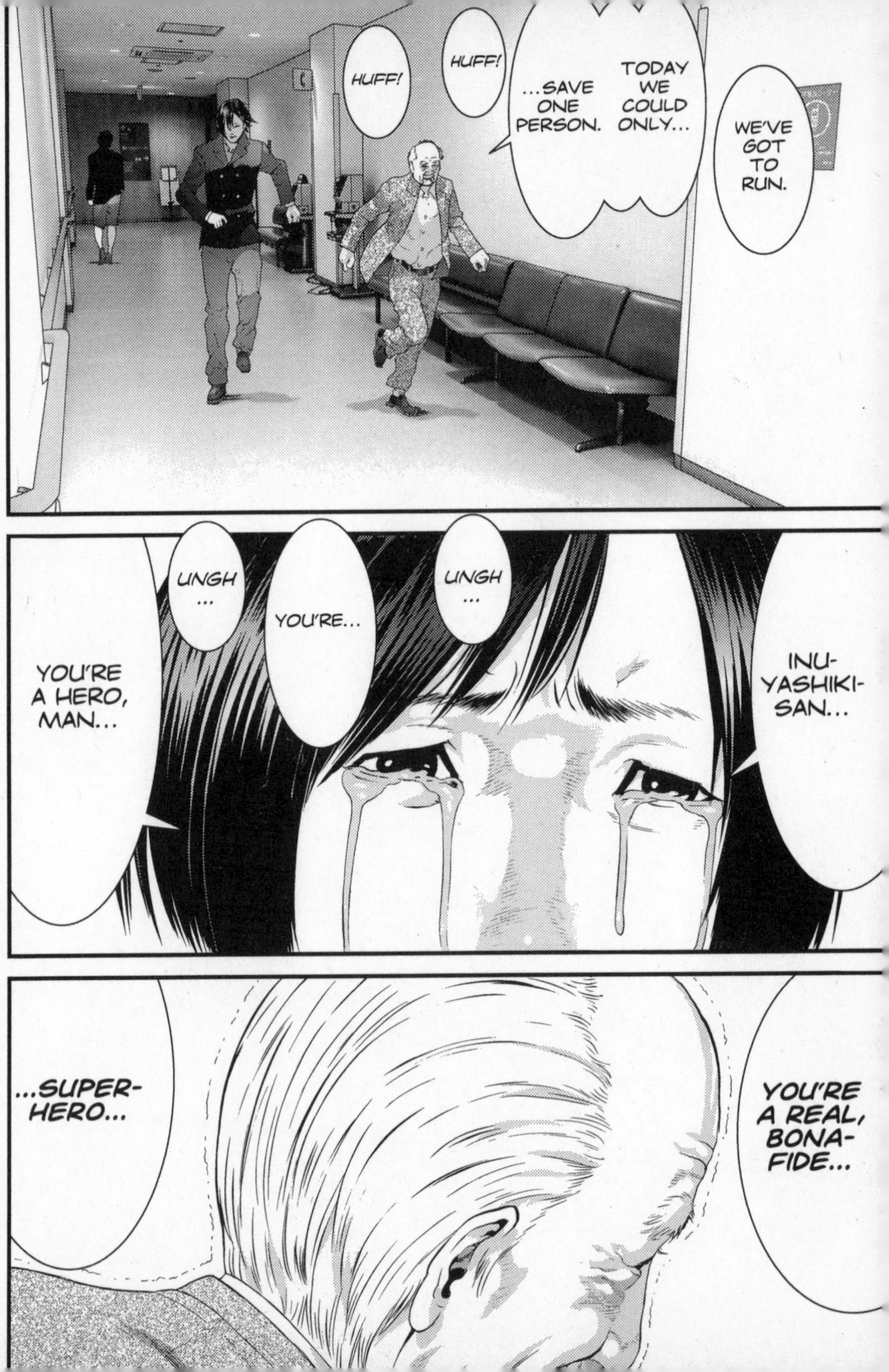
WE'VE GOT TO RUN.
TODAY WE COULD ONLY...
...SAVE ONE PERSON.
HUFF!
HUFF!
INU-YASHIKI-SAN...
UNGH...
YOU'RE...
UNGH...
YOU'RE A HERO, MAN...
YOU'RE A REAL, BONA-FIDE...
...SUPER-HERO...

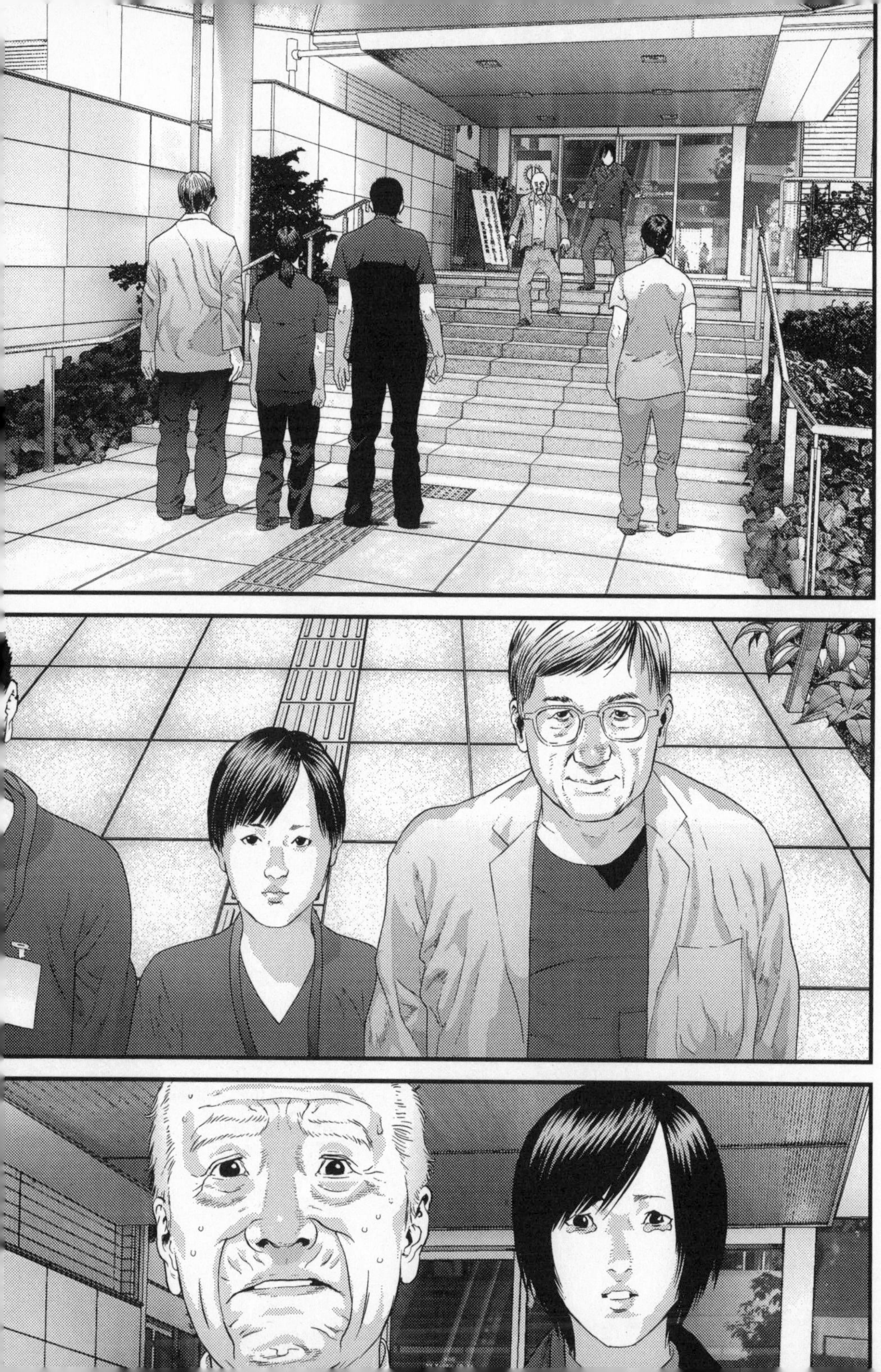

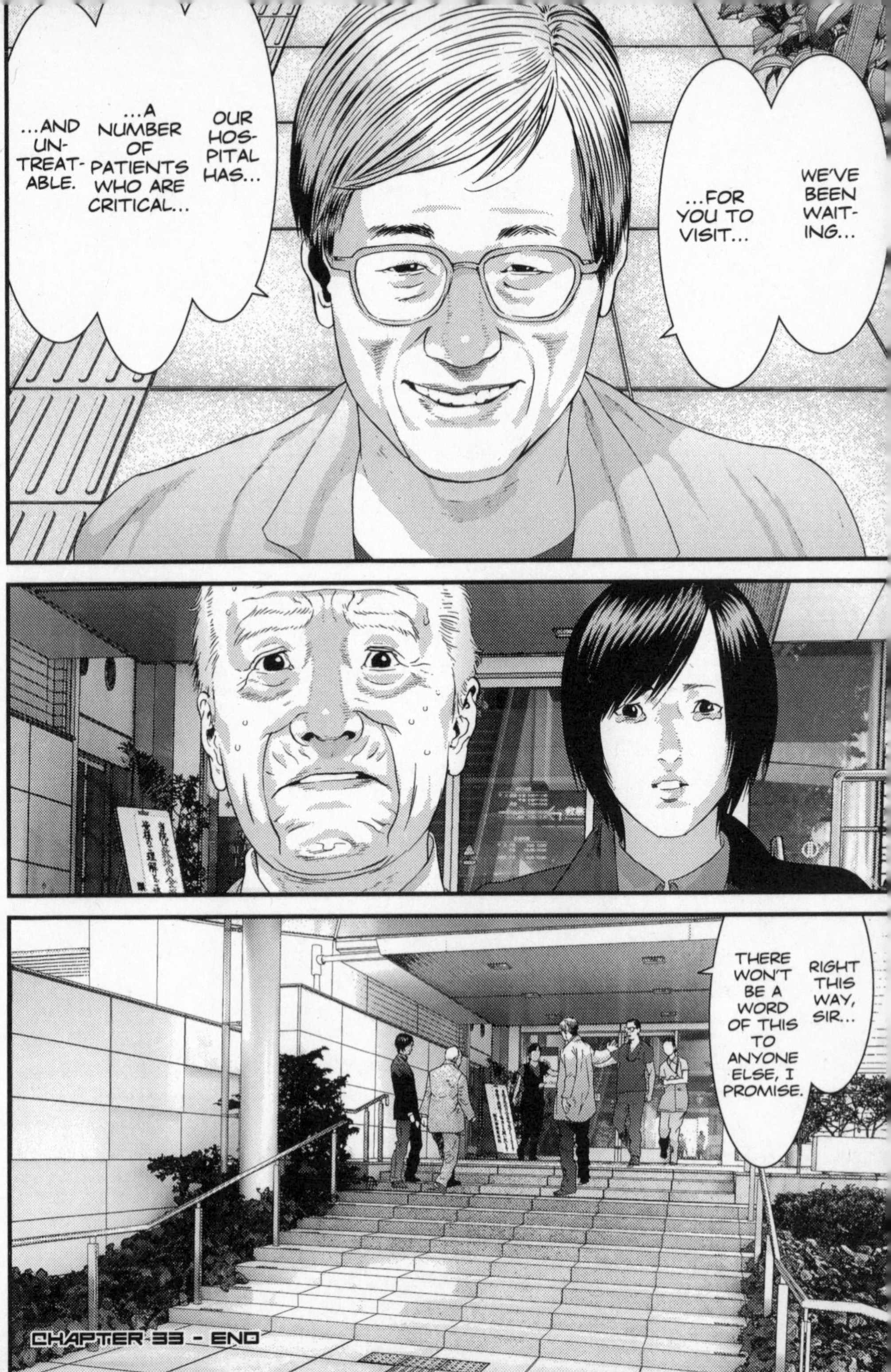
WE'VE BEEN WAIT- ING...
...FOR YOU TO VISIT...
OUR HOS- PITAL HAS...
...A NUMBER OF PATIENTS WHO ARE CRITICAL...
...AND UN- TREAT- ABLE.
RIGHT THIS WAY, SIR...
THERE WON'T BE A WORD OF THIS TO ANYONE ELSE, I PROMISE.
CHAPTER 33 - END

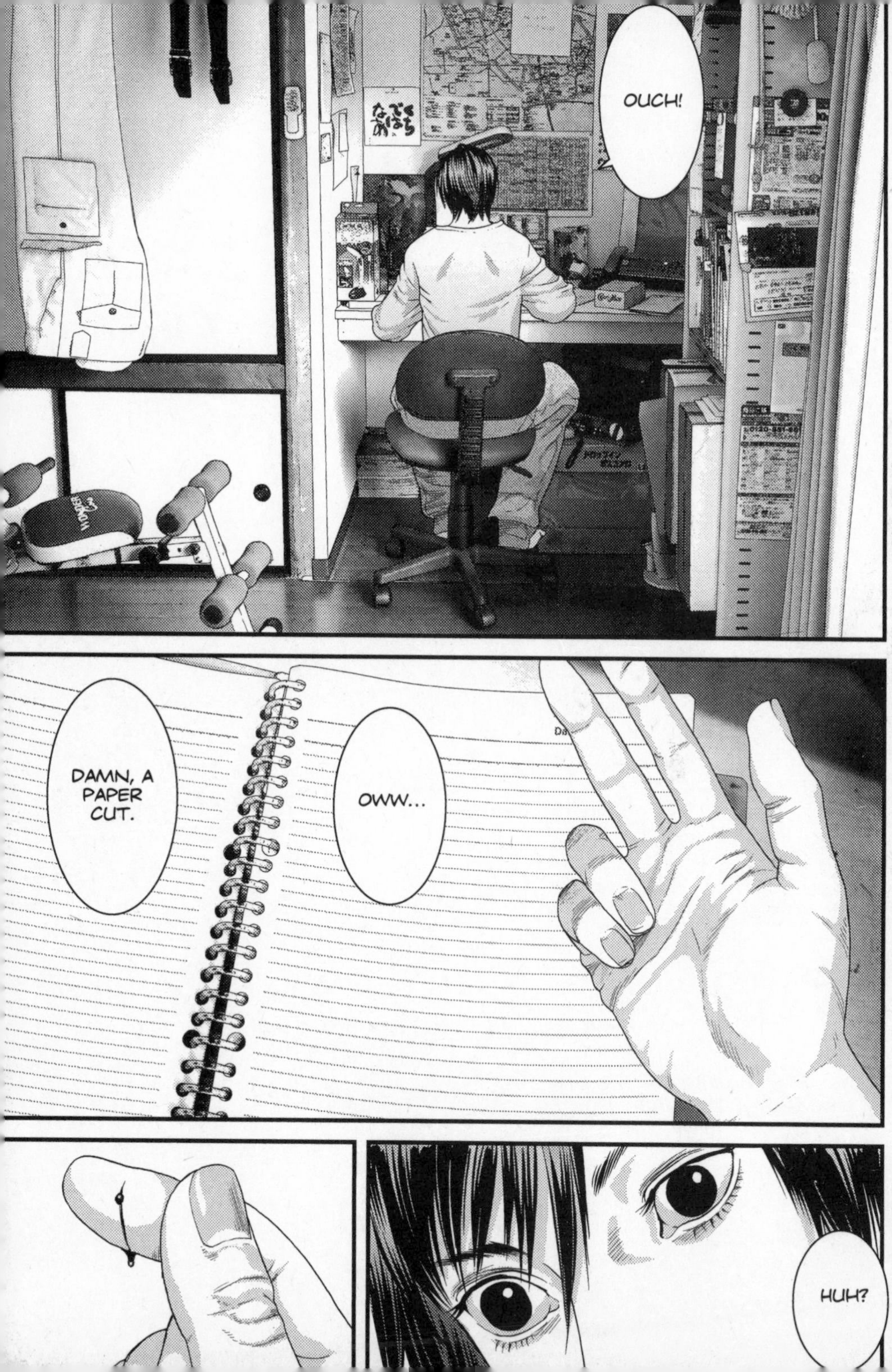
OUCH!
OWW...
DAMN, A PAPER CUT.
HUH?

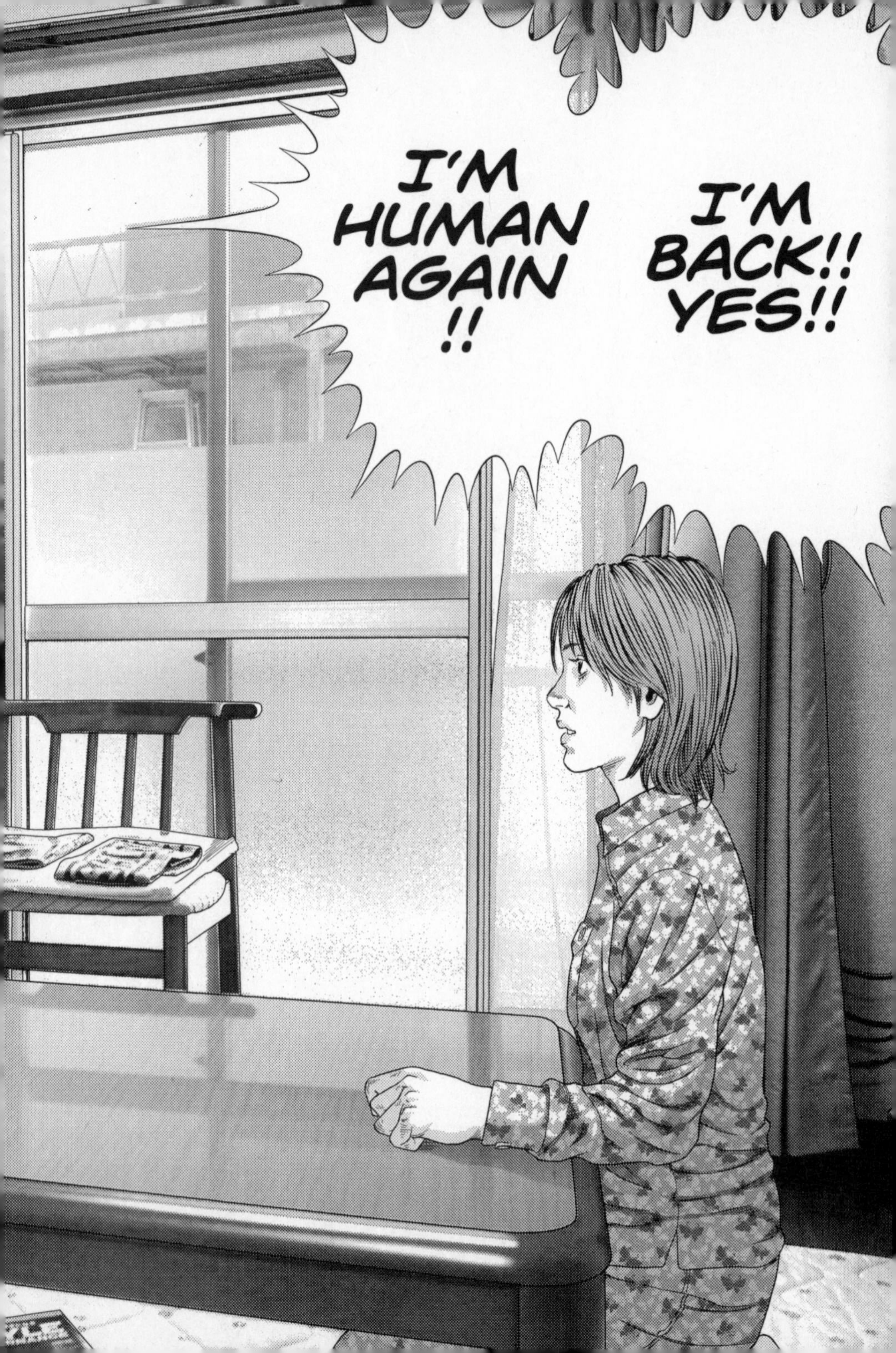
I'M BACK!! YES!!
I'M HUMAN AGAIN !!

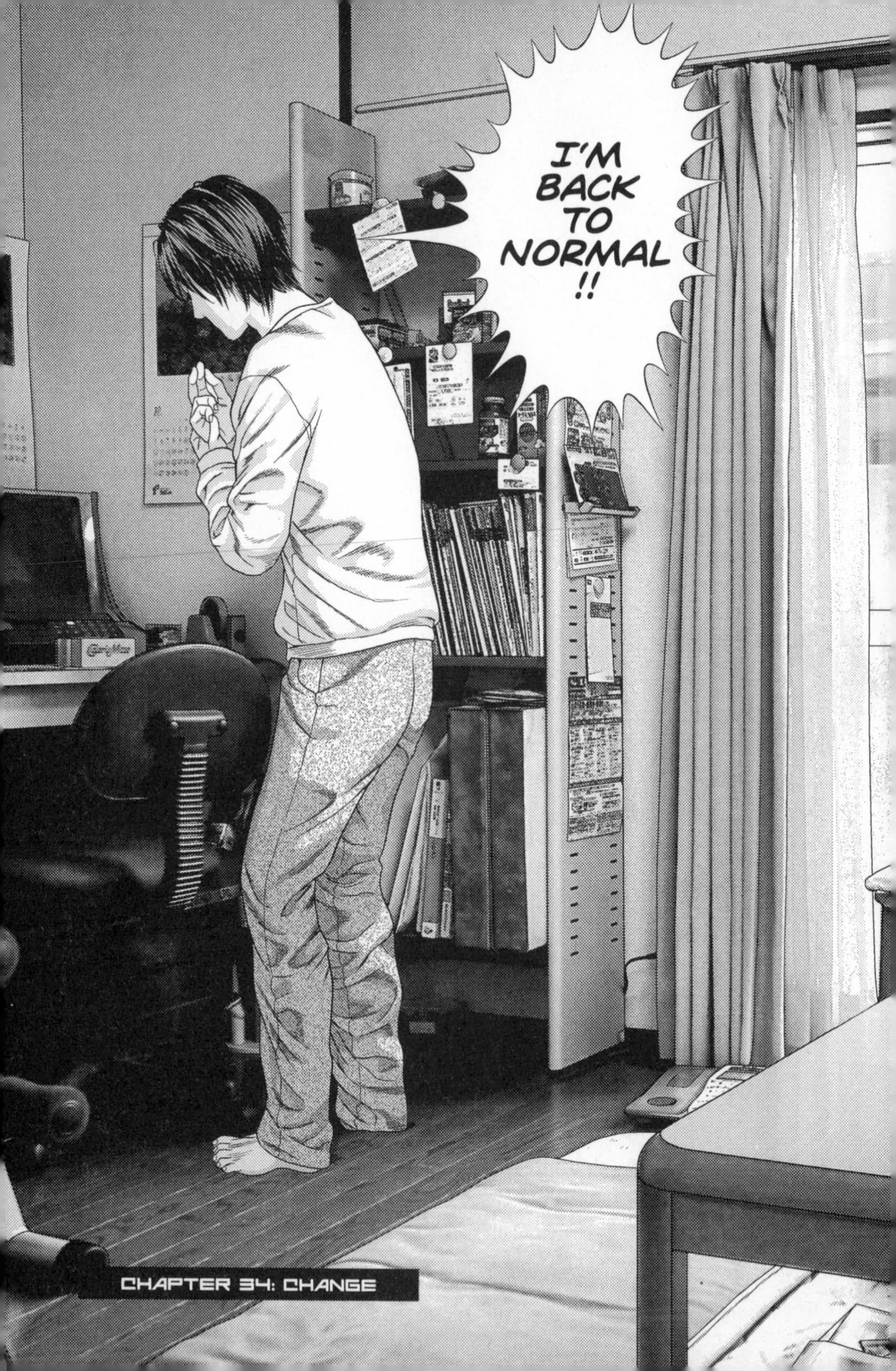
I'M BACK TO NORMAL !!
CHAPTER 34: CHANGE

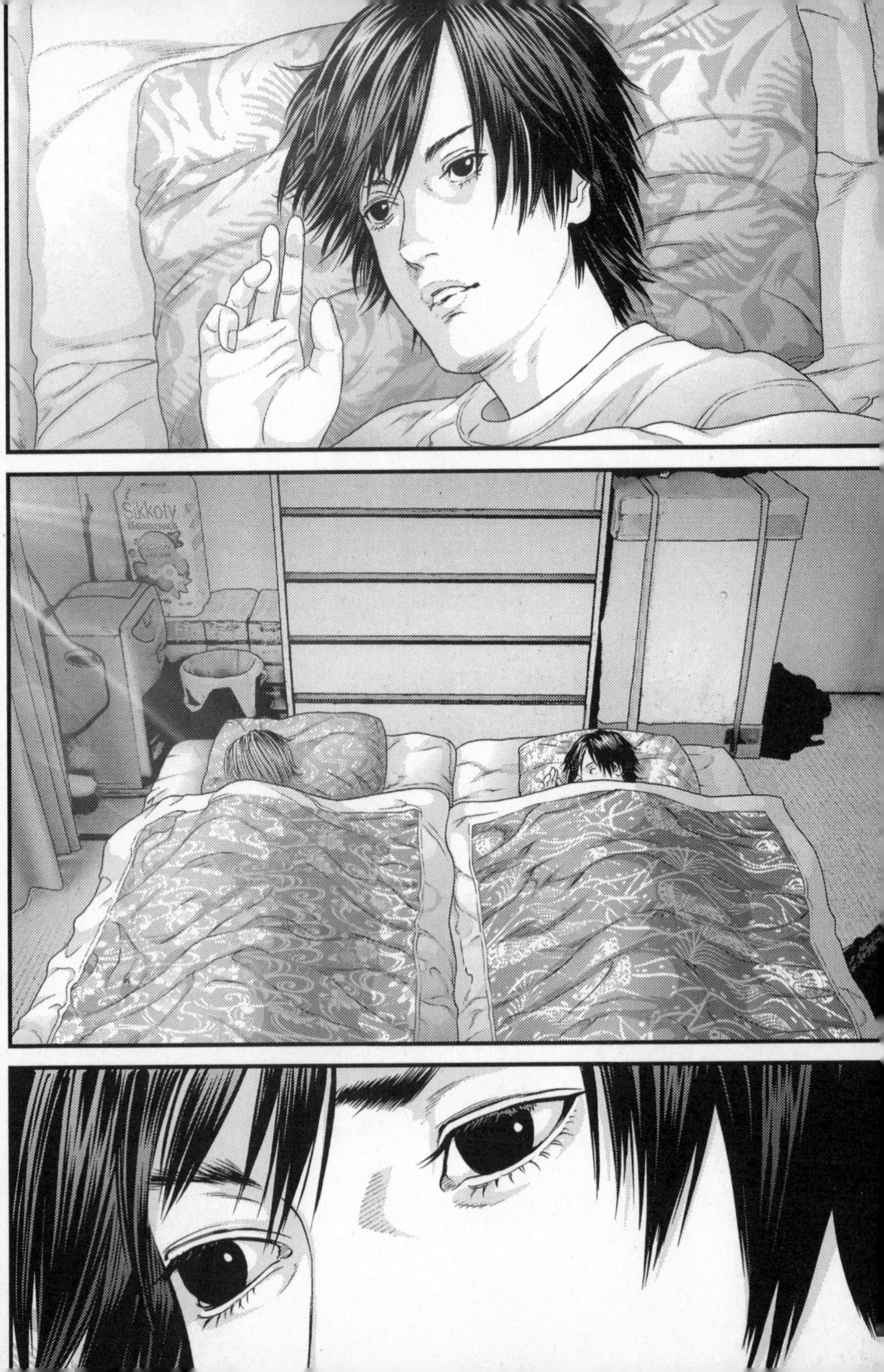

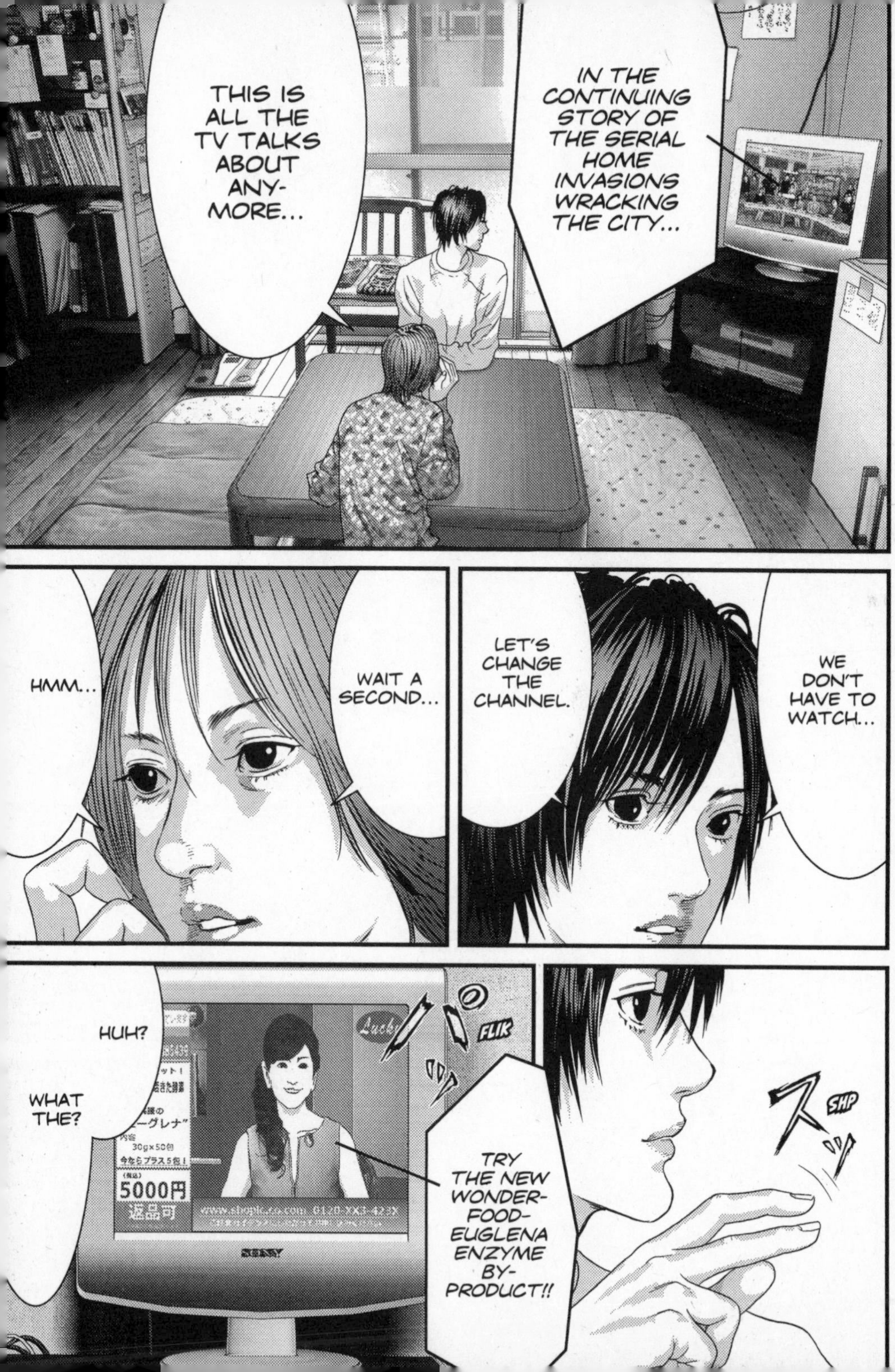
IN THE CONTINUING STORY OF THE SERIAL HOME INVASIONS WRACKING THE CITY...
THIS IS ALL THE TV TALKS ABOUT ANY-MORE...
WE DON'T HAVE TO WATCH...
LET'S CHANGE THE CHANNEL.
WAIT A SECOND...
HMM...
SHP
TRY THE NEW WONDER-FOOD-EUGLENA ENZYME BY-PRODUCT!!
FLIK
30gx50包
今ならプラス5包！
5000円
返品可
HUH?
WHAT THE?

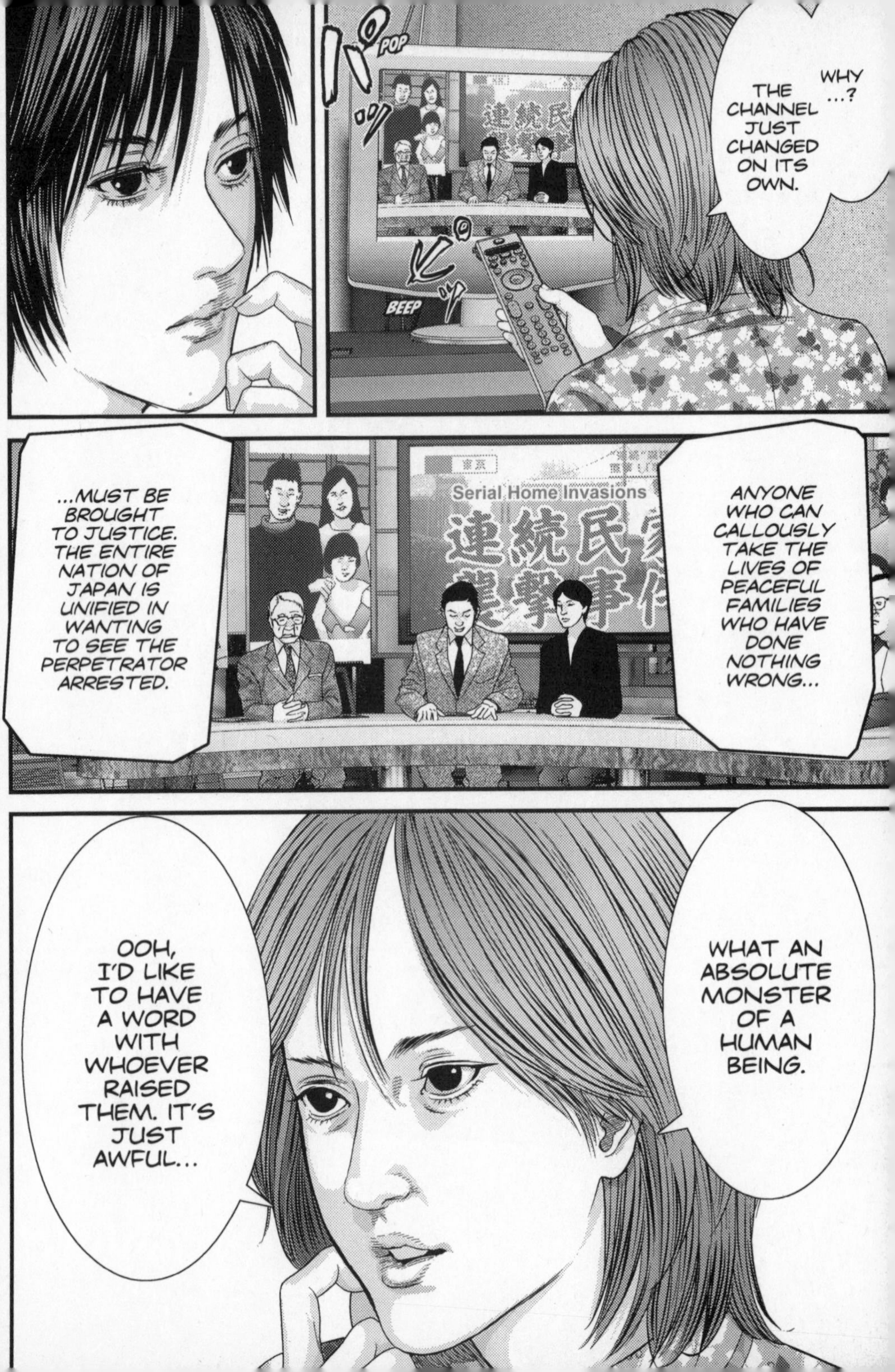
WHY ...?
THE CHANNEL JUST CHANGED ON ITS OWN.
POP
BEEP
ANYONE WHO CAN CALLOUSLY TAKE THE LIVES OF PEACEFUL FAMILIES WHO HAVE DONE NOTHING WRONG...
Serial Home Invasions
...MUST BE BROUGHT TO JUSTICE. THE ENTIRE NATION OF JAPAN IS UNIFIED IN WANTING TO SEE THE PERPETRATOR ARRESTED.
WHAT AN ABSOLUTE MONSTER OF A HUMAN BEING.
OOH, I'D LIKE TO HAVE A WORD WITH WHOEVER RAISED THEM. IT'S JUST AWFUL...

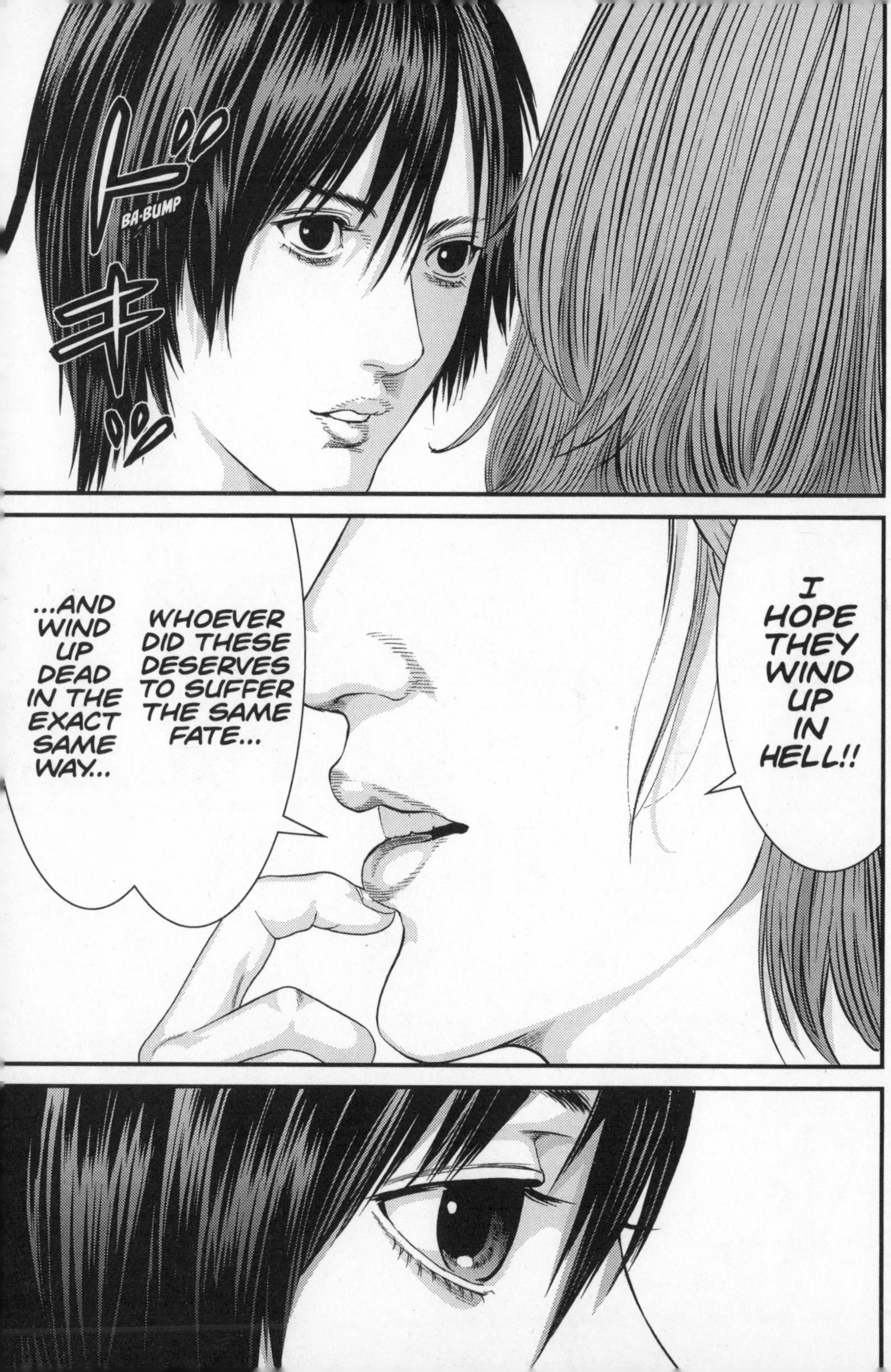
BA-BUMP
I HOPE THEY WIND UP IN HELL!!
WHOEVER DID THESE DESERVES TO SUFFER THE SAME FATE...
...AND WIND UP DEAD IN THE EXACT SAME WAY...

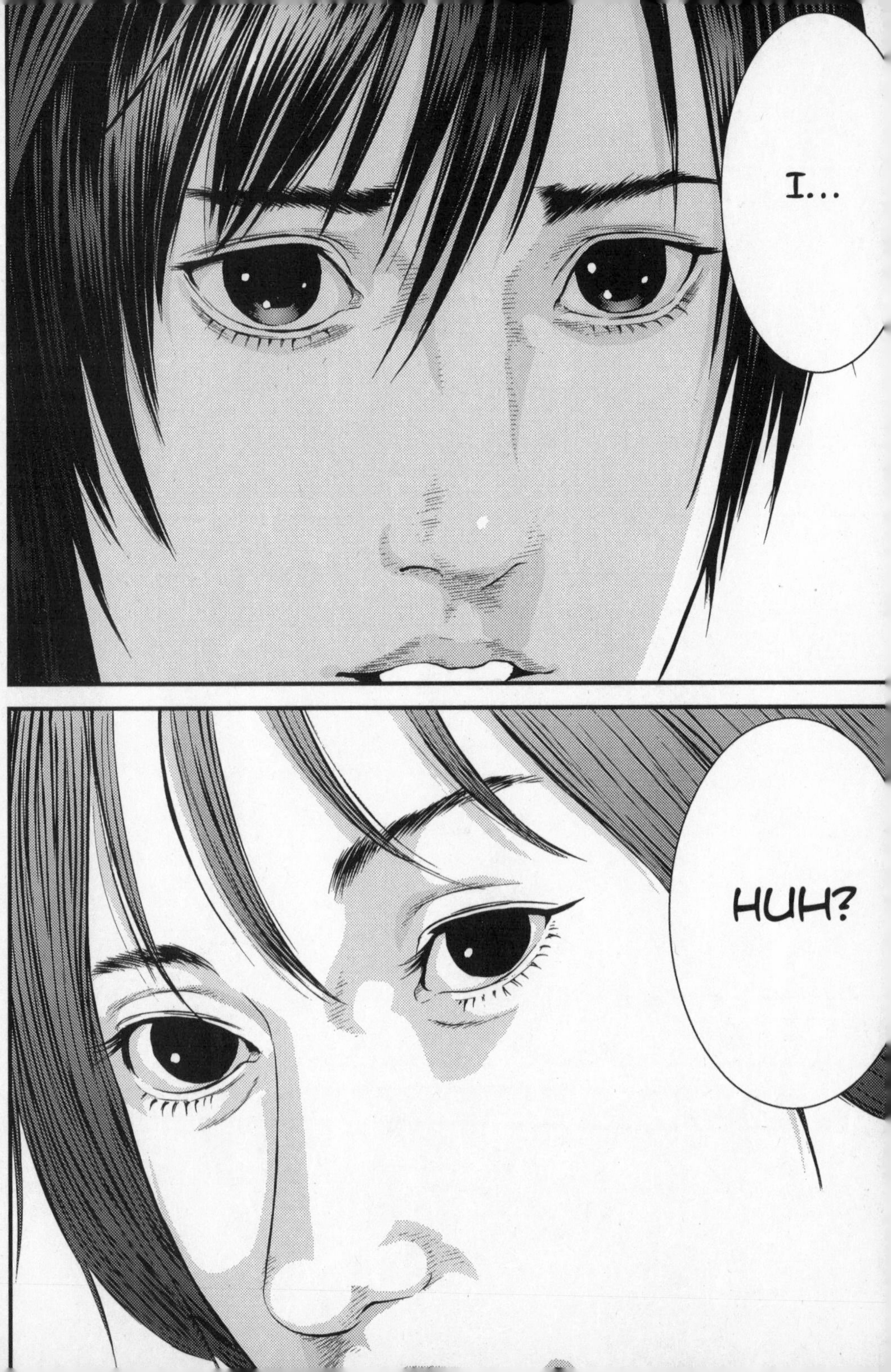
I...
HUH?

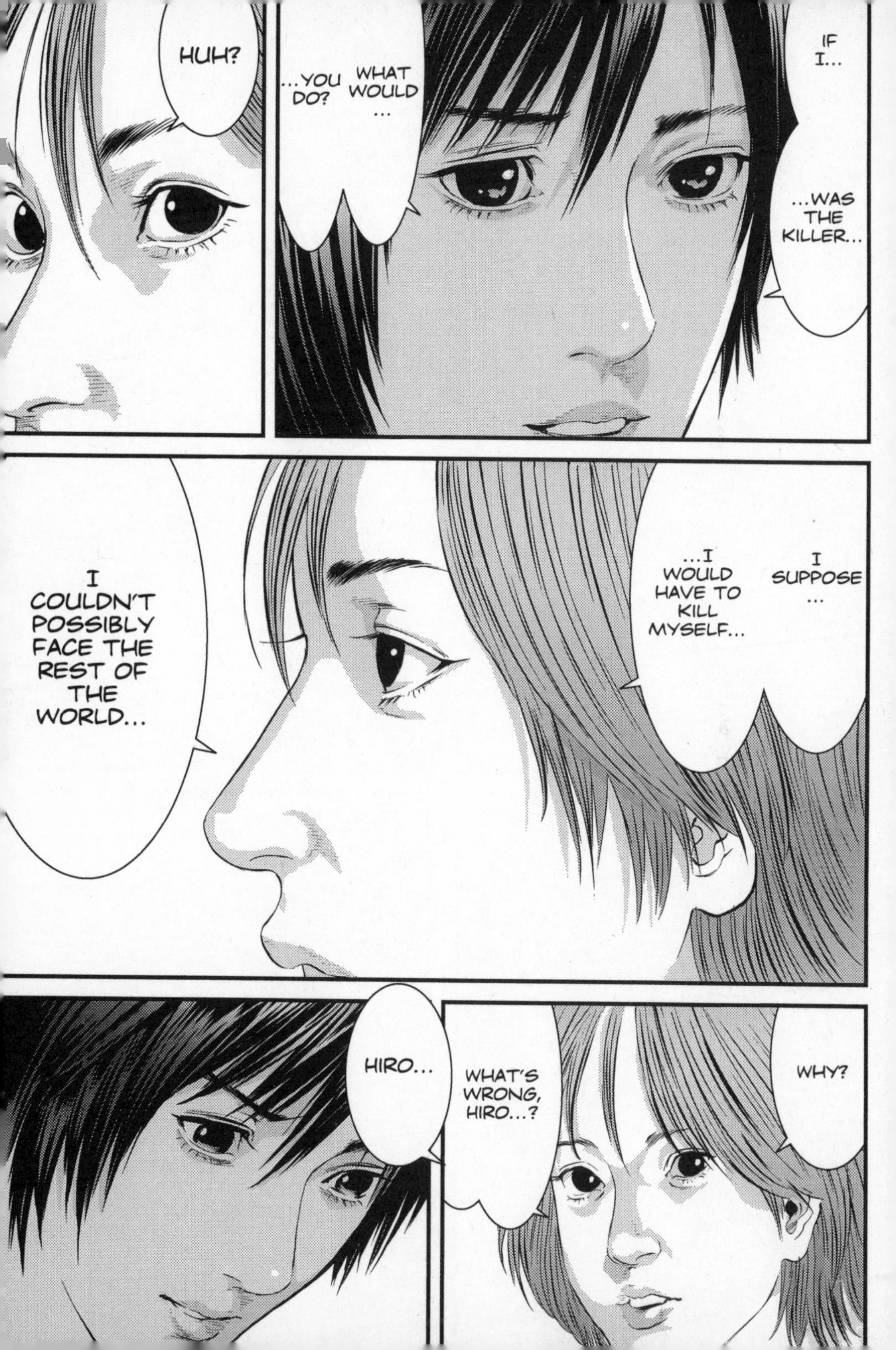
IF I...
...WAS THE KILLER...
WHAT WOULD ...
...YOU DO?
HUH?
I SUPPOSE ...
...I WOULD HAVE TO KILL MYSELF...
I COULDN'T POSSIBLY FACE THE REST OF THE WORLD...
WHY?
WHAT'S WRONG, HIRO...?
HIRO...

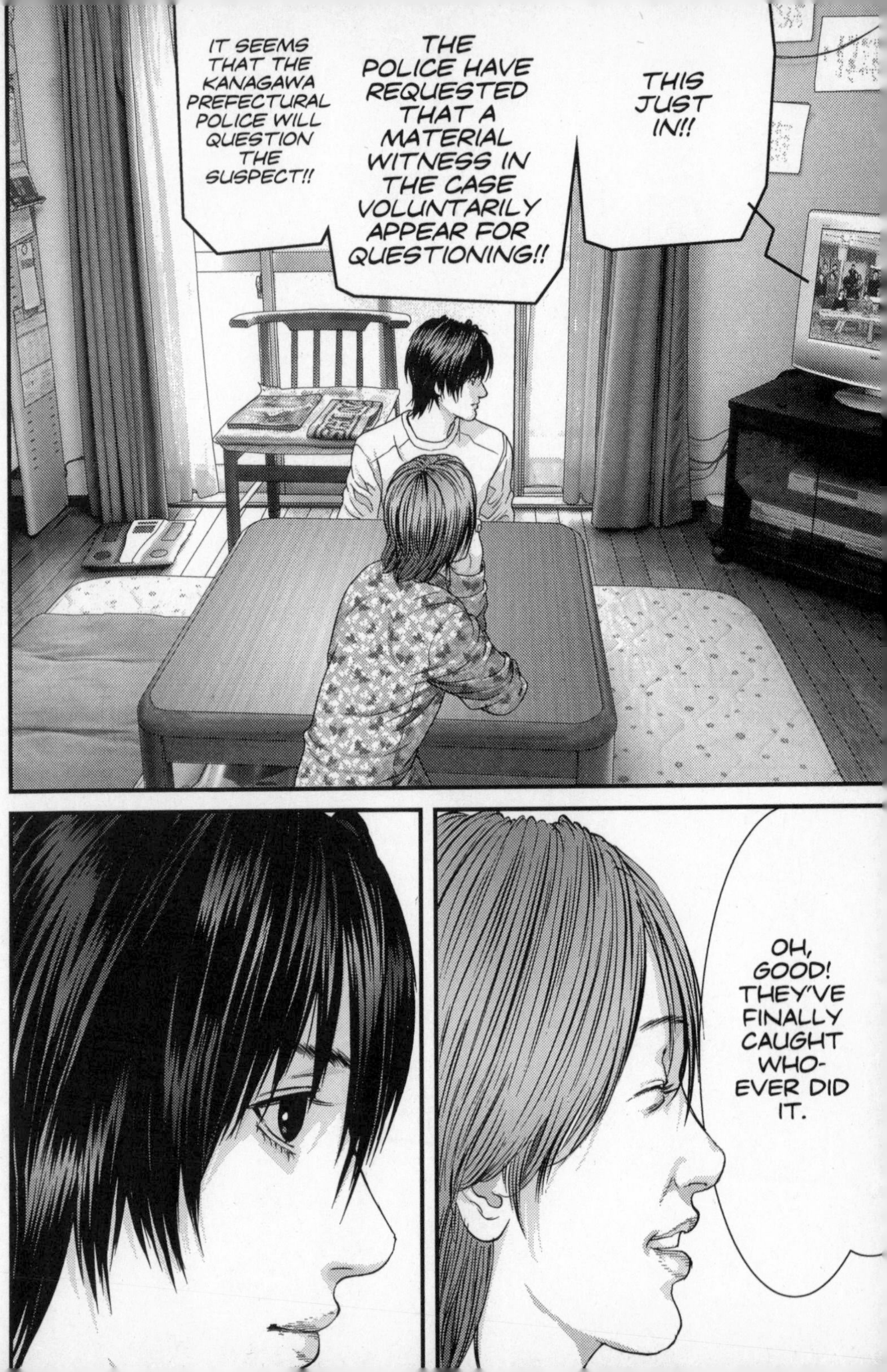
THIS JUST IN!!
THE POLICE HAVE REQUESTED THAT A MATERIAL WITNESS IN THE CASE VOLUNTARILY APPEAR FOR QUESTIONING!!
IT SEEMS THAT THE KANAGAWA PREFECTURAL POLICE WILL QUESTION THE SUSPECT!!
OH, GOOD! THEY'VE FINALLY CAUGHT WHO-EVER DID IT.

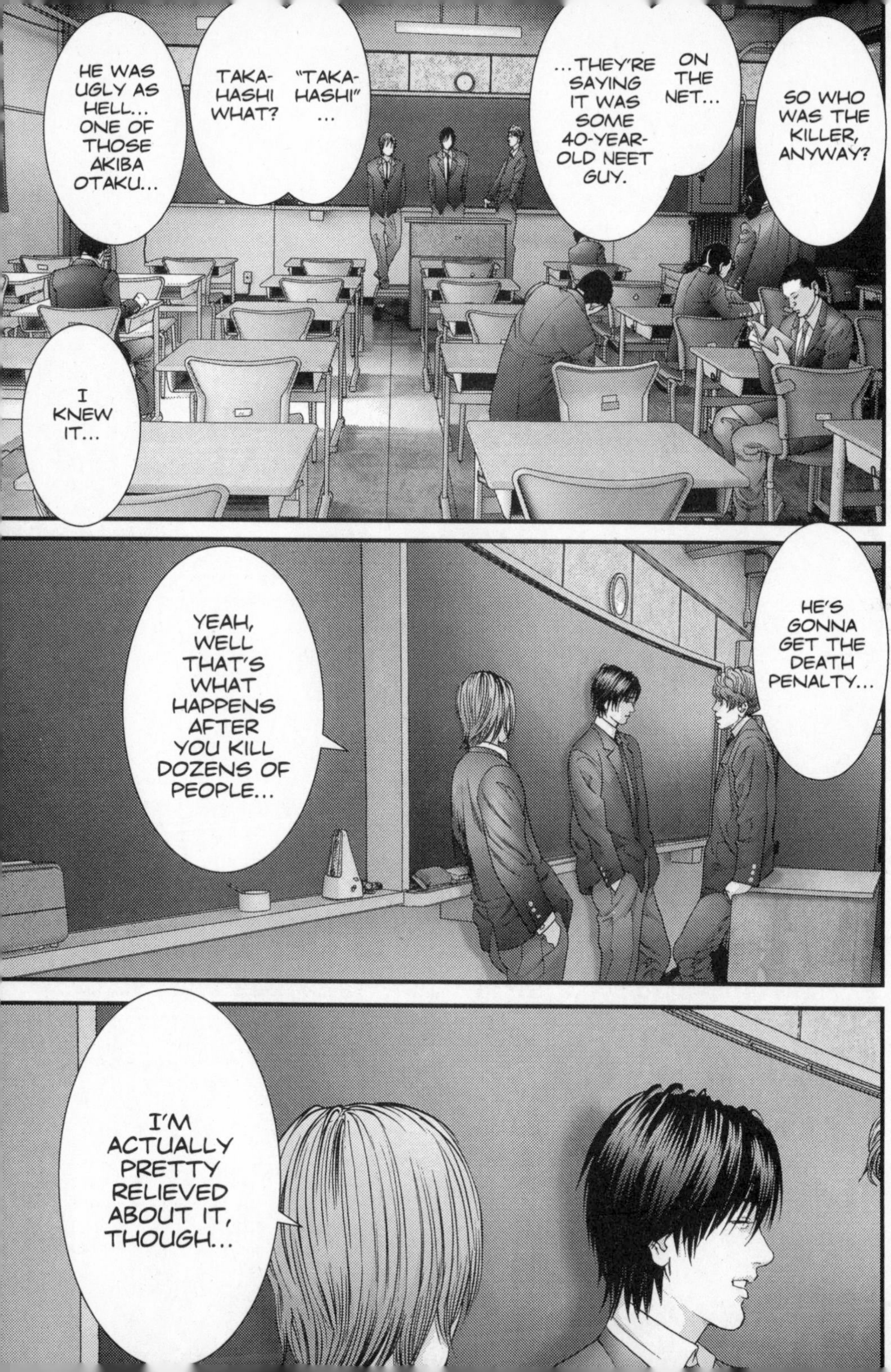
SO WHO WAS THE KILLER, ANYWAY?
ON THE NET...
...THEY'RE SAYING IT WAS SOME 40-YEAR-OLD NEET GUY.
"TAKAHASHI"...
TAKAHASHI WHAT?
HE WAS UGLY AS HELL... ONE OF THOSE AKIBA OTAKU...
I KNEW IT...
HE'S GONNA GET THE DEATH PENALTY...
YEAH, WELL THAT'S WHAT HAPPENS AFTER YOU KILL DOZENS OF PEOPLE...
I'M ACTUALLY PRETTY RELIEVED ABOUT IT, THOUGH...

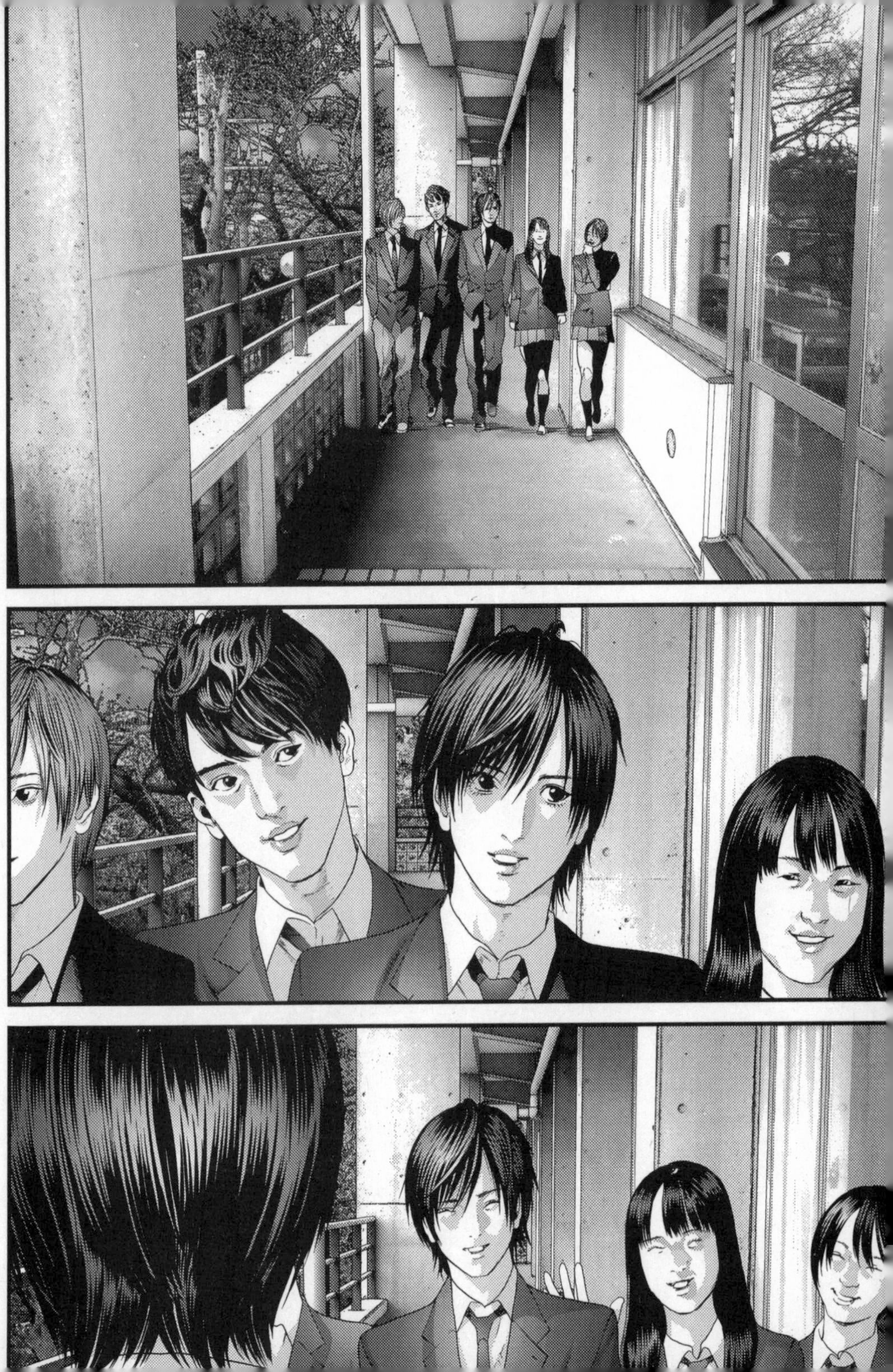

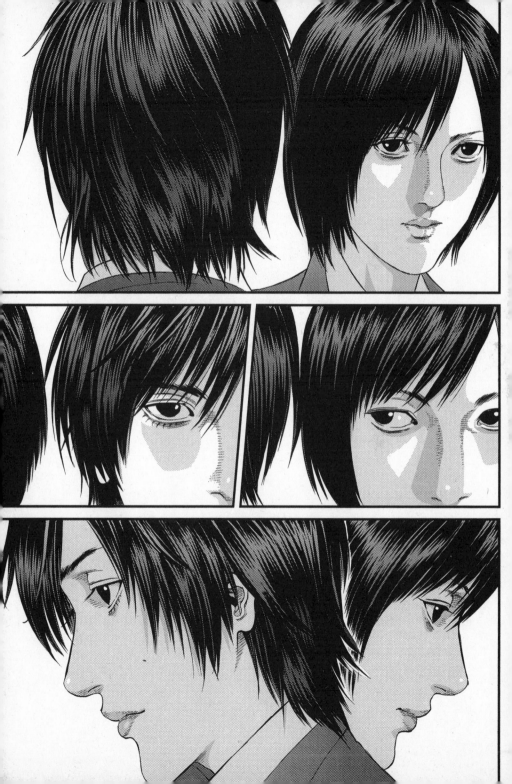

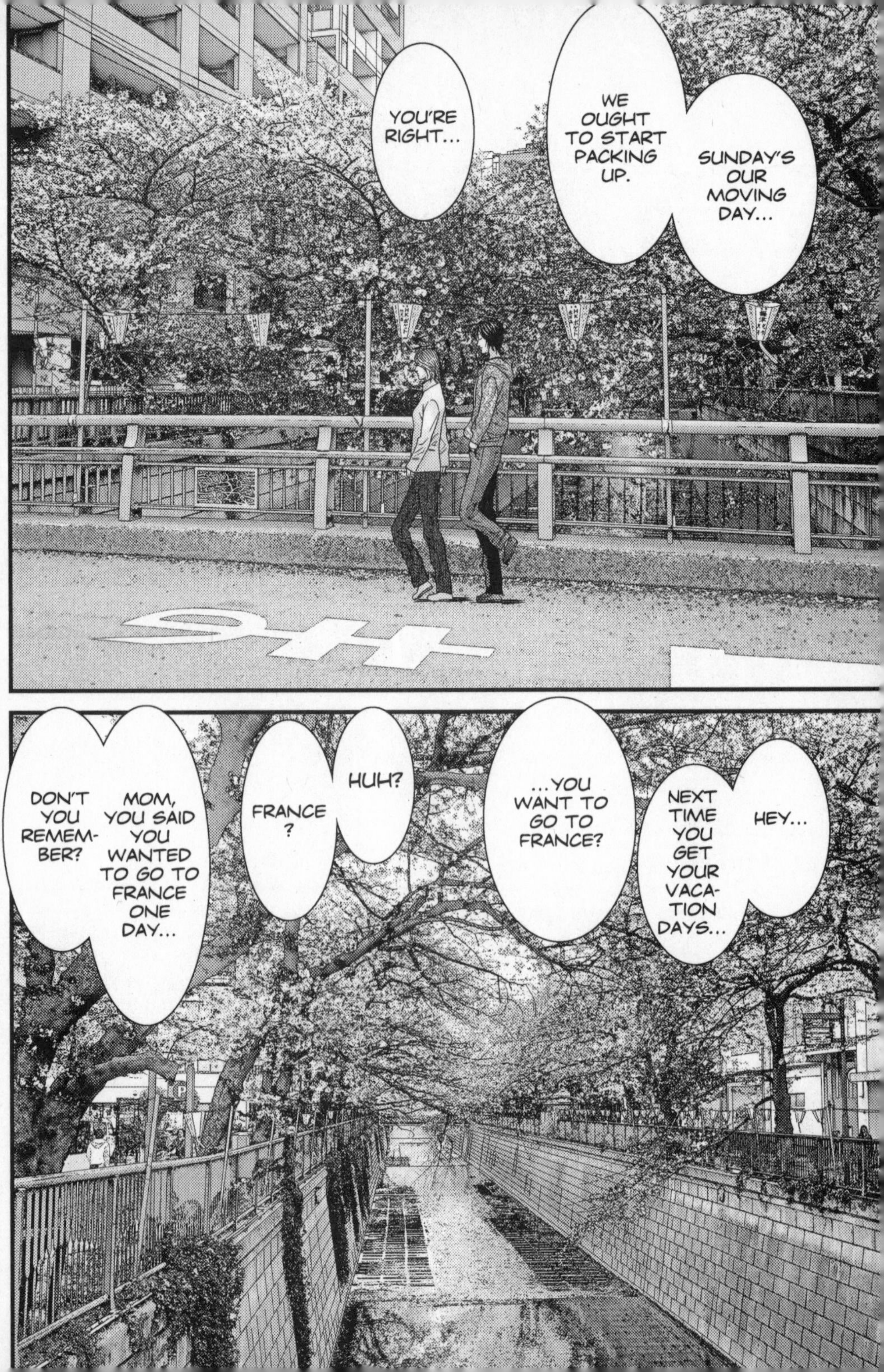
SUNDAY'S OUR MOVING DAY...
WE OUGHT TO START PACKING UP.
YOU'RE RIGHT...
HEY...
NEXT TIME YOU GET YOUR VACATION DAYS...
...YOU WANT TO GO TO FRANCE?
HUH?
FRANCE?
MOM, YOU SAID YOU WANTED TO GO TO FRANCE ONE DAY...
DON'T YOU REMEMBER?

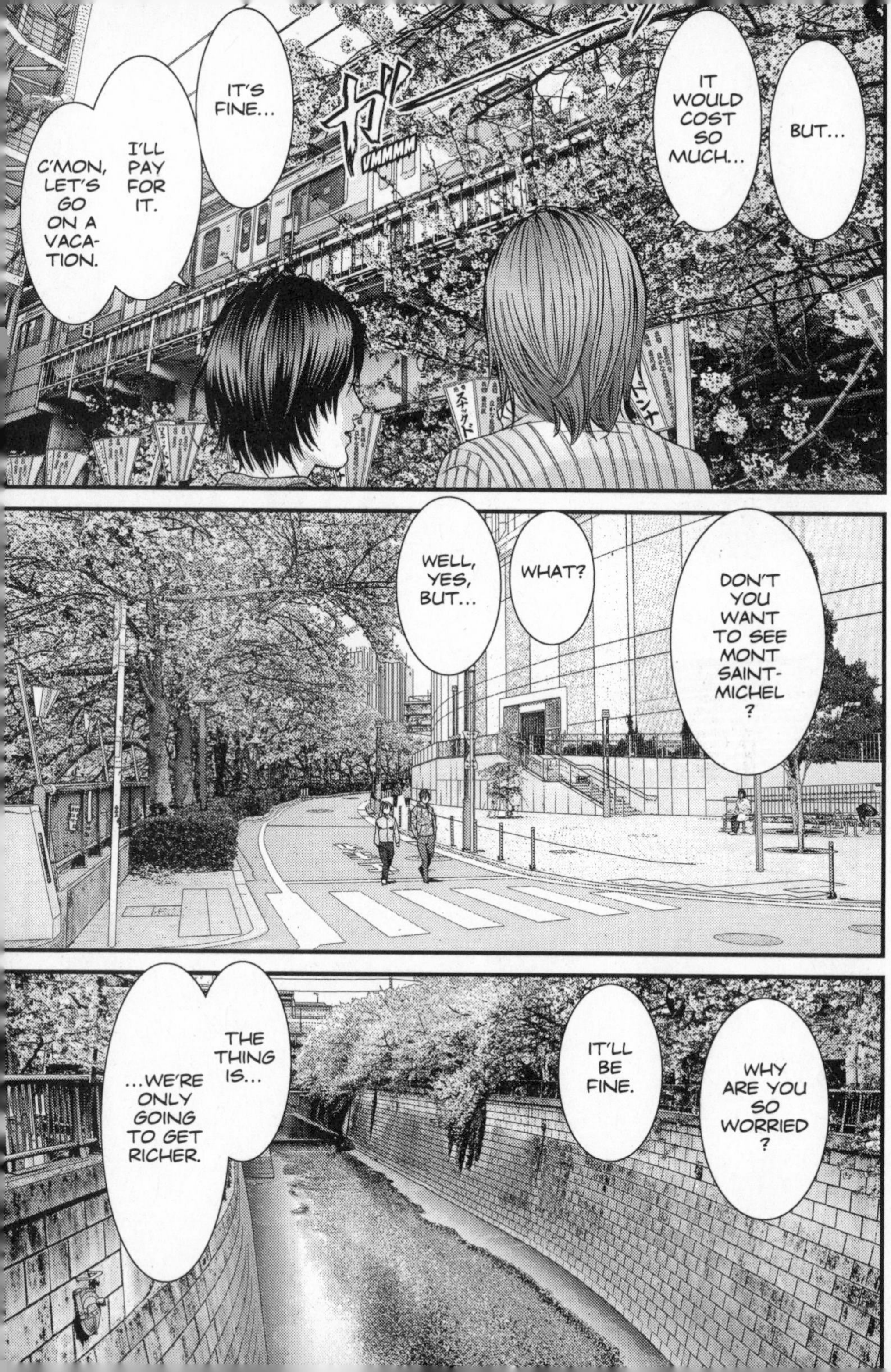
BUT…
IT WOULD COST SO MUCH…
VMMMM
IT'S FINE…
I'LL PAY FOR IT.
C'MON, LET'S GO ON A VACATION.
DON'T YOU WANT TO SEE MONT SAINT-MICHEL?
WHAT?
WELL, YES, BUT…
WHY ARE YOU SO WORRIED?
IT'LL BE FINE.
THE THING IS…
…WE'RE ONLY GOING TO GET RICHER.

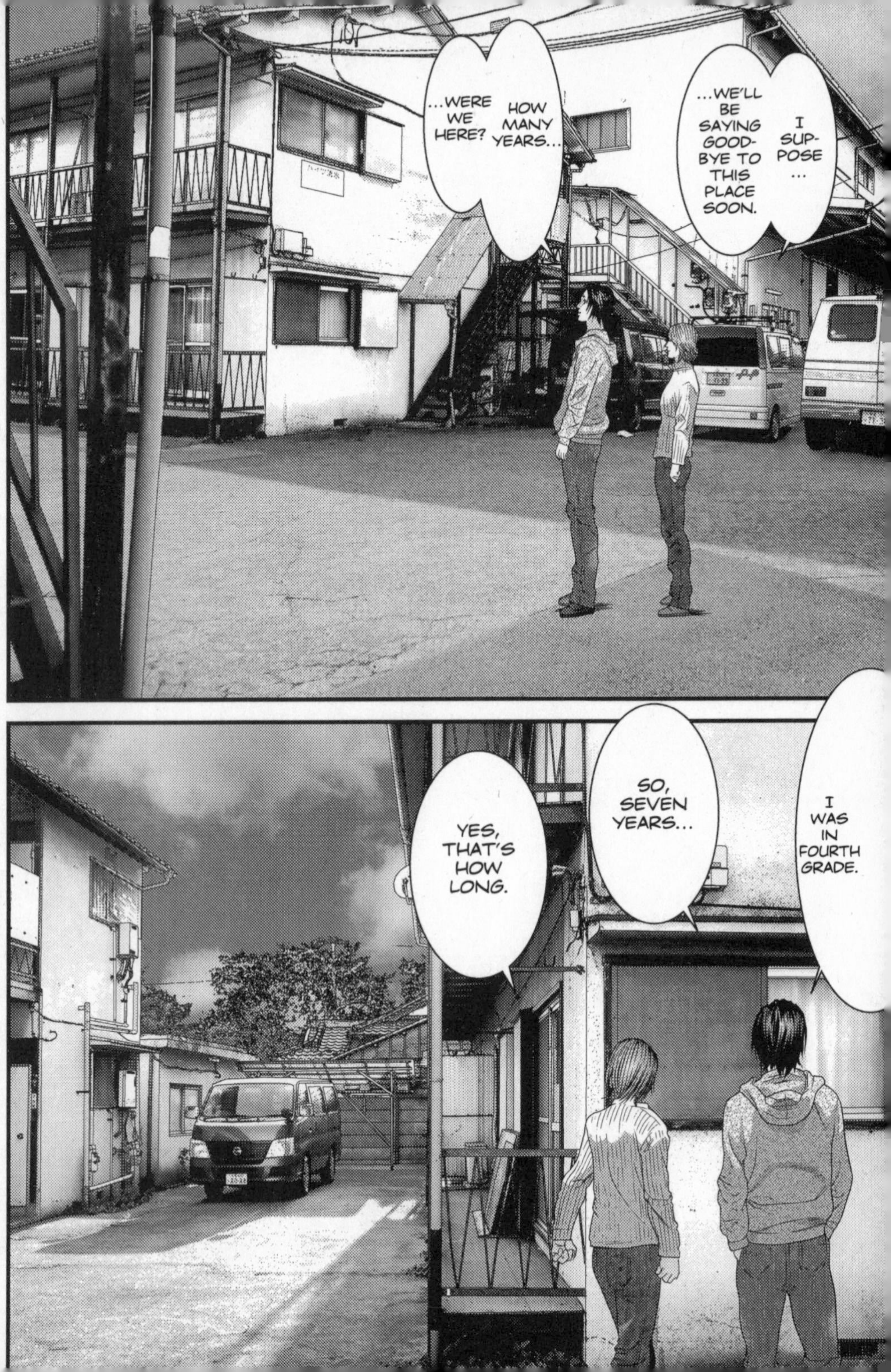
I SUP-POSE ...
...WE'LL BE SAYING GOOD-BYE TO THIS PLACE SOON.
HOW MANY YEARS...
...WERE WE HERE?
I WAS IN FOURTH GRADE.
SO, SEVEN YEARS...
YES, THAT'S HOW LONG.

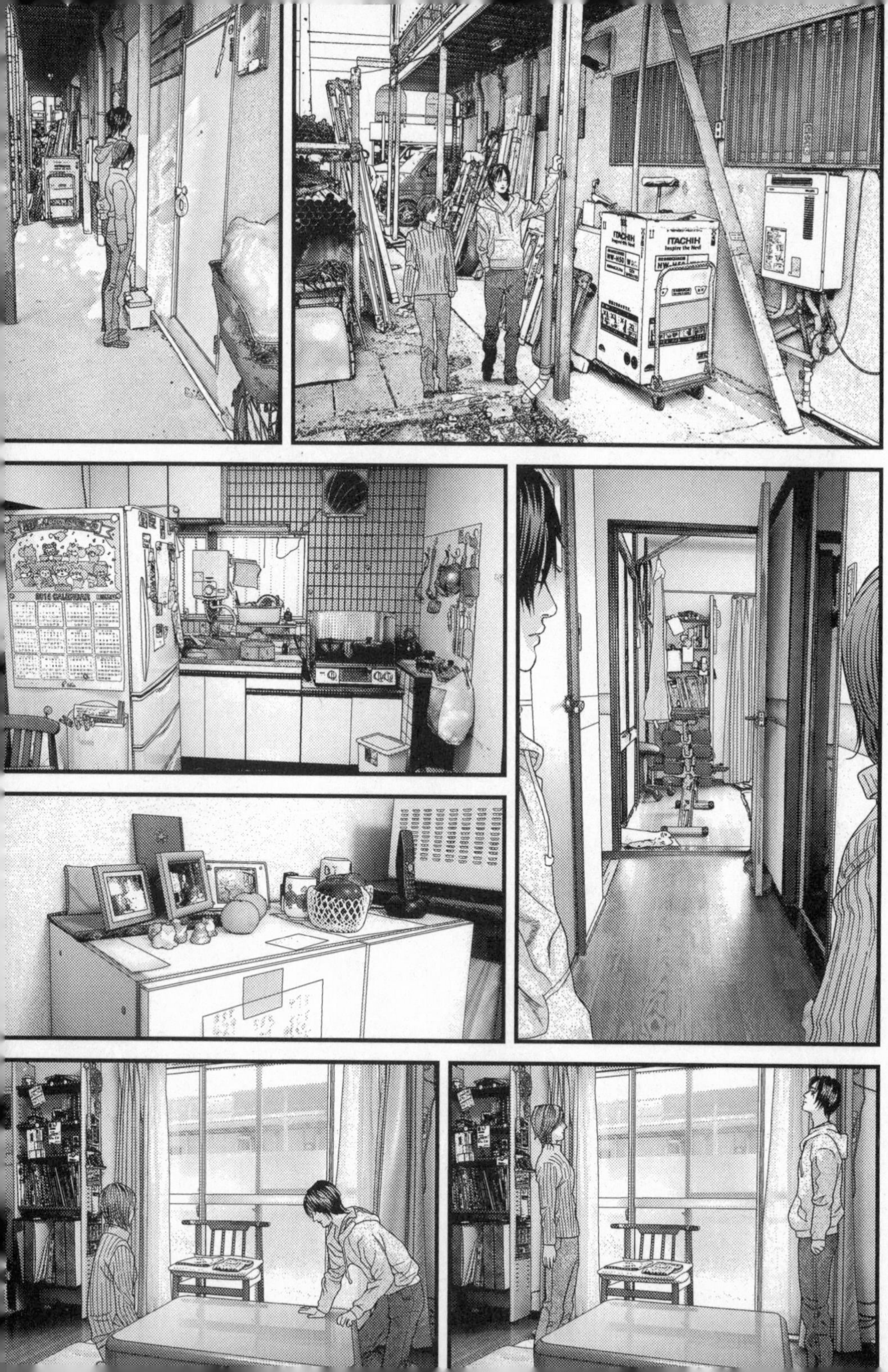
ITACHIH
Inspire the Next

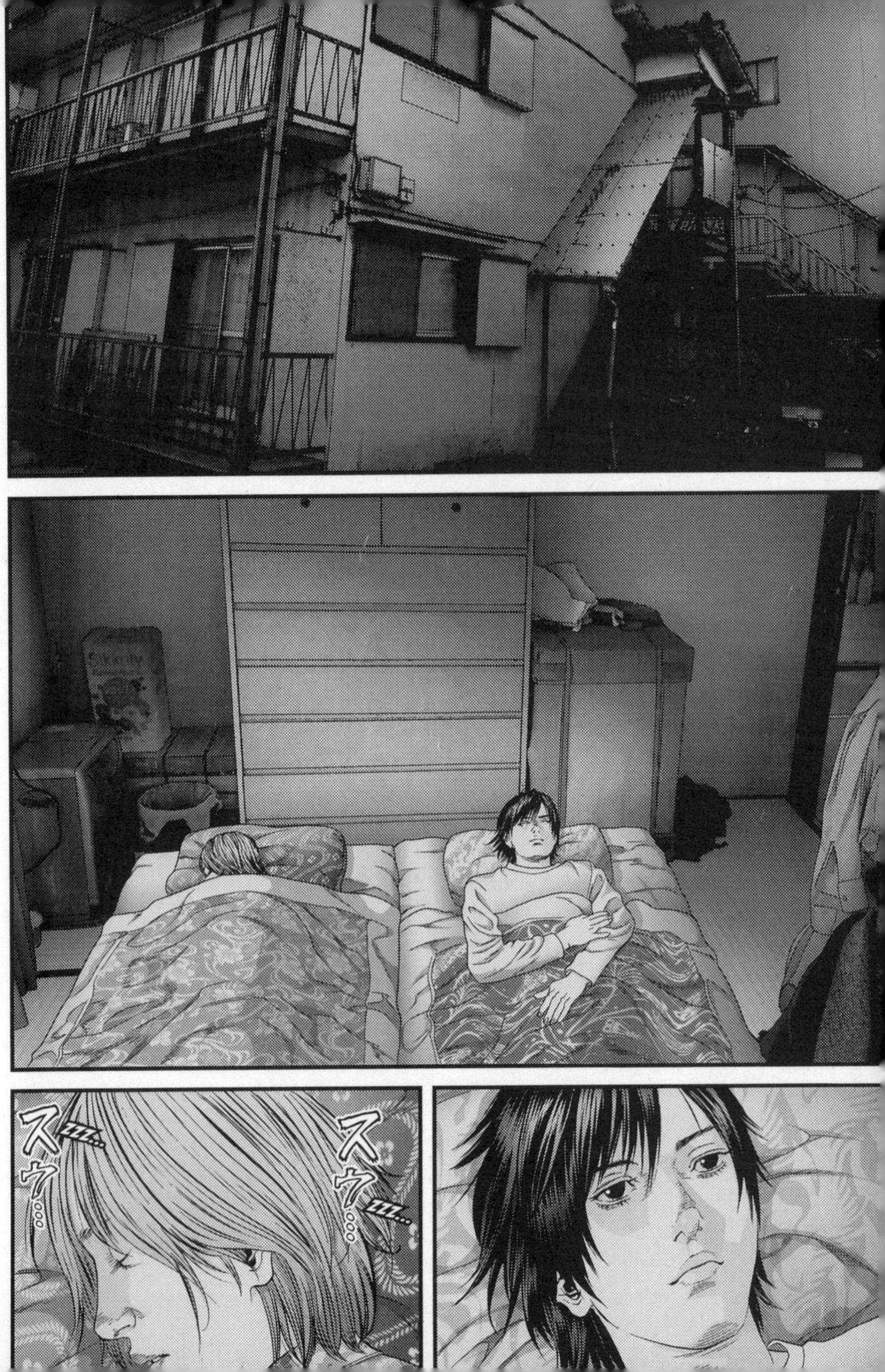
スゥ…
zzz…
スゥ…
zzz…

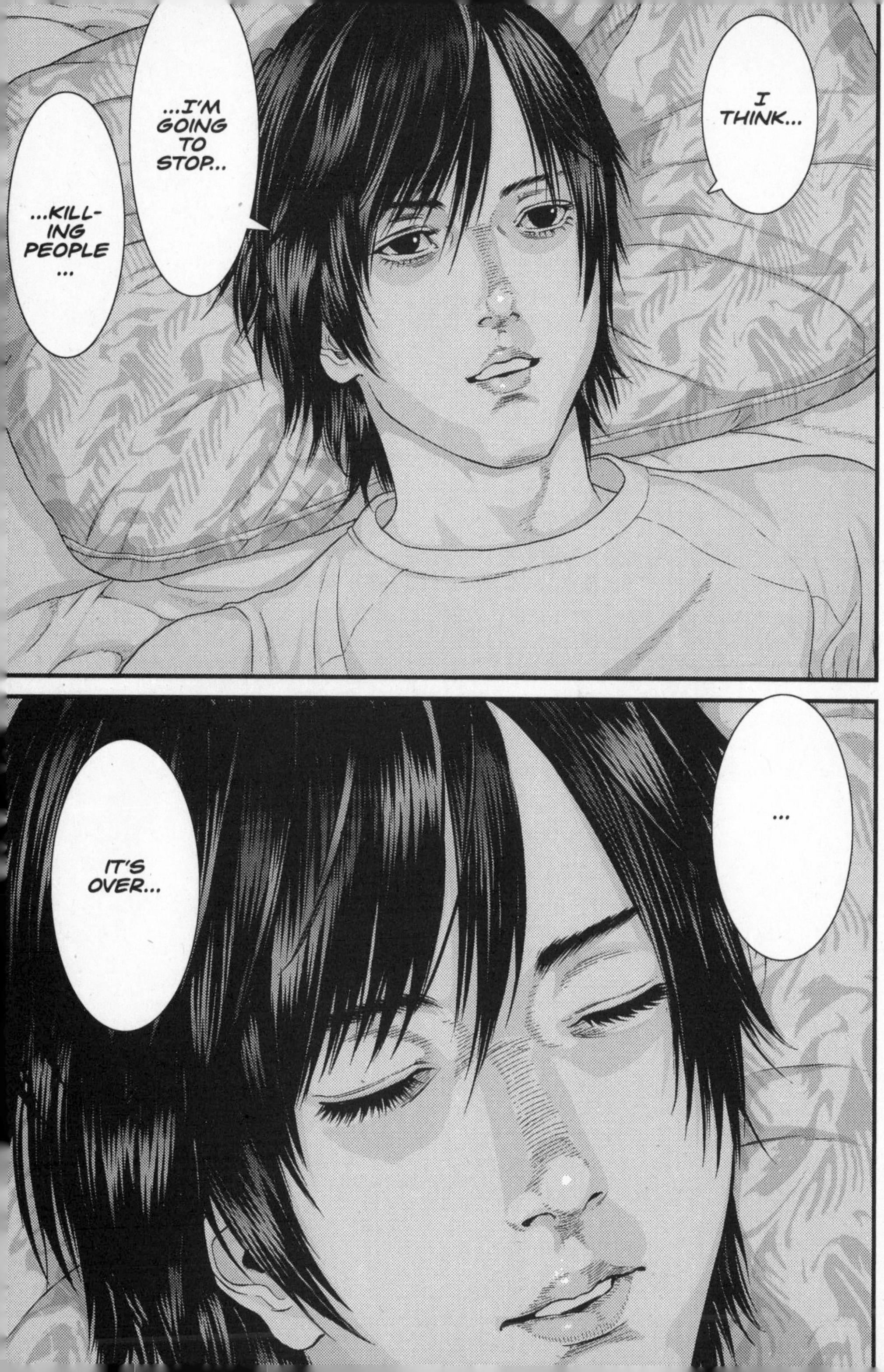
I THINK...
...I'M GOING TO STOP...
...KILL-ING PEOPLE ...
...
IT'S OVER...

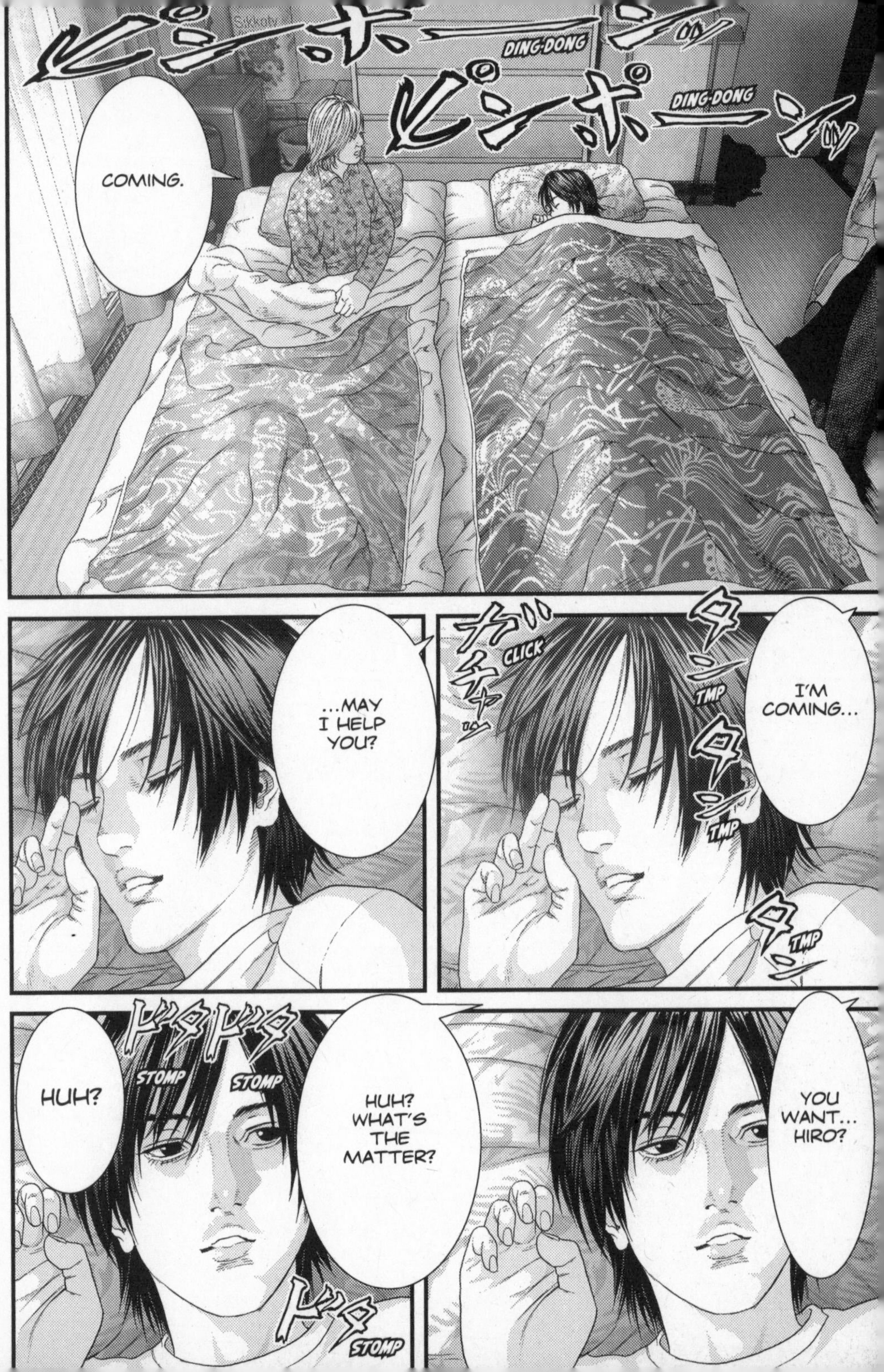
DING-DONG
DING-DONG
COMING.
CLICK
I'M COMING...
TMP
TMP
TMP
...MAY I HELP YOU?
YOU WANT... HIRO?
HUH? WHAT'S THE MATTER?
STOMP
STOMP
HUH?
STOMP

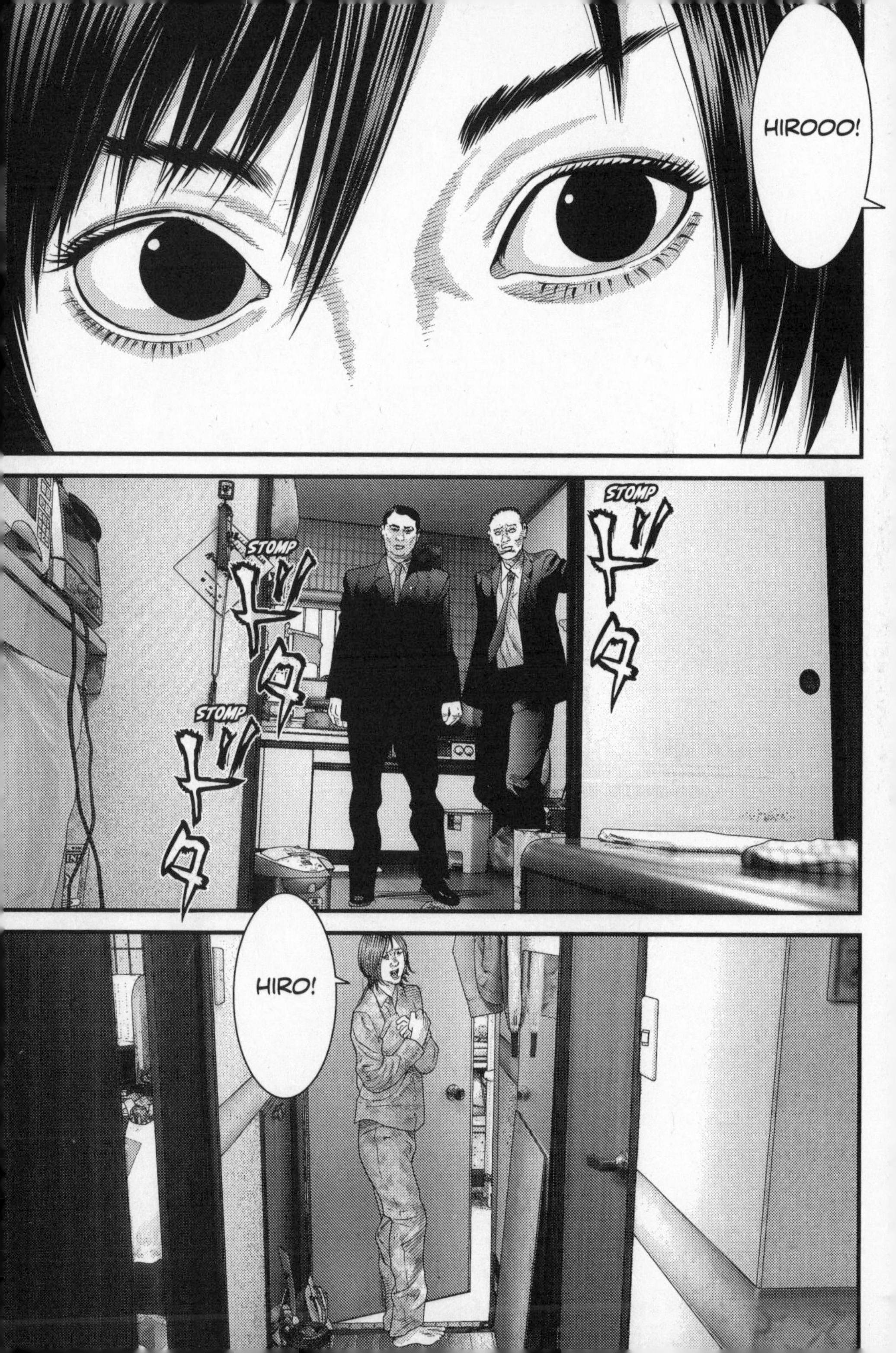
HIROOO!
STOMP
STOMP
STOMP
HIRO!

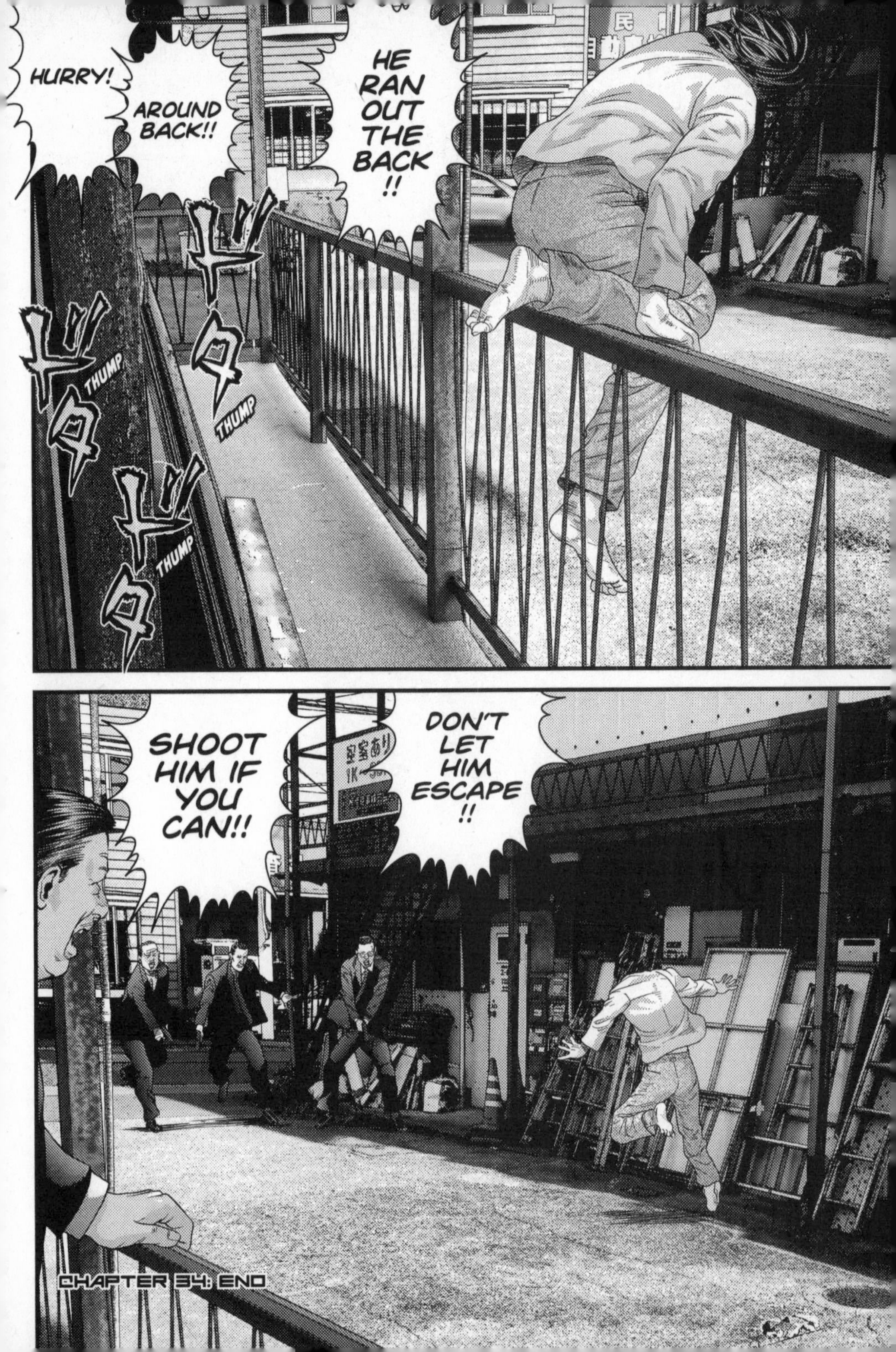
HE RAN OUT THE BACK!!
AROUND BACK!!
HURRY!
THUMP
THUMP
THUMP
DON'T LET HIM ESCAPE!!
SHOOT HIM IF YOU CAN!!
CHAPTER 34: END

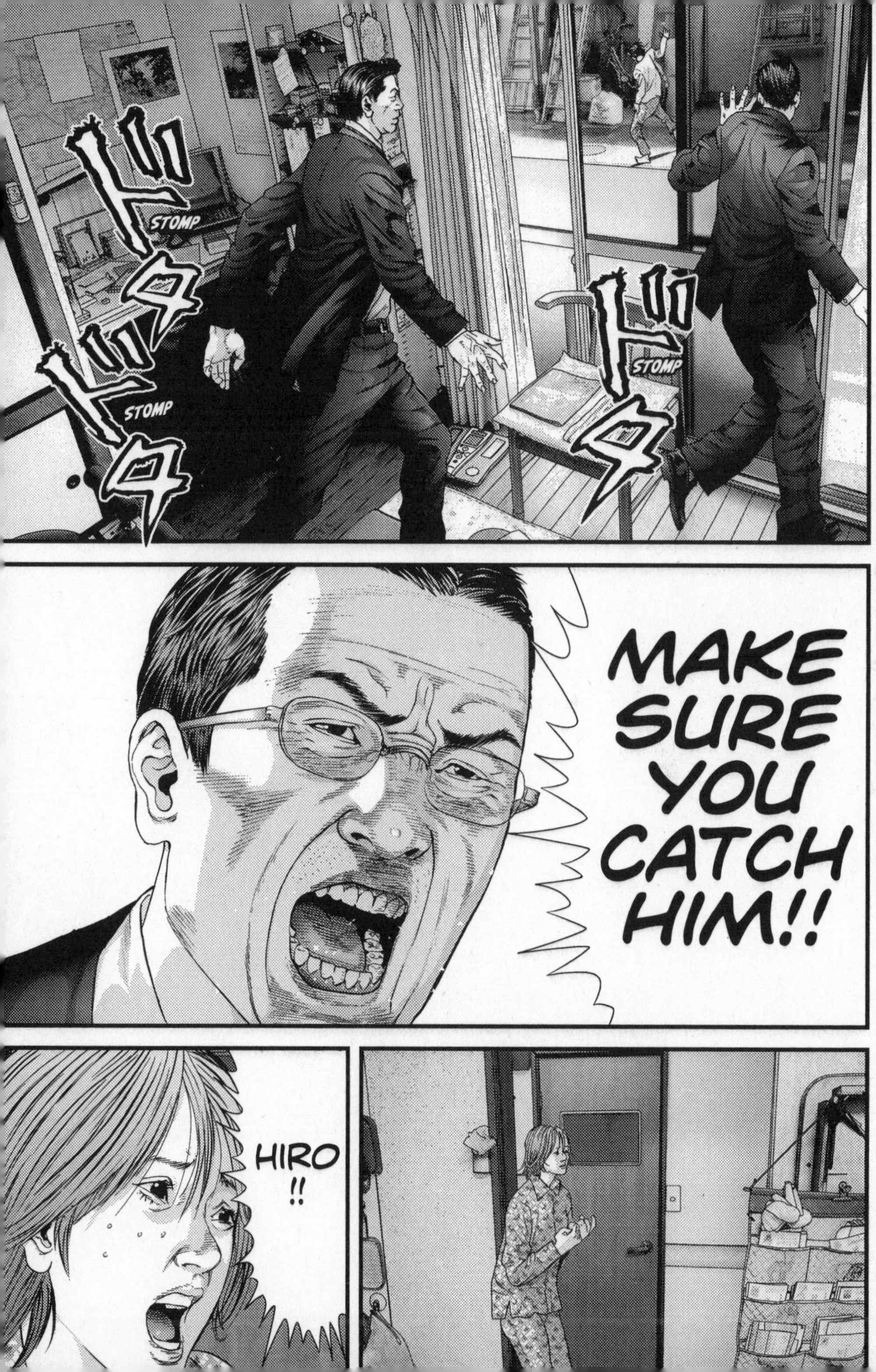
STOMP
STOMP
STOMP
MAKE SURE YOU CATCH HIM!!
HIRO !!

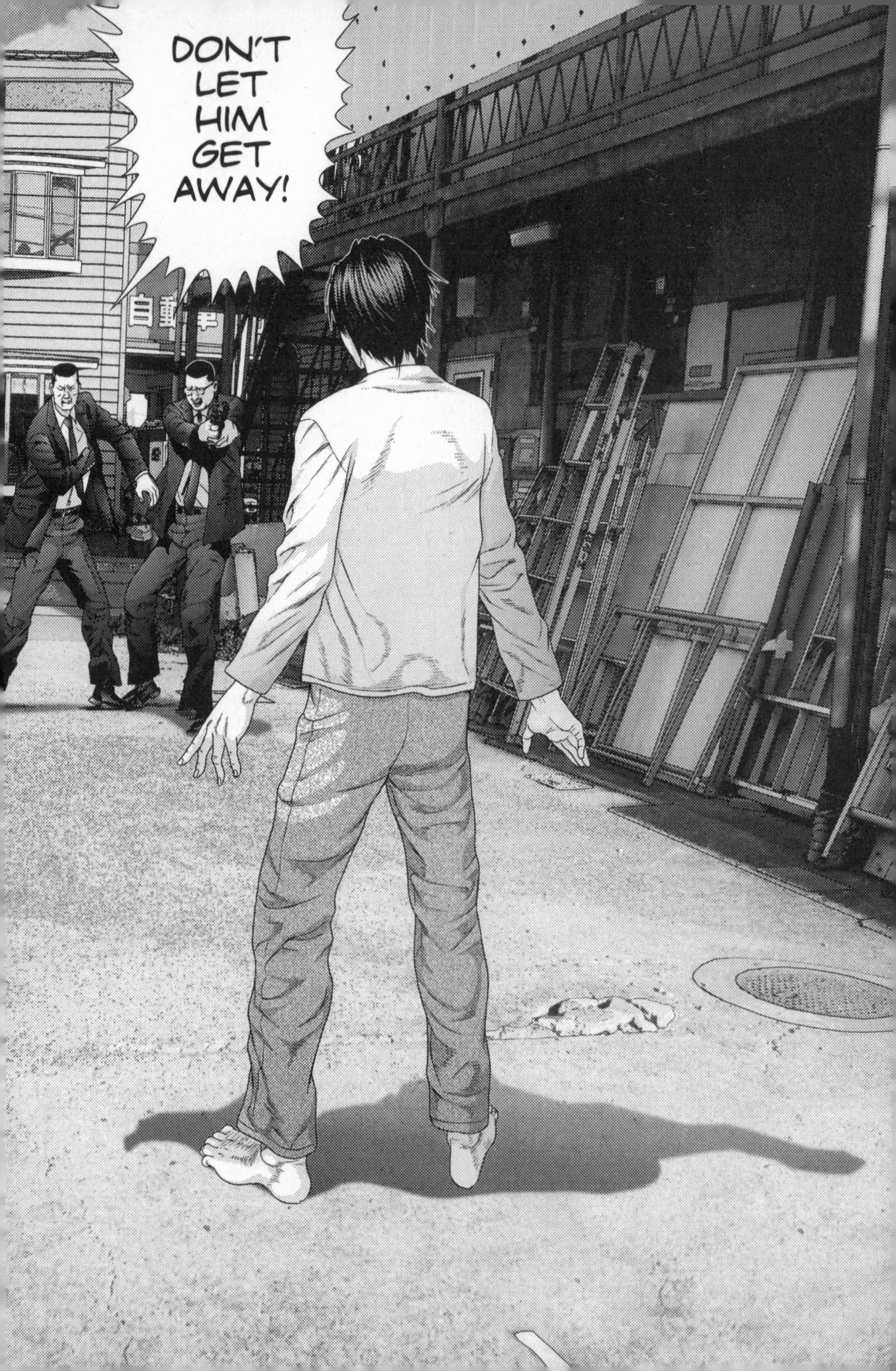
DON'T LET HIM GET AWAY!

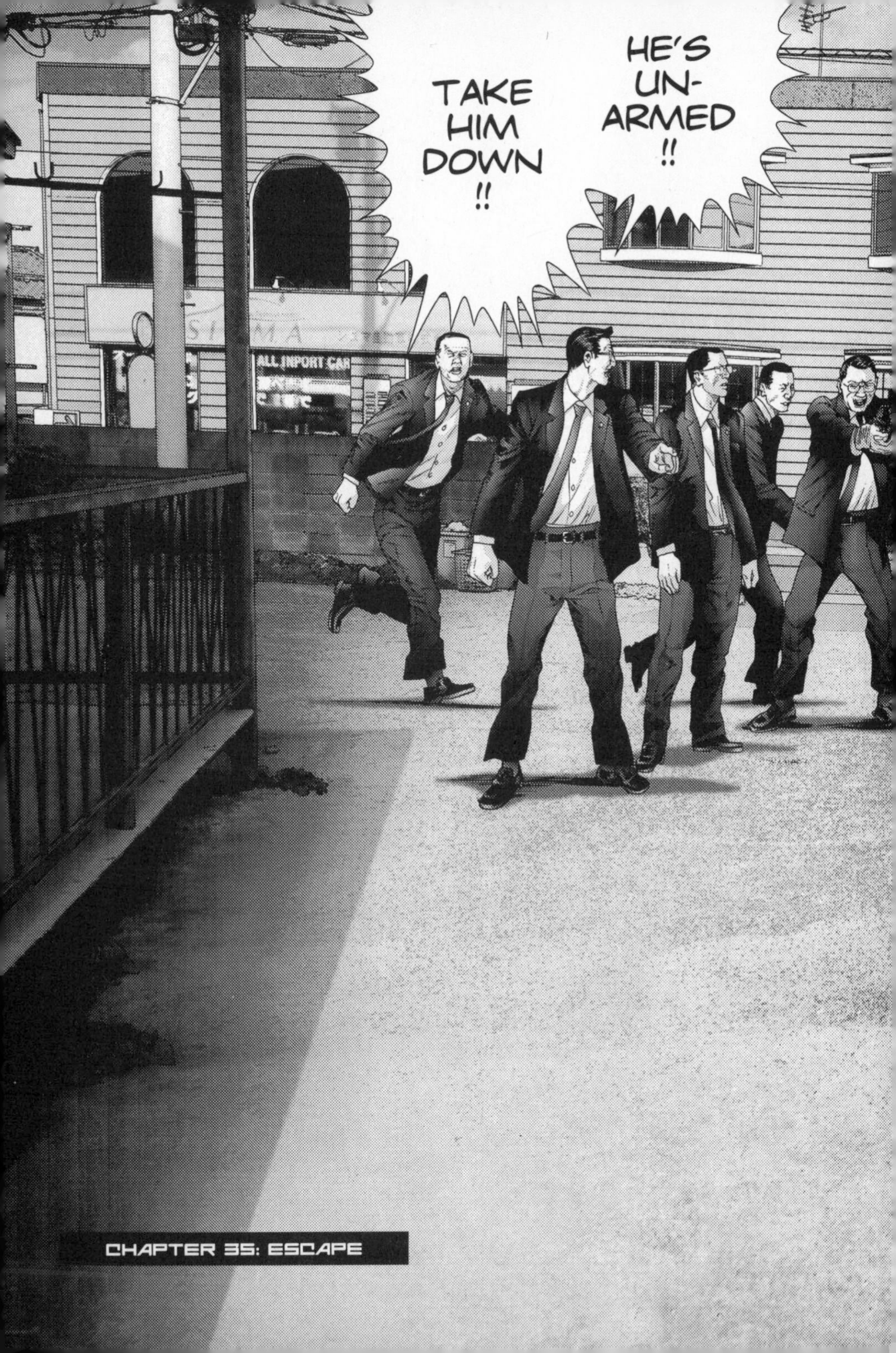
HE'S UN-ARMED!!
TAKE HIM DOWN!!
ALL INPORT CAR

CHAPTER 35: ESCAPE

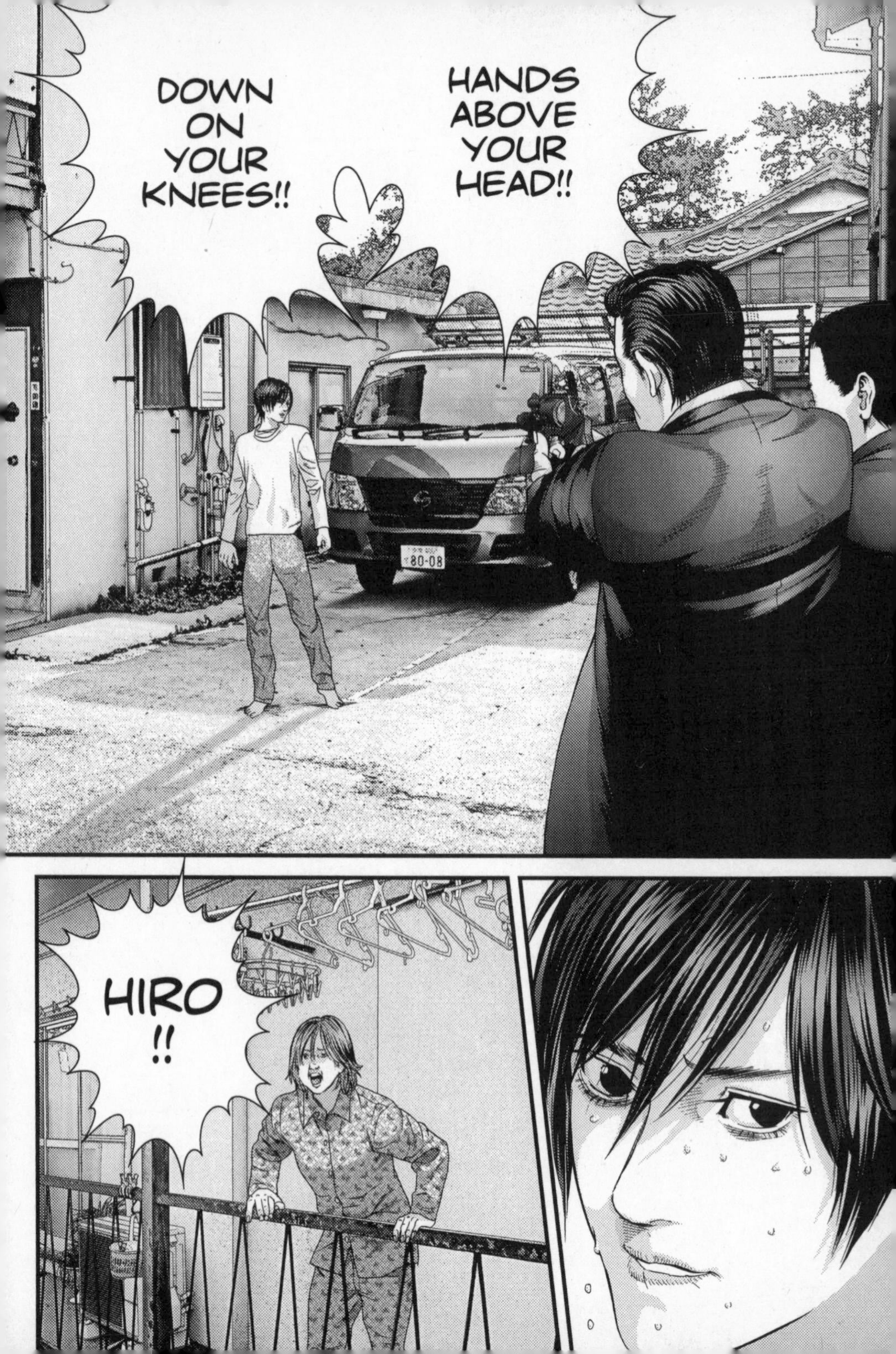
HANDS ABOVE YOUR HEAD!!
DOWN ON YOUR KNEES!!
HIRO !!

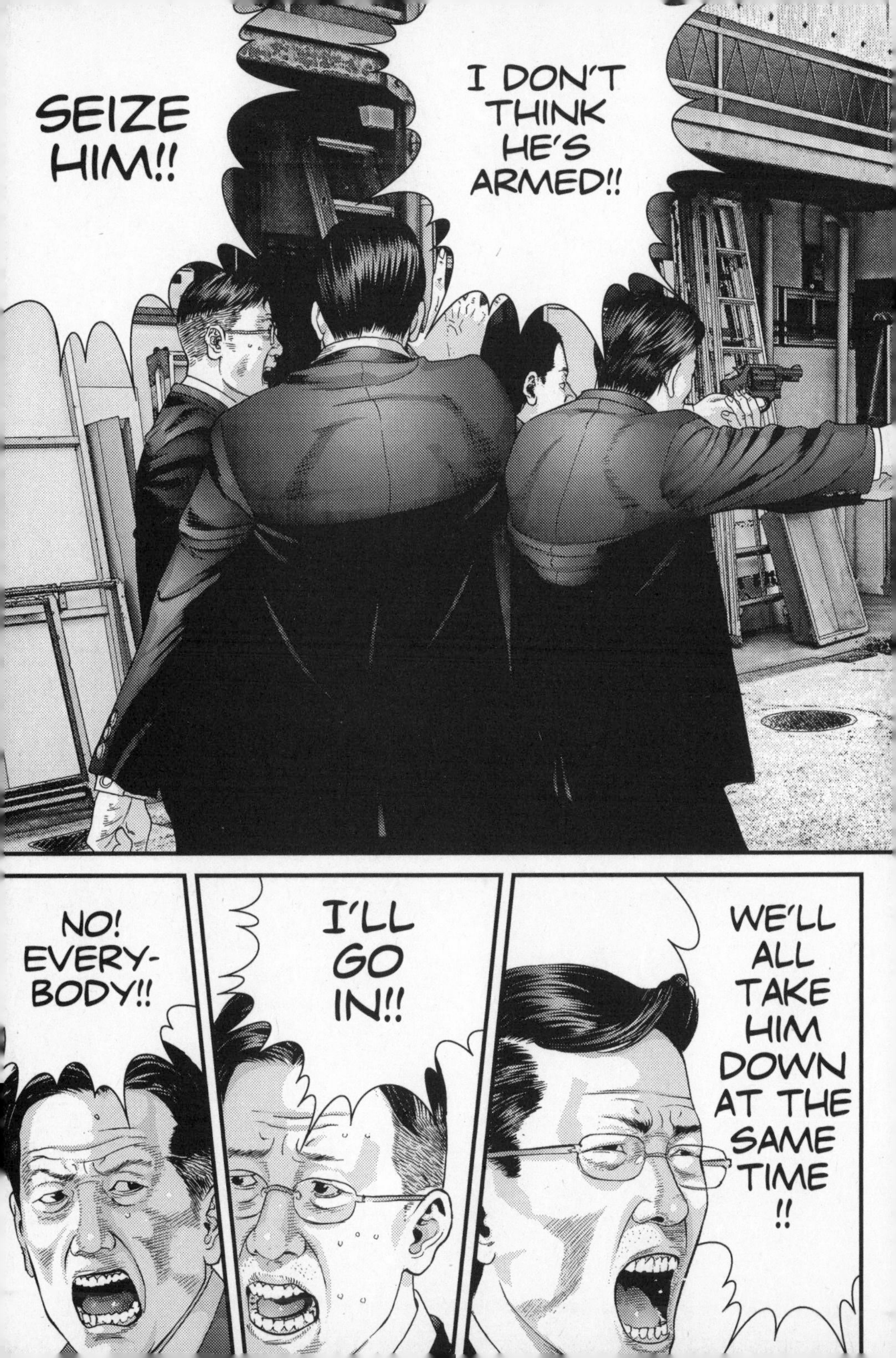
I DON'T THINK HE'S ARMED!!
SEIZE HIM!!
WE'LL ALL TAKE HIM DOWN AT THE SAME TIME!!
I'LL GO IN!!
NO! EVERY-BODY!!

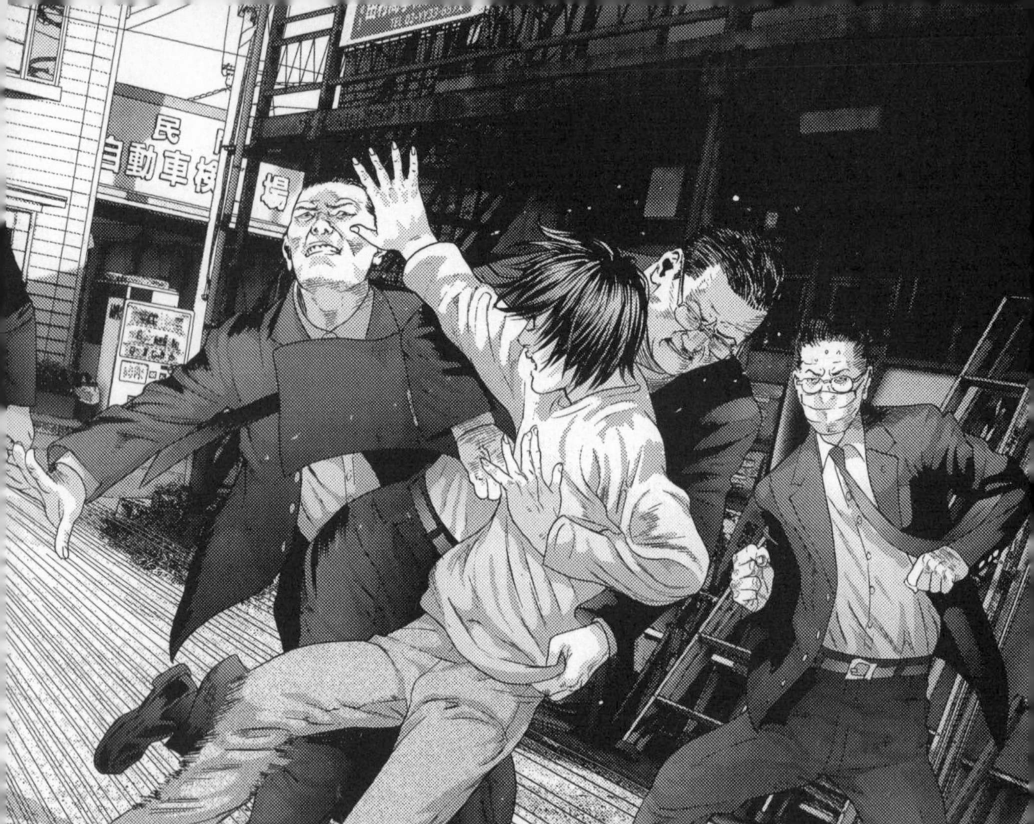
民
自動車校
場
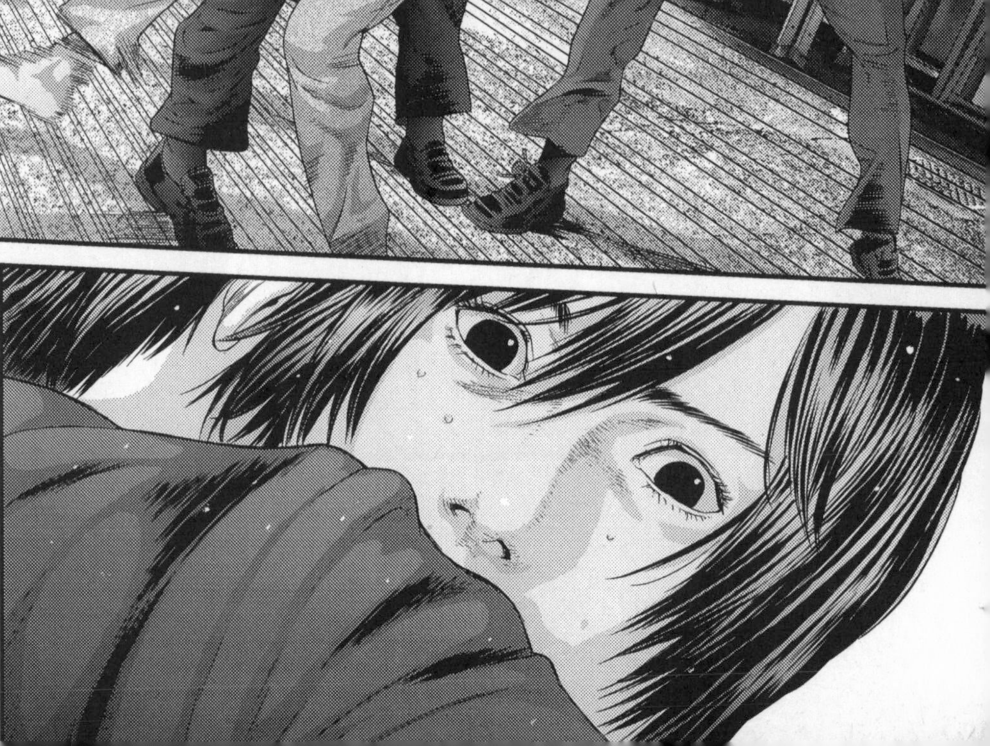

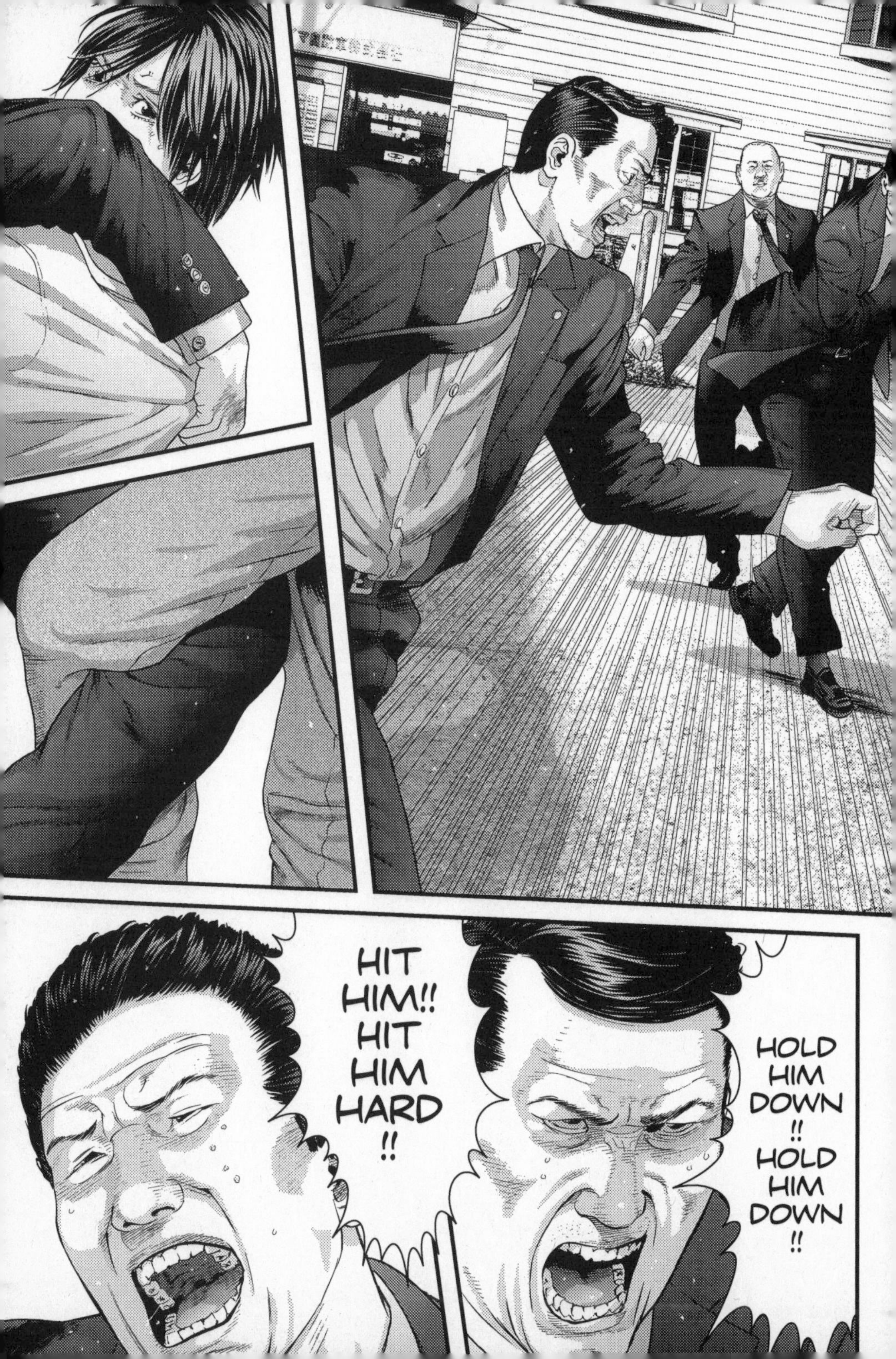
HOLD HIM DOWN!! HOLD HIM DOWN!!
HIT HIM!! HIT HIM HARD!!

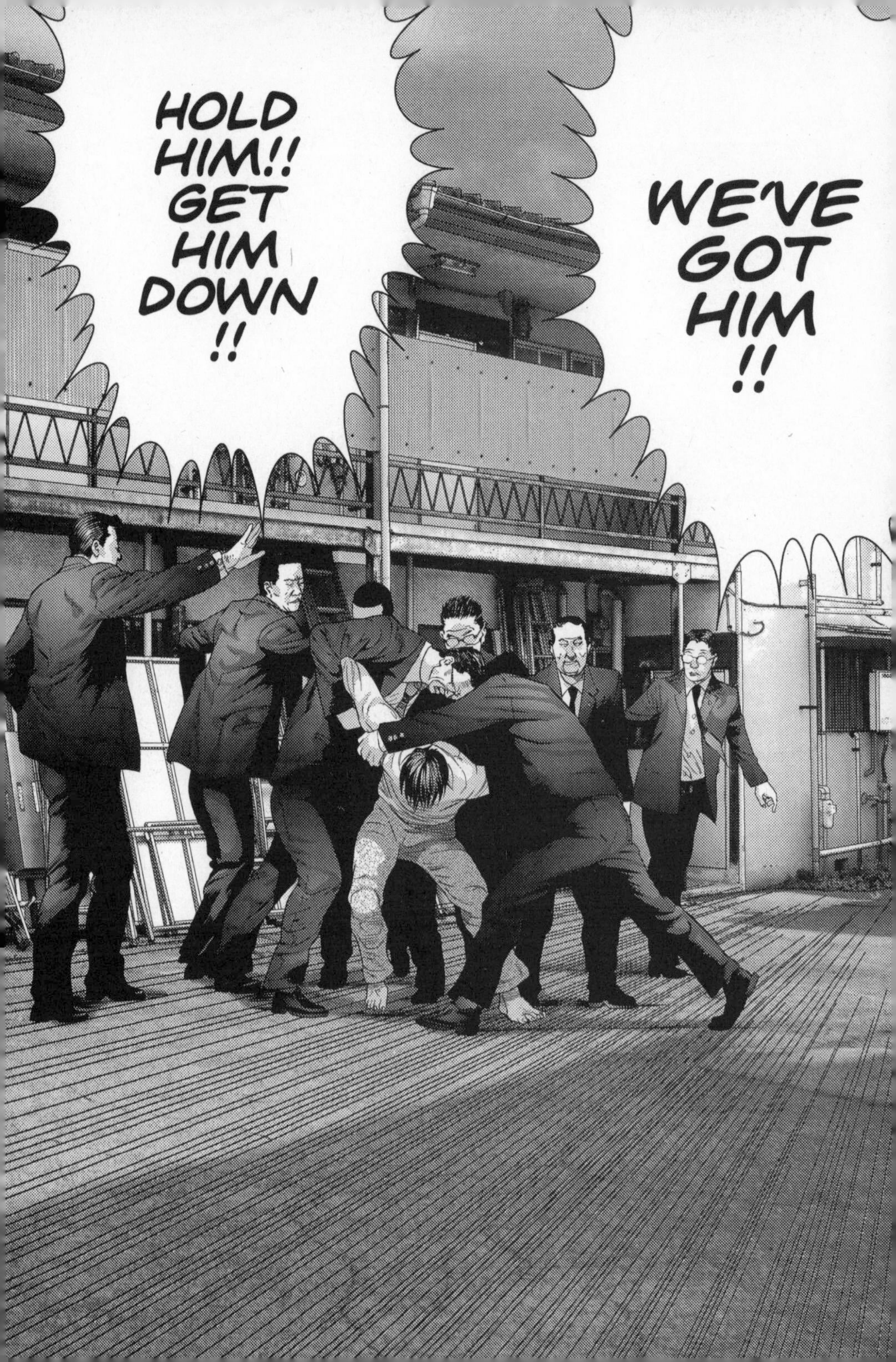
WE'VE GOT HIM!!
HOLD HIM!! GET HIM DOWN!!

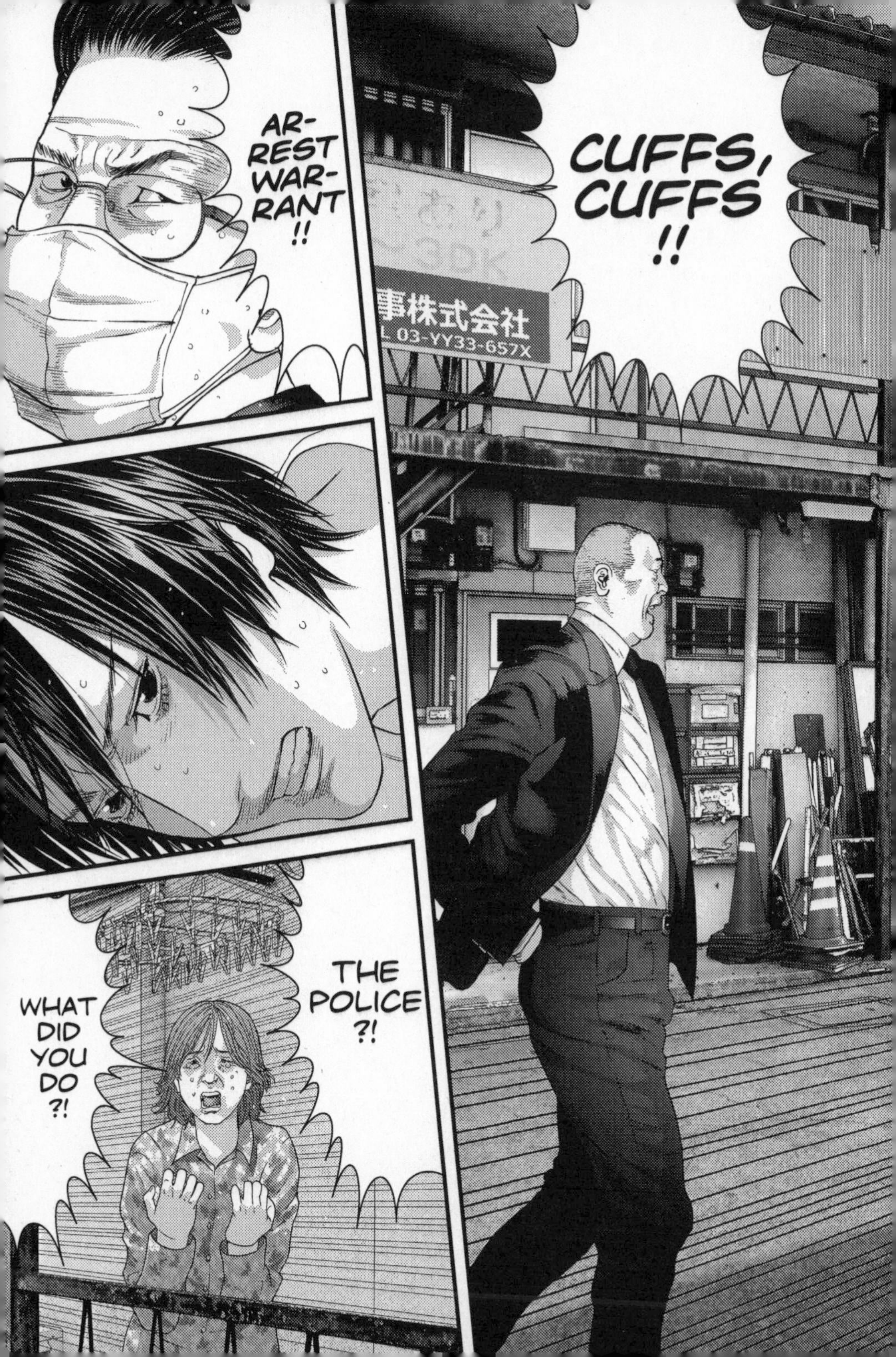
事株式会社
L 03-YY33-657X
CUFFS, CUFFS!!
AR-REST WAR-RANT!!
THE POLICE?!
WHAT DID YOU DO?!

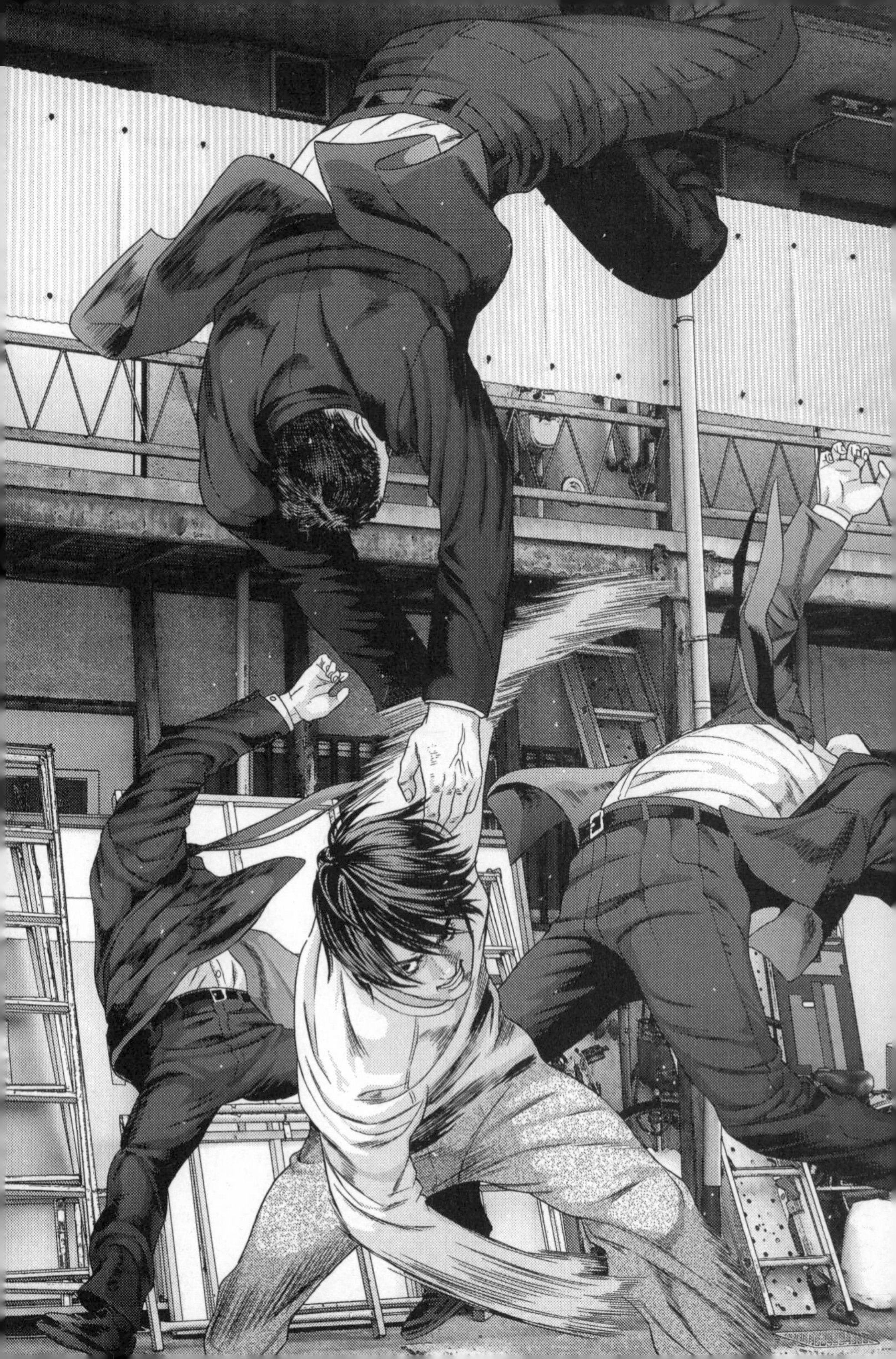

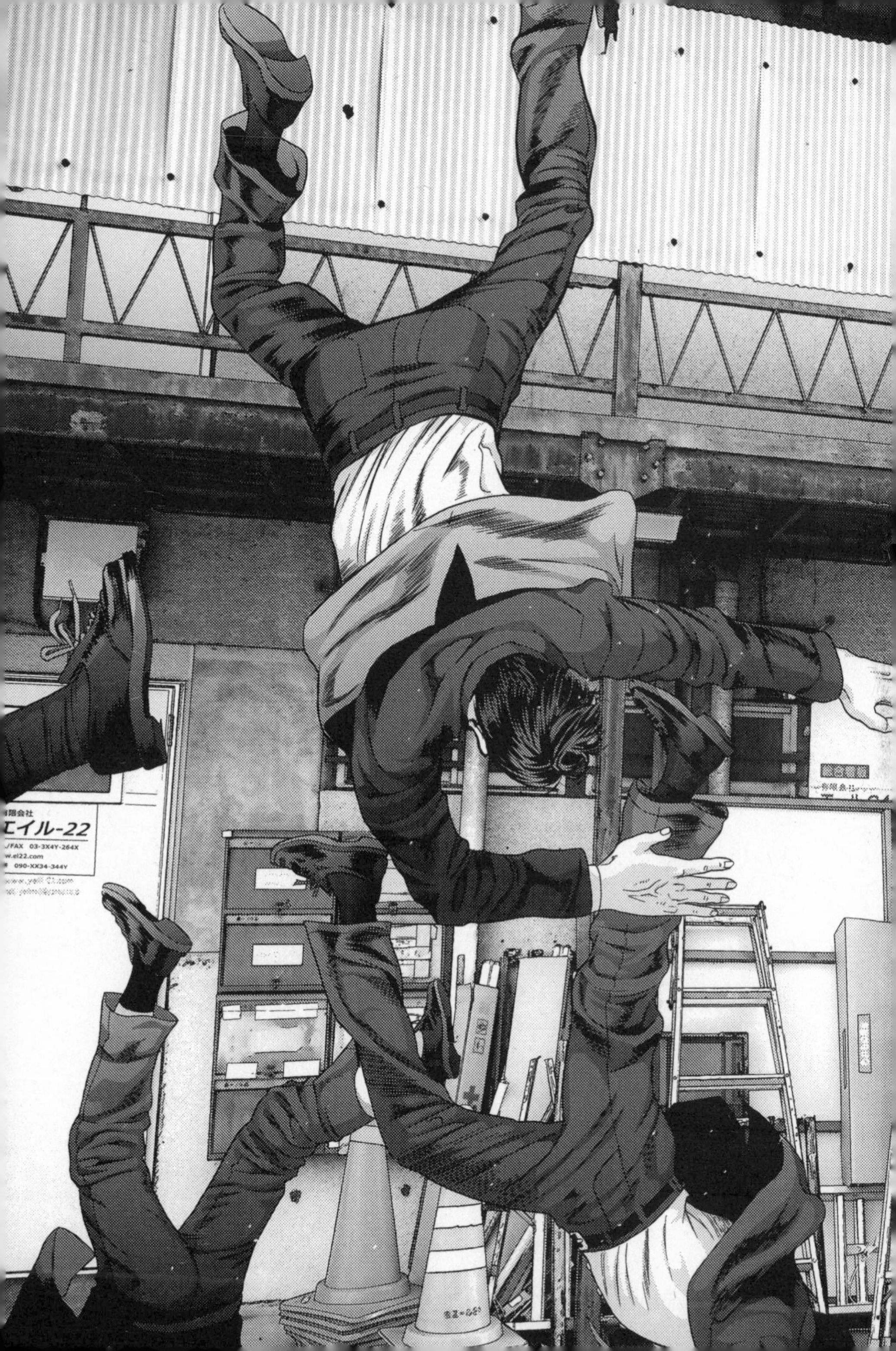
限会社
エイル-22
/FAX 03-3X4Y-264X
w.el22.com
090-XX34-344Y

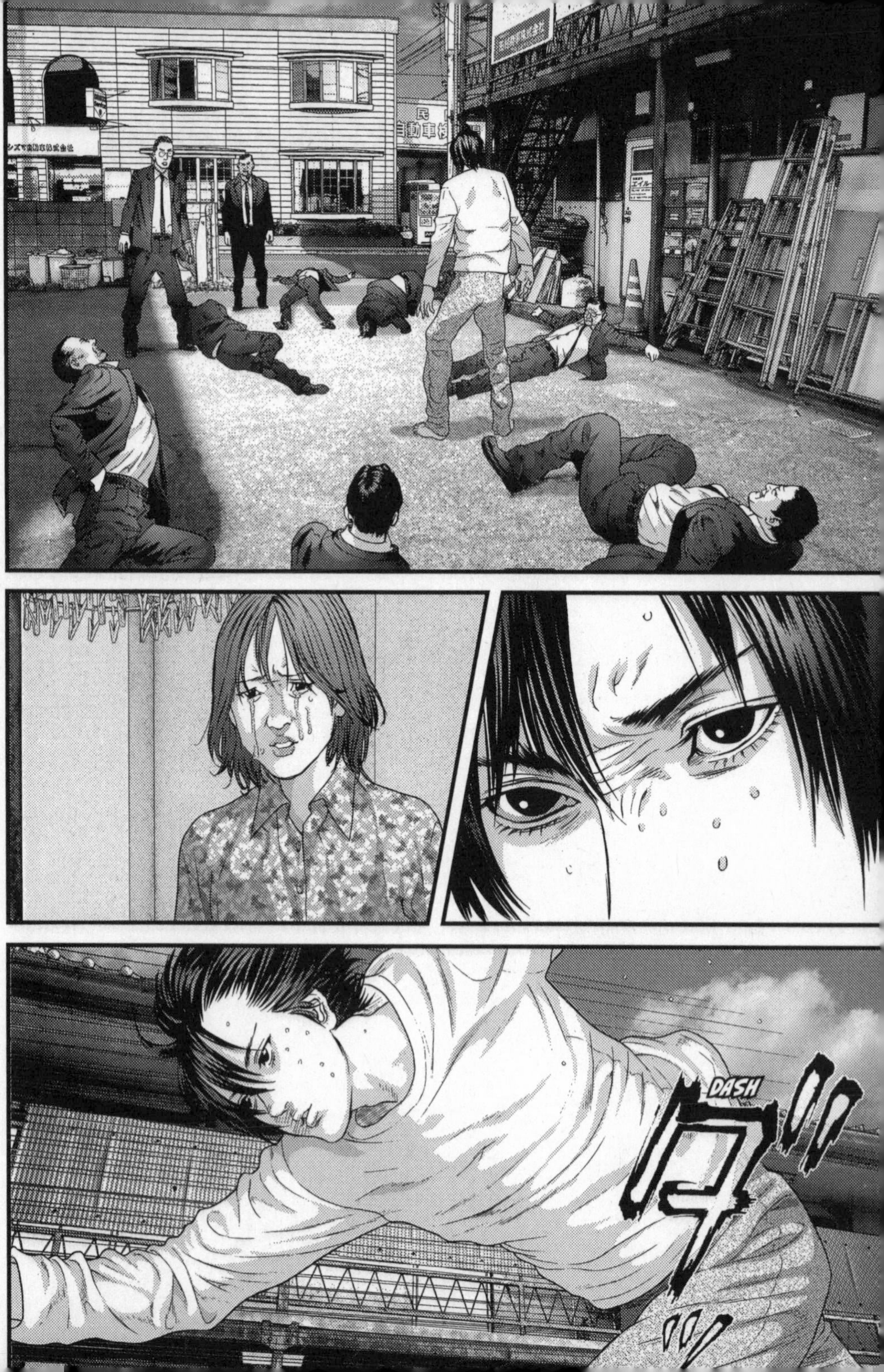
DASH

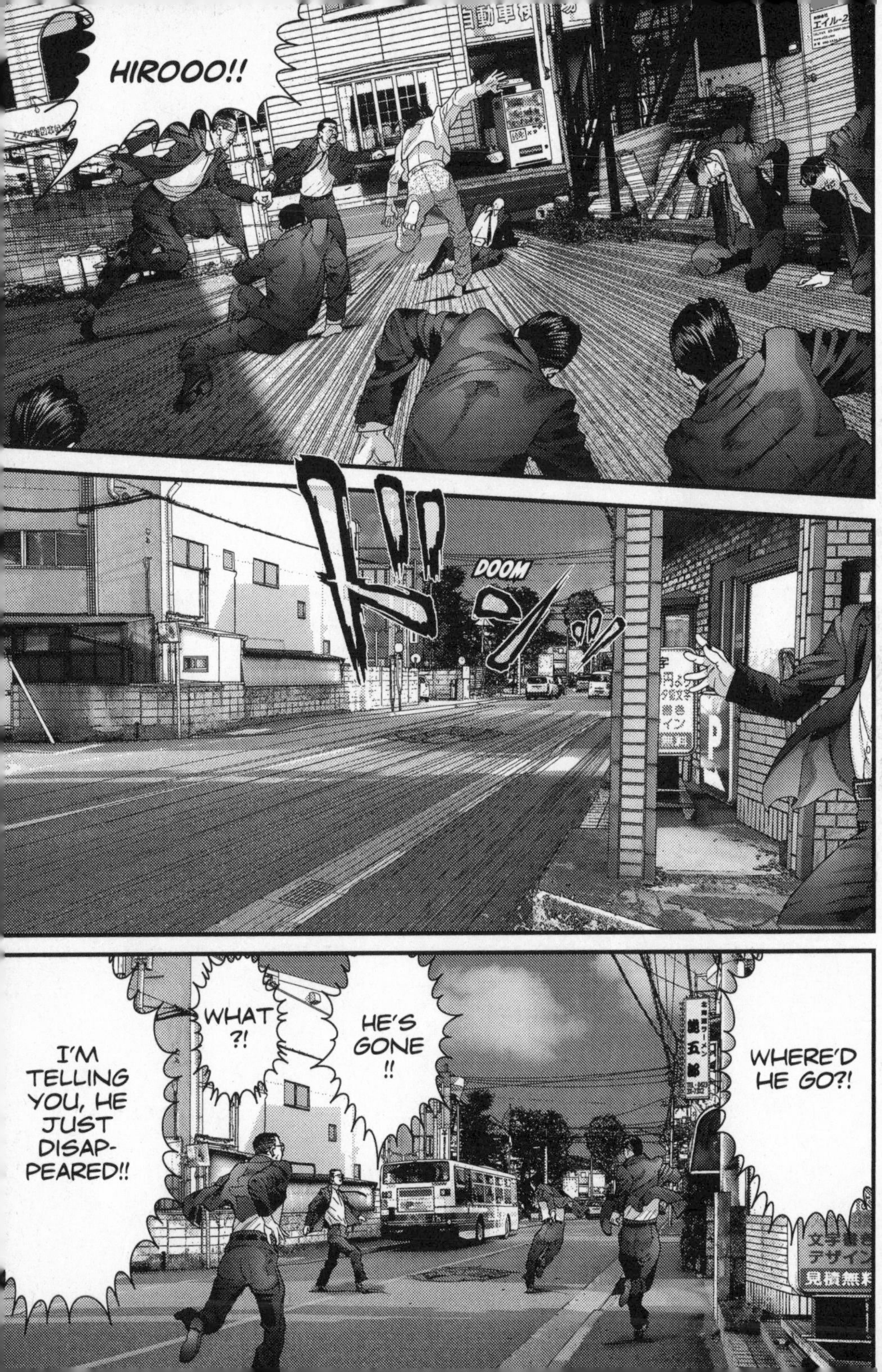
HIROOO!!
DOOM
WHERE'D HE GO?!
HE'S GONE !!
WHAT ?!
I'M TELLING YOU, HE JUST DISAP-PEARED!!

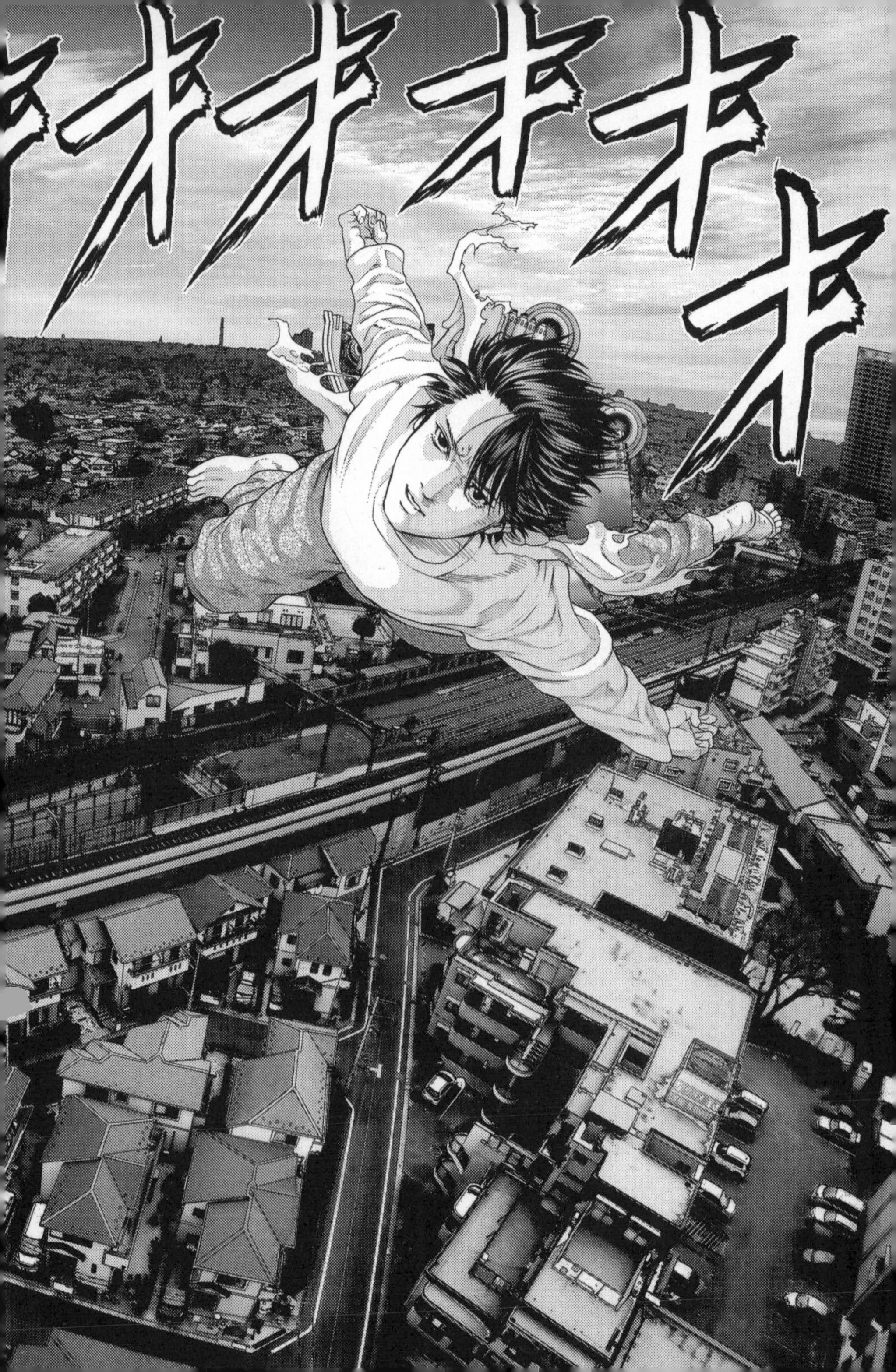
オオオオオ

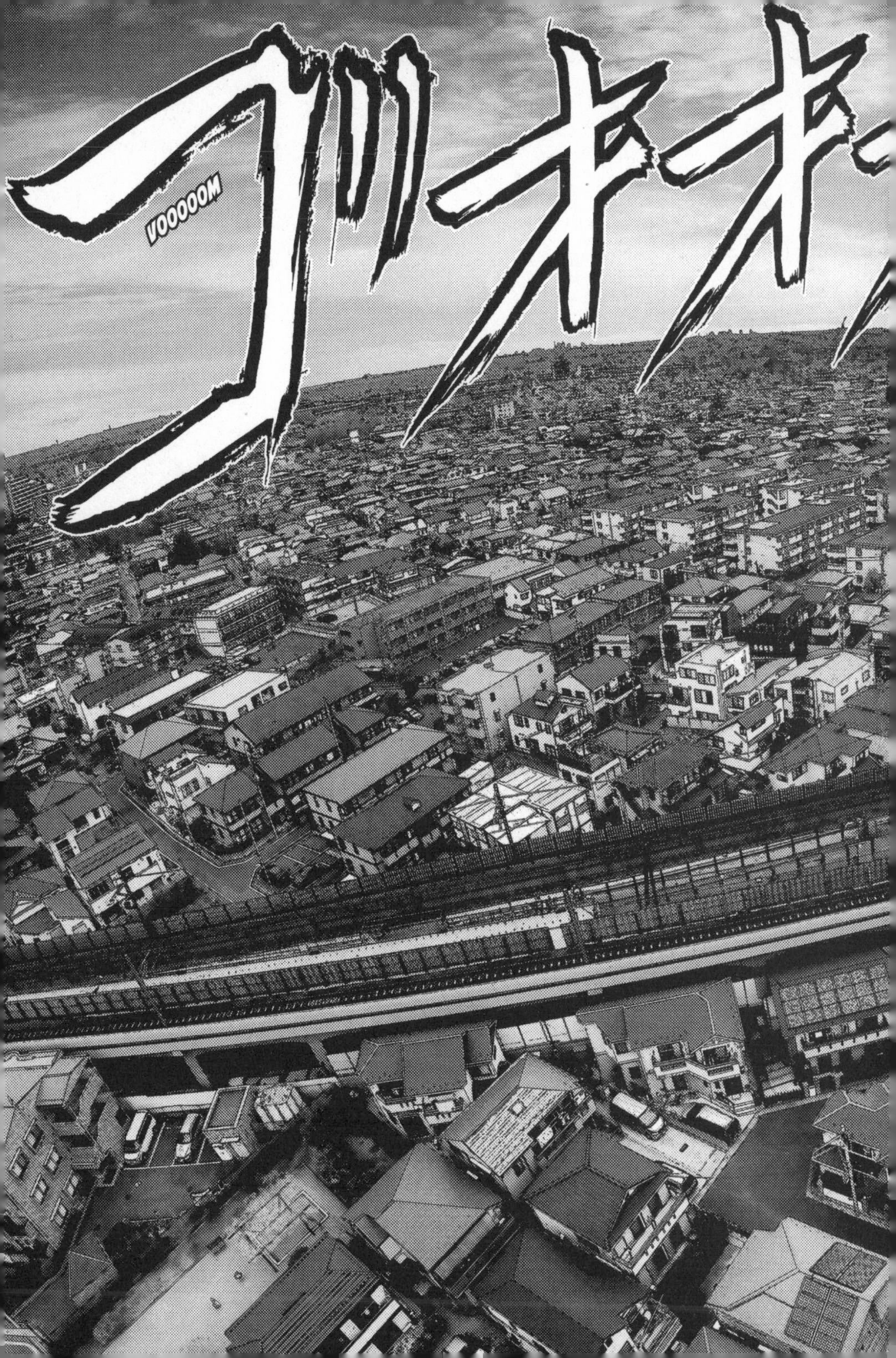
ゴオオ
VOOOOOM

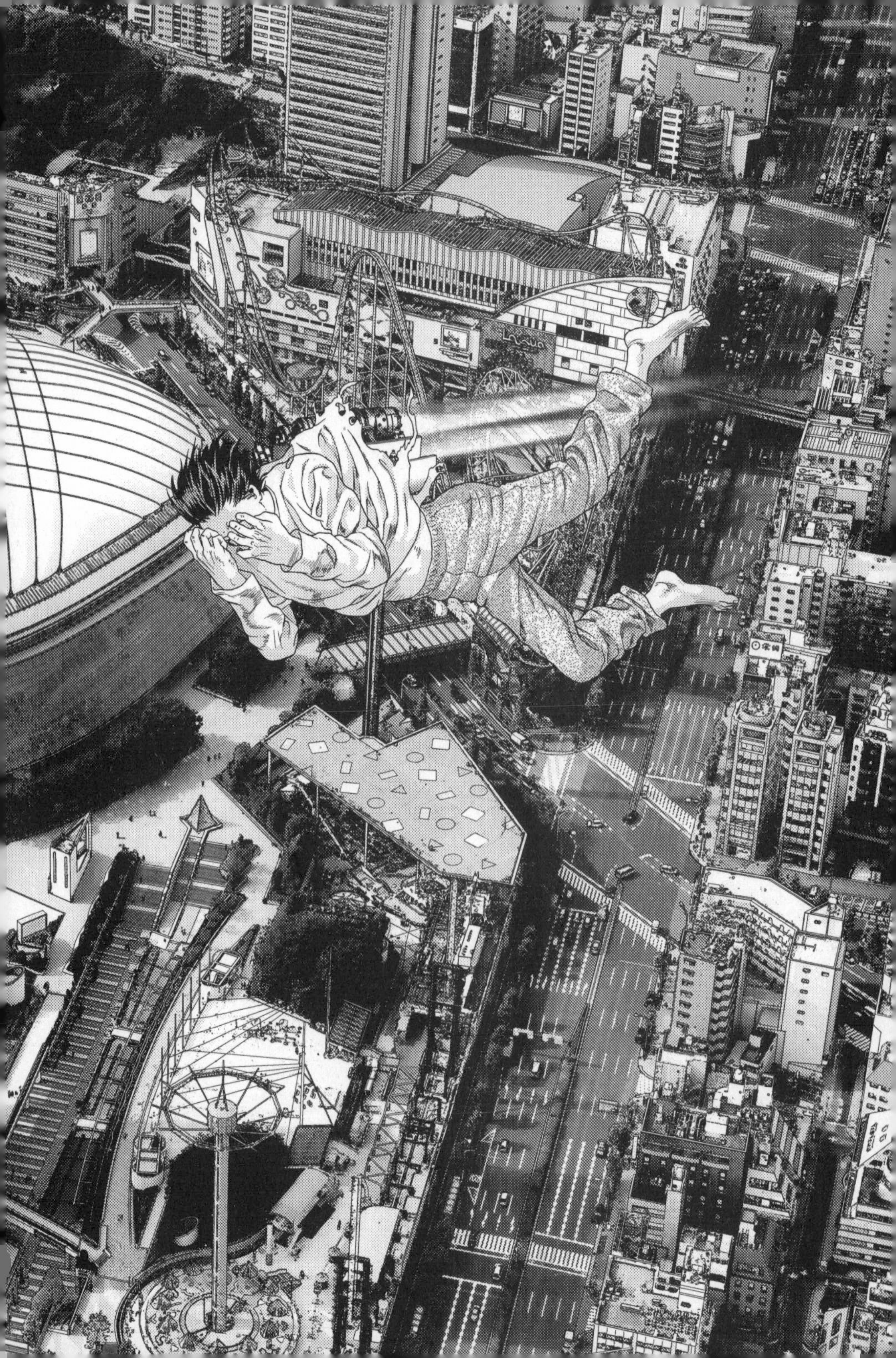
LaQua

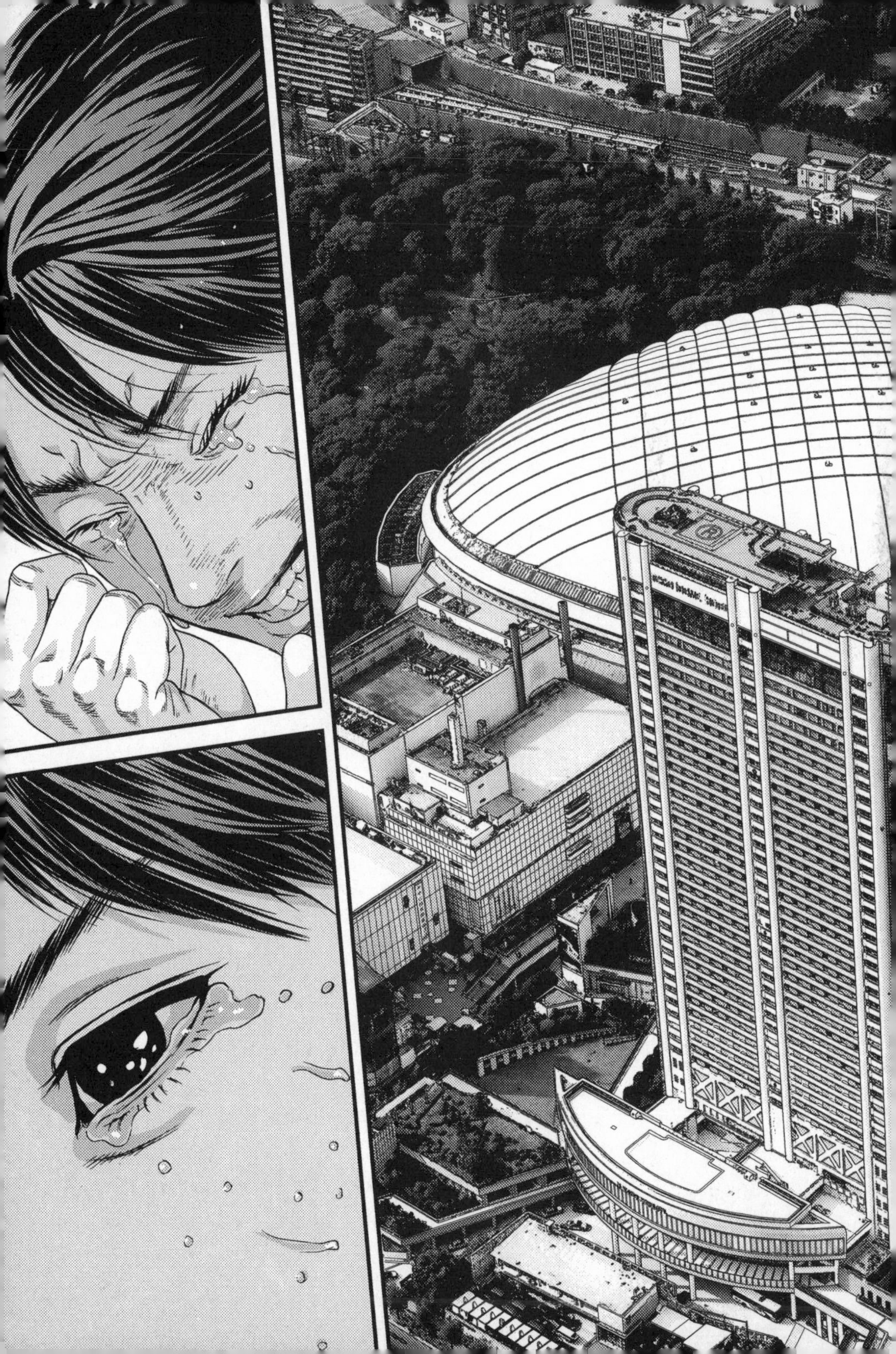

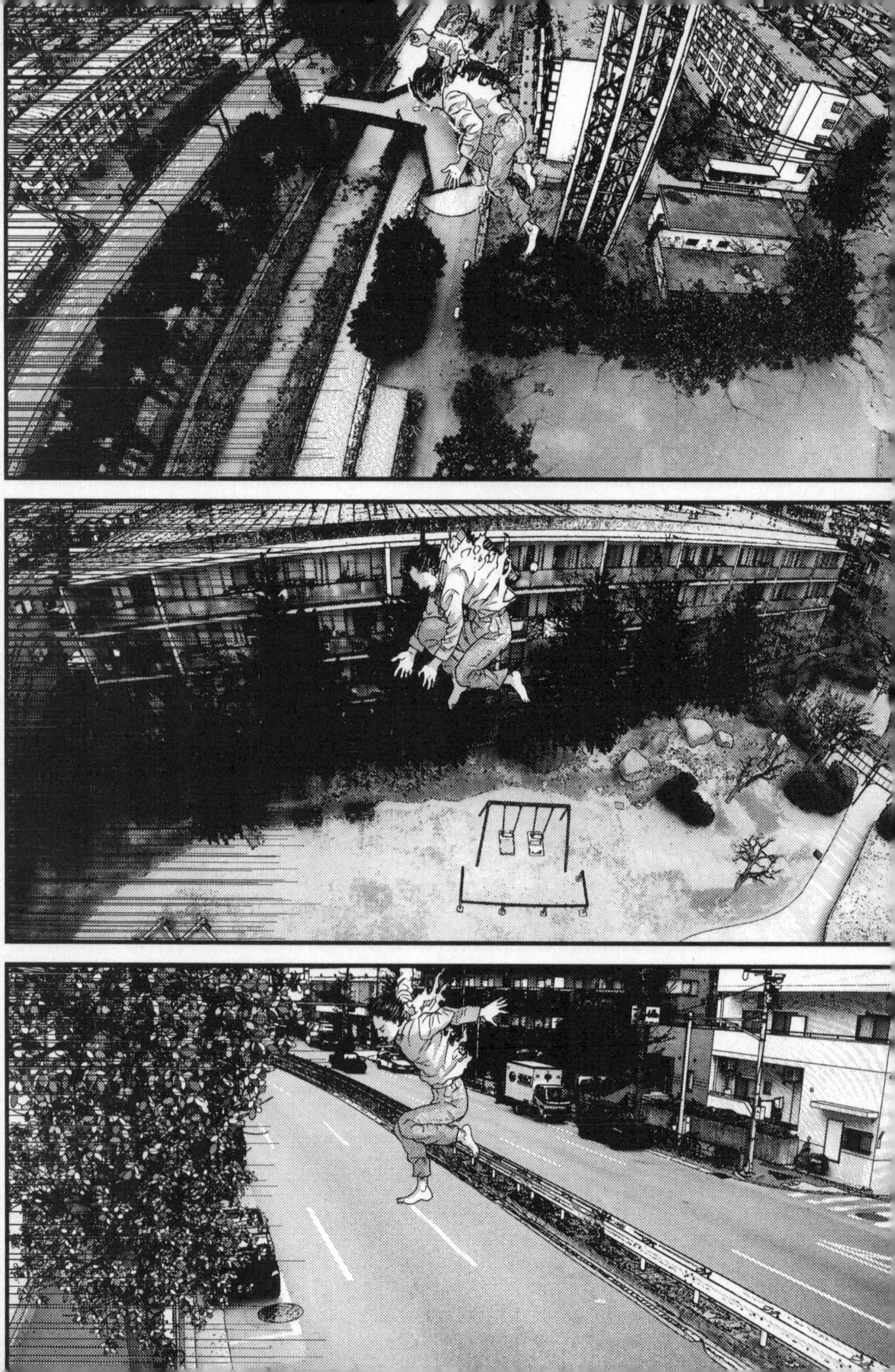

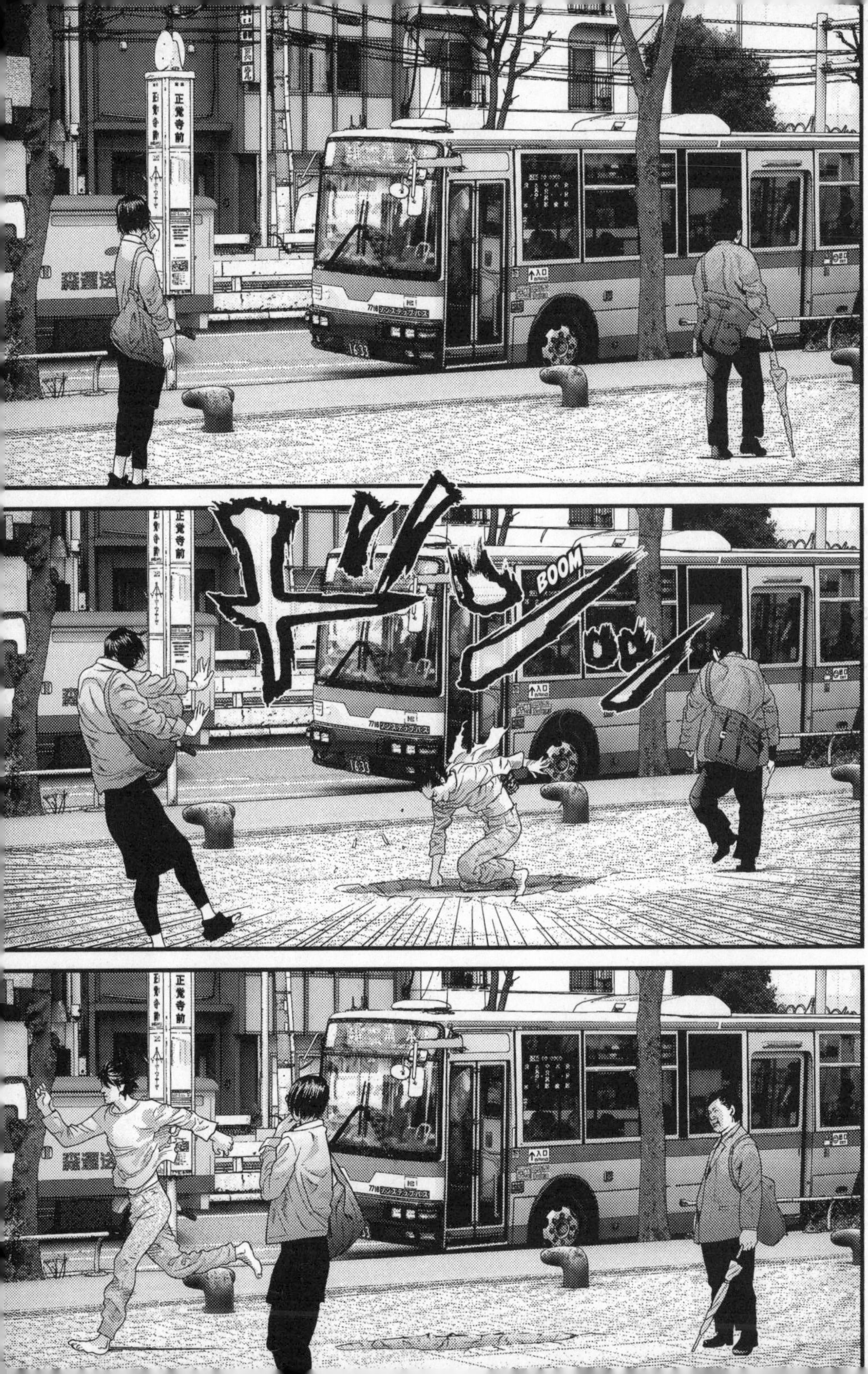
正覚寺前
BOOM

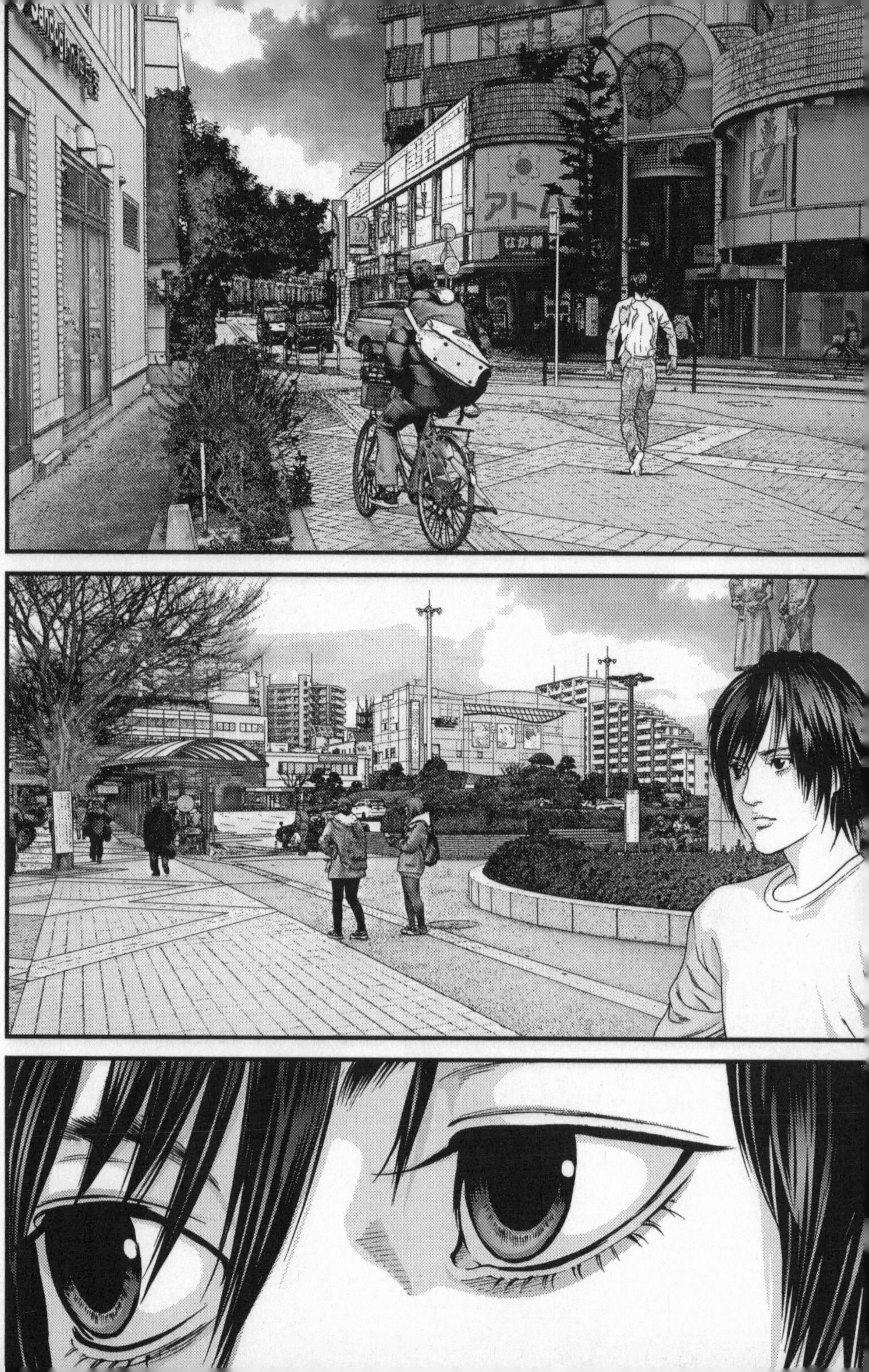
アトム

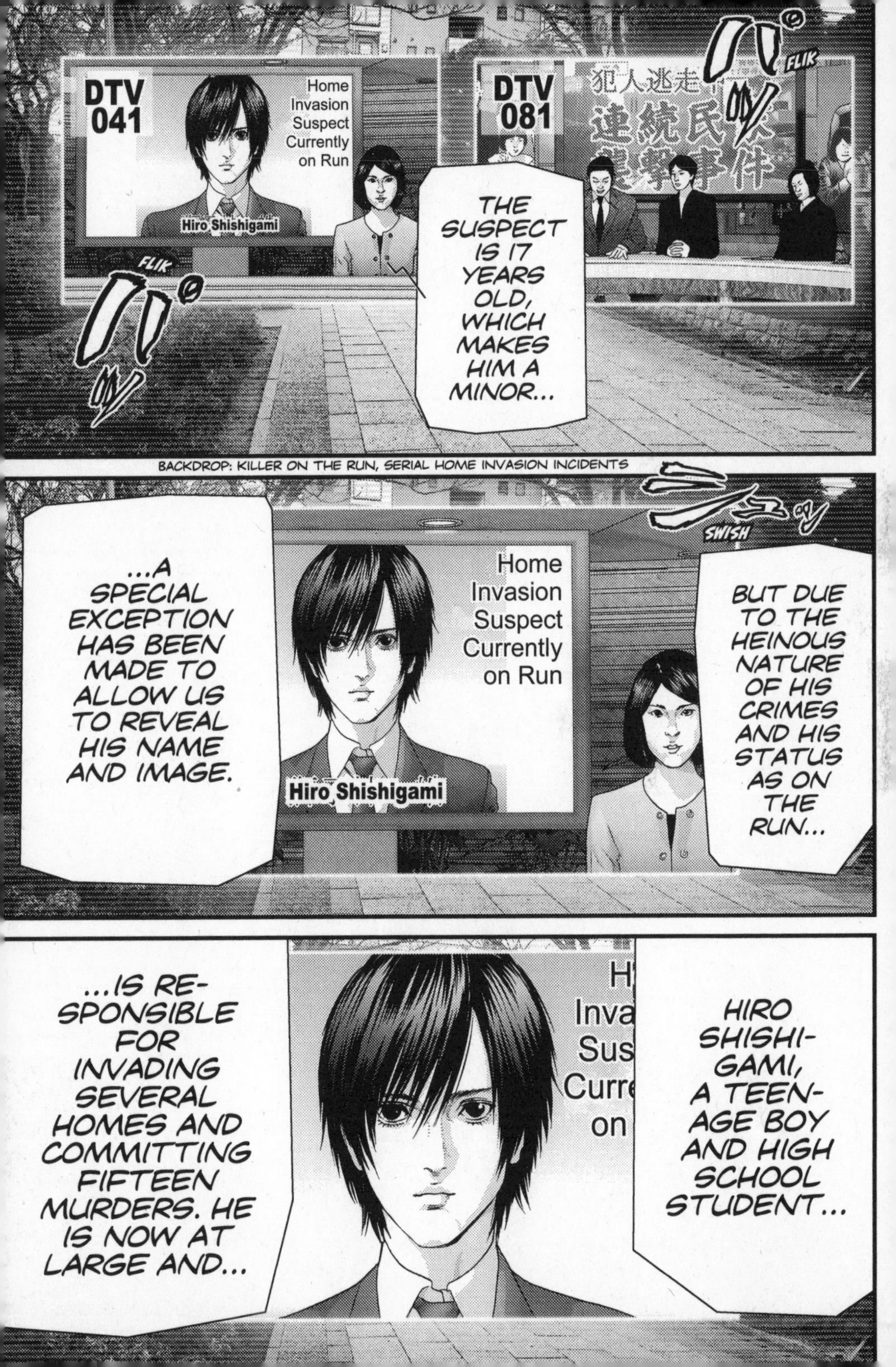
FLIK
DTV 081
犯人逃走！
連続民家襲撃事件
DTV 041
Home Invasion Suspect Currently on Run
Hiro Shishigami
THE SUSPECT IS 17 YEARS OLD, WHICH MAKES HIM A MINOR...
FLIK
BACKDROP: KILLER ON THE RUN, SERIAL HOME INVASION INCIDENTS
SWISH
BUT DUE TO THE HEINOUS NATURE OF HIS CRIMES AND HIS STATUS AS ON THE RUN...
Home Invasion Suspect Currently on Run
Hiro Shishigami
...A SPECIAL EXCEPTION HAS BEEN MADE TO ALLOW US TO REVEAL HIS NAME AND IMAGE.
HIRO SHISHIGAMI, A TEENAGE BOY AND HIGH SCHOOL STUDENT...
...IS RESPONSIBLE FOR INVADING SEVERAL HOMES AND COMMITTING FIFTEEN MURDERS. HE IS NOW AT LARGE AND...

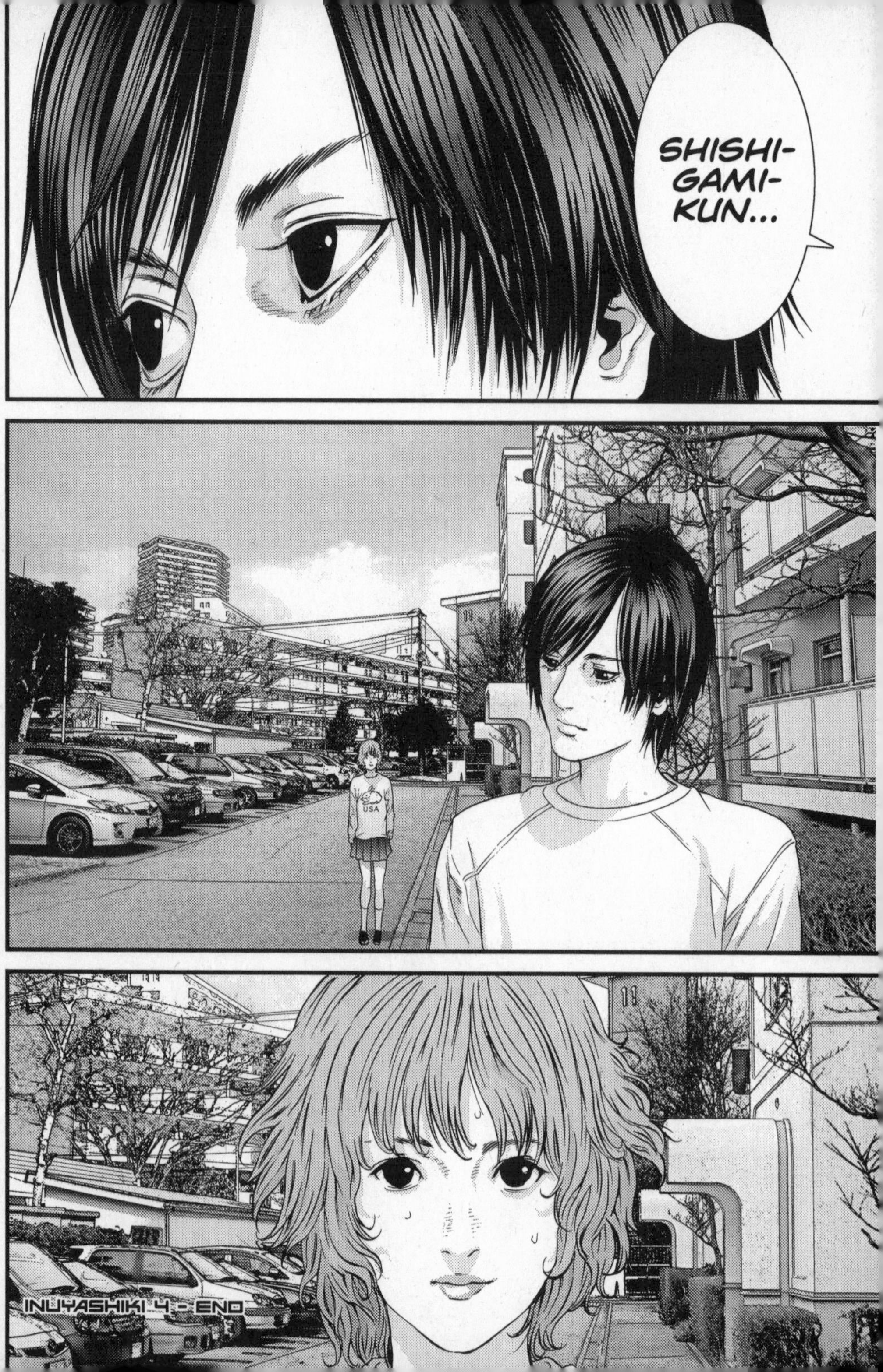
SHISHI-GAMI-KUN...
USA
INUYASHIKI 4 - END

Translation Notes

Kodankai, page 23

A MEETING OF THE KODANKAI, A GOVERNMENT-DESIGNATED, DANGEROUS ORGANIZED CRIME GROUP, WAS ATTACKED RECENTLY.
ALL 278 MEMBERS OF THE GANG, INCLUDING THE TOP BRASS, SUFFERED DAMAGE TO THE EYES AND CERVICAL VERTE-BRAE.

Most existing yakuza groups have a name ending in either -gumi (meaning "association" or "union") or -kai (a similar term meaning "party" or "assembly"). What is amusing about this particular group is that the "Kodan" in Kodankai are the same kanji from the name of the publisher Kodansha.

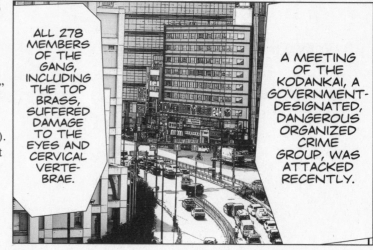

LDK, page 115

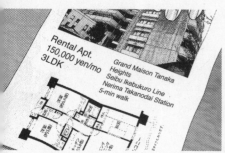

Rental Apt.
150,000 yen/mo
3LDK
Grand Maison Tanaka Heights
Seibu Ikebukuro Line
Nerima Takanodai Station
5-min walk

The "LDK" classification is a Japanese system of interior designation for the purpose of real estate advertising. LDK stands for Living, Dining and Kitchen, the term for the general kitchen/common-room area, and is preceded by a number that signifies the other rooms (bedrooms or other purpose). In this case, a 3LDK means that the apartment has three rooms, plus a main kitchen-attached room.

Sukiyabashi Jiro, page 128

One of the most celebrated and lauded sushi restaurants in Japan and owner of a coveted three-star rating from Michelin. Its reputation internationally was boosted by the documentary film *Jiro Dreams of Sushi*, which explored owner Jiro Ono's dedication to his craft.

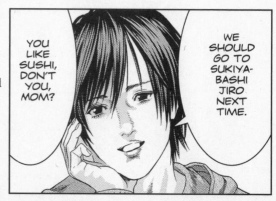

WE SHOULD GO TO SUKIYA-BASHI JIRO NEXT TIME.
YOU LIKE SUSHI, DON'T YOU, MOM?

NEET, page 157

An acronym meaning "Not in Education/Employment/Training." It refers to a person who is not a student or employed, and is not seeking work, either.

SO WHO WAS THE KILLER, ANYWAY?
ON THE NET... ...THEY'RE SAYING IT WAS SOME 40-YEAR-OLD NEET GUY.
"TAKAHASHI" ... TAKAHASHI WHAT?
HE WAS UGLY AS HELL... ONE OF THOSE AKIBA OTAKU...
I KNEW IT...

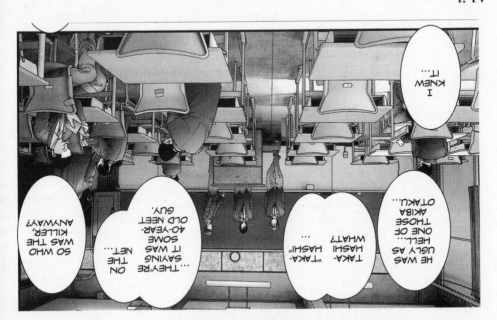

Akiba, page 157

A shortening of Akihabara, the tech-centered neighborhood of Tokyo that is the cultural cente of the otaku subculture, based on its plentiful manga/anime-centric retailers, arcades, maid cafés, and so on.

AUG — 1 2017

Inuyashiki volume 4 is a work of fiction. Names, characters, places, and incidents are the products of the author's imagination or are used fictitiously. Any resemblance to actual events, locales, or persons, living or dead, is entirely coincidental.

A Kodansha Comics Trade Paperback Original.

Inuyashiki volume 4 copyright © 2015 Hiroya Oku
English translation copyright © 2016 Hiroya Oku

Published in the United States by Kodansha Comics,
an imprint of Kodansha USA Publishing, LLC, New York.

Publication rights for this English edition arranged through Kodansha Ltd., Tokyo.

First published in Japan in 2015 by Kodansha Ltd., Tokyo, as *Inuyashiki* volume 4.

ISBN 978-1-63236-263-6

Printed in the United States of America.

www.kodanshacomics.com

9 8 7 6 5 4 3 2 1

Translator: Stephen Paul
Lettering: Scott Brown
Editing: Ajani Oloye
Kodansha Comics Edition Cover Design: Phil Balsman